CHAUCER AND THE ART OF STORYTELLING

CHAUCER AND THE ART OF STORYTELLING

LEONARD MICHAEL KOFF

UNIVERSITY OF CALIFORNIA PRESS
BERKELEY   LOS ANGELES   LONDON

University of California Press
Berkeley and Los Angeles, California

University of California Press, Ltd.
London, England

© 1988 by
The Regents of the University of California

Library of Congress Cataloging-in-Publication Data

Koff, Leonard Michael.
  Chaucer and the art of storytelling.
  Bibliography: p.
  Includes index.
    1. Chaucer, Geoffrey, d. 1400.   Canterbury tales.
2. Chaucer, Geoffrey, d. 1400—Technique.   3. Story-
telling in literature.   I. Title.
PR1875.S75K64 1988   821'.1   87-19099
ISBN 0-520-05999-9 (alk. paper)

Printed in the United States of America

1   2   3   4   5   6   7   8   9

*To my father
and
the memory of my mother*

Contents

Acknowledgments

I would like simply to name here those teachers and friends who have given me encouragement and truth, a blessed combination in any life: F. W. Dupee, Moses Hadas, Bert M-P. Leefmans, Carle Hovde, and Donald Frame, teachers at Columbia whose searching spirit I hope lives in this book. Anne Middleton, at the University of California, Berkeley, a powerful mentor and a rare friend. Ojars Kratins, at Berkeley, a steadying intellectual hand, and Stanley Fish, a teacher of indomitable spirit. Paul Sheats, Edward Condren, Andy Kelly, and Lynn Batten, friends at UCLA who live the collegial ideal. Jean Aroeste, now Associate University Librarian at Princeton, a sure intellectual support during the hours I spent at the University Research Library, UCLA.

I owe deep personal thanks to Gloria Gross, at California State University, Northridge, who saw me through difficult times, to Laurie Koff, my dear sister, to Stephen Goldstein, Lon Engelberg, and Richard Taruskin, fine friends, and to Jennifer Michaels-Tonks, at Grinnell College, who perhaps heard more about Chaucer than she imagined she ever would. I owe professional thanks to Stanley Chyet, Director of Graduate Studies, Hebrew Union College, and Mark Dworkin, at Hillel Macor, UCLA, for giving me the occasion to talk about Chaucer's Prioress at Hebrew Union College.

I wish to thank the readers for the University of California Press, Christian K. Zacher and John Ganim, for their responsive and acute analysis of my work. The care they generously showed it gave me much encouragement. Doris Kretschmer, Barbara Ras, and Stephanie Fay guided this book to the public, a happy voyage. My copyeditor, Peter Dreyer, saved me from many blunders, and Kate Gross helped me index. And Jeanette Gilkison, at the Department of English, UCLA, who typed so many versions of this book, never once faltered—we did it!

One sad note attends the publication of this work. Donald R. Howard, of Stanford University, died before he could see it in print. He was a wise and intuitive friend in learning who sustained me for many seasons with a gift for speaking openly and listening well. I miss him very much.

Finally but not last, to Joyce, as ever, poet, lover, wife—a divine trinity—who gave me a deadline.

Introduction

I offer this study, divided into seven chapters, as an introduction to certain Chaucerian ideas about stories and storytelling. Its aim is to shift the ground on which some long-held assumptions about Chaucer and Chaucerian narrative rest. In general, the first three chapters are historical, theoretical, and sometimes speculative. The last four offer extended close readings of specific Chaucerian tales, or parts of tales, to illustrate ideas developed in the first three chapters and briefly outlined here.

Chapter 1 begins by examining one of the most persistent misunderstandings of Chaucer criticism—that Chaucer requires us to read him "deeply" because, so the argument runs, his opinions, as guides to the meaning of the text, emerge only obliquely. Indeed, both D. W. Robertson, Jr., and Charles Muscatine read Chaucer as if his narratives asked readers to decode them. But Chaucer, as we shall see, is not an ironist. He is not coy, though he can be both playful and perceptive. Chaucer's presence in his own work is valuable for what we do with his self-characterizations and with his characterization of the storyteller who cannot tell stories, the "man noght textueel." As a guide to his own narratives, Chaucer's storyteller always disappoints. Although we need not abandon the idea of dramatic irony or structural irony or irony of manner in Chaucer—this last is characteristic of medieval declamation—we should not assume that for Chaucer irony is deviousness and that for insiders deviousness is a direct line to Chaucer himself.

Wherever he is, Chaucer's storyteller is always the worthy servant of "olde bokes" on behalf of the community of social beings that

1

reading creates. In talking about Chaucer as a storyteller, we should recognize both that Chaucer's idea of telling stories is linked to the publicness of stories and that to preserve the integrity of traditional tales, Chaucer tells them aloud, in an extended sense, because they are not purely his. Chaucer is forever giving up his magical omniscience as a performer of his own work and providing a way for all performers, public and private—all readers—to give up the power they may claim for themselves to make the narrative mean in a certain way. Chaucer's storyteller in the text cannot guide for reasons that have nothing to do with Chaucer's "coyness." Moreover, Chaucer's telling stories aloud implies that he sees himself fulfilling an important public charge; he understands in what sense a man of words is dedicated to traditional matter, to the truth of "olde bokes" as the "keye of remembraunce" for the body social created and re-created through public reading. Indeed, the drive to community is not just understandable; it is laudable. The impulse to create a community of men, which reading does, is worthy of us *as men.* To talk about the "hermeneutic potential" of Chaucer's text is thus to assert that his text is as important for the truth or truths it is said to embody or point to as for an audience seeking truth. Meaning is always the vehicle that sustains a community of people; our undertaking to understand something written affirms that we value it. A text seems, as we probe it, to put us in our best light; as we read, we become social beings and thinkers.

In Chaucer's day, reading, even private reading, was a social event—a "good" event because it was a civilized and civilizing one. Moreover, authors like Chaucer had to control the literal level of a story, since it bound the members of the community one to another, and to the story. The literal level of a written text for Chaucer was thus important both to individual readers so that each could read, make connections to something "deeper" (deeper in themselves, as we shall see) and to readers as a community defined by their reading together. A coherent literal level actually created for Chaucer's work the community of literate men in the sense I mean it, most visibly when a story was performed (or performed at home) as part of, say, an evening's entertainment. No text ever completely loses a literal sense, though critics can argue—they have about Chaucer—that the literal level of a story is valuable for its capacity to take readers through or beyond or behind it to something deeper, better, truer, more real. None of such models for reading puts any stock in a literal sense that can both define and mirror a community of readers, so that stories are deep to the extent that people think deeply about themselves and the world.

It is always dangerous to grasp at Chaucer's intentions; still, his sense of himself as a servant of "olde bokes" and his confounding of our expectations for guidance imply that his concern for the intelligibility of stories reflects his concern for their formative and connective powers. Thus for their readers' sake old books are public and reflect, for readers who react to what they read, what each one may be. Such a view of Chaucer's art imputes to its publicness a value beyond that of mere historical fact—we know Chaucer performed his work—and to Chaucer as a public poet a value for the community of readers who remember their past by reading traditional matter. As a storyteller, Chaucer creates the conditions for performance, even at home. His narratives are occasions for reflection.

In these terms, I think, we can recover the significantly historical context of Chaucerian performance—shared, and shareable, sociability, for us often only a wished-for condition of reading and living. Chaucer had, I believe, both biblical and medieval traditions for his art of storytelling, an art that did not encourage an author, or a reader, to confound the literal sense of a tale to make it meaningful, an art that encourages us, in reading Chaucer, to observe a conceptual distinction between what I call allegorical reading and parabolic listening. Chapter 2 discusses these terms, though I should emphasize here that parabolic listening in Chaucer is not uniquely dependent on Chaucerian performance—private readers, too, can listen, can cooperate with an author, can share in the "public" circle of interpretation and reflection storytelling creates—though parabolic listening is an idea that performance seems naturally to give rise to. Such listening defines textual communities. Moreover, the distinction between allegorical reading and parabolic listening (a distinction I think Chaucer knew, though not, of course, in these terms) tells us much about Chaucer's intentions as a storyteller—about the sense in which his stories are public: about their presentation and about a reader's *use* of them. This distinction, as far as I can tell, is new to Chaucer criticism, though not to medieval literary theory, to certain modern theories of literary hermeneutics, and to biblical criticism. It derives from attempts to formulate theories about both the interpretation of narrative and the development of narrative in the Middle Ages from biblical parables.

Furthermore, we can theorize, using current literary criticism and hermeneutics, and Chaucer's own texts, that Chaucer's narratives, as fictions of projection and discovery, put readers on the testing end of truth—both about themselves as readers and about the historical texts they read. Again, readers see this truth in fiction designed not to be read as a code for something else but fiction that creates something public by being a mirror of, and making shareable, human thought, speech, and behavior. Chaucer's narratives teach by encouraging us to use them as records of human presence in the world—our own, Chaucer's, and that of Chaucer's "medieval people." In this way, they are moral fictions, as chapter 3 explains, whose good lies in their credibility as make-believe and in our power to bring them to ourselves as both self-revealing and historically descriptive performances.

The first of the four chapters that offer extended close readings of Chaucerian texts discusses the Merchant's Tale and the Wife of Bath's Prologue and Tale. It examines such notions as the simultaneity of voice in Chaucer, the collateral serialization of the Chaucerian text—which the *House of Fame*, for example, illustrates and *Troilus and Criseyde* defines—and what I call the sexuality of performance. My discussion of the Wife of Bath's Prologue and Tale illustrates in some detail how that work permits us to make sexual and self-aware moral and social values that define us as masculine and feminine and that define the Wife of Bath as an "open" Chaucerian type. Chapter 5 pairs two of the *Canterbury Tales*—the "Pardoner's 'Prologue'" and the Knight's Tale—to suggest that the distinction between "pure voice" and "pure bookness" in Chaucer is misleading. Chaucer's text has a voice everywhere, and the voicing of the text reveals us to ourselves. Voicing enables us to interpret Chaucer just *because* we can hear our own views; it allows us to tell the tale—that is, to fulfill its deflections and limitations by giving it moral and historical realization in us. Chapter 6 examines aspects of two *Canterbury Tales*—the Franklin's Tale and the Prioress's Tale—to show some of the ways we as readers in a particular time and place recover the literature of another time—what values we can find in it, what truths we can express about it.

The final chapter looks at the closure the Parson's Tale gives to the *Canterbury Tales* and offers a new reading of Chaucer's "leave-taking" at the end of the work. It sees that passage as analogous to the end of the *Troilus*, for both "conclusions" reinforce the co-operative storytelling of a narrative designed to give each reader a text to use—one to stand on as the center of a defining world.

Chapter One

Irony, Declamation, and Chaucer's Presence in His Own Work

A modern reader may find it difficult to imagine a simpler problem than understanding Chaucer. Chaucer's narratives seem easy enough to follow if one starts at the beginning and reads to the end. To begin at the beginning seems both a natural and logical way to proceed, for Chaucer is a storyteller.

Nevertheless, there is a persistent strain in the academic criticism of Chaucer that refuses to begin at the beginning. The argument runs something like this: one should distinguish between telling and meaning when reading, and writing about, Chaucer. His narratives operate on at least two levels. There is an "outer story" and an "inner meaning." The two are not the same, although they are inseparable. What a Chaucerian tale may be about is thus not necessarily what it means. Meaning must be looked for "within" the story, as if it were something the story was designed to cloak or protect. Meaning cannot be found by simply "reading the story," for it is deeper than the story. It "uses the story" to reveal itself, since the story is being told only for the sake of the meaning yet is consciously hiding it.

There are at least two versions of this argument, the patristic and the symbolic. They are surprisingly similar even though they are supposed to represent two ways of approaching Chaucer—one is an adaptation from medieval literary theory, the other from modern theory. D. W. Robertson, Jr., is the spokesman for patristic exegesis. He describes Chaucer's poetry as an allegory of "fruyt and chaf" in which the reader is asked to proceed through the "chaf," or outer story, which delights, to get to the "fruyt," or inner meaning, which teaches. The process of reading that Robertson describes is one of discovery through discarding; Robertson's reader eagerly penetrates the "chaf" of the story, only to discard it for something better. Although seeming to begin at the beginning, the reader actually reads deeply and unilaterally "into" the story, looking for the key to its meaning "as a whole." Though there is always the sense with Robertson that good readers know what they are looking for, the "Robertsonian" story is made delightfully obscure on purpose—it cannot be understood on the surface alone—so that the reader can penetrate the kernel of patristic wisdom hidden in the story for the reader's own good. The "unwrapping" process tests the reader's moral judgment; only those who are not seduced by the pleasing "chaf" can pass the test, and passing means both knowing the difference between "chaf" and "fruyt" and being patient and thorough enough to sort one from the other. In this way, Robertsonian discovery gives firm and confirming truth.

Although, unlike Robertson, Charles A. Owen, Jr., does not distinguish so strictly between inner and outer meaning, he has found the key to Chaucerian narrative in the one or more passages in a story "that at once embody and expose the limited vision of created character and creating narrator." These passages, Owen says, "foreshadow in the unwitting speech or opinion of a character the outcome of the plot and help create symbolic values that give the narrative an added and unifying dimension. They are in a sense symbolic of the whole work."[1] Although Owen sees symbolic irony in the "significant" speeches of the *Canterbury Tales*, his hypothesis that Chaucer is to be read deeply and symbolically has been taken to apply to all of Chaucer's work. Owen is neither the only spokesman for this view nor the only typical spokesman, although he is a very good one. Chaucer, he argues, writes nonlinear stories that must be read as unfolding symbolic structures playing on the contrast between what *is* and what men see.

Although both the patristic and the symbolic arguments are sophisticated, neither is altogether sound. First, the symbolic argument confuses narrative and lyric, or rather attempts to read narrative as if it were a lyric. Thus critics like Owen talk about the symbolic center of a Chaucerian tale, using the word *symbolic* in a sense that is pure *symboliste*. But a Chaucerian tale is not "distilled" from some center of truth or emotion distinct from the story that is said to embody it. Even Robertson, whose allegory of "fruyt" and chaf" is medieval enough, does not see that the process of reading "chaf" provides the key to the "fruyt," unlocking the meaning. The distinction between "fruyt" and "chaf" in medieval theory is always made after the experience of reading, not before or during it. Although Robertson requires that the reader who knows how to read have doctrinal preconceptions, the actual process of reading allows readers to find and test their understanding of doctrine actively and sequentially, not once and for all. Boccaccio himself makes this point:

But I repeat my advice to those who would appreciate poetry, and unwind its difficult involutions. You must read, you must persevere, you must sit up nights, you must inquire, and exert the utmost power of your mind. If one way does not lead to the desired meaning, take another; if obstacles arise, then still another; until, if your strength holds out, you will find that clear which at first looked dark. For we are forbidden by divine command to give that which is holy to dogs, or to cast pearls before swine.[2]

For Boccaccio, the distinction between "fruyt" (what the text means) and "chaf" (how the text says what it means) becomes clear only in the process of reading. Some might call Boccaccio's process a wrenching of the text to make it give up, or open up, a meaning Boccaccio already knows is there and must be there. But the process, which entails a thoroughgoing appropriation of the text—it keeps pearls from swine—yields meaning only after the process has been concluded—that is, after the reader is satisfied that he has found what he already knew was there. "Chaf" itself has value as the outer covering—the inner-outer distinction is emblematic only— because "chaf" serves to disguise the "fruyt." "Chaf" diverts the reader from the truth, of which it is the pleasing and seducing part.

Moreover, that the "fruyt" may be altogether traditional does not, or at least should not, make the search for it pro forma. To find what is "always true" is to the medieval mind, if not to some modern ones, a real search and a real joy. The activity of discovering the universal confirms that we are not, with respect to our thoughts, doomed to our own reading of the world. That is why Boccaccio would not object to our calling his reading "using the text." Indeed, the text was written to be used. "Fiction," Boccaccio says, "is a form of discourse, which, under the guise of invention, illustrates or proves an idea, and, as its superficial aspect is removed, the meaning of the author is clear. If, then, sense is revealed from under the veil of fiction, the composition of fiction is not idle nonsense."[3] Even though an author may be unaware of the meaning a reader may insist is there, a reader must, while reading, ferret out meaning, as Boccaccio says, because such diligence—learning where to look—gives both truth and pleasure at having found hidden answers.

It was Raymond Preston who suggested that Chaucer as a storyteller was an ironist "who kept in reserve, at a given point in his story, the completeness of the narrative and of possible attitudes toward it."[4] For Preston, the telling of a story from multiple points of view that defines Chaucer's complexity also defines Chaucer's skeptical intelligence, intelligence that is "neither unbelief nor frozen doubt" but curiosity that examines all "sides of a question" so that it "can think of them all together." Although Preston does not suggest that "keeping in reserve" means concealing, there may be at least a temporary concealment in a Chaucerian tale that can be read as if the operation of Chaucer's skepticism, his "spiritual laughter," implied disbelief or doubt,[5] rather than inquiry, suggesting to the attentive reader, who takes the hint of ironic juxtaposition as a sign of deeper veins of meaning, that Chaucer is encouraging us to mine for hidden points of view.

It is not that Chaucer cannot be trusted to speak openly. Because his narratives encourage varied judgments even as we read them, we assume that steady intellectual effort will lead us to discover the covert ("real") meaning in ironic juxtaposition. Irony conceals on purpose. There is a clear connection, for example, between Preston's ironic Chaucer and Charles Muscatine's "ironic" Gothic Chaucer. Indeed, Muscatine works out a stylistic criticism on the assumption that "keeping in reserve" means keeping "something" in reserve: another set of stylistic idioms—hence attitudes— that Chaucer encourages an audience to hear as intended contrast to what it reads. As Muscatine argues, Chaucer's complexity depends on attention to style: we know the one through the other.[6]

What Muscatine, for example, says about the "double irony" of Pandarus's and Troilus's existence in and through style—"Pandarus never quite *becomes* the farcical clown" and "Troilus never *becomes* impossibly melodramatic"[7]—explains their stylistic doubleness as the irony of juxtaposed idioms, a stylistic feature of *Troilus and Criseyde*. Moreover, Gothic juxtaposition for Muscatine defines segmentation in Chaucer on the basis of distinctly identifiable narrative idioms put into the "mouths" of characters in the narrative. Like Owen, Muscatine implicitly assumes G. L. Kittredge's analogy to drama in defining narrative idioms in Chaucer.[8] For Muscatine, Chaucer is always a dramatist when he is being a stylist—Chaucer as Gothic stylist is controlled by Chaucer as dramatist.[9] Muscatine has difficulty hearing in Chaucer an informing voice other than that of conventional style. That difficulty seems to me a serious and dangerous example of the inversion of voice and code that Paul Ricoeur argues structuralists like Muscatine make all too readily.[10] Implicit, too, in Muscatine's appeal to the dramatic principle is an attempt to give Chaucer a coherence, a storial and psychological roundness, that Muscatine senses is undermined by the very idea of Gothic juxtaposition, a "modern" critical idea rather than a Victorian one.

But Chaucer is an imperfect dramatist. Because it is not grounded on the idea that Chaucer's narrative need not maintain a fixed point of view, Gothic juxtaposition as a theory of "inorganic" and implicitly ironic juxtaposition of parts, or even as a theory of "dramatic" juxtapositions of styles, really only explains our "discomfort" with narrative that does not maintain a consistent point of view. Critics who argue for Muscatine's idea of Gothic juxtaposition do so because they assume that the narrative discontinuity in Chaucer is an obstacle to sense. A manuscript in Chaucer's day would have proceeded episode by episode, each "complete in itself," because each episode occurred as a public event delivered by a performer and graspable by listeners as a unit.[11] Whatever patterns of radical and not-so-radical juxtapositions were created as each episode met the next would seem ordinary enough to an audience accustomed to listening in parts, although an individual juxtaposition might well seem new or surprising, or even ironic.[12] Narrative segmentation in Chaucer, and particularly in the *Canterbury Tales,* a work that has come to define the organizing principle for all of Chaucer because it is taken as his maturest achievement, is thus not satisfactorily explained by the idea of juxtaposed "voices" or idioms of conventional medieval styles put into the "mouths" of characters in a Canterbury "drama." For Muscatine the problem is the coherence, buttressed where necessary by dramatic coherence, of two styles, the Bourgeois and the Courtly; for Robert M. Jordan it is the breaking down of narrative voices and their appropriate idioms, even within speeches that have been explicitly given to characters in the narrative.[13] But for both, whether or not Chaucerian drama is sustained, the juxtaposition of parts depends on clarifying problems of narrative point of view in Chaucer. Though both critics use as their implicit analogy visual rather than temporal models—ornament in pictures or architecture—both Muscatine and Jordan (Jordan explicitly disavows dramatic presuppositions) want their models to help clarify how we apprehend the Canterbury journey, if only, perhaps, as an architectural journey through ideas.

If any narrative voice must be said to distinguish one part of the narrative from another, it ought not to be any of the voices of the Canterbury pilgrims in the "drama of their journey" to Canterbury. It should be instead the voice of a performer declaiming the part of a storyteller and then proceeding to impersonate, sometimes unevenly but often quite convincingly and with an obvious self-consciousness that would fool no one and delight everyone, the individual pilgrim "narrators" and the fictional characters in "their" fictions. Clearly, such impersonation is not drama. Chaucer's listeners may have thought that at a live performance they heard, say, the Wife of Bath speaking as she might have spoken were she a real woman. But what we surely mean when we say that the Wife is "dramatic" or "alive" is that whoever declaims her part—it might be a man reading the Wife's part at home—brings to life her particular "spoken" idiom so completely that the Wife seems to become a person in her own right on the stage, as it were, of the imagination. No Wife in costume performs on a real stage—a minor observation, perhaps, but important for keeping distinct the literal and the figurative. A medieval performance of the kind we see in the *Troilus* frontispiece from the Corpus Christi College, Cambridge, MS 61 of that work must surely have been characterized by mimicry, public and spoken, by a series of steady (intermittent but firm) impersonations of character—literal impersonations, not theoretical (linguistic) impersonations of the voices of a text in the Derridaean void. Nowadays someone giving a recitation pretends to be acting; he looks either at an invisible presence beside him, if he is supposed to be talking to someone, or at a presence in front of him, beyond or above the audience, if he is supposed to be talking to himself about himself or talking to a higher power. But in Chaucer's day, a performer looked at his audience as he declaimed, for he did not have the idea of acting as we know it; he played to the audience in ways only bad actors might. He was self-conscious.

Now declamation necessarily gives to the performer one irresistible quality—omnipresence. The performer simulates drama by performing all the spoken parts and being the narrator too. He makes the audience "auditors" and "imaginers" who, if a performance is going well, "see double"—see one man looking directly at them, convincingly impersonating someone else, whom they imagine. When interrupted, however, by the very man who makes them see double (see and imagine), the audience sees only him. To talk fully about the "playfulness" of a Chaucerian tale, about its self-consciousness as a form and its resemblance to a play—it is drama "in someone's head"—we should make a conscious effort to assign interruptions of the narrative to a live performer, like Chaucer himself. In this way we can create, even as we read alone and to ourselves, the sense of the publicness of the work. It takes real imagination to bring the idea of public performance to mind, for as we read alone and to ourselves, we can easily think of the *Canterbury Tales* as an almost-novel or almost-play. Being alert to such intrusions in the text as "he said" should, of course, help us remember that Chaucer's work is a presentation.

In such a public performance, a live presentation, the performer, despite his position on stage, does not have to provide a narrative thread like that of a printed text. The word *coherence*, as we use it, is defined by the printing press that gives us books without live speakers, though not without a voice, or voices. The coherence of printed matter means an intelligible arrangement of the text, a discernible and developing, usually logical, line of sense. In declaimed narrative, the performer provides another kind of coherence; he is the medium through which words, and the illusions the words create, pass from one mind to another. He is a real person whom we know and one to whom we give enough of our trust, at the outset, to allow him to take us where he will. I suppose because he is human, we assume he will make sense.

Unfortunately, we no longer have a ready vocabulary to talk about the magical coherence a public figure can bring into being. Walter Benjamin makes a similar point in talking about storytelling as a species of craftsmanship:

The storytelling that thrives for a long time in the milieu of work—the rural, the maritime, and the urban—is itself an artisan form of communication, as it were. It does not aim to convey the pure essence of the thing, like information or a report. It sinks the thing into the life of the storyteller, in order to bring it out of him again. Thus traces of the storyteller cling to the story the way the handprints of the potter cling to the clay vessel. Storytellers tend to begin their story with a presentation of the circumstances in which they themselves have learned what is to follow, unless they simply pass it off as their own experience.[14]

For Benjamin, the storyteller as artisan embeds his words *in* his performance, crafting them so that they become ours through him. The listener's relation to the storyteller is controlled by his interest in retaining what he is told, for according to Benjamin, "the cardinal point for the . . . listener is to assure himself of the possibility of reproducing the story."[15] And, we might add, the listener hopes to reproduce, through recounting or retelling, the excitement of the performance that has embedded his experience of listening in his own mind.

A live performance is not a "happening"—the participatory theater of the sixties—and magical coherence does not make digressions either sensible or tolerable. But if we like the man who is telling us a story, we shall probably like the story he tells and give him time to tell it. A live narrator, performing from a prepared text, will not make sensible what is in fact incoherent. But his reading will bring us a narrative with amplifications and intrusions and commentary and digressions that might seem unclear if the text were not read aloud. We want texts with a thread. Without such a line to the center, we would want to know why a text was meandering. It would seem to need streamlining to bring it into accord with the way we think the mind should work when it is working clearly. But a public text does not necessarily meander. It may seem to wander because it has to pass through a performer to listeners—a performer may have memorized it, or parts of it; it may seem to be caught up in the present through digressions and commentary. But since it literally passes from one mind to another—it is not grappled with, independent of the personality of the performer—it can easily mirror the progressive and recessive sequence of thought. In presenting the content, then, a performer has an omnipotence that is easily read as ironic control *just because* the performer as storyteller appears and disappears as a performing part in the text itself.

Now the coherence that actual presentation gives to a text makes Chaucer's narratives different from, say, Langland's. Unlike Chaucer, Langland hardly seems to have paced his verse on the rhythm of speech he might have learned from performing his own work. Langland's narrative fumbles from one scene to another, as he confronts "the religious and social issues raised by his conscience."[16] To be sure, Langland has imagined a performative structure to his narrative, but he has taken it upon himself alone to interpret what he "hears." He is both author and audience to himself in an often unmanageable narrative solipsism. His work lacks a clear sense of real "public location," not the point-of-view coherence of a printed page but the coherent and intrusive presence of a live performer presenting his illusion of real-life scenes—an oral sequencing learned by actual performance. Langland probably did not learn his narrative techniques in a public forum; his knowledge of performative structure comes from books. Perhaps because Langland cannot fix his oral presentation in the real world—reading aloud would have helped him do that—his narrative is finally disjointed. There is a difference not yet understood between discontinuity in public narrative and the disjointedness in an imagined oral narrative that has not been presented publicly. The principle of organization in Chaucer so sorely wanting in Langland is really the intelligibility achieved by a writer who puts in manuscript for a medieval reader, even a private one, a public narrative the writer experiences critically and aesthetically as performed because he has performed it.

A change in reading habits in the fifteenth century may account

in part for Langland's popularity, for like Lydgate, whose work is
also characterized by centerless digressions, Langland's narrative,
or narratives—he reworked his manuscript three times—is suited
perfectly to an audience of readers who can still imagine public
performance even if they have never participated in one. To the
fifteenth century, neither Langland nor Lydgate may have seemed
disjointed, though each seems nowadays to have pushed public
narrative, without the benefit of actual performance, to its limits.
For us, both Langland and Lydgate can be unmanageable, and it
takes all our concentration to thread the narrative with the narrator
every "oral" text is supposed to have built into it. By contrast to
Langland and Lydgate, Chaucer seems remarkably lean and directed—eminently readable. What accounts for his "unity" is the
constant presence of a storyteller with an identifiable storytelling
manner as a discontinuous part *in the text*. Chaucer's own experience with live performance gave his narratives a coherent "oral"
form we can easily imagine as capable of being performed and so
capable of being followed.

Despite Chaucer's magical coherence, however, critics like Robertson and Owen read him as if he wrote narrative not serially in
time but for "technological space," in Hugh Kenner's phrase, "on
printed pages for which it was designed from the beginning," as if
he wrote storytelling "discourse discontinuously in space."[17] Both
Robertson and Owen, as patristic and symbolic readers of Chaucer,
hold that hidden communications with the reader are present in
the text and are kept in reserve just because the Chaucerian text is
consciously a collage of voiced styles (Muscatine's argument using
Kittredge). Moreover, whatever is kept in reserve is not altogether
clear to Chaucer himself, who is seen as the earthly voice for other,
larger and deeper, voices—either the voice of Christian morality
(the voice of *doctrina*) or the voice that is at once human and universal. Although Muscatine is not generally thought of as sharing
much with Robertson, the two nevertheless share an assumption
about the role of difficulty in Chaucer. Muscatine sees it as a stimulus to learning the vocabulary of conventional styles; Robertson
sees it as the stimulus to learning how to sift "fruyt" from "chaf."
Both see it as part of learning to read Chaucer deeply.

Now a "deep" reading—one that is correct because it is complete—implies that the reader must move away from the text.

Structuralists like Muscatine implicitly talk about moving *above* it; the "mixed style" points to perspectives and "wholes" in Chaucer that are finally Chaucer's subject.[18] Allegorists like Robertson talk about moving *through* (into and beyond) the text, as if the text were a covering to be removed. Indeed, both structuralist and allegorical readings are alienated in the same way, though the directional analogies implicit in each ("above" versus "through") suggest that structuralist readers and allegorical readers move in opposite ways: for Muscatine, Chaucer embodies the idea and the virtue of comprehensiveness; for Robertson, the idea and the virtue of a single informing code. But for each, art finally serves ideas—the ideas of wholeness or morality—in ways that make Chaucer's art touch us because it is conceptual (illustrative) and because it moves us away from its engaging (varied and diverting) surface to help us understand it—to show us what it is.

In defining the word *irony*, H. W. Fowler has also defined the hidden answers that Muscatine, Robertson, and others assume when they attempt to read Chaucer closely—that the idioms or ideas Chaucer's narratives keep in reserve are revealed only to some of his readers. These critics hypothesize an informed audience, medieval and modern, who can read Chaucer, or learn to read him, both deeply and correctly by taking advantage of his particular cast of mind. Chaucer's narratives are said to be ironic because Chaucer has conceived them ironically. As Fowler puts it, irony is a literary mode that depends upon "a double audience, consisting of one party that hearing shall hear and shall not understand, and another party that, when more is meant than meets the ear, is aware both of that more and of the outsiders' incomprehension."[19] In Fowler's sense, irony describes the relation not between parts of a work but between the work itself and the audience. Irony for Fowler (and for Muscatine and Robertson) is a mode of informed understanding that establishes an intimacy between an author, or authorial voice, and the knowing audience; it presumes that there are hidden or delayed communications in a work that the author and some members of the audience know, or expect to know, but that other members of the audience and the critics in the universities are busily looking or waiting for.

The notion that those who have not fully understood Chaucer's narratives look for the key to their occasional mystification seems, if a bit devious, nonetheless plausible. It accounts in a general way for Chaucer's always appearing, as a storyteller, to keep his audience "in mind." His poetry is public, even in manuscript, and he repeatedly addresses "readers" as "listeners" and refers to the circumstances of performance. Moreover, the notion of "special meanings" implicit in Fowler seems to explain how a "rhetorical" poem may be "symbolic," even in a modern sense: Chaucer's narratives, so the argument runs, purposefully deflect their "meaning" while still being public, if only for the initiated. Furthermore, the notion of hidden meaning seems to explain clearly why Chaucer's deepest appeal is to "right readers," medieval or modern. That such a view of Chaucer's literary method reflects a form of elitism in otherwise good critics—the flattering assumption that a hidden style wants to bring only the best readers closer to it and to its author because it operates covertly—is obvious enough. Muscatine perhaps falls victim to a more generally accepted form of elitism than Robertson, one that welcomes intelligent (sufficiently learned) readers into an "open coterie." We may feel that Muscatine is more generous to us than Robertson, but both, I think, believe in the fiction that there is an informed reader for Chaucer's work who can, or can learn to, dig deep and think big.

The problem of irony in Chaucer—finding answers in a literature consciously hiding them—is misconceived. The problem itself is one that, curiously enough, modern readers of printed books unwittingly create for themselves when they read Chaucer, for one of the assumed axioms of the criticism of fiction is that the printed page, which has no "rhetor" in the literal sense, must have a point of view. For the sake of coherence, an apparatus that provides point of view must be built into a text that circulates in book form. Elizabeth Eisenstein has argued that the impulse to systematize manuscripts for readers existed *before* printing and that the printing press only made it simpler to achieve "bookness."[20] She argues that although "early printers took over functions performed *both* by copyists *and* by stationers (or 'publishers')," printers probably thought that they were merely making available to more people a library of books whose medium of presentation their new technology was not altering.[21] What the printing press finally changed, Eisenstein says, was dependence on an author to present his written work (literally his manuscript) to a public that could not, before printing, have an exact copy of a text or experience the ease with which we negotiate one without authorial or editorial—another reader's—point of view. Indeed, it is often an editor who makes an author accessible in printed books by making books self-sufficient. The standardization of the text, with its attendant editorial clarifications and "making orderly," and the increasingly wider dissemination of texts through new modes of promotion reflected as much as caused changes in reading habits; one could read privately before printing. A well-coordinated book (an edited one) made performance more easily portable and private than it had been, though not necessarily silent, since one might want to simulate a performance at home. An edited book made an actual public performance less and less necessary, however wished-for. The idea of performance entails the notion that there was a time when reading could be seen to bring people together and that the rhetoric of fiction was once happily literal, not simply nostalgic.

How soon after printing people began to think of reading as a longed-for performance is not settled, though I suspect it was probably rather late, perhaps not until the eighteenth century. Certainly we think of it that way. Walter Benjamin, for example, would distinguish what he calls "story" from the "novel": the former, he says, is a reminiscence, a communal and traditional event; the latter is a remembrance, a private act.[22] In these terms, Chaucer's manuscript narratives are "stories." They do not require a guiding voice. Because of the circumstance of performance, their live storyteller provides immediacy of effect rather than a consistent point of view. Not that parts of a Chaucerian narrative are juxtaposed with no center of focus; rather a performer, who was the center of consciousness even for the private reader in Chaucer's day, reads, or is imagined as reading, the parts of "others" and comments on them.

Because the hand-copied manuscripts in which Chaucer's poetry circulated well into the middle of the fifteenth century resemble the form of the printed book in which his poetry is read today— both are bound volumes that might be read without a performer— critics persist in treating the Chaucerian performance as they would treat reading Chaucer in print. Not finding an obvious and consistent point of view in him, critics postulate not-so-obvious points of view that give the narrative coherence. Chaucer's narratives are thus said to be both elaborate and deep, possessing real inner form. Although M. B. Parkes explains that readers in Chaucer's day

were in the habit of "working through" a text by inserting, for example, their own paragraph marks with corresponding marks in
the margins accompanied by numerals or headings such as *contra*
and *responsio* to indicate the stages of the argument, or adding
running titles, or dividing the text into chapters and indicating subordinate topics in the margin, or compiling their own *tabula* (al-
phabetical index), or inserting their own synoptic table of contents,[23] they were not, I believe, reading in quite the same spirit
as we read. To be sure, readers before printing were like modern readers—think of students with magic markers—making texts
graspable privately, though they were closer to real performance
than we are. The readerly activity Parkes describes in discussing
the *Canterbury Tales* as a compilation is an example of scholastic
lectio—a "process of study which involved a . . . ratiocinative scru-
tiny of the text and consultation for reference purposes";[24] nonetheless, such readerly activity might not entail any sense of what I
would call the disassociation of publicness.

I hope I have not allowed a distorting historicism to inform my
treatment of Chaucer, though I am sympathetic to Walter Benjamin's distinctions. Still, I believe that nowadays readers and critics
have to marshal systems of understanding to feel themselves a part
of some community of readers. They must ferret out meaning, revealed to them as members of a coterie of right readers who, because they are divided from one another by great silences, become
more special to each other as they read and interpret. Indeed, they
must construct around reading a web of analogies of performance
and sociability that reflect the degree to which performance and
sociability are merely wished-for social and intellectual conditions
of reading and living. The potential for being an insider is apparently infinite.

Perhaps, then, we ought to tender here a distinction between
private performance in Chaucer's day and private reading in our
own. The first was a developing aspect of the aural reception of
literature and not only describes how reading occurred in Chaucer's time, but tells us how Chaucer's readers thought of their reading habits. Private performance is not equatable as an idea with
private reading, to which critics nowadays feel obliged to give an
inner, almost secret, rhetoric. Private performance and private
reading entail different notions of how the reception of ideas deter-

mines one's sense of participation in social and intellectual life. No reader today who made a point of reading aloud would seriously imagine himself participating in a performance in which reading was the socially and intellectually central public act, though some of Chaucer's readers might have imagined such a situation, particularly if they were outside his "primary audience."[25] Perhaps only the weekly public reading of the Gospel in church (or the portion of the five books of Moses in synagogue) is for us comparable to the performance of words that create a communal event, because the words performed belong to the community—a historical as well as a divinely ordained community.

Noticing that one is subvocalizing, that one is reading aloud, is for us, I think, a surprising, even an embarrassing, moment of awareness. It disturbs the silence of reading, what we take to be thoughtful interiority—the mental space of reading and thinking. And it *feels* illiterate. Hearing our own voice as we read does not suggest that we are participating at home in a public act, that we are being communal and intelligent because we are re-creating public words in our own voices. If anything, hearing ourselves read is an act of memory, not of replication; for in hearing our words, we remember how far we have come from public performance and the idea of public activity informed by words said, or at least heard, together. Private performance in Chaucer's day repeated at home what was in fact public performance. It implied that the private performer—we can call him a reader, though we mean something special by that term—was participating, and was continuing to participate (consciously, through the sound of his own voice), in a public act of storytelling that constituted for him the civilized life of the community. Nowadays we have to construct theories of understanding that surround the act of private reading, for we are continually plagued by the need to rationalize the private and the personal, to show readers how their responses, though they may feel private, are public and shareable, not lonely.

It is only because we are so thoroughly private as readers that the injunction in the Prologue to the Miller's Tale that "whoso list it nat yheere, / Turne over the leef and chese another tale" (3176–77) seems to anticipate the natural consequence of movement toward an enlarged public and the written (printed) word.[26] In a way it does; Chaucer was performed in his own day privately from hand-copied manuscripts that circulated like books. And Chaucer as an author who performed his work had a sense of words existing on the handwritten page. In the Squire's Tale, for example, the falcon says "as I have seyd above" (540) rather than "as I said before," but this "error" may have occurred while Chaucer was writing the Squire's Tale and may reflect, at the moment it was written, Chaucer's sense of himself as the author of a handwritten manuscript rather than the narrator of an "oral" one. But the "slip," if that is what it is, is clearly no argument against the idea of the actual performance of the Squire's Tale from manuscript in a group or at home. Then, too, the "slip" may suggest the way Chaucer saw the text making a public and performing image of itself, like a banner unrolling, so that the text speaks ("as I have seyd") about itself ("above") as *words presented*. Chaucer, I would argue, never thought that his manuscript leaf was not public (performable and performing).[27] Still, it is easy to see (or disregard) borderlines retrospectively, whereas prospectively things look, as I think they looked for Chaucer and his audiences, very much unchanged from what they had always been. In Chaucer's day, people behaved at reading performances as if public and private readings were similar: private readers performed aloud; we would call such performance mumbling. Performance in Chaucer's day would have been public even when it took place at home—performance is not the same as the silent study of a text—just as for us, I suspect, reading is private (thought of as intended for each member of the audience), even when it happens to take place in groups. It is impossible to pin down exactly when private performance became (or rather came to be thought of as) private reading. But the distinction between the ways private readers and performers think about what they are doing suggests itself to me precisely *because* the effort to recover publicness in the process of reading often seems so difficult. A number of important critics nowadays write about reading as if there has in fact been a disassociation of publicness.[28] Moreover, when we remember, for example, that millions of people may be reading a best seller at one time, the idea that our thoughts are finally shareable comes to us with a surprise akin to suddenly seeing a panorama—the panorama of social life.

For us, then, as readers, and as readers of Chaucer, it is not difficult to imagine Chaucer's poetry as a private text whose juxtaposed parts lead us into a purposefully ironic maze of concealments. Indeed, some of our best Chaucerians think that Chaucer's "being ironical"—commenting covertly in his own narratives in any number of ways: Muscatine's or Robertson's or Charles Owen's—implies that he (Chaucer) "sees things as ironic." Chaucer, as we know, has an eye for incongruity, but it is far from clear what he intends *us* to make of his perception of the variableness of people, circumstances, and ideas. If Chaucer is ironic, his irony is the irony of the teacher, not the gamester. The gamester teases in order to be found out; his use of irony betrays a habit of mind that consciously hides in order to be caught. The teacher backs away from his audience—backing away only looks like teasing and coyness—in order to make the audience pursue his work, not him. And Chaucer's work, as Charles Koban puts it, creates fictional worlds ("persuasive structures") that permit, indeed invite, an audience to explore the logic of choices.[29] Chaucer expects members of his audience to develop a sense of intellectual and moral judiciousness just *because* his tales are never morally prescriptive; they do not ask specific moral questions that require either specific or allegorized answers. Rather they pose abstract and speculative questions in the form "What is the nature of . . .?" They do not ask, "What should be done in such and such a given instance?" What is edifying in Chaucer is the occasion to develop powers of mind and reflection, not to come up with a right answer.[30]

It is indeed just the distinction between teacher and gamester that Bertrand Bronson, who has written so persuasively on these very matters in Chaucer, seems to have missed. "In perhaps no other poetry ever written," Bronson says, "has an author established between himself and his audience a bond so immediate, so personal, so amusing, so teasingly full of nuance, so deceptively transparent, so delicately elusive—in a word, so highly civilized."[31]

Granted all this, does Bronson suggest that we hunt for Chaucer because he is there? In a way, yes, for unfortunately Bronson does not see that the civilizing force of Chaucer's immediate, personal, and elusive nuances is to move us away from him (Chaucer) and closer to his stories—not as objects or things, but as ideas. One of the thrusts of Bronson's work as a critic has been to dispel the notion of a static Chaucerian persona, a fixed Chaucerian self on a page, and about that he is right. But what results when he argues that "we are very personally involved" with the narrator and "with his entire assistance," since "he is almost the only figure in his 'drama' . . . who truly matters to us," is our headlong movement into the Chaucerian maze of concealments.[32] We cannot know, of course, what Chaucer believed, nor does indeterminancy finally make Chaucer available to us. Our not listening to him tell a story, our second-guessing his intentions and his meanings (indeterminacy continually gives us Chaucer *and takes him away*) is a sign, not of our delight with Chaucer's deceptive authorial bonds, but of our impatience with him—our fear of his range, his comprehensiveness, and our own limitations.

Would a medieval audience have shared our critical concerns with reading "deeply"? Probably not. Chaucer's medieval audience would certainly have had a sense of the "real Chaucer" at all times. Confined to a written text that we read but do not hear declaimed, however, we often find the real Chaucer, the man with the truth, emerging from the text, but then disappearing with an impersonation, or series of impersonations, that frustrates as much as it intrigues. We pursue and create "presence" where there is "absence," and where indeterminacy creates perpetual absence. The Chaucerian style only draws attention to itself and its author to thrust us away from a search for Chaucer's opinions. It renders him, for all his irony of whatever mood, serious or happy, charmingly open and curiously absent—a special kind of Jamesian "polished mirror."

A. C. Baugh suggests that Chaucer's characterization of himself as a simpleton—ignorant, credulous, earnest, or enthusiastic, usually self-disparaging and overscrupulous, a bookworm who knows next to nothing about love or life—is the most obvious and simplest self-mockery. It resulted, Baugh thinks, from the court's personal knowledge of Chaucer the man and the nature of literary publication in the fourteenth century, the idea of which we see in the Corpus Christi College, Cambridge, MS illumination showing Chaucer reciting his *Troilus and Criseyde*. Baugh insists that in trying to recover the personality of Chaucer in his narratives, we ought to distinguish between "what has a good chance of being real and what is almost certainly fictitious, introduced for humorous or dramatic effect."[33]

There is, however, a finer distinction than Baugh's that does *not* reopen the "controversy" between Bronson and E. Talbot Donaldson over Chaucer's persona and oral delivery, something Baugh himself, I think, was trying not to do.[34] It is the distinction between an ironist like Chaucer who presents himself as an ingénu, perhaps for the sake of the humor it will evoke because the pose is an amusing mockery of his keenness of perception (Baugh's point), and an ironist, also like Chaucer, who impersonates a simpleton storyteller to be regarded in performance as distinct from himself. The former is, of course, as much an impersonation as the latter and both are self-conscious poses that may shade off into each other, particularly if we imagine Chaucer performing his work and naming himself in it.[35] But what is important here is neither the idea of a live author speaking behind the mask (or masks) he has created for himself nor the idea of someone else speaking behind Chaucer's self-created mask in the text, but what an author seems to ask an audience to do when it encounters his "other self" (or "selves"), no matter who is reading.[36] Thus Chaucer's presentation of himself as an ingénu, an amusing self-impersonation, encourages us to intuit what Chaucer really thinks. It invites an audience, as the part is being read by Chaucer, or anyone else, to move "through the mask" to the author, and although it disappoints, it does permit us the illusion that we find Chaucer. That illusion guides our reading and strengthens our interpretation of the narrative because we feel that our judgments are Chaucer's too. Chaucer's mask is indeed removable—Chaucer is *not* an ingénu, and what we see he probably saw. But unmasking Chaucer only confirms our own reading of his narratives; it does not give us Chaucer's reading except as it makes us confident in our own.

Like Chaucer's presentation of himself as an ingénu, the creation of a puppyishly enthusiastic or bemused or bookish storyteller as a part in the text anyone might read also invites an audience to unmask the performer, but it permits us the illusion that in doing so we know *more* than the storyteller. Chaucer "in his own poetry" has been described variously, as we know, but what critics have not understood is that attempts to describe him *in one place* in his poetry—as, say, the shy, uneasy elvish teller of Sir Thopas, or the sociable companion of his fellow pilgrims in the General Prologue, or the man of little worldly experience in the early poems and the

Troilus, or the bookish and credulous, sometimes comic and foolish debator of the "praise-of-marriage" passage in the Merchant's Tale, where he is not even named—all result in not grasping what his multiple characterizations require of us. Whether we imagine Chaucer, or someone else, performing the part is not the issue. In the first case, we might feel teased by the self-consciousness of the pose—Chaucer wrote the part for himself; in the second case, we might feel amused by its ineptness. But in either case, our judgments, as we read Chaucer's work, will be confirmed. It hardly matters whether we think we see the truth Chaucer sees, or see more than a simpleton storyteller sees. What matters is how we handle our own sense of omniscience. As Baugh suggests, Chaucer's presentation of himself is always comic and intermittent—how often we think we hear him may vary widely—but his special presence seems so delightful that we always single it out in our memory as the example of Chaucer "in his work." The part of a narrator who cannot command confidence in *his* omniscience, though he seems to be everywhere, is comic, too, but it also let Chaucer, when he performed the part, as it would let anyone who performed the part, intentionally confound expectations of guidance, an expectation that performance itself (listening or reading) always creates.

It is true that Chaucer's self-characterization as an ingénu is, in a narrow sense, a kind of withholding; what Chaucer seems to be saying about himself is not on the face of it true. In book 2 of the *House of Fame,* for example, Chaucer, using his own Christian name, tells how he is tutored in Boethian physics ("Geffrey, thou wost ryght wel this" [729]). Chaucer, who was in his own lifetime known to be a competent astronomer, would probably not have needed instruction from a "divine" guide who figuratively swoops down upon him from heaven:

> Thus I longe in hys clawes lay,
> Til at the laste he to me spak
> In mannes vois, and seyde, "Awak!
> And be not agast so, for shame!"
> And called me tho by my name.
>
> (2.554–58)

Chaucer's guide is hardly Dantesque. His "awak!" is appropriately schoolmarmish, but Chaucer is only comically the class dunce.

Again, in the *Parliament of Fowls*, Chaucer is put upon by a guide, this time for his indecisiveness:

> Ferde I, that nyste whether me was bet
> To entre or leve, til Affrycan, my gide,
> Me hente, and shof in at the gates wide,
> And seyde, "It stondeth writen in thy face,
> Thyn errour, though thow telle it not to me."
>
> (152–56)

But Chaucer's curiosity probably did not need outside encouragement—a physical "shof." Chaucer was always eager to explore literary gardens. His stance in relationship to his fictional guides, either the Black Knight, the Eagle, or Scipio Africanus, betrays a self-conscious and, in that sense, ironic ineptitude that his audience would have perceived with little difficulty. It does not reveal something about his power of mind that he had always kept, or meant to keep, hidden.

Those passages in Chaucer's poetry that name him and thus seem to describe him personally—identification here would seem unmistakable—are relatively few in number, confined for the most part to the *Canterbury Tales*. In the portrait of Chaucer in the Prologue to Sir Thopas, for example, Chaucer is described both as abstracted in manner ("Thow lookest as thou woldest fynde an hare, / For evere upon the ground I se thee stare" [696–97]) and as corpulent in body ("Now war yow, sires, and lat this man have place! / He in the waast is shape as wel as I" [699–700]). Chaucer has become here, for the moment, a pilgrim-storyteller in his own tale about pilgrims, but what that means about the truth of his self-characterization is far from clear. There may, on the one hand, be some truth to the idea that Chaucer was actually plump. He makes fun of his own figure in at least three passages in his work and, if we keep in mind that Chaucer read before an audience whose good humor and geniality he would have been courting, then obvious and lighthearted self-mockery, particularly of something as apparent as his amplitude, might be fitting. Chaucer as "popet" in line 701 of the Prologue to Sir Thopas, for example, suggests that Chaucer was a "dainty" man, who may have had a plump midsection. Indeed, it is a portly Chaucer the Eagle in the *House of Fame* swoops down upon ("Me carynge in his clawes starke / As lyghtly

as I were a larke" [2.545–46]). Then, too, in the *Lenvoy de Chaucer a Scogan,* Chaucer links himself with Scogan and "alle hem that
ben hoor and rounde of shap" (31). The real point, of course, about
Chaucer's passing references to his own amplitude is the "moral"
use to which he himself could have put them. A chubby man is, or
ought to be, sociable. In this "ought" lies our predisposition to like
Chaucer; it gives us, as it were, what Chaucer wants us to believe
about him—his prepossessing nature.

Chaucer's "reserve," on the other hand, unlike his plumpness,
may almost certainly be fictitious, introduced for the humor of the
idea, and not something that might have been true, or something
Chaucer would want us to imagine as true. Even though Harry
Bailly remarks that Chaucer, among the company of pilgrims, appears "elvyssh by his contenaunce" (7.703), the circumstances of
Chaucer's public life do not confirm the idea that he was self-
absorbed ("For unto no wight dooth he daliaunce" [7.704]). Although Chaucer's portrait in the margin of the Ellesmere manuscript of the *Canterbury Tales* seems to confirm the Host's verbal
picture of him—Chaucer's face is mild and rather sad; its pensive-
ness is accented by a wistful expression—perhaps both the Host and
"the Ellesmere miniaturist attributed to Chaucer the conventional
character of a poet, that of a dreamer, dazed by the visions of un-
earthly beauty or of moral truth which provide the subject-matter of
so many medieval poems."[37] Being "elvyssh" may have been only a
pose. Line 703 does not, as has been argued, support a view of
Chaucer as a poet whose self-ironies knowingly hide opinions that
an ironic stance (being "elvyssh") happily aids and that are only revealed to an initiated few who see "elvishness" for what it is.[38] The
line does not reveal something about the importance of Chaucer's
mischievousness as a poet that we ought to believe and that his
work bears out because it is "dark," like the "elvysshe craft" (751)
of the Canon's Yeoman's Tale, the hermetic alchemical art that depends on imaginative penetration for its credence. If line 703 suggests that Chaucer's wistful ignorance is a mask for his real acute-
ness of perception, his amusing pose is at most a deliberate and
purposeful stance distancing Chaucer the man from Chaucer the
performer, and giving us the freedom to accept his omniscience.

Indeed, Chaucer's portrait in the Prologue to Sir Thopas may
imply that if he was as full "in the waast" as the Host, Chaucer

should have behaved more like the robust tavern keeper. For Harry Bailly size is sociability and an "elvyssh" manner is rude, perhaps because it is intellectual and uppity. That is not to say that Chaucer the man behaved like the fictional Harry Bailly. Rather, Chaucer, as thoroughly social a person as any, could count on the fact that he would be familiar enough to his listeners to portray himself as bemused, incompetent, and somewhat inexperienced in the world, all of which was certainly not true. Whatever else it may be, Chaucer's self-portrait in the Prologue to Sir Thopas is comic and endearing, not false, but slightly, though harmlessly, distorted—"ironic" only in the sense that it is happy feigning. In a similar way, the Man of Law's disparaging remarks about Chaucer's work—its "lewed" style (2.47–50) and its voluminousness (2.51–55)—and about Chaucer's own poetic program, like the Host's virulent response to Chaucer's "rym dogerel" (7.925), Chaucer's Tale of Sir Thopas, and Africanus's remark about Chaucer's "connyng for t'endite" (167) in the *Parliament of Fowls*, only draw happily ironic attention to what Chaucer in fact wrote and wrote so well.[39] As Alfred David argues, the Man of Law, as well as the Eagle in the *House of Fame* and the God of Love in the Prologue to the *Legend of Good Women*, represents Chaucer's "ironic portrait of critics who favored him with condescending praise and gratuitous advice."[40] David subscribes, as do I, to John H. Fisher's suggestion that the Introduction to the Man of Law's Tale is "Chaucer's good humored response to Gower's displeasure at the new direction of Chaucer's poetry."[41]

Now the relatively few explicit references to "Geffrey" throughout Chaucer's work are inevitable in public performance. They refer to Chaucer in performance making a conscious and harmless mockery of himself as man and storyteller. But even those passages where Chaucer is not named—where Chaucer's storyteller openly and honestly lays bare his unique limitations *as a storyteller*, limitations that need not have any bearing on the man (or woman) who performs the part—might have been taken in Chaucer's day as personal references. Chaucer wrote the part of the "man noght textueel" for himself, although anyone can perform it believably. Its *locus classicus* is the General Prologue, 725–46, echoed in the Manciple's Tale and elsewhere.[42] What is created in the General Prologue and elsewhere, is *both* an ironic portrait of Chaucer in performance, who could feign if he chose to, *and* the part of a well-

meaning storyteller, a pilgrim among many pilgrims, whose limitations as narrator ("My wit is short, ye may wel understonde" [746])
necessarily shift the burden of interpreting stories from himself,
because he simply cannot do so, to the members of his audience.
All anyone can expect from such a fictional storyteller, even if
Chaucer read the part, is that the storyteller will do his best to do
the very least he can—to report the words of others correctly,
copying, as it were, the book of nature ("To telle yow hir wordes
and hir cheere, / Ne thogh I speke hir wordes proprely" [728–29])
and not being arbitrary ("He moot reherce as ny as evere he kan /
Everich a word, if it be in his charge" [732–33]) or partial ("He
may nat spare, althogh he were his brother" [737]). One cannot assume, as we read, that such a storyteller will *not* do more because,
for some reason never clarified, he chooses not to do so. Chaucer's
storyteller, as a part in the text that can be re-created without him,
does not tell us something about Chaucer that Chaucer cannot, or
will not, tell us directly. Chaucer's storyteller is not a "dark presence." And there is no reason to assume, as so many do, that the
storyteller knows more than he tells, when he says he does not.

Interpretation of Chaucer's narratives is thus cooperative by de-
fault of the storyteller, because he cannot do it. That is Chaucer's
fiction, which amuses *and* disappoints. As a part he wrote for himself, and performed, it both makes light of his discerning eye and
throws readers back on themselves, confounding expectations of
guidance, because the simpleton narrator never becomes wiser.
The fiction of incompetence, which is a kind of played-out authorial
indeterminacy, never fades to reveal its performer, *even if he is
Chaucer.* Indeed, any performer can bring to life Chaucer's "man
noght textueel"—a storyteller whose fidelity to the words of others, in spite of what he says (he is a bit priggish), will be at best
painstaking, both because it is, in his view, a feature of decorum
and of truth, biblical ("Crist spak" [739]) and classical ("Plato seith"
[741]), that "the wordes moote be cosyn to the dede" (742) and because his own powers of "feigning" and interpreting are circum-
scribed. Even if we identify a "heightened, philosophizing voice"
in the opening eighteen lines of the General Prologue, the voice
of "authoritative literary tradition" linking the natural, the erotic,
and the social spring in broad, explanatory syntax (the "whan . . .

thanne" construction), giving voice to "a general longing" in us "for a wise, full vision of the human condition and even for entrance into the recesses of divine privity," that "clerkly articulation of the poet's task is abruptly truncated."[43] We hear the voice of Chaucer's storyteller in the nineteenth line of the General Prologue ("Bifil that in that seson on a day"). High authorial confidence summarily vanishes.

Even within a limited circle, Chaucer's narratives in manuscript probably circulated in his own day without him, and someone reading Chaucer aloud might well have attempted, if he had heard Chaucer read (this is a fascinating possibility), to impersonate Chaucer performing his tales.[44] Such a medieval performer, perhaps a member of a noble family, or one of Chaucer's friends, might remember one of Chaucer's performances the way we remember our favorite actor doing, say, *King Lear,* when we sit down to read the part or try to act it out. This possibility—remembering Chaucer performing—is naturally unavailable to us, though anyone who performs Chaucer's work (reads it to himself) might pretend any number of things. Indeed, even if the reader of Chaucer pretends he is Chaucer (who can honestly resist?), the protestations of ignorance from Chaucer's storyteller, faithful to the words of others—"I was there" is his truth claim—only encourage the reader to pursue the intent of words he hears from a less than omniscient voice.[45] What Chaucer's omnipresent storyteller can buttress is only the reader's belief that both he and "Chaucer unmasked" know the truth. That is *not* discovering Chaucer's point of view in Chaucer's "hidden openness," but discovering, happily enough, one's own. It has even been suggested that Chaucer's words in the General Prologue imply, like the words of Vincent of Beauvais in his *Speculum maius* ("Nam ex meo pauca, vel quasi nulla addidi. Ipsorum igitur est auctoritate, nostrum autem sola partium ordinatione") that, *because* Chaucer as storyteller in his own work takes the voice of a compiler, the *Canterbury Tales* invites studying. The *mise-en-page* of the work—I can hardly hope to improve Parkes's fine phrase—encourages any reader to pursue Chaucer's text in the spirit of a highly witty vernacular version of scholastic *lectio.*[46] This kind of reading entails not merely our learning to sort out the author's voice from his impersonation as compiler (either as "repor-

tour" or as outsider),[47] but to take on, as we listen to Chaucer, what
a compiler implicitly expects his readers to do with the words of
others—to entertain them seriously. What is amusing, too, about
the idea of Chaucer as *compilator* is that we know that he is also an
auctor. The order in which he sets out to report the words of others
(the *compilatio* of the *Canterbury Tales*) is forever breaking down,
so that order in Chaucer—the ordering of tellers and tales—finally
tells us less about how Chaucer thinks, or wants us to think, about
his *matere* than about how we can, or can choose to, read it. Indeed, Chaucer's *compilatio* serves an individual ordering, a personal and personalized *ordinatio.*

Not even Chaucer's "vehement opinions" guide our reading in
a certain direction. In the Nun's Priest's Tale, for example, there
are outbursts that, because they seem entirely uncharacteristic of
Chaucer, "must be Chaucer himself" in sneak appearances as an
irrepressible minor prophet.[48] One of these is unmistakably frank:

> Allas! ye lordes, many a fals flatour
> Is in youre courtes, and many a losengeour,
> That plesen yow wel moore, by my feith,
> Than he that soothfastnesse unto yow seith.
> Redeth Ecclesiaste of flaterye;
> Beth war, ye lordes, of hir trecherye.
>
> (3325–30)

If the Nun's Priest's Tale does allude to the murder of the duke of
Gloucester and the subsequent quarrel between Henry Bolingbroke and Thomas Mowbray,[49] then this apostrophe might have
touched a medieval audience in a particularly pointed way. But the
allusions to contemporary events in the tale are, as J. Leslie Hotson
himself points out, merely a "few well-chosen strokes," scattered
throughout, never a "weary parallelism,"[50] so that Chaucer's outburst might refer either to the susceptibility of Henry Bolingbroke
to flattery, if Chauntecleer is read as representing Bolingbroke, or
to the general moral decay in the court of Richard II, who was cor-
rupted by his circle of friends, if the tale is dated in October or
November 1398, shortly after the departure of Bolingbroke and
Mowbray. Moreover, passages of fully given commentary are so
characteristic of performance in general that these remarks may

simply be an example of the way a faithful and bookish storyteller freely interrupts his story just to comment wisely on public matters in general. Such a performer becomes part of a community of listeners that includes us.

Now Chaucer, I think, understood both the power of performance—what we allow, perhaps want a performer to do with a text—and the value that derives from our not being closed off from a story by a performer's charisma. In Chaucer we become part of the community of men who read and remember not by being made to feel at first outsiders to it and then special inductees as we move through poses of secretive all-knowingness to become one with Chaucer himself as interpreter, arbiter, and guardian of tales in a kind of private ownership of human tradition. Indeed, we may be, like Chaucer's Petrarchan Clerk—for Anne Middleton "an emanation and creation of his own books, a man wholly of letters"—individual guardians of tradition.[51] But that does not make us self-sustainingly possessive. Rather our communal membership is made possible by a Chaucerian storyteller in the text working against any performer's assumptions of all-knowingness—a sense of monopoly on understanding, and hence leadership in interpretation. We can see this in Chaucer's first poses as dreamer and ingénu, as faithful, bookish narrator in need of guidance. And we can see it, too, in his later work, in the *Canterbury Tales*, for example, where Chaucer works against his own magical omniscience as performer, and the omniscience of all subsequent performers (all readers), by giving any performer the part of a storyteller who cannot guide because he is, on his own account, unable to. Passages of apology (affirmations of inadequacy) in Chaucerian narrative enable an audience to manage its inevitable tendency to hear a point of view from Chaucer's storyteller. For guidance, Chaucer substitutes cooperative story-making between storyteller in the text and audience, for which the performer, or the reader himself performing, is the public (voiced) link.

Chaucer's narratives would probably have become obscure long ago had readers come to feel they could not understand Chaucer's stories without him. We know they have not, though something like obscurity attends them when a reader looks for Chaucer in his work to help him grasp them. It is a special reader indeed who

can let Chaucer go and see in Chaucer's narratives a simpleton
storyteller handing over a text to him in order for him to imitate, as Donald R. Howard says, Chaucer's "thinking presence,"[52]
not so much a storyteller who has opinions on this or that, but
a storyteller—puzzled, bookish, tentative, wide-eyed, credulous,
observant—who has an opinion on how to have opinions. Chaucer's storyteller shows the reader, in a kind of parody of wisdom,
how to maneuver through the Chaucerian landscape. The storyteller's charming deflections give him a certain naïveté and render
him incapable of being a guiding voice. His remarks ("I am a man
noght textueel") create the characteristically Chaucerian protesta-
tion of incapacity,[53] feigned, yes, because we know that Chaucer as
author was not blind to the possibilities of artistic illusion, but not
feigned in order that we pursue a Chaucer who is hiding from us.
Narrative openness of this kind invites us to amend opinions and
judgments that are insufficient—to complete tales and passages
in tales, even seemingly static ones, that a storyteller leaves unfinished.

Alfred David has shown how the puppyish narrator in the General Prologue to the *Canterbury Tales* encourages readers to set up
a scheme of values that judge Chaucer's pilgrims, something the
narrator, for all his opinions, does not do. David's idea about *our*
amending the narrator's shortcomings makes precisely my point
and seems to me particularly nice because it describes cooperative
reading in a portion of the *Canterbury Tales* that seems to be merely
a catalogue of participants in the narrative, hardly a performance
that would engage us by its liveliness.[54]

Although Chaucer does not denounce the vices of his age in the
General Prologue, he is not morally sly. I disagree with David's
view that Chaucer slowly, but inexorably, broke with medieval
conventions about the ultimate morality of art and its higher purpose.[55] But David is right when he says that "the most comprehensive standard of judgment we may apply [to Chaucer's Canterbury
pilgrims] is that of 'worth' in general, thereby borrowing Chaucer's
own thematic word 'worthy,' which appears nine times in the por-
traits and occurs in the first line of the first portrait," so that the
General Prologue becomes "an essay in 'worthinesse'" that listeners have to work through.[56] How do we do it? Patricia Eberle has

suggested how Chaucer's audience may have done it. She has observed that Chaucer's descriptions of the Canterbury pilgrims in the General Prologue assume commercial values Chaucer's noble audience found implicitly acknowledged there. In this way, the General Prologue becomes a self-revealing mirror of values, both nostalgic and contemporary, for Chaucer's audience. Eberle, too, reads the General Prologue as an essay in worthiness. "The mixture of courtly and commercial languages in the *General Prologue*," Eberle says, "evokes in the mind of an audience a mixed world unlike the world of either the romance or the *fabliau*, a world where both a knight and a merchant can be called 'worthy,' a term of praise traditional for the nobility but, at the same time, a term with its ultimate roots in the world of finance."[57] On the one hand, as Eberle says, the mixture of courtly and commercial values in the General Prologue reveals to us Chaucer's implied audience. On the other, if the mixture describes Chaucer's actual audience, it reveals to us how they may have seen themselves and their values in a text that shows their own values to them, perhaps in surprising ways. Eberle rightly insists that her stylistic observation is not *her* argument for the rise of the middle class, as reflected in Chaucer.[58] If anything, it is an argument for an ethos of mercantile projection that implicates Chaucer's aristocratic audience in the capitalist values it wants to see as characteristic of others.[59] By assuming for both its narrator and its audience "a lively interest in the world of getting and spending money, the world of commerce,"[60] Chaucer's text confronts his court audience, who in Chaucer's day *had* commercial interests, with the evaluative complexity of their economic behavior—in what sense they as *both* knights and merchants are "worthy." Would Chaucer's audience, for example, have made a medieval descriptive and moral distinction between productive and commercial capitalism or seen the distinction between less and more revolutionary kinds of capitalism in their own day, as we see it in theirs, as the reflection of mixed feudal and capitalist values?[61] Perhaps. Chaucer's text invites such evaluative entanglements. Indeed, for Chaucer's audience, the Parson's definition of commerce— for him it is a species of Christian grace, neither productive nor commercial capitalism—surely misses an obvious point about the capacity of money to earn money and give both freedom and power:

Of thilke bodily marchandise that is leveful and honest is this: that, there
as God hath ordeyned that a regne or a contree is suffisaunt to hymself,
thanne is it honest and leveful that of habundaunce of this contree, that
men helpe another contree that is moore nedy.

(10.778)

Chaucer's wider audience, in his own day and ours, would, of
course, make of the Parson's high-minded omissions in justifying
commerce and the stylistic conflation Eberle has rightly noted in
the General Prologue their own self-revealing moral and historical
context. Because he is unlike Gower or Langland in moral zeal,
we should not assume that there is nothing like a "moral Chaucer."
Donald Howard has found him.[62] And I hope to suggest in some
detail a way to find him too—in us.

Chapter Two

Medieval Storytelling

More clearly than any other passage in Chaucer, the Prologue to Melibee defines the idea of the Chaucerian performer as public servant: the idea of a man declaiming a manuscript impossible to mass-produce, but nonetheless community property, for the sake of his listeners. "Old stories" in Chaucer's day were available to everyone in the sense that members of any reading audience, Chaucer's included, might have read or heard them before.[1] In this respect, an author like Chaucer might claim that his story was original, or one of a kind, but only insofar as it was his retelling of an older story. Indeed, Chaucer never claims anywhere in his canon that he has written something wholly new; rather he asserts that he has literally, through his retelling of them, brought old stories to the public. His retelling—the actual writing of a manuscript and the performance of it—is thus, in some measure, dedication to old stories; retelling stories preserves them by making them known again publicly, for Chaucer always sees himself as serving the story he is writing. What he must "pass on" through his text and his performance is the sense of the "old story," not his skillful elaboration of it. Chaucer is thus, as he says in the *Parliament of Fowls*, the cultivator of old stories, keeping them alive by reading them:

> Of usage—what for lust and what for lore—
> On bokes rede I ofte, as I yow tolde.
> But wherfore that I speke al this? Nat yoore
> Agon, it happede me for to beholde
> Upon a bok, was write with lettres olde,

> And therupon, a certeyn thing to lerne,
> The longe day ful faste I redde and yerne.
>
> (15–21)

Chaucer reads for "usage"—use—he says. And if the distinction
he makes between "lust" and "lore," of which so much has been
made, implies that Chaucer reads either for entertainment or
for learning—a specific and knowable kind of entertainment and
learning he is intent on finding—it also implies that entertainment
and learning are the happy products of reading. Indeed, Chaucer
may be either entertained or instructed by books—much would
depend on the spirit in which he read—but his dedication to books
("with lettres olde") does not necessarily depend beforehand on
finding either "lust" or "lore." This point is important, for books for
Chaucer are places where wisdom, as he also says in the *Parliament of Fowls*, has grown, and is growing still, and from which
wisdom ("newe science") may be harvested:

> For out of olde feldes, as men seyth,
> Cometh al this newe corn from yer to yere,
> And out of olde bokes, in good feyth,
> Cometh al this newe science that men lere.
>
> (22–25)

Reading for Chaucer entails a kind of matching activity. Chaucer
comes to a book with "a certeyn thing to lerne" (20) because he has
already assumed there is learning to be had there. Old books cooperate with readers. For this reason old books, as the places where
wisdom is encountered, not just as the place where wisdom is
stored, deserve the dedication, the time and labor, Chaucer gives
them ("The longe day ful faste I redde and yerne"). The likening of
books to fields that grow new corn, not to storehouses where grain
already harvested by someone else has been stored, is justly memorable because it implies the nourishing continuity of books and
the value readers and writers derive from producing ("growing")
new works—new words ("corn")—from them. A book is less valuable as a place subject to raiding when one is hungry (bereft of
ideas), a kind of last-resort granary, than as a field for harvesting.

In the Prologue to Melibee, Chaucer explains that he has based
the manuscript of his Melibee on another manuscript (961–64). He
thus implies that some members of his audience may have heard

the Melibee before. Earlier in that same prologue, Chaucer explains precisely what he meant by the idea of basing his "murye
tale" (964) on "this tretys lyte" (963). His explanation of what we
would call his version of the Tale of Melibee—a translation that
allows for some latitude in the actual recounting of the story, but
not in the conveying of the sense of it—finds justification in what
are the variations of the four Gospels, whose authors, like himself,

> Ne seith nat alle thyng as his felawe dooth;
> But nathelees hir sentence is al sooth,
> And alle acorden as in hire sentence,
> Al be ther in hir tellyng difference.
>
> (945–48)

It is difficult to tell whether the justification for what the author of
another version of the Tale of Melibee had done was meant to answer actual allegations of authorial distortion; like any writer, Chaucer may "varie" (954) in his speech. Indeed, his variation, a gloss on
the work retold (the original), a retelling that embodies Chaucer's
understanding of what he has read, makes of his version something
new and original with him. Thus Chaucer's version of Melibee gets
at the sense of the original by being a retelling of it—an active cultivation of it as if it were, to return to Chaucer's analogy, a field for
growing corn. To cultivate "olde feldes" (Chaucer's metaphor for
the act and value of reading and writing) is to remember and, by
remembering, to make present and useful. Retelling an original
story does not in theory distort the original. It recovers it and
makes it public (present) and useful, useful for the audience who
will come to hear it performed, or perform it, just as it is useful for
an author whose métier it is to comb and cultivate the record of
human memory. That an author's retelling may fail to catch the
sense of the original does not in theory falsify the idea of a translator's will to fidelity, an idea that springs from a conscious and
laudable impulse to join and recover (cultivate and uncover) the literary and human past—the will to establish history in the self. In
this way, the actual practice of manuscript copying, which an author like Chaucer would undertake when he intended to write his
own version of a story, and his justification for it (for his variation),
is understandable. And we can perhaps see in the Prologue to
Melibee an explanation for the relationship between any of Chau-

cer's manuscript narratives and their immediate sources—a theory of writing and of its use and value.

The problem raised in the Prologue to Melibee is, of course, merely one part of the general problem of the "forme of speche" as raised in book 2 of the *Troilus*. After explaining that "to wynnen love in sondry ages, / In sondry londes, sondry ben usages" (27–28), Chaucer addresses any in the audience who *may* have felt— Chaucer *is* being gamesome here—either that Troilus's choice of words will not be efficacious because they are "wonder nyce and straunge" (24) or that Troilus's behavior as a lover is foreign to their understanding of how lovers generally act:

> And forthi if it happe in any wyse,
> That here be any lovere in this place
> That herkneth, as the storie wol devise,
> How Troilus com to his lady grace,
> And thenketh, "so nold I nat love purchace,"
> Or wondreth on his speche or his doynge,
> I noot.
>
> (29–35)

The reference to "any lovere in this place" may tease the members of Chaucer's audience by flattering them; it implies that they are all lovers. The reference follows book 1 of the *Troilus*, where everyone has heard Troilus sound very much in love. Still, the problem of believing in the effectiveness of Troilus's words and behavior may be at some time an obstacle to the credibility of the love story. The reference to "any lovere" presumes that readers, despite Troilus's apparently complete command of the range of love's moods, judge Troilus's behavior. The point is not that any reader would be puzzled by some of Troilus's acts, but that he *might be*, since public behavior and public language change. Chaucer's response to a problem he seems to anticipate about the intelligibility of his text is not rigged—Chaucer is not being coy here, but inviting—for in light of the circumstances of reading before a public and the fears that Chaucer expresses in his *Wordes unto Adam, His Owne Scriveyn*, the problem of the "forme of speche" either in *Troilus and Criseyde*, or anywhere else in his work, can only be "solved" and the story preserved, made intelligible to the public, by accommodating a manuscript narrative to all varieties of readers. Through his reference to broad historical changes, Chaucer is, of course, calling attention here to the textuality of his work—the fact that it is written down and can only "happen" as we listen to it and imagine. Chaucer's *Wordes unto Adam*—one copyist addressing a somewhat more pedestrian one—reveals, for example, some of the concerns that beset any author before the invention of printing and have beset any author since:

> So ofte a-daye I mot thy werk renewe,
> It to correcte and eek to rubbe and scrape;
> And al is thorugh thy negligence and rape.
>
> (5–7)

But Chaucer's obvious care about the transmission of his work at the hands of a "sloppy" copyist reflects real and legitimate fears about the unsettled state of English in his own day, not just about a copyist's (an editor's, not merely a printer's) possible errors. For Chaucer the intelligibility and hence popularity of a narrative is directly related to the degree of actual dialectical difference in the language. As Chaucer says in the *Troilus* (5.1793–98), to "myswrite" is not only to "mysmetre" the narrative, but to run the risk of making it misunderstood. Meaning in Chaucer is always negotiated in the public forum *as* a narrative is read. A Chaucerian tale is built in the mind both out of what the performer says—and the authority the performer's magical omniscience may give to what he says—and out of what the participating listener understands. Between the copyist and the performer, there is the chance of compounded error.

A manuscript narrative, I should emphasize, is not only one book, but many; the modern equivalent to a medieval manuscript might be the scenario of a story rather than a word-for-word printed edition of it. A scenario, like a medieval manuscript, is realized as it is read, taking full shape only as it is performed. Like a medieval manuscript, it requires the response of an audience to complete it. A public manuscript is not published and then read; it is published by being read.[2] The author of the story will, therefore, pace the narrative so that an audience can follow it and "fill it out." Reading cooperatively does not imply that the author is incompetent, but only that he cannot possibly make the entire narrative explicit to everyone, given the nature of language and the circumstances of public narration.

Although nothing about the circumstances of its presentation would require such a course, a novelist may also ask readers to complete a story in their imaginations. In this case, the novelist treats narrative as participatory in the same sense as the author of a declaimed manuscript. On the one hand, keeping the narrative open to readers ensures that the novel can be read by many people. On the other hand, however, a novelist does not ask readers to co-operate in the telling of the story in exactly the same way in which Chaucer might ask his audience to "read with him." Even if retelling an older tale, a novelist generally views the retold version as one of a kind, claiming the "aura" of an original for the work, as Walter Benjamin puts it.[3] For Chaucer, however, cooperation implies dedication to the idea of the "old story" being retold to preserve it, and to preserve the civilized community who hear it, because an "olde boke" is the "keye of remembraunce," not because it is an original piece or a reproduction. Reading ensures continuity for Chaucer. Memory, as Benjamin says, "creates the chain of tradition which passes a happening [a story] on from generation to generation."[4]

Thus Chaucer's stories create companionship and are built *as texts* to create it. Portions of the narrative that repeat, clarify, or summarize, as well as extra-verbal performative devices such as facial expressions, hand gestures, and body motions in general, which animate what is being read, make Chaucer's work accessible to those who may not understand at first hearing, but who want to. Listeners cannot put a manuscript down while it is being performed; they are, in this sense, its captive audience. Actual experience with declamation would enable an author to sense how long he should sustain his narrative before some kind of break, just as practice in reading publicly enables a performer to adjust his pace, his inflection, and his capacity to give his story life to the mood—the patience or impatience—of his audience. Like an author's literary sense of declamation, a performer's magical omniscience can be made to serve the story rather than the author's ego or the performer's presence. If the author is, in his own mind *as author*, subordinate to the story he is retelling, the performer is, in his mind, subordinate to the author, for the performer's part is given him. Although he can, through his public reading, interpret the story he presents, he is bound, like the author, to an idea of guardianship over the integrity of the text he holds in his hands. Actors today understand this, as do some teachers; the idea is not foreign to us.[5]

Thus a manuscript narrative performed is ideally paced to the comprehension of all; it has to be socially accommodating, and if we are "reading aloud to ourselves," it accommodates the many persons in each reader, the socially flexible self, rather than romantic uniqueness ("privetee"). In theory, everyone ought to be able to read it, and a public (or private) performer, who reads for everyone, takes pains to make sure everyone understands. In book 5 of the *Troilus*, the storyteller actually pauses to gloss a word:

> And but if Calkas lede us with ambages,
> That is to seyn, with double wordes slye,
> Swiche as men clepen a word with two visages,
> Ye shal wel knowen that I naught ne lye.
>
> (897–900)

The narrator explains that the phrase "lede us with ambages" means leading with equivocation ("with double wordes slye"), although the narrator has taken the opportunity to clarify ("that is to seyn") while simultaneously being amusingly literal ("a word with two visages"). For a performer, the part of the storyteller *in the text* plays well as a bookish man; I do not hear Diomedes in these lines, and I suspect I am not supposed to. Verbal equivocation, the storyteller explains, is the use of one word with two "faces," because one is led by an image, not by a sound. The impulse to clarify for the benefit and amusement of listeners has momentarily taken precedent over the story itself, for clarification is an essential aspect of Chaucer's real concern for the intelligibility of his text. The storyteller's pause in order to clarify is admittedly awkward for a modern reader—the witty literalism does not help either—but it is nonetheless thoroughly in keeping with the aim of broad narrative accommodation.

We can thus see that a manuscript narrative declaimed is always explaining itself to its audience because it has a number of people reading it at once—some will understand more than others; some faster than others—and it must ideally be understood by all of them. A printed book, because it neither is nor need be in so direct a relationship to its audience, lends itself much more tolerably as a form to the self-expression of its author and less to the immediate demands of an audience who must hear and understand the first time. The proem to book 2 of the *Troilus* concludes with one of the narrator's characteristic expressions of humility ("but syn I have bigonne, / Myn auctour shal I folwen, if I konne" [48–49]), but the problem Chaucer sees for himself as a translator of the books of others is a real one. He must gauge his own version of a manuscript narrative, for the sake of the story, to the capacity of his audience to understand a text declaimed; his demands are always of the moment.

Thus when Chaucer in book 3 of the *Troilus* argues for the impracticality of a full-blown realism by an appeal to his "auctour," he gives each reader a place in the story:

> But now, paraunter, som man wayten wolde
> That every word, or soonde, or look, or cheere
> Of Troilus that I rehercen sholde,
> In al this while unto his lady deere.
> I trowe it were a long thyng for to here;
> Or of what wight that stant in swich disjoynte,
> His wordes alle, or every look, to poynte.
>
> For sothe, I have naught herd it don er this
> In story non, ne no man here, I wene;
> And though I wolde, I koude nought, ywys;
> For ther was som epistel hem betwene,
> That wolde, as seyth myn autour, wel contene
> Neigh half this book, of which hym liste nought write.
> How sholde I thanne a lyne of it endite?
>
> (491–504)

Because his author has not given him the letter, Chaucer says, Chaucer cannot reproduce it. Although the argument is amusing, it is not rigged. It perhaps would not advance the point of the interchange between Troilus and Criseyde to give details that may obscure and delay; it would certainly leave readers less active in pursuit of the story, readers who can well imagine "every word, or soonde, or look, or cheere / Of Troilus." Love letters contain secrets, and it is superior devising for Chaucer to be silent, and thus intimate, about matters we all surely know firsthand. To say anything would be to let textuality get the upper hand, for Chaucer is interested in the performative (imaginative and cooperative) aspect of Criseyde's letter, not its verifiable content.

Now there is a curious reference to the "redere" in book 5 of the *Troilus* that, in light of Chaucer's role as public servant to his narrative, we can perhaps clarify. After explaining that it is beyond his powers of expression to "telle[n] aright or ful discryve" (267) Troilus's woe at having to be separated from Criseyde, Chaucer as author and performer addresses his audience directly:

> Thow, redere, maist thiself ful wel devyne
> That swich a wo my wit kan nat diffyne.
> On ydel for to write it sholde I swynke,
> Whan that my wit is wery it to thynke.
>
> (270–73)

Although "redere" is singular, Chaucer's intention is probably not to single out one "reader" from among his listeners. Chaucer's use of the familiar "thow" reflects some sense of intimacy with all his readers; we might say "each one of you." The familiar address enlists sympathy and help for Chaucer's "failing verbal powers"; it appeals to any reader's concern for the story he hears—his sense of its accuracy, authenticity, truth, and value. If we imagine this passage in the hands of a private reader, the reference to the "redere" does not essentially change the thrust of the invitation. Listeners and readers—both have a manuscript conceived as narrative declaimed, whether or not actually declaimed—are asked to cooperate with the author as performer in bringing an "old story" to the public.

Indeed, a passage in the Prologue to the Second Nun's Tale defines the distinctly medieval version of the idea of making a tale public:

> Yet preye I yow that reden that I write,
> Foryeve me that I do no diligence
> This ilke storie subtilly to endite,
> For bothe have I the wordes and sentence
> Of hym that at the seintes reverence
> That storie wroot, and folwen hire legende,
> And pray yow that ye wole my werk amende.
>
> (78–84)

The word "amende" here may have substantive meaning—it may not be merely polite invitation—for it suggests that the members of the audience ought both to "correct" the tale for inaccuracies, because of what they may know about the story of St. Cecilia from other manuscript sources, or from other reading, and to "amplify" the tale by filling it out and thus interpreting it, for the sake of the story; the idea of amending the tale is thus an invitation to be like the author himself, a vehicle for the manuscript story. Listeners may well attempt to follow the pattern of the narrator's apologies and read without assuming a monopoly on interpretation. In book 3 of the *Troilus*, Chaucer specifically asks readers who may know more about love than he does—although he knows something—to correct or amplify his version of the story:

> But soth is, though I kan nat tellen al,
> As kan myn auctour, of his excellence,
> Yet have I seyd, and God toforn, and shal
> In every thyng, al holy his sentence;
> And if that ich, at Loves reverence,
> Have any word in eched for the beste,
> Doth therwithal right as youreselven leste.
>
> For myne wordes, heere and every part,
> I speke hem alle under correccioun
> Of yow that felyng han in loves art
> And putte it al in youre discrecioun
> To encresse or maken dymynucioun
> Of my langage, and that I yow biseche.
>
> (1324–36)

Chaucer here invites us to do the best we can with his text, just as he has done the best he can with *his* author's text. Both he and we are assumed to be knowledgeable about love (from life *and* books) and serious about understanding, making an old text (and a new one)—there will be newer ones, too—clear.

In book 5 of the *Troilus*, the narrator even suggests that if anyone is in doubt about the accuracy or sense of what he is reading, he should look at the original:

> But trewely, how longe it was bytwene
> That she forsok hym for this Diomede,
> Ther is non auctour telleth it, I wene.
> Take every man now to his bokes heede;
> He shal no terme fynden, out of drede.
>
> (1086–90)

The point is not that anyone would look for a "terme" in the sources to Chaucer's *Troilus*, but the idea that an author's narrative, because it is based on another manuscript narrative, or narratives, is as accessible to anyone as it was to him—that is, accessible to interpretation. The medieval storyteller did not, of course, pretend to subjective originality; he merely happened to be the man most skilled verbally in bringing a manuscript narrative before the reading public. He was its actual literary servant—the "copyist" of the words of others—more than a scribe, but scribal in his approach to literary composition. The medieval author was both the transmitter and the spokesman, though not final arbiter, of the manuscript narrative he used in the writing of his own version of the same story.

Indeed, the narrative stance in Chaucer is often a kind of knowing equivocation to permit a number of possible interpretations, since the text is a book for everyone. In book 1 of the *Troilus*, for example, the narrator backs away from easy interpretation:

> But how it was, certeyn, kan I nat seye,
> If that his lady understood nat this,
> Or feynede hire she nyste, oon of the tweye;
> But wel I rede that, by no manere weye,
> Ne semed it as that she of hym roughte,
> Or of his peyne, or whatsoevere he thoughte.
>
> (492–97)

In this passage, Chaucer not only explains that the information his sources provide does not allow him to form an opinion, but implicitly acknowledges that it is likely a reader may wish to understand more than Chaucer can specify here; Chaucer recognizes that it is emotionally and judgmentally crucial to know whether Criseyde is innocent or playing obtuse, but that it is also impossible to determine. A reader may decide one way or the other, but either way, Chaucer reminds him, a reader has no actual basis for his judgment in the "boke" itself. Chaucer and his audience together, as it were, are up against a text that refuses to specify an important fact about Criseyde's knowledge.[6]

The only passage where Chaucer explicitly calls himself the "servant" of anything occurs in lines 15–21 of the proem to book 1 of the *Troilus*. Line 15 ("For I, that God of Loves servantz serve") has been identified as a paraphrase of the papal title *servus servorum*

Dei, and, in the context of the narrative, the narrator stands in relationship to lovers who serve the God of Love as Chaucer does to
his real audience.[7] Although the storyteller in the *Troilus* explains
that he himself is not a lover, he says that he can, through the story
he narrates, serve those who "worship" love:

> But natheles, if this may don gladnesse
> To any lovere, and his cause availle,
> Have he my thonk, and myn be this travaille!
>
> (19–21)

The idea of serving Love's servants makes performance a rite of
"religious" affirmation, the erotic-secular equivalent to hearing the
gospel or the lesson in church. Chaucer as the "servant of the servants of love" knows the old words necessary for worship.

In book 2 of the *House of Fame*, there is also a reference to
Chaucer's service to the God of Love—Chaucer is not specifically
called a servant, although that is the implication—this time made
on behalf of Jupiter by the Eagle who is speaking to Chaucer:

> Certeyn, he hath of the routhe,
> That hou so longe trewely
> Hast served so ententyfly
> Hys blynde nevew Cupido,
> And faire Venus also,
> Withoute guerdon ever yit,
> And never-the-lesse hast set thy wit—
> Although that in thy hed ful lyte is—
> To make bookys, songes, dytees,
> In ryme, or elles in cadence,
> As thou best canst, in reverence
> Of Love, and his hys servantes eke,
> That have hys servyse soght, and seke.
>
> (614–26)

Chaucer has not directly explained in this passage how he serves a
public through declamation—the secular equivalent to religious
worship—although he has made it clear that he has written his
"bookys, songes, dytees" for the sake of those intent on serving
love. In book 2 of the *House of Fame* as in the *Troilus*, Chaucer
asserts that he has not personally experienced love. The Eagle
makes the point:

And peynest the to preyse hys art,
Although thou haddest never part.
(627–28)

Chaucer is thus only the servant of servants. Still, in his public
reading of love poems, he can speak for those who worship in a way
analogous to that in which a celibate priest can perform marriages.

In the F Prologue to the *Legend of Good Women*, Chaucer is
actually "condemned" by the God of Love for having written what
are, according to the latter, heresies against his law, and for having,
in particular, defamed women by composing the *Troilus* and trans-
lating the *Roman de la Rose*. Thus, when Chaucer kneels by Love's
flower, he is upbraided for his disservice (315–18). From the point
of view of the God of Love and, by analogy, from the point of view
of Chaucer's audience, Chaucer's role as performing poet can either
"help" or "hinder" the worship of love through the stories Chaucer
tells. In the F Prologue to the *Legend of Good Women*, Chaucer is
on trial for what he has failed to write; the God of Love has asked
for unequivocal *exempla* and feels he has gotten, in the *Troilus* and
the *Romaunt*, something less. Robert Frank has argued that from
the point of view of the God of Love and those in Chaucer's audience who expect Chaucer to be exemplary, Chaucer offers less than
foursquare *exempla* in the *Legend of Good Women*.[8] What is implied in the God of Love's rebuke, however, is the idea that the
role of the performer is sacerdotal. Not that the author or performer has in himself some special genius—something godlike, pe-
culiar to him alone as a literary man—but that the author and performer have a public trust. The role is hypothetically available to
everyone, but not everyone can perform it. The author thus articulates for the community what each man cannot say singly; here perhaps the analogy between the writer as servant of God *and* the God
of Love is more than figurative. Reading is done for the community
of men by a public man. Public reading is not like the worship of
God; it is not directed to another being, although in its own way it
consecrates the body social. It is devoted to remembering old stories, and although it is without the deep solemnity of worship, it
nonetheless demonstrates that declamation, a social activity, gives
the community of men an occasion to hear of its past and judge
what is more than particular about it—to learn in effect what is

timeless about it and what ought, therefore, to be common knowledge. This is not being taught something outside of a context that includes us. Indeed, this is only teaching (being taught something) because we are the focus of a story's effect on us. And we are in history.

In the G Prologue to the *Legend of Good Women*, Chaucer says his aim as author and performer is to lay bare the idea of the text, the "sentence" of the story, which all his readers, including himself as author, are trying to get at:

> For myn entent is, or I fro yow fare,
> The naked text in English to declare
> Of many a story, or elles of many a geste,
> As autours seyn; leveth hem if yow leste!
> (85–88)

The idea of making a text "naked"—open so that its inner point is available—surely gives us something of the reason Chaucer has "reverence" (82) for "olde aproved storyes" (21), as he says in the G Prologue to the *Legend of Good Women*. Because these stories have been heard before, hearing them again aligns readers with the ancient and general human tradition the stories seem to embody. Reading defines performer and listener as social and historical beings—people with active (and acting) memories. Indeed, it is just *because* stories have been heard before and been approved of that they ought to be listened to again. "Aproved" has the ring of truth for the community of men that stories serve to create and re-create as they are read. It is perhaps for this reason that Pandarus says, in book 2 of the *Troilus*, that, despite the "subtyl art"— perhaps the pleasure of literary embellishment—that often makes stories appear to lack a clear intent, no story is altogether pointless:

> How so it be that som men hem delite
> With subtyl art hire tales for to endite,
> Yet for al that, in hire entencioun,
> Hire tale is al for som conclusioun.
> (256–59)

Pandarus has not, of course, specifically said what stories must teach, although he insists that they are told for some reason, no matter how "entertaining" they are. And that reason implicates us.

Instead of the kind of allegorical reading Chaucer's text is usually given, a reading that implies a private decoding of the text—a raid on it as if it were a storehouse rather than a field—I think Chaucer's narratives require what I call parabolic listening. My distinction does not rest on the quibble between reading Chaucer privately and listening to him declaim, something we can only imagine. Nor does it rest on a distinction between a Robertsonian reading of Chaucer and an "anti-Robertsonian," Muscatinian one in which it is claimed that the variegated vitality of life is itself Chaucer's moral norm.[9] Both kinds of readings raid the text. My distinction between allegorical reading and parabolic listening rests on certain recoverable assumptions about medieval storytelling implicit in the special forms of address of the parables of Jesus and in the value of the literal surface of a text as argued for in the exegetical theory of Hugh of St. Victor. Moreover, there is evidence that Chaucer knew and understood the implications of such biblical and medieval storytelling assumptions and that these assumptions lie at the heart of his storytelling. Furthermore, I have made the distinction between reading and listening to suggest that, unlike parabolic listening, which in fact establishes us within a historical circle of understanding, allegorical reading requires an intellectual diligence and interpretive translation that devalues the literal surface of a text and its shareable alignments of text and reader and world.

As I mean the term, allegorical reading of a text requires that the naturalistic details of a story be translated into a pattern of ideas that replaces the story so that the story can *mean something*. Both Robertsonians and anti-Robertsonians see Chaucer illustrating maxims—his narratives are about morality, Christian or humanist, God-given or universal, using the literal level of his stories to mirror the ideational. Indeed, both Robertsonians and anti-Robertsonians, as we know, leave Chaucer without subject matter other than general maxims, for both assume that the literal level of a story is only a make-do structure until the mind can accommodate itself to the ideas that the literal level embodies and points to, and for which it has value. Allegorical reading never denies the realism of the literal level, but for an allegorist what actually happens in a story does not explain in what way the events are significant. For an allegorist, realism is *there*, in the story, so as to charge it with meaning, and interpretation is intended to put the text to its proper use, not only for the ideas the text is said to have and point to, but also for the allegorist, for whom interpretation is a testimony to faith. To an allegorist, interpretation is witness to a conviction in the meaningfulness of the story—it has meaning to be gotten and understood—and in the meaningfulness of God, who has given the allegorist, through the world, the elements of the story. Interpretation for the allegorist is a sign of commitment to meaning. And to interpret with the requisite faith in the meaningfulness of the text brings blessedness—the honor of humility and wisdom.

Now a parabolic listener, though also committed to meaning, comes to a story expecting to hear it for what it is, not to decode it or make it what it *ought to be*, as if it were a cryptogram. For the parabolic listener realism has its own interest; it is there to help— to confer similitude, give topicality—and it is not finally without a point. But the parabolic listener—a private reader can listen para- bolically, too—need not do even the most benign kind of violence to the literal sense to make a story that seems to see "truth in con- crete pictures" rather than "in abstractions,"[10] a story possessed of a certain guileless naturalism, mean in a way that implies a need to recover a hidden original true sense now concealed on purpose.

Edgar de Bruyne makes an important distinction between kinds of allegory, much overlooked by Chaucerians and modern critics of allegory, that seems to have been commonplace in medieval aes- thetic theory. Dante certainly knew it, and Chaucer, I can only suppose, did also.[11] De Bruyne says that there was a difference be- tween what he calls religious allegory (what Dante calls the alle- gory of theologians) and parabolism (what Dante calls the allegory of poets). The former, says de Bruyne, is "directly concerned with objects" that have "a dual structure, to which, obviously, corre- sponds a double meaning." Moreover, that meaning "is the cre- ation of the will of God and imposes itself upon the human intel- lect, which is powerless to change it."[12] Religious, or theological, allegory only refers to "real objects"; it is genuine allegory based on the "objective structure of the world created by God," a double re- ality "at once physical and supernatural."[13] Parabolism, or the alle- gory of poets, or "classical" allegory, "concerns only words," which can have a "literal and a figurative meaning"; it is a "human in- vention."[14] It is not a mysterious "true" bridge to creation itself, nor are its elements—its literal level—"real" events.

Given de Bruyne's distinction between kinds of allegory, there follows a difference in the way one approaches each. One reads religious allegory as if one were reading a "holy text" (i.e., the Scriptures themselves or the book of nature). One is "passive" to the text. Meaning is already given—religious allegory is authoritarian—and is merely discovered. It is, in effect, imposed on the mind of the reader. By contrast, one reads the allegory of poets "actively," in the sense that one takes delight in the power of a gifted intellect to make connections that are both true and thrilling. Moreover, a joy in the power of the mind, an aesthetic exhilaration that does not cloud over, indeed belongs to, the perception of truths hidden in a fiction, accompanies this reading experience. Religious allegory inspires awe and a certain humility before the doubleness of creation itself, a doubleness the text literally mirrors. In his reading of Chaucer, Robertson, the modern proponent of Chaucer as allegorist, has rejected de Bruyne's aesthetic and historical distinction, so that what he offers as "Chaucer the allegorist" is, on theoretical grounds, shaky. Robertson's exegetical reading links the pleasures of discovery, "the pleasure of search, surprise, and astonishment" in Chaucer, without making clear whether one has discovered that which is "imposed" on the mind by God or what is "made" by the inspired human mind alone.[15] Clearly what should be at issue for a Robertsonian are Chaucer's own claims for his work. For to use patristic exegesis on a text other than the Scriptures or the book of nature implicitly assumes that the author of the text claims for his work a status like that of Scripture. Joseph Mazzeo has shown that Dante makes that claim for the *Divine Comedy*,[16] but does Chaucer for any of his work? I do not find any evidence for thinking so, at least not about the *Canterbury Tales*. Donald Howard does not think so either. He has written about the "Canterbury" tales as tidings in a way that both amplifies his own sense of them as lies and anticipates my sense of them, and of all of Chaucer's narratives, as fictions of discovery and testing.[17] "Tidings," Howard says, "are where events and language meet, where the world becomes preserved in words. They are the end of action; they are the beginnings of legends and fictions, the raw stuff of literature."[18] The idea that the "tales of Canterbury" are tidings—"not each is true, but each is authentic," with "a person behind it even if that person is a liar"—strongly suggests that Chaucer's nar-

ratives are fictions of self-discovery. In reading them, "we have to
seek out and decide upon the truth or authenticity of tidings, and
so reading literature demands of us an act of will: the truth of a
poem, if it is written 'for our doctrine', must be in *our* idea of it."
The distinction here between truth and authenticity is nice indeed.
Reading Chaucer demands of us an engagement that will decide
truth as value for us, since a tiding is given, as Howard says, as a
stance "that invites and permits."[19] Howard has here touched on
the way verisimilitude itself calls on us to use it. Realism in Chaucer points with, and through, detail to a reality that calls forth, indeed demands, interpretation, not a reading *through*, but a reading *with*.

Moreover, the idea of tales as tidings—fictions—strongly suggests that if Chaucer's narratives are fictions of self-discovery, mirrors of (and for) us, they are not fictions that lay claim to the "true
doubleness" of creation. Given de Bruyne's aesthetic distinctions,
then, both Robertsonians and anti-Robertsonians are religious allegorists. Both read *through* Chaucer's text in order to make clear
and applicable either God's truth or humanist value. Indeed, the
structuralist humanism I see in Muscatine—the claim he makes
for juxtaposition as the technique in Chaucer that reveals multiplicity—is a ready example of the doctrinal use of literature. Both
the idea of religious allegory and the allegory of poets entail ideas
about the nature of art and the world that readers bring to texts and
to objects. De Bruyne's distinction is a distinction of mind as well
as of genre (things). The point is that texts (or the world) can be
conceived (grasped) in many ways—"read" as religious allegory
(used up, as it were) or "listened to" (put to use) as a veil or as
words (or signs). The distinction rests not on assumptions *in* texts
or the world, but assumptions brought *to* each by a willful power of
mind. The antithesis, for example, that de Bruyne says was drawn
in the Middle Ages between "allegory" and "integument" is only a
difference *within* the larger, too often neglected, distinction between religious allegory and parabolism—a distinction at the heart
of the matter.[20]

It is instructive here to observe how a theory about the demands
and difficulties of the literal surface can explain how Chaucer's narratives are parabolic in C. H. Dodd's sense. For Dodd, a story is
parablelike if it is an elaboration of a single comparison, "a meta-

phor or simile drawn from nature or common life, arresting the
hearer by its vividness or strangeness, and leaving the mind in sufficient doubt about its precise application to tease it into active
thought."[21] All the details of such a story are designed "to set the
situation or series of events in the clearest possible light, so as to
catch the imagination" and direct it:[22]

All is true to nature and to life. Each similitude or story is a perfect picture of something that can be observed in the world of experience. The
processes of nature are accurately observed and recorded; the actions of
persons in the stories are in character; they are either such as anyone
would recognize as natural in the circumstances, or, if they are surprising,
the point of the parable is that such actions *are* surprising.[23]

Dodd explains that the realism of the parables of Jesus "arises from
a conviction that there is no mere analogy, but an inward affinity,
between the natural order and the spiritual order." Because nature
and the supernatural are one, any "part in that order" can illuminate the whole. New Testament parables teach that now, since
Jesus, "the Kingdom of God is intrinsically *like* the processes of nature and the daily life of men," so that one need not make up "ar-
tificial illustrations" for the truth of God.[24] The parables of Jesus
present "the ministry of Jesus as 'realized eschatology', that is to
say, as the impact upon this world of the 'powers of the world to
come' in a series of events, unprecedented and unrepeatable, now
in actual process."[25] These parables "enforce and illustrate the idea
that the Kingdom of God had come upon men there and then. The
inconceivable had happened [and is still happening]; history has
become the vehicle of the eternal; the absolute was clothed with
flesh and blood."[26]

Unfortunately, Dodd's thesis about the realism of the parables of
Jesus has not yet been brought to bear on the study of storytelling
in the Middle Ages. For if he has defined a uniquely Christian view
of history and of art—for the Jews the best the world can illustrate
are the "things to come"—he has defined storytelling as an occasion to meet God in nature and history. In Dodd's view, "Christian
realism" is both realistic and moral; for him there is a major current
in medieval thinking that sees no inherent conflict between being
realistic and being moral; in fact being both is inevitable, since God
is in history now, and in the art that mirrors history. As such, inter-

pretation should not, because it does not, violate the realism of the parable. Interpretation does not depend either on giving an independent (timeless) moral significance to each detail or on assuming that realistic details argue for the humanist (human and timeless) value of realism itself. Application of the parable to moral life is effected "through a judgment on the imagined situation," without any necessary "decoding of the various elements in the story" to make them illustrate some principle.[27] All parables entice "a reader to a judgment upon the situation depicted,"[28] where all is true to nature. The idea of judgment here does not mean "passing judgment" once, and finally, so much as the "taking into account" of the particular circumstances of the case; judgment means judging, successively and piecemeal, where judgment itself does no violence to nature, though it may change the reader. Indeed, the argumentative or provocative character of parables always demands decisions. If a reader "elects the parabolic world, he is invited to dispose himself to concrete reality as it is ordered in the parable, and venture, without benefit of landmark but on the parable's authority, into the future."[29]

Now parables have always been thought of as tests of their hearers' understanding. If, for example, we compare Matthew's explanation of the Parable of the Sower with Mark's explanation, we can see something of the idea of parabolic intention. In Mark, the Parable of the Sower is explained as if to keep some men outside the sense of the narrative:

And he said unto them, Unto you it is given to know the mystery of the kingdom of God; but unto those who are outside, all these things are done in parables, / That seeing they may see, and not perceive; and hearing they may hear, and not understand; lest at any time they should be converted, and their sins should be forgiven them. (4:11–12)

In Matthew, the parable is explained as if to make the truth accessible—to create insiders, since outsiders are dull-witted:

Therefore speak I to them in parables, because they seeing, see not; and hearing, they hear not, neither do they understand. (13:13)

But in both cases, the Parable of the Sower is "about" exclusion. It both seems to offer itself and is offered (in Matthew at least) as explicit, yet it seems to speak darkly; it both proclaims itself openly and conceals enigmatically. Thus in Matthew, Jesus speaks in similitudes ("in parables") so that those who need to know the mystery of the Kingdom of God will understand the parable as a defense against those who do not know the mystery; it is a vehicle for teaching *if* its meaning is already clear, or rather a vehicle for affirmation or reinforcement. In one way, Mark *feels* intolerant, for he seems to say that Jesus speaks "in parables" (in riddles) in order to damn outsiders. But this may be the uncharitable reading of Mark; for if the mystery of the Kingdom of God is precious (and it is), then both the understanding and the reality of it, gained in part through the understanding, ought to be sought after. We need not, of course, seek after meaning by wrenching the literal sense of a parable; we need not become allegorical readers in order to get to, and show how we have gotten to, understand and "live" the mystery of the Kingdom of God. *That* seems to be God's gift, which our wanting cannot will Him to give, though He gives it, whether we are allegorical readers or parabolic listeners.

We can see the allegorical view of Mark's idea of a parable clearly enough in St. Augustine's *On Christian Doctrine*, where Augustine exalts, as a sign of our blessedness, our laboring to make a text promote the reign of charity. But Augustine's version of Mark is not implicit in the Marcan explanation of the Parable of the Sower:

Many and varied obscurities and ambiguities deceive those who read casually, understanding one thing instead of another; indeed, in certain places they do not find anything to interpret erroneously, so obscurely are certain sayings covered with a most dense mist. I do not doubt that this situation was provided by God to conquer pride by work and to combat disdain in our minds, to which those things which are easily discovered seem frequently to become worthless.[30]

If, indeed, Augustine felt some of the frustration of the Marcan view that parables are only for insiders, so that he offers a way for us to demonstrate that we understand *how* to understand a text ("what is sought with difficulty is discovered with more pleasure"), he nonetheless asserts in the same sentence that "for the present, however, no one doubts that things are perceived more readily through similitudes."[31] Here is an apparent conflation of the Marcan and Matthean views of parables as if there were no differences, for indeed the implication of both Mark and Matthew, whatever their differences, is that parables, indeed all stories, need interpreting. They are dark and speak obliquely. Between Mark and Matthew, we are thus given (for all stories, because exegesis is still with us)[32] a reason for both the "darkness" of narrative—it has precious meaning only for insiders, who must learn to read "into the story"—and the seeming guilelessness of it—it has meaning that the "eyes and ears," the senses for which it was written, will make understandable. Furthermore, for both Mark and Matthew, understanding brings health; that is, it completes what we know, or should know, about ourselves, and so completes, or fulfills, the story, since understanding the biblical story—being an insider rather than an outsider—is itself either the vehicle for (if we insist on following Matthew) or the test of (if we follow Mark) an awakening of the reader.

More than ten years ago, John T. Irwin and T. D. Kelly, in applying the idea of parabolic intention, showed how biblical parables,[33] one kind of *exemplum* that does not give truth, in J. A. Mosher's sense,[34] so much as admit us to it, became for other storytellers in other contexts a model of storytelling that consciously puts the reader on the challenging end of doctrine. Irwin and Kelly do not trace a direct line of descent from New Testament parables to any of Chaucer's work, although they do trace one to both *Cleanness* and *Patience*.[35] These are religious poems; still, Irwin and Kelly suggest that the biblical parable, because of what it assumes about the presence of God in the world *now* and the way Christ talked to Christians, provided a specifically Christian rhetoric for any medieval storyteller who had something to say: a way to talk to those who are in the presence of the truth so that what is said will reveal to everyone, particularly those who listen, how completely they understand:

In their original setting (Christ's public ministry) the parables were used by Christ as a linguistic device to initiate the separation that was their subject, the separation of the few who are to be included in the kingdom of heaven from the many who are to be kept out. This separation, which becomes final at the Last Judgment, begins on earth in the varying responses of those who hear Christ's parables. The few who have been given the knowledge of the kingdom of heaven understand the parables and accept Christ, while the many who have hardened their hearts against the

word do not understand the parables and reject Christ. The final separation is brought about by a divine judgment, the present separation by a
human judgment. They are not the same judgment, but one grows out of
the other, for God judges of us on the last day according to the way in
which we have judged of Christ's teachings. Thus in judging Christ's parables we pass judgment on ourselves.[36]

Irwin and Kelly argue that biblical parables, and all stories that
work like New Testament parables—as I think Chaucer's narratives
do—require the reader's judgment on the story—parables are stories that initiate the reader into truth—and the reader's evaluation
of that judgment—parables are stories that define who the reader
is. Biblical parables and parablelike stories are mirrors for the
reader—mirrors for those who understand what is hidden and who
recognize that an act of understanding is an act of self-definition.
By *not* telling us what to think or how to behave, parables, in Irwin
and Kelly's sense, tell us what we know and who we are.[37] The special feature of New Testament parables—the teller who confounds
expectations for simple moral guidance in the interest of our spiritual awakening—is the special feature of all parablelike stories, the
feature that makes them at once recognizable *as stories* and as
stories that serve truth.[38] Through them we recognize the world,
ourselves, and ourselves in the world.

We have our version of the idea of stories as truthservers. The
idea is not new to us; no matter how consciously we read a story
for its "slice of life," we still like, for example, to comment on the
story we read and see what our comments tell us about ourselves.
We are in a way heirs to the eschatology of the parable, for to see
how a story comments on us as we read it is surely to hold some
view of the immanence of truth—to claim that truth is available
to us now in the world as we live in and judge it. Indeed, to recognize ourselves in stories is to judge the world of which we are a
part and about which stories seem to talk. The idea of parabolic
listening as an approach to Chaucer thus has the double virtue of
encouraging the reader's thoughtfulness while not taxing the author's or reader's ingenuity. No one, either author or reader, need
make a text, which is already "about something"—its literal level—
mean something else in a better (or deeper) way. Indeed, allegorizing Chaucer's stories, consciously making them mean something else, as both Robertsonians and anti-Robertsonians do, is in

itself quite perverse, for Chaucer intended his stories neither for the church nor for the schoolroom (where one might want, and be encouraged, to read through the text, as if it were a window). Allegories invite by virtue of being closed and offering a reader an insider's understanding. They are not provocative, except insofar as they are closed, and complete closure may be inviting. For the man of faith—and the allegorist has faith in the rightness of his interpretive acts—to be an insider gives both power and humility, confidence and universality. Parablelike stories invite by being open (breaking open), by "extravagance," as Paul Ricoeur says, speaking of biblical parables,[39] and offering readers the occasion to demonstrate how they become insiders. Allegories allow insiders to demonstrate that they are insiders, too, but not with the same necessary urgency to show or witness that mystery is accessible, understanding possible.

In book 6 of his *Didascalicon*, Hugh of St. Victor teaches the necessity of knowing, through study and meditation, the literal sense of the Scriptures before beginning to expound their deeper meaning. While he acknowledges that the student of the Scriptures should "adhere staunchly to the truth of the spiritual meaning and that the high points of the literal meaning, which itself can sometimes be wrongly understood too, should not lead him away from the central concern in any way whatever," Hugh offers his particular exegetical program so that interpretation of the Bible's spiritual sense can be "grounded" (Hugh's word) in the literal (surface) meaning of the text and thereby be guided by language itself *and* history, the word he uses to define "not only the recounting of actual deeds but also the first meaning of any narrative which uses words according to their proper nature."[40] Hugh thus values the literal and historical, what we would call the literary (fictional) level of a sacred text because, for him, it helps avoid ingenious scriptural exegesis, what we would call allegorical decoding. "It is necessary both that we follow the letter in such a way as not to prefer our own sense to the divine authors, and that we do not follow it in such a way as to deny that the entire pronouncement of truth is rendered in it."[41]

For Hugh, exegesis begins with the letter and, in a foursquare developmental way, proceeds to the spirit. The result is a kind parabolic use to which the religious text is put to stimulate and shape

both critical thinking and spiritual meditation. Religious life begins
in textual (literary) scholarship, Hugh's *lectio divina:*

First you learn history and diligently commit to memory the truth of the
deeds that have been performed, reviewing from beginning to end what
has been done, when it has been done, where it has been done, and by
whom it has been done. For these are the four things which are especially
to be sought for in history—the person, the business done, the time, and
the place. Nor do I think that you will be able to become perfectly sensitive to allegory unless you have first been grounded in history. Do not
look down upon these least things. The man who looks down on such
smallest things slips little by little. If, in the beginning, you had looked
down on learning the alphabet, now you would not even find your names
listed with those of the grammar students. I know that there are certain
fellows who want to play the philosopher right away. They say that stories
should be left to pseudo apostles. The knowledge of these fellows is like
that of an ass. Don't imitate persons of this kind.[42]

When he cites St. Augustine in chapter 11 of book 6, Hugh
makes a remarkable plea for letting the text guide readers—remarkable, that is, for its literary humanism:

When, therefore, we read the Divine Books, in such a great multitude of
true concepts elicited from a few words and fortified by the sound rule of
the catholic faith, let us prefer above all what it seems certain that the
man we are reading thought. But if this is not evident, let us certainly
prefer what the circumstances of the writing do not disallow and what is
consonant with sound faith. But if even the circumstances of the writing
cannot be explored and examined, let us at least prefer only what sound
faith prescribes. For it is one thing not to see what the writer himself
thought, another to stray from the rule of piety. If both these things are
avoided, the harvest of the reader is a perfect one.[43]

Hugh is here "criticizing the Gregorian tradition, with its sublime
disregard for the letter of Scripture."[44] For Hugh, even the most
theoretical teaching must originate in a sense of the text grounded
in a kind of matching theory of truth consonant with the text and
the teachings of faith, both learned and untutored. Hugh's description of his own method in two of his treatises on Noah's Ark may
make us think, as Beryl Smalley says, "of the Kindergarten. We
smile when Hugh, with the gravity of one in the forefront of a scientific movement, rejects Origen's figure of the ark as top-heavy,
and when he proposes 'little compartments', round the outside, for

the amphibious beasts. Our smile is mistaken: a scientific movement is really afoot."[45] Hugh is making the literal surface a proper
subject for study, perhaps even for a sanctioned imaginative (literary) play—a fleshing out that is grounding. Hugh wants us first to
visualize the literary surface in order to explain it. I suspect that
Hugh would not have thought of his expounding the literal surface
of a sacred text as literary because he regarded what we see as an
incipient literary hermeneutic as a powerful intellectual exercise of
piety. Any distinction between a sacred, or even a serious, text and
a purely literary one, a distinction Hugh himself makes, is not the
issue here. What Hugh at first objects to in works he calls "appendages of the arts"—what we would call literature—is their seeming
preoccupation with eloquence that obstructs passage from a clear
and strong literary surface to some inner truth.

Occasionally, it is true, they [the "appendages of the arts"] touch in a scattered and confused fashion upon some topics lifted out of the arts, or, if
their narrative presentation is simple, they prepare the way for philosophy. Of this sort are all the songs of the poets—tragedies, comedies, sat-
ires, heroic verse and lyric, iambics, certain didactic poems, fables and
histories, and also writings of those fellows whom today we commonly call
"philosophers" and who are always taking some small matter and dragging
it out through long verbal detours, obscuring a simple meaning in confused discourses—who, lumping even dissimilar things together, make,
as it were, a single "picture" from a multitude of "colors" and forms.[46]

Hugh is making a distinction here similar to one we usually make,
in a generic sense, between classicism and mannerism. But since
he wants to find all intellectual expression appropriate to philosophy as he understands it, he finally accepts the literary arts:

It appears to me that our effort should first be given to the [seven liberal]
arts . . . which comprise the tools of philosophy; afterwards, if time affords, let these other things be read, for sometimes we are better pleased
when entertaining reading is mixed with serious, and rarity makes what is
good seem precious. Thus, we sometimes more eagerly take up a thought
we come upon in the midst of a story.[47]

Even Hugh's stylistic distinction between philosophic writings
and the literariness of the Scriptures, which should occupy us when
we begin to study the Bible, is a distinction based on the value a
sensible and plain style holds for our enlightenment.

The writings of philosophers, like a whitewashed wall of clay, boast an attractive surface all shining with eloquence; but if sometimes they hold forth to us a semblance of truth, nevertheless, by mixing falsehoods with it, they conceal the clay of error, as it were, under an over-spread coat of color. The Sacred Scriptures, on the other hand, are most fittingly likened to a honeycomb, for while in the simplicity of their language they seem dry, within they are filled with sweetness. And thus it is that they have deservedly come by the name sacred, for they alone are found so free from the infection of falsehood that they are proved to contain nothing contrary to truth.[48]

Hugh's sense of what we would call explication de texte is serious and orderly.[49] Indeed, any text that did not permit his method must have seemed to him trivializing because the literal level of the text was not admitting us to the spiritual. In this way, Hugh is *not* playful like allegorists or deconstructionists: his method would not violate the integrity of the literary surface. Hugh finds potential value in all books.

Do not scorn at least to read a book, if you have the time. If you gain nothing from it, neither do you lose anything; especially since there is, in my judgment, no book which does not set forth something worth looking for, if that book is taken up at the right place and time; or which does not possess something even special to itself which the diligent scrutinizer of its contents, having found it nowhere else, seizes upon gladly in proportion as it is the more rare.[50]

Moreover, Hugh expects us to read and think with a studious humility.

There is no one to whom it is given to know all things, no one who has not received his special gift from nature. The wise student, therefore, gladly hears all, reads all, and looks down upon no writing, no person, no teaching. From all indifferently he seeks what he sees he lacks, and he considers not how much he knows, but of how much he is ignorant.[51]

For Hugh, finally, any distinction between a purely sacred and "literary" text—some non-sacred writings are more serious than others—is less important than the sacred use of the imagination in opening up our connection to a text that matters, sacred or profane.

Unfortunately, the Victorine program, which Hugh set forth, failed. It implied, as Smalley says, "too high a tension between the academic and the religious life." Hugh's ideal exegete was "a com-

bination of Paris master and contemplative religious which only exceptional circumstances could produce. We know that by the end
of the century the mystical anti-scholastic current at St. Victor had
conquered the more intellectual current that Hugh represented,
while in the schools theology was breaking away from exegesis."[52]
There was thus no sustaining Victorine influence on religious or
scholastic life and certainly no traceably direct influence on literary
life and culture.[53] Moreover, the Victorines seem to have developed their sense of the use and value of the literal surface of a text
independent of influences from the kind of interpretative engagement with the parables of Jesus that I have called parabolic listening. Even Joachim Jeremias acknowledges that "at a very early
stage the process of treating the parables as allegories had begun, a
process which for centuries concealed the meaning of the parables
under a thick layer of dust."[54] As we know, allegorical reading and
parabolic listening do not grow out of one another, and although
the latter may be a welcome antidote to the sometimes fantastic
and arbitary interpretations of the former, it is not a necessary or
final one. The Victorines represent a valuable, albeit isolated, recovery of the sensible ground on which interpretation and, for
them, piety rested. And for a time the Victorines flowered as a distinctly medieval acknowledgment of the use and value of the textual surface, though they themselves literally died out.

Still, Hugh reflects and defines the idea of a textual community
broadly enough and soundly enough that his ideas can describe any
community of readers for whom a text embodies shared moral or
social values and for whom the reading and interpretation of texts
constitutes a civilized and renewing public activity. I would even
suggest that the distinction between allegory and figuration is powerful not because it should be maintained in explaining the interpretive practices of a religious community (the distinction is implicitly seen to explain how alienated exegesis can become;[55] it is
sometimes a distinction of danger and potential disappointment,
even for Auerbach)[56] but because it implies, as the Victorines demonstrated, that even a religious community could, and sometimes
did, ground itself in its own Christian and sensuous history. Thus
Brian Stock extends Hugh's idea of the textual community to the
general religious and secular—the bookish or textual—life of the
mind, and I would extend it to describe how Chaucer's narratives

create and sustain such a community of readers. Both kinds of textual communities are importantly self-reflective. Reading engages the community in uncovering shared assumptions, values, meaning, and direction. Stock, of course, talks about the restorative value of Hugh's textual community, a healing goal a literary and secular community need not necessarily pursue with any degree of consciously religious zeal: "Man, so to speak, not only anguished over a new separation from the paradise of familiar relations in Eden, which were oral, intimate, and free from interpretive superstructures. Texts, as Hugh of St. Victor suggested, or rather, reading, study, and meditation based on them, offered him a technical instrument for helping to restore the lost spiritual unity with God."[57]

Stock's historical arguments about the change from an oral community to a visibly textual one seem to me specious.[58] The human condition is always and finally textual. Even memory and unwritten codes, formulaic patterns of social and moral behavior, and the words that accompany such behavior and the imaginative re-creation of it, are a kind of lived text. We need not postulate an immediate, ritualistic, and unconsciously oral condition, an Edenic wholeness from which we have fallen (been thrown out), in order to establish that reading and writing, conditions of distance and absence, create critical thinking. Indeed, too much has been made of the supposed immediacy of act and action in a so-called state of orality, an electronic version of the medieval state of nature, that does not, it is said, permit self-consciousness. Our current notion of orality reflects our Rousseauist nostalgia for a state of nature in which language is not the catastrophic sign of our disconnection from consciousness. Such a view of the mixed condition of literacy—our self-consciousness is implicitly our fall from consciousness—throws us on the horns of a paradox; self-consciousness is both the symptom of our fall and the path of our recovery to an Edenic wholeness. Moreover, such a view of literacy is, I think, historically inaccurate.[59] My point is that texts in oral communities, like literal texts in verbal communities such as Hugh's, or Chaucer's, encourage participatory thinking, what I call parabolic listening. My use of listening here is, of course, intended to stress the cooperative nature of even the most isolated reading, not to make a misleading distinction between reading in groups and reading alone and to ourselves. Texts, religious or secular, exercise our best capacity, our highest

reach of will and intellect, to understand ourselves and the contexts, God-given and man-made, that govern us. They rectify us,
which, even in a religious community like Hugh's, is our responsible use of them. God does not compel us to read His word as
moral zombies. Allegorization of a text may be simply the way a
dull—a literal, not necessarily an interestingly literate—mind
works. Chaucer's readers, like God's (students of Scripture), can al-
legorize. But they can also listen.

Declamation, as we know, was the medium of Chaucer's textual
community, although no reference in his work clearly indicates
which narratives were in fact declaimed—whether all of them,
some of them, or parts of some of them—or clearly establishes the
actual circumstances and expectations of a public reading—where
it took place, whether it was a special occasion, who was actually
present, whether there were pauses during the reading or discussion of the reading afterwards, and how attentive the audience was
or was expected to be.

The little scene in book 2 of the *Troilus* (78–84) that describes
Pandarus having found his niece Criseyde at home with her friends
("two othere ladys" [81]) being read to in a kind of private declamation of a text ("Herden a mayden reden hem . . . / . . . while hem
leste" [83–84]) illustrates in broad outline some historical details of
the literary habits of Chaucer's day. We are perhaps accustomed to
thinking of Chaucer declaiming before a court audience in the kind
of "command performance" we see pictured in the *Troilus* frontispiece. But the imagined "public" reading in the *Troilus* itself takes
place in the morning in Criseyde's "paved parlour" (82), suggesting
that reading in Chaucer's fourteenth century might have taken
place at any time during the day, not simply at or after a royal supper, and be a public occasion even at home. The phrase "while
hem leste" even suggests that reading (being read to) might be interrupted at the pleasure of the audience.

We know also that readers in Chaucer's day read alone, though
they probably did not read silently unless they wanted their reading, like Criseyde's private and silent reading of Troilus's letter
(2.1173–79), to be purposefully asocial. Silent reading was a kind
of withdrawal. Chaucer, for example, in book 2 of the *House of
Fame* (656–60), is described by the Eagle as a dedicated bookworm who has read and learned privately. Although "domb as any

stoon" (656) probably means that Chaucer was silent when he read
by himself—both his account books at the customshouse and his
"scholarly" books at home—the phrase is curious, because reading
alone and silently was not characteristic of even private sociable
reading in Chaucer's day. We have, contemporary with Chaucer,
Froissart's description of the lover in his *L'Espinette amoureuse*
coming upon a maiden reading the romance of *Cléomidès* alone
and silently—not moving her lips to read aloud.[60] And indeed we
have, well before Chaucer as a kind of early medieval adumbration
of the idea of silent and asocial reading, St. Augustine's testimony
in his *Confessions* that he saw St. Ambrose reading silently—not
moving his lips, nor vocalizing—although his eyes moved across
the page.[61] But these two instances of silent reading are special.
Augustine was surprised at Ambrose's practice. Perhaps he thought
that Ambrose read silently because he wanted to avoid being questioned by listeners when he needed to concentrate. Perhaps Ambrose wished to preserve his voice, which easily became hoarse. In
Augustine's mind, Ambrose's silence was *not* a matter of stand-
offishness, though his having to explain Ambrose's habits so fully
suggests, I think, that others might have interpreted them as such.
Perhaps, too, Augustine saw in Ambrose's silence the kind of private perusal of the meaning of a text ("his heart explored the meaning," as Augustine says) that came in the Middle Ages to constitute
a distinctive kind of private and essentially asocial reading we would
call meditation.[62]

By contrast, the lover in Froissart sees silent reading as a manifestation of his lady's aloofness. Perhaps because lines 656–60 from
the *House of Fame* describe Chaucer's abnormal absorption in his
books, the phrase "domb as any stoon" implies that Chaucer's tire-
less and persistent reading meant that he had foregone both the
gratification of the ear, the socially pleasurable part of reading, and
the sharing of knowledge. Chaucer's dedication to books in the
House of Fame is not only excessive; it may be antisocial. It is obviously "monkish." Perhaps Chaucer is ironically suggesting that
had he been a more "social" man, he would have read out loud to
himself. The point is that declamation was both the medium of
Chaucer's textual community and the imaginative norm of all shareable reading, public and private, in Chaucer's day.

We should add, too, that when Chaucer, in roughly his own day, is pictured as reading aloud to others, he is shown as noticeably thoughtful—not private, but reflective. Again, declamation for a textual community, not a purely bookish one, means recitation of a publicly shareable text and a re-created (lived) textuality. The illuminator of the *Troilus* frontispiece suggests, I think, that Chaucer is listening to his own story while he is telling it; he is clearly thinking about something. Indeed, Chaucer is not reading from a manuscript with his eyes lowered to the page, but both re-citing and gesturing. There seems not even to be on the pulpit a manuscript from which Chaucer might read. He is not literally act-ing out a part, but declaiming, and declamation does not depend on a book. Chaucer's head is cocked to one side—he has a thoughtful air—and he is using his right hand to gesture, bringing his narrative, or part of it, *to* his audience, perhaps in imitation of a minstrel's "sleight-of-hand."[63] There is both movement here and reflection, which suggests to me the dual nature of medieval story-telling; the man who recites an "olde boke," or his version of an "olde boke," which the *Troilus* is, plays himself like the instrument of a minstrel and listens to the modulations, in tone and theme, of his own voice. Eustache Deschamps, Chaucer's French contempo-rary, seems to have thought of his performances similarly, as a kind of "comedie du *Moi*," in which "il propose au public la mise en scène parfois douloureuse, mais souvent comique de sa propre existence."[64]

For Deschamps, such a performance demands a sociability al-most innate, the "instrument" of which is, as Deschamps says, the human voice ("une musique de bouche").[65] Moreover, the perfor-mance is *not* visual, except insofar as it is an imaginary seeing. Al-though there is no sure way of telling exactly how elaborate Chau-cer's hand gestures and body motions may have been—Poirion suggests that Deschamps's performance was a kind of "dance du corps"[66]—medieval declamation was not drama, even in a medie-val sense.[67] Unlike a play, which can stage our illusions, however hard we try to let it lead us through the visual to the idea embodied on a stage—this is how medieval theater was in theory meant to be seen—a live performance, by its very nature, always works against our illusions.[68] However convincing a performer is, he cannot es-cape our eyes, nor does he try to. Live performance is not concep-

tually more intricate than a play, but it may be harder to do well.
Voice and idea must carry all.

Moreover, live performance calls on the faculty of memory—in
the Middle Ages a faculty of imagination and reflection—perhaps
more fully than a play, and in ways that have hardly been examined. In a special sense, the live performance of a written text always takes place "in the past"; that is, it evokes images from sense
experience retained in memory and sets into operation our judgments and understanding, also held in memory, as St. Augustine
says in his *Confessions* 10.17, as "knowledge" there "of itself."
For Augustine, the working of memory is the vehicle for our self-
knowledge; it is a kind of inner mirror of the self—the physical self
through time (our senses and our emotions), as well as our innate
knowledge:

The power of the memory is great, O Lord. It is awe-inspiring in its profound and incalculable complexity. Yet it is my mind; it is my self. What,
then, am I, my God? What is my nature? A life that is ever varying, full of
change, and of immense power. The wide plains of my memory and its
innumerable caverns and hollows are full beyond compute of countless
things of all kinds. Material things are there by means of their images;
knowledge is there of itself; emotions are there in the form of ideas or
impressions of some kind, for the memory retains them even while the
mind does not experience them, although whatever is in the memory
must also be in the mind. My mind has the freedom of them all. I can
glide from one to the other. I can probe deep into them and never find the
end of them. This is the power of memory! This is the great force of life in
living man, mortal though he is![69]

Memory is thus for Augustine the "place"—he likens it (*Confessions* 10.8) to a "great field," a "spacious palace," a "storehouse for
countless images of all kinds"—over which the mind can roam or
be guided, by itself or by others, in its search to know itself.[70] I
would argue that this idea, as a kind of picture of thinking, had very
deep consequences, for medieval aesthetics and religion,[71] even
though Augustine does not settle on one image. Frances Yates observes that although "one must be extremely careful to distinguish
between art and the art of memory, which is an invisible art, yet
their frontiers must surely have overlapped. For when people were
being taught to practice the formation of images for remembering,

it is difficult to suppose that such inner images might not sometimes have found their way into outer expression."[72] Conversely, it
is equally likely that we can see in the visual arts of the Middle
Ages, particularly the Christian didactic art, a reflection of those
very images of memory. Yates even conjectures that "this inner art
[the art of remembering] which encourages the use of the imagination as a duty surely must have been a major factor" in the evoca-
tion of images:

Can memory be one possible explanation of the mediaeval love of the grotesque, the idiosyncratic? Are the strange figures to be seen on the pages
of manuscripts and in all forms of mediaeval art not so much the revelation
of a tortured psychology as evidence that the Middle Ages, when men had
to remember, followed classical rules for making memorable images? Is
the proliferation of new imagery in the thirteenth and fourteenth centuries related to the renewed emphasis on memory by the scholastics?[73]

Chaucer is a literary artist whose "pictures" are solely of the
mind. Perhaps the act of remembering that first gave him his people
and his scenes—fresh and remarkable by medieval standards—can
also give them, as mental images formed in response to verbal
stimuli, to listeners (readers) with the same singularity and keenness.[74] There is perhaps for readers, as there was first for an author, a memory act that hearing words or reading fosters. This act is
both a re-seeing of the striking and memorable images (*imagines
agentes*) by which, according to the medieval theory of memory
and faculty psychology, one first conceives and remembers things
"sensible" and a *re*-awakening of the knowing and judging faculties
of the mind—the things "intelligible."[75] In Chaucer we get both
descriptions and voices that call up people for the *oculus imagina-
tionis*, or as Chaucer says in the Man of Law's Tale "thilke eyen of
[the] mynde" (552). Like Lady Grace-Dieu in Guillaume de Deguileville's *Le Pèlerinage de la vie humaine*, Chaucer too

> . . . shal (yiff that I may)
> Boothe thyn Eyen take away,
> and hem out off her place fette;
> And in thyn Erys I shal hem sette.[76]

Chapter Three

Chaucer's Circle
of Understanding

In book 2 of the *Troilus*, Criseyde plays out in her head, as we would say, a scenario of immense private and public importance *for her:*

> Now sette a caas: the hardest is, ywys,
> Men myghten demen that he loveth me.
> What dishonour were it unto me, this?
> May ich hym lette of that? Why, nay, parde!
>
> (729–32)

Criseyde is here imagining how her behavior to Troilus might be understood by others and how she might be forced to understand her behavior, and behave, in order to explain herself. She is constructing the fiction she has the power to make real. I take this as a paradigm for Chaucerian storytelling as I have been describing it; putting cases—posing instances—shapes, and is shaped by, reality. Indeed, *life* becomes art when we read, in a medieval sense—read into—life, as if it were a story that needed interpretive gestures to be created and understood. In the Renaissance, Sir Philip Sidney explicitly likens the poet's fable to the lawyer's hypothetical case of "John Doe"; for it, like the poet's fable and the clerk's story, "nothing affirmes,"[1] though it projects worlds. It takes Criseyde only four lines to propose a reality, to put a case that includes—encircles and explains—her, and then, for the moment, to reject it. Reality in Chaucer is textually enclosed because mind is. Such encirclement of the world gives us the world and ourselves in it. From inside that circle, understanding is possible.

Criseyde's words, of course, only give us imaginary pictures. We imagine her thinking, which is imagining her acting. Her voice gives us scenes to which we give bodies. Although we participate in imagining, there is in Criseyde's four lines no tyranny of sight, no single perspective that creates a single angle of moral judgment. Perhaps because there is in Chaucer no staging of what we imagine, or any attempt to stage it, there is no sustained objectivity— no "frontal, upright, horizontal" and moving extension encouraging us to compare and contrast an object of our attention visibly given us. Seeing, as in the visual arts and in drama, is "preeminently a distancing, judgmental act."[2] Hearing and imagining encourage pictorialization, too, but they require, not the illusion of objectivity, but the beginning of self-objectifying subjectivity. They play to the inner eye of self-definition. Like parables, Chaucer's narratives simply "put the case," the imagined situation, and ask that we interpret it. Moreover, Criseyde is to her scenario ("Now sette a caas") as Chaucer's storyteller is to his: both propose a reality, put a case, or cases, and invite interpretation, their own and that of others. Because Chaucer's storyteller in the text cannot make them, judgments—judging as a series of self-objectifying acts of mind and feeling—fall to the audience. Notice how literary and legalistic models of speaking ("Now sette a caas") are conflated here; the poet's case, and the lawyer's, are public speaking. Both make worlds. Indeed, Chaucer's narratives seem as puzzling and one-sided to the storyteller as they may be to some members of the audience. Judgments do not belong to the narrator, who cannot "explain the text"—decode it in order to make it understood. Moreover, although it encourages thoughtfulness, a Chaucerian narrative does not demand that readers choose to be thoughtful in one way and not another *before the story begins*—that is, choose to read morally or realistically as a way to manage Chaucer.

The idea of storytelling as case-putting is particularly significant for the theory of the early novel and important for us because Chaucer is often read *as if* he were novelistic rather than parabolic. Knowing the difference does not mean distinguishing between actual pieces of realistic detail that might turn up in either a novel or a parablelike narrative, but knowing how realistic detail is being used—what it implies about Chaucer's own literary theory and what we assume is Chaucer's justification for including a detail from everyday life. Chaucer does claim, as we know, an overt moral verisimilitude *and* a covert actual one, but he does not *falsely* maintain, as early novelists felt obliged to do, or as recent novelists (the so-called new journalists) want to do, that a fiction is not a fiction at all. Chaucer does not claim that the literal surface is merely a thin veil of signification—he is not an allegorist—in order to avoid raising the issue of the truth or falsehood of the literal surface. Unlike allegories, parablelike narratives such as Chaucer's are both thought-provoking—meaningful, but not necessarily doctrinal—and true to nature; they are not a way for an author to be "realistic" in order to talk about something else (as both the Robertsonian and the anti-Robertsonian views of Chaucerian narrative assume).

Furthermore, unlike news, out of which the novel as we know it is said to have developed,[3] parablelike narratives do not literally have to "keep up with the passage of time"[4]—that is, they do not necessarily have to be verifiable. Chaucer's readers are not then concerned with the issue of establishing, in a journalistic sense, the truth or falsehood of works of fiction, but with the application of such fictions to individual lives and to communal life as seen through each man. The issues that beset the readers of early fiction and those that engaged Chaucer's medieval readers were not, I think, the same. As Lennard Davis has shown, the "demands of the plain style" of prose news to create "an ongoing, coterminous account of reality through the use of seriality, continuity and recentness" led to the abandonment, in Michel Foucault's words, of the notion of a "Primary Text open to interpretation and polysemousness, and with it the entire, inexhaustible foundation of the words whose mute being was inscribed in things; all that remains is representation unfolding in the verbal signs that manifest it, and hence becoming discourse."[5] No hermeneutic drive to see below or beyond the literal surface of a fiction to morality or truth *alone* defined the novel as a genre. "True-speaking" in the novel, as Davis says, "had much more to do with language and politics in news, in a growing concern about the accuracy of detail, and a growing legal mechanism to define, analyze and contain the nature of representation."[6]

Although the phrase "circle of understanding" is not Chaucer's,

Chaucer does come to something like the same idea about the use and value of his work. Like most writers, Chaucer, too, theorizes about the notion of *where* (in what place and in what activity) the morality of his work lies. The evidence is indirect, but in his own work Chaucer seems to have taken on, much as a critic might take on, the question of the status, or "being," of a work of art. First, there is the passage in book 1 of the *Troilus*, translated from the opening lines (43–46) of Geoffrey of Vinsauf's *Poetria nova:*[7]

> For everi wight that hath an hous to founde
> Ne renneth naught the werk for to bygynne
> With rakel hond, but he wol bide a stounde,
> And sende his hertes line out fro withinne
> Aldirfirst his purpos for to wynne.
>
> (1065–69)

Although in context Chaucer uses the lines from Geoffrey to describe the way Pandarus lays the groundwork for the love affair between Troilus and Criseyde, the lines from the *Poetria nova*, a handbook, as we know, on the art of literary composition, explain how a writer of "fictions," like Chaucer, and a creator of them, like Pandarus, first make their plans, then execute them *and*, all the while, expect us, as readers or observers, to understand the process of both creation and execution. There is an implicit comparison in book 1 of the *Troilus* of a writer, Chaucer himself, and Pandarus, which Pandarus's plotting and manipulation of the action between two lovers and his vicarious response to each throughout *Troilus and Criseyde* bears out; Pandarus is the narrator's counterpart in the story.

Like a writer, Pandarus begins, Chaucer says, with an idea and then, also like a writer, whose creation in Geoffrey of Vinsauf and in Chaucer is compared to a house, works out his idea "in the world." In a sentence Chaucer does not use in the *Troilus*, though he surely knew it, Geoffrey of Vinsauf, sounding very much like the medieval "aesthetic theorists" Erwin Panofsky discusses, says that a literary idea is an archetype before it is "real":

> Status ejus / Est prius archetypus quam sensilis.
>
> (47–48)[8]

An idea, he says, is first in the mind and then in the "sensible" world. Pandarus, like the writer, will build his idea in the world—

work it out between two people—but it will be shaped by the already completed form of it as a mental plan. Geoffrey uses "status ejus" in the same sense, I think, in which we would talk about the "being" or existence of a work of written fiction, like the *Troilus* itself, which is conceived first, and then written down, not with "rakel hond," but with a "hertes line," or builder's plumb line.[9] In Chaucer's translation of *De consolatione philosophiae*, Boethius says:

For ryght as a werkman that aperceyveth in his thought the forme of the thing that he wol make, and moeveth the effect of the work, and ledith that he hadde lookid byforn in his thought symplely and presently, by temporel ordenaunce; certes, ryght so God disponith in his purveaunce singulerly and stablely the thinges that ben to doone.

(4. Prosa 6.82–89)

God "disponith in his purveaunce" just as the workman does in his mind *beforehand*, not before creation (cognition), but before its working out. Chaucer seems to have felt comfortable with the idea of the mentalistic status of things, not only art, but of the world itself. He does not make issue of the mental, as opposed to the purely physical, status of an art object, but rather sees one as the natural, indeed inevitable, fulfillment or shaping of the other. Purpose can go amiss, as Chaucer himself admits in book 5 of the *Troilus*, where he says he hopes that his reader will take care to understand his *Troilus and Criseyde*, just as he took care in writing it to understand his "auctor." ("And red whereso thow be . . . / That thow be understonde, God I biseche!" [1797–98].) But for Chaucer there is *potentially* the possibility that what is thought can be put on paper and, through reading (hearing), be transferred to another mind. The "Hous of Fame," Chaucer says, is a place where,

> Whan any speche ycomen ys
> Up to the paleys, anon-ryght
> Hyt wexeth lyk the same wight
> Which that the word in erthe spak,
> Be hyt clothed red or blak;
> And hath so verray hys lyknesse
> That spak the word, that thou wilt gesse
> That it the same body be,
> Man or woman, he or she.
>
> (*House of Fame* 2.1074–82)

Although Chaucer may seem charmingly literal in this passage—
the idea is for us almost cartooned—the germ of the idea is serious;
for Chaucer here suggests not only that ideas pass from one mind
to another, but that the "body," or being, of the mind that first conceived the idea is accessible to someone else. Chaucer does not
mean that the physical body is visible, but that the potential for
understanding how, and perhaps why, an idea was conceived, is
available to one who hears it. One can thus work backwards from
the written page to the idea itself *and* to the mind that first conceived the idea and talk about authorial intention—what was in the
author's head when he first formulated his thought, now "built like
him" (as an intention). This little passage from the *House of Fame*
tells us much about how we can set a work of written fiction in its
mental birthplace and "see" the writer himself—the "same body"—
in his work. What makes a writer available to us is thus *how* he is
heard, and it is the reading of the text that makes all the difference
in the way a writer will "take shape" in our minds. Air, Chaucer
says in the *House of Fame*, is the medium through which sound
reaches our ears, and ideas our brain; it is through the voice, air
engaged by the vocal chords and the movements of the organs of
articulation, that the mind controls what we hear.[10] "Pointing" a
text, Chaucer says in a passage in the *Romaunt* not found in the
French original, creates the occasion when one mind meets another:

> Now is good to here, in fay,
> If ony be that can it say,
> And poynte it as the resoun is
> Set; for other-gate, ywys,
> It shall nought well in alle thyng
> Be brought to good undirstondyng.
> For a reder that poyntith ille
> A good sentence may often spille.
>
> (2155–62)

The verb "poynten" here means to punctuate, to read a manuscript
so that the sense of it ("resoun") is not obscured. We still say "point
out" when we talk about clarifying the sense of something, perhaps
by elaborating the point we wish to make. Chaucer understands
this sense of the word too, I think. Of course, "poynten" in Middle
English also means to "stab" or "pierce," but using the word in this

way is not far afield from the idea that someone who is reading a text, a public performer or a private reader, must catch the sense of a line or passage and "say it" so that the "resoun" of the text is apparent to whomever is listening. The idea of stabbing or piercing a passage also carries with it the idea of setting lines on a manuscript page—that is, pointing where line ruling goes in order to indicate margins and establish a passage materially as a text.[11] But this sense hardly excludes the notion of establishing a passage as an idea; indeed, one depends on the other since the performer or reader reads *from* the page (from the page to the mind). It is all the fashion today to show how a modern "silent" reader tries out a sentence "in his head"—negotiates it, so to speak, before he comfortably and reasonably settles on its meaning. A performer, who knows how his reading of a text may fix meaning, does virtually the same before he goes before the public (when he is practicing his part); he is always attentive to himself as a performer and public arbiter of meaning. Although his magical omniscience is compelling, it must never work against his "good undirstondyng" of a text.

Oddly enough, the position of the word "set" at the beginning of line 2158—we land heavily on the word—suggests that there is meaning to a line or passage we may or may not hit on, and I think Chaucer believes that. The metrics of lines 2157–58 from the *Romaunt* force on us the idea that the "resoun" of a text can be grasped, that there is a way to read particular lines that corresponds to some idea in an author's head. Thus any reader who "poyntith ill" may give to someone, including himself, a mistaken understanding of the text he reads; he may "spille" a "sentence," as if meaning—like liquid, another medium that conducts—needed a container of the right size and shape, the right inflection and inference on the performer's part, to convey it to someone.[12] Chaucer falls in with those who believe that texts have meaning that readers—authors themselves, fictional narrators, performers, and private bookish men—must all bear a responsibility for making understandable (public), and that if meaning slips away, it must be sought after. It is thus not so important to argue that Chaucer falls victim to some "intentional fallacy"—I do not think he does—as to suggest the social and intellectual implications of such a theory of cooperative pursuit for both a writer and his readers, all of whom must come to a text with the assumption that it means something, partly because it has meant something before and partly because, as Chaucer says, ideas give us the "bodies" of those who think and speak. Meaning may elude us, but it is precisely because it may that we participate in social and intellectual ventures, like reading, to pursue it. The idea of "out thereness," George Steiner says, is the necessary fiction of situation for reading: "The reader proceeds *as if* the text was the housing of forces and meanings, of meanings of meaning, whose lodging within the executive verbal form was one of 'incarnation'. He reads *as if*—a conditionality which defines the 'provisional' temper of his pursuit—the singular presence of the life of meaning in the text and work of art was 'a real presence' irreducible to analytic summation and resistant to judgment in the sense in which the critic can and must judge."[13] Moreover, the idea of "out thereness" is also the necessary situation—for Chaucer it is not a fiction—that generates humanness. By reading we define ourselves as human—committed to the meaningful and to the occasions when we can demonstrate how we find it.

Now Canterbury tale-telling, as we know, is entertainment for a company of men and women who have been asked to make a game of it, and the game has a point, at least for Harry Bailly. His stipulation in the General Prologue that whoever "telleth in this caas / Tales of the best sentence and moost solaas, / Shal have a soper at oure aller cost" (797–99) makes entertainment requisite. But it also makes entertainment and Harry Bailly's willful orchestrations of it a valuable, in his mind, public act. Indeed, for the Host, making life sociable for the Canterbury pilgrims *is work*—the Host's work is the pilgrim's play. Of course, what is really only clear from Harry Bailly's terms for storytelling is that the terms of judgment are his, even though everyone will pay for the victory dinner. "And which of yow that bereth hym best of alle," the Host first says (796), which *he* glosses as telling "tales of best sentence and moost solaas." There will be a ranking—perhaps a worst as well as a best tale—but Harry Bailly judges. The pilgrim who wins the game must bear himself best in the Host's judgment—be as social as Harry Bailly fancies himself? That is not clear. Indeed, it is not clear if one tale has to have both "sentence" and "solaas," or if these are separate evaluative standards. What is, I believe, more important than such slippery details of judgment is the *idea* that judging, like the hierarchical order of storytelling in the *Canter-*

bury Tales—the Host asks the Knight to begin and then the Monk, but the Miller breaks rank—will go awry. Harry Bailly's binary categories of judgment, his moral and social architecture, and his orchestration of the after-pilgrimage supper—he is indeed a kind of social director—are immodestly idiosyncratic. His judgments burst from him; they are not deduced. We should add, too, that Chaucer's other uses of "sentence" all suggest that the word does not mean something specifically, pointedly moral, but implies that some process of interpretation, even reiteration, must be undertaken so that what something means, its point, will be revealed. The Parson, for example, uses "sentence" in this way:

> But nathelees, this meditacioun
> I putte it ay under correccioun
> Of clerkes, for I am nat textueel;
> I take but the sentence, trusteth weel.
>
> (10.55–59)

And so does the narrator in the *Troilus:*

> But soth is, though I kan nat tellen al,
> As kan myn auctour, of his excellence,
> Yet have I seyd, and God toforn, and shal
> In every thyng, al holy his sentence.
>
> (3.1324–27)

"Sentence" in these two examples means, rather broadly, the essential meaning, the point, of the words themselves. Indeed, "sentence" may mean the point of the literal level, not its decoded meaning (if there is one), since that so-called deeper or better meaning must depend on an intelligible literal surface. If "sentence" is being used in this way, then "sentence" and "solaas"— what Chaucer's allegorists have assumed to mean the "fruyt" and the "chaf" of his stories—are not different. What is entertaining may be engaging, even useful, like a bran muffin.

Beginning then as entertainment—at least readers may expect entertainment—Chaucer's narratives both inevitably and invariably take a turn to the thoughtful, and that turn draws readers into Chaucer's circle of understanding. The invitation to interpret and reflect on the imagined situation (the "caas") reveals each reader's conceptual scope and judgmental power. The turn is conscious, but not so broad that the story becomes simply an excuse to moralize. The turn marks an occasion for readers to think—to come to see the point or "knotte" of the imagined situation, as Chaucer says in the Squire's Tale (401–8). The change of emphasis is not strictly temporal, although initially there is a kind of time sequence to it. A turn may come almost immediately, or at any time after the audience has settled into the narrative, and there may be more than one. Turns may be signaled by a rhetorical question, or the storyteller's comment on what has just gone before, or a momentarily arresting juxtaposition that only seems voiceless (both Muscatine's and Robertson's misunderstanding of structure in Chaucer). Turns mark both in the text *and in us* the unfolding of parabolic narration and are, in this sense, where structure is really textuality, the formal features of Chaucerian narratives. The actual court or courtly circumstances of medieval presentation would, I believe, have precluded Chaucer's being morally heavyhanded at each turn, and his storyteller never avows that he is making a "moral" point, patristic or humanist. He does not guide in matters of interpretation, though he invites it.

There is a wonderful momentary equality between the Black Knight in the *Book of the Duchess* and the storyteller, when the knight acknowledges that his lady is dead and the storyteller offers his compassion ("Be God, hyt ys routhe!"), that illustrates what I mean by a Chaucerian circle of understanding. Just at the moment of the open acknowledgment of death and pity, a kind of community of moral men that the reader has been anticipating, but from which both the Black Knight and the storyteller bolt, is created on the word "routhe" (1310):

> And with that word ryght anoon
> They gan to strake forth; al was doon,
> For that tyme, the hert-huntyng.
>
> (1311–13)

The *Book of the Duchess* has figuratively been about hearthunting—the play on the word "hert" (hart and heart) is transparent—not only for the Black Knight and the storyteller, both of whom are "in sorwful ymagynacioun" (14). The reader, too, goes hunting, but finds his heart much sooner than anyone in the narrative. His patience, until the others know themselves as well as he knows himself and them (himself *through them*), is the finest sign of his compassion and humanity. The *Book of the Duchess* in fact flatters and praises the reader. Like a parable, it thrusts him into positions of foreknowledge, compassion, understanding, and power, so that what he sees in the resistance and dullness of others is his own anticipation of genuinely human values, which *he* can display. The *Book of the Duchess* is both a mirror for the reader and a "place" where he can be at his best, as he takes it upon himself to read and understand.

Even when there are seeming voices of authority in the Chaucerian narrative, like Chaucer the pilgrim or Harry Bailly, the reader is still encouraged to participate in the communal life of the mind and the public world of judgment. Chaucer the pilgrim in the Prologue to the Miller's Tale, for example, makes the same defense of storytelling as he does in the General Prologue (725–46). His retreat into foresquare textuality, dutiful and morally neutral, invites readers to choose, and so does his foresquare morality ("The Millere is a cherl, ye knowe wel this; / So was the Reve eek and othere mo" [3182–83]). We are not told who the other Canterbury churls may be. We can only guess, and our list would be telling for us. As judge of the Canterbury tale-telling game, Harry Bailly, like Chaucer the pilgrim, is always himself, *though that is his value*. His presence creates an alignment of pilgrim-narrator, Canterbury listener, and participating reader that works to encourage judgment of an imagined and imaginary circumstance, not the triggering in the reader of some prior commitment to a coded "deep" reading. Despite what the Host implies about his capacity to be fair, Harry Bailly's judgment is neither simple nor deep, but woefully personal. Although the pilgrims as a company at least nominally agree in the General Prologue, before the pilgrimage begins, that he "wolde been oure governour, / And of oure tales juge and reportour" (813–14), individual pilgrims do not seem bound by the Host's opinions. Harry Bailly's confident announcement in the Prologue to the Nun's Priest's Tale ("And wel I woot the substance is in me, / If any thyng shal wel reported be" [2803–4]) proves disappointing, for his notion of a "wel reported" tale is purely his.

The introduction to the Pardoner's Tale, for example, both gives us and takes away the Host's evaluative presence in the *Canter-*

bury Tales. Harry Bailly would be his own physician. Because the
tale of Virginia is too painful for him, he says, he requires either a
drink or another story:

> By corpus bones! but I have triacle,
> Or elles a draughte of moyste and corny ale,
> Or but I heere anon a myrie tale,
> Myn herte is lost for pitee of this mayde.
>
> (314–17)

As a self-involved listener, the Host serves as a model for response,
not because his opinion is prescriptive, but because it is forthright.
As a "reader," Harry Bailly sees himself as deeply pious and his
righteousness is characteristically aggressive. He condemns Clau-
dius ("fals cherl") and Apius ("fals justise") outright ("As shameful
deeth as herte may devyse / Come to thise juges and hire advo-
catz!" [289–91]). His expresson of sorrow for Virginia is swift ("Al-
gate this sely mayde is slayn, allas!" [292]), but his gloss of the tale,
which follows directly, seems roundly off base:

> Allas, to deere boughte she beautee!
> Wherfore I seye al day that men may see
> That yiftes of Fortune and of Nature
> Been cause of deeth to many a creature.
> Hire beautee was hire deth, I dar wel sayn.
> Allas, so pitously as she was slayn!
> Of bothe yiftes that I speke of now
> Men han ful ofte moore for harm than prow.
>
> (293–300)

For Harry Bailly, the Physician's Tale is a comment on the treach-
ery of good looks, as if Virginia's beauty, her gift from Dame Fortune, capricious and testing, was her fault—both the cause of
Apius's lecherous passion and her own decapitation. I think the
Host links the gifts of fortune and nature just *because* he wants to
make beauty a lure, something desirable and something dangerous
(for Apius), something bestowed and something to feel guilty about
(for Virginia). It is only partly true here that Harry Bailly is a misogynist; he sees Virginia's fortunate beauty as the occasion to in-
dict fortune and nature as the cause of harm for man in general.
Virginia's is only an especially pitiful case. Indeed, it is difficult to

pinpoint the direction of the Host's ejaculatory response. He exclaims "allas!" three times (292, 293, 298), as if his religious moralizings are for himself alone. He sounds self-absorbed. He tells the Physician that the excessive emotion caused by the "pitous tale" (302) of Virginia has given him palpitations:

> Seyde I not wel? I kan nat speke in terme;
> But wel I woot thou doost myn herte to erme,
> That I almoost have caught a cardynacle.
>
> (311–13)

Bailly is much moved, but far from upbraiding the Physician for arousing his anginal piety, he praises him with a characteristically masculine celebration of bodily fluids—urine and liquor:

> I pray to God so save thy gentil cors,
> And eek thyne urynals and thy jurdones,
> Thyn ypocras, and eek thy galiones,
> And every boyste ful of thy letuarie;
> God blesse hem, and oure lady Seinte Marie!
> So moot I theen, thou art a propre man,
> And lyk a prelat, by Seint Ronyan!
> Seyde I nat wel?
>
> (304–11)

The linking of urinary vessels ("urynals") and chamber pots ("jurdones"), perhaps vessels used in diagnosing diseases by uroscopy, a cordial ("ypocras"), perhaps an aphrodisiac, composed of red wine, spices, and sugar, and medical remedies ("galiones" and "letuarie"—the latter perhaps a kind of confection one licks) unites the Host with a man he admires ("a propre man"). He thinks of the Physician as a "prelat," and he swears by "Seint Ronyan"—a pun, I believe, on "rognon," the French for "kidneys." What is celebrated here is masculine power, felt as liquids consumed and spent. The Physician is the celebrant. Semen is not mentioned, but it is, I believe, implicit in the Host's idea of masculine juices. When he turns to the Pardoner, he wants a kind of consolation for his heart "lost for pitee of this mayde" (317), and the Host expects the Pardoner to help him recover it ("Telle us som myrthe or japes right anon" [319]). We can only, of course, believe the Host is overcome with "pitee" if we grant him a masculine bravado confirmed by his personal reading of the Physician's Tale—his special kind of triumphant railing at private, but for him generalizable, wrongs of fortune. No one objects.

Thus Harry Bailly, as a reader, is happy *because* he enacts the proposition that literature has a therapeutic effect, and that the "patient" must, as Pandarus says in book 1 of the *Troilus,* "unwre his wownde" (858)—uncover himself, read personally—in order for the "triacle" to work. What the Host encourages is initiative in making personal responses. His decidedly idiosyncratic responses actually work against interpretations of the "Canterbury" tales that are strict and doctrinaire. The fiction of the oral presentation of the tales among the Canterbury pilgrims makes the *Canterbury Tales* into a kind of *speculum libri;* it presents a mirror to the world of books, showing how books were read in Chaucer's day—how they were listened to, and perhaps how "life" was. Indeed, if anything about what the pilgrims say ought to be a topic among critics, it is not simply what their tales may tell us about their psychology, somehow conceived without reference to their sociability. Rather, the pilgrims' opinions of other pilgrims' tales show us the way listening to others reveals us to ourselves, if we are attentive. The pilgrims' personal reactions—their enthusiasms, blind spots, amorality, high-mindedness—give us a clue to the way stories awaken both sociability and judgment in all readers, fictional and real.

We cannot say, of course, that the Host encourages the Knight to speak the way the Host may encourage us to read. But like the Host's reaction to the Physician's Tale, the Knight's reaction to the Monk's Tale expresses the medicinal effect of the story both on himself and on society in general, as he understands it. Here is a second example of special reading, this one from a man the Host sees as his social, and perhaps evaluative, better. It illustrates idiosyncratic reading that can define social status because it *is* personal, not because it should not be: the Knight is no more objective than the Host, nor should he be expected to be merely because we assume he has a nobler social conscience:

> "Hoo!" quod the Knyght, "good sire, namoore of this!
> That ye han seyd is right ynough, ywis,
> And muchel moore; for litel hevynesse
> Is right ynough to muche folk, I gesse.
> I seye for me, it is a greet disese,

> Whereas men han been in greet welthe and ese,
> To heeren of hire sodeyn fal, allas!
> And the contrarie is joye and greet solas,
> As whan a man hath been in povre estaat,
> And clymbeth up and wexeth fortunat,
> And there abideth in prosperitee."

(7.2767–77)

There is perhaps an intentional play in this passage on "disese" and "ese." In one sense they are antonyms: in Middle English, "disese" meant both "displeasure" and "disease." For the Knight, who is expressing his view of the function of art, a story is good if it reinforces the socially positive. Telling the story of fortune's tragedies is, therefore, not as "gladsom" (2778) as recounting fortune's comedies; it is a great discomfort to the body social because it implies the futility of renown, the connection between the past and the present, between books and "life." Like the Host, the Knight listens personally, although unlike Harry Bailly here, the Knight presumes to generalize his reactions to the Monk's Tale for the community of men. In this sense, the Knight's response conflates the hygienic and recreational justifications of literature Glending Olson has shown are the twin aspects of the medieval view of literary pleasure.[14] The Knight sees the literature he values as promoting bodily good ("ese," not "disese"). It gives health and mental cheerfulness. One depends on the other. The Knight's justification is not an effort "to create a category of aesthetic delight or to define literary pleasure as an end in itself." His justification of literary pleasure is a justification of literature's good. For the Knight, literary pleasure remains "distinctively medieval" in its moral concern.[15]

We should note two things here: first, the Knight's idea of literary pleasure is not preparatory to a higher or better kind of serious use of literature. Literary pleasure is not an adjunct to literary value. It is not a kind of time off before one begins more serious work. Second, the Knight's view of valuable literature is unabashedly personal. He prefers stories of good fortune, not because they have no moral purpose, not because they are trivial and cannot teach, but because they can. The Knight values the personally and socially positive, and would have literature do the same—he stops the Monk abruptly ("good sire, namoore of this!"), because the Monk is not gladsome. We have not, of course, found the only answer to the literarily sober-minded in the Knight's response to the Monk's Tale. We have perhaps found one of the best responses to readers whose sense of moral value requires they be disciplined as they read. In no sense, of course, is the Knight's response to the Monk's Tale and the literary pleasure it implies Chaucer's view, though one cannot help feeling that Chaucer would be more sympathetic to the Knight than to the Monk. If he can be said to be championing one view of art over another, it is a view that sees literary pleasure and literary seriousness (not "pain") as complementary demands of literature providing us as people and as thinkers with a text to stand on. For Chaucer, literature teaches and delights because it engages readers in a hermeneutic circle of interpretation and reflection.

For all his desire for literary pleasure, the Knight is not an irresponsible reader of the Monk's Tale. Nor is Harry Bailly, who agrees with the Knight's judgment of the tale—and "knowing him" we expect that—but whose objection to it seems to grow out of his natural impatience with people who complain.

> He spak how Fortune covered with a clowde
> I noot nevere what; and als of a tragedie
> Right now ye herde, and, pardee, no remedie
> It is for to biwaille ne compleyne
> That that is doon, and als it is a peyne,
> As ye had seyd, to heere of hevynesse.
>
> (2782–87)

What is done is done. The Host in no way understands the import of the idea of *de casibus*—falling from good fortune into bad. That idea is not a lesson to him about the instability of the world. Indeed, dwelling on the unfortunate seems unrealistic to the Host— gloomy and antisocial—because brooding, in his mind, does no good. Unlike the Monk, and unlike those who take on *de casibus* stories and treat them seriously as stays of experience,[16] the Host would keep the wheel of fortune turning up, at least imaginatively; he wants only stories of good fortune. He even suggests, after the Knight has interrupted the Monk, that the Monk start again, but this time talk about something jolly, like hunting (2805). Perhaps the Monk's tales came both as an annoyance and a surprise to Harry Bailly. Judging from his remarks to the Monk in the Prologue to the Monk's Tale, Harry Bailly expects a good story, perhaps a racy one, from the Monk, whose sexuality is unmistakable to the Host:

> Thou woldest han been a tredefowel aright.
> Haddestow as greet a leeve, as thou hast myght,
> To parfourne al thy lust in engendrure,
> Thou haddest bigeten ful many a creature.
>
> (1945–48)

But the tale the Host gets, the tragedies of fortune the Monk "gives birth to," brings him (the Host) down. Harry Bailly probably thinks that men will be, or should be, hearty, no matter what their métier. Hence his annoyance and surprise.

Like the Host, critics are always surprised by the Monk's tales, but of course for different reasons. They usually find the satiric Chaucer here, but do not take their cues from the Host's assumption that the Monk is brimming with sexuality but lacks "leeve" to exercise it. They look both to the portrait of the Monk in the General Prologue and to the Monk's Tale for their arguments to satire. Indeed, the fact that the Monk is an outrider and might have sexual "leeve" has not led anyone, except the Host, to wonder about the Monk's sexual stamina, though everyone seems to agree that the Monk is "tied to the earth."[17] I suspect that for Harry Bailly, whose manliness is a kind of abstract fetish for him, one never has enough "leeve" to "bigeten ful many a creature," even as an outrider. More to the point, I think, is that the Host sees the kind of Monk *he* needs; his Monk is by extension the Monk of the General Prologue—the one we may see. In keeping with his personal reading of character and stories, the Host assimilates the Monk's "monastic contradictions" to his own "identity theme."[18] And critics do the same. Thus Chaucer as satirist is always thought elusive, for what he has given his readers are multiple guides to the same "naked" text. Neither the Host nor the Knight can fully clothe the text, give it a husk, as it were. Neither the Host nor the Knight can guide with an omniscience we can believe in because it is sustained, though the personal opinion of each is crucial for getting interpretation started.

Because Chaucer has a "tendency to fictionalize the process of exemplification itself,"[19] to take the part of narrative guide, divide it up, and pass it around among those who tell stories and those who listen to them, knowledge of the motives for reading one way or another is as important to our understanding of something read as our dogged concentration on the text itself. The Canterbury pilgrims should not be upbraided because of the way they exhibit what psychologists call "group dynamics." The "knowledge of their motives" in listening is "sufficient to deflect" to us the "exemplary bearing of their tales."[20] Harry Bailly asks the Monk to "quite with the Knyghtes tale" (1.3119), a suggestion to "repay" or "reward" the Knight's Tale for its value as a "noble storie, / And worthy for to drawen to memorie" (3111–12). But when the Miller insists that he precede the Monk in order to "quite the Knyghtes tale" (3127), his paying back comes to sound like a competitive drive for self-justification as a pilgrim who can tell a "noble tale for the nones" (3126). The Miller's drunken interruption has the ring of inferiority. Only then does "quite" seem to me an appropriate affirmation of status and nobility in a social game, not a kind of capturing and recasting of another's story in order to remake it. It may, indeed, be valuable for Chaucer's sense of the uses of storytelling that the noble design of Canterbury tale-telling the Host envisions, his dream of hierarchy and human stability, goes awry. The Miller's drunken interruption disturbs the Host's "medieval" social order, but it releases creative power that each pilgrim, including the Miller and the Host, expresses through telling and listening to stories. "Canterbury" tales may burst forth as a kind of answering weapon for grievances, real and imagined, personal and intellectual, petty and high-minded, but storytelling yields a kind of greater peace. Art catches, embodies, and releases for our observation the urges to power and creativity (re-creation), godlike and dangerous if not made to engage our sense of social caring and a storyteller's sense of projected power and choice. Storytelling makes and remakes the world each time a story is told or retold ("quite"). In this pluralist sense, storytelling is a responsible act of human understanding.

Recently, Anne Middleton has observed that *because* Ricardian poetry generally "envisions a society composed of members whose differing stations, functions, and ways of life yield different perspectives on the common world, which it is the aim of the speaker to respect, to bring to mutual awareness, and to resolve into common understanding," whatever common understanding we, "each

of us in the presence of the others, can see about our common condition, the world we share *as a people,* becomes the poetic subject."[21]
Middleton sees the social and literary values that find expression
for her in public poetry represented "in Chaucerian fiction only, as
it were, in indirect discourse, assigned in various ways to several
characters in the Canterbury fiction—and thereby greatly qualified."[22] Her chief examples of Ricardian publicness are those "baggy
monsters," Gower's *Confessio Amantis* and Langland's *Piers Plowman.* And it is precisely their "bagginess," which she sees not as
looseness but as accommodation, that is for her their openness.
Still, the *Canterbury Tales*—as a form not baggy, but perhaps
"incomplete"[23]—can also, I think, be placed under the Ricardian
rubric. Indeed, the idea of storytelling for a community of men that
storytelling in part fashions—a kind of social explanation for the capaciousness of Chaucer's tales—is, to my mind, a third example of
Ricardian publicness. Even the *Troilus,* with whose storyteller we
puzzle out the motives and manners of characters, and even the
genre of the work, is in the spirit, if not the letter, of Ricardian
public poetry.

Bringing to common understanding is for Middleton the radiating feature of what she calls the "bourgeois style," not any single
piece of verbal or visual decor, but a "social sense" in the author
that puts readers on the testing end of truth—the feature of style
Chaucer's narratives share with parable—and makes parabolic listening—not so much what one listens for (that would be telling, of
course), but the listening itself—both personal and, because it is
personal, social too. Because the bourgeois style, which commends
the virtues of comparison—"suffraunce" (mutual toleration, compromise, forgiveness)—is for Middleton "a coherent set of ethical attitudes toward the world—experientially based, vernacular,
simple, pious but practical, active," it can designate "the poetry
that gives expression to this essentially high-minded secularism."[24]

Middleton's view has much in common with Morton Bloomfield's humanism[25] and the hermeneutics of Hans-Georg Gadamer.
Indeed, Gadamer's notion that "it is not so much our judgments as
it is our prejudices that constitute our being" may serve to explain
how the voices of Chaucerian fiction, always partial, often disruptive, are in fact "the biases of our openness to the world." The nature of the hermeneutical experience "is not that something is out-

side and desires admission. Rather, we are possessed by something and precisely by means of it we are opened up for the new, the different, the true."[26] Gadamer's concept of prejudice is crucial to an understanding of his idea of the hermeneutic circle, the circle of interpretation and reflection in which Chaucer's work intentionally encloses his audience—his fictional audience (like the Canterbury pilgrims), his intended audience (Chaucer's immediate historical circle), and his actual audience (his historical readers and us).[27] Indeed, Middleton's notion of a distinctively Ricardian mode of address, literary and social, is just such a Gadamerian hermeneutic circle that encloses both Chaucer and Gower without either "Gowerizing" or "humanizing" (universalizing) Chaucer. Her metaphysic of reading helps delimit the worldly context in which Chaucer and Gower, and hence Chaucer's intended and actual (historical) audience, may have lived as men of letters—readers and thinkers— themselves and the context we can and cannot share with them. In the discussion that follows I hope to suggest specific ways in which Chaucer and his historical audience would have used, and would have been expected to use, the narratives we assume they read and valued. In a way, I am reconstructing, as it were, their hermeneutic circle, suggesting what they found engaging, revealing, and educative in Chaucer in order to open up my own circle of interpretation and reflection. I offer my historical discussion to historicize us.

From a Memoranda Roll list compiled in 1384–85, we know that Richard II at that time owned fourteen books,[28] primarily in French, though several were in Latin. Richard seems "to have been anything but an assiduous book collector," and the list really tells us little about his personal tastes, though "for entertainment reading the staple was romance."[29] Richard purchased none of the books himself. All fourteen were inherited from his grandfather, Edward III, and recovered from their custodian, John Bacon, during the first six years of Richard's reign.[30] Richard Firth Green notes that "eleven of them had been pawned or sold within a year of their passing into his possession."[31] Richard's taste may have been influenced by his tutor, Sir Simon Burley, a list of whose books for 1388, the year Burley was executed, a victim of the Merciless Parliament and the Lords Appellant, V. J. Scattergood provides.[32]

Unfortunately, no work of Chaucer's appears either on any list of books belonging to Richard II or in the inventory of Burley's books; indeed none appears on any book list of those associated with the court.[33] It is highly improbable that Richard knew any of the classics, although it is likely that they formed part of his concept of a man of learning. In 1395, for example, he commissioned a Latin epitaph for his tomb in Westminster Abbey in which he compared himself to Homer ("Omerus").[34] The comparison is extravagant. Richard was certainly neither a Homer nor a "patron of Homers," which may be what the word implies.[35] Richard's literary tastes— French, courtly, and, in that sense, according to Elizabeth Salter, international—can be said to have governed the culture that developed in and for his court circle only obliquely,[36] though Salter does suggest that Chaucer's use of English is a "triumph of internationalism"—his creation of a "high-prestige vernacular literature" for which Richard's patronage meant providing an occasion for Chaucer's speaking in English to a court accustomed to hearing learned and significant matter in French, the first great vernacular literature of Europe.[37]

Salter has perhaps exaggerated Richard's intellectual and social support for the literary arts[38] and Chaucer's direct presence before the king. Moreover, if we can generalize from the available book lists, the "culture of the court was still overwhelmingly Latin and French, and French of a somewhat old-fashioned sort. . . . There are no Italian books." English had apparently not "acquired any sort of prestige,"[39] despite, for example, legislation in 1362 that made it theoretically, if not actually, the language of pleading in the law courts.[40] Indeed, it may well be that to choose to write in English, as Gower did in the *Confessio Amantis,* and as Chaucer did habitually, "was felt to be somewhat anomalous and *avant garde.*"[41] Still, we can perhaps talk about Chaucer's literary internationalism, even if we cannot link it to the king as a cultural force, as Chaucer's "high-prestige" vernacular hope—a gesture of broad connection that invites English readers into an international community that includes Latin, French, and Italian works, among them the works of Chaucer's contemporaries,[42] much beyond the narrow "medieval" internationalism of the Ricardian court. It is altogether possible, too, that Chaucer's readers in his own time did

not understand the significance of his capaciousness of genre and
style. Chaucer's "Englishing" is, in this sense, a daringly wide gesture of cultural inclusion.

We know Richard commissioned the first version of Gower's
Confessio Amantis, but we have no similar charge for Chaucer.
Besides the statement in the colophon of 1390, composed when
Gower finished this version of the *Confessio*, which says that the
work "was made at the instance of his most serene highness, the
aforesaid king of England, Richard II," thirty-three of the forty-
nine extant manuscripts of the *Confessio* describe the boating party
on the river at which Gower was asked to undertake his poem.[43] I
cite the passage in full because it is the best account we have of
Richard as royal patron.[44]

> In Temse whan it was flowende
> As I be bote cam rowende,
> So as fortune hir tyme sette,
> My liege lord par chaunce I mette;
> And so befel, as I cam nyh,
> Out of my bot, whan he my syh,
> He bad me come in to his barge.
> And whan I was with him at large,
> Amonges othre thinges seid
> He hath this charge upon me leid,
> And bad me doo my besynesse
> That to his hihe worthinesse
> Som newe thing I scholde boke,
> That he himself it mighte loke
> After the forme of my writynge.
>   (39*–53*)[45]

The scene is flattering enough to Richard, and Gower's couplets
tranquilly record the event, though the passage probably does not
do justice to Richard's sense of his own largeness of spirit. This was,
in its way, a grand moment for patron and poet alike, for the assign-
ment took place on the royal barge on the Thames. But the real
point for Gower, I suspect, is the fortuitousness of the commission
("So as fortune hir tyme sette") to "boke" something substantive for
the education of his king.[46] We are even invited in the above passage to imagine with Gower *his* happy conception of royal power
meeting and putting into the service of the kingdom a poet's time

and labor. That for Gower is a poet's dream, and a meeting on water is marvelously apt. In his own eyes, Gower's commission has the touch of destiny. Whether or not the *Legend of Good Women* was written at the request of Richard's queen, Anne of Bohemia, there is a kind of dedication to her in the F Prologue (496–97). And it has been suggested, though I am more intrigued than convinced, that perhaps "the young royal couple at this time [on the barge?] conceive[d] the idea of having the two premier poets of the kingdom write parallel poems in praise of love," through which they could, and do, offer advice on the conduct of kings.[47]

The case can be made, I think, for Gower's and Chaucer's shared concern, in the years following the Merciless Parliament of 1386, for the condition of kingship in England. There are clear parallels between Chaucer's only extended political commentary, the thirty-six lines in the F Prologue to the *Legend of Good Women*, and three works: Gower's *Mirour de l'omme* (the best background for the opening lines of Alceste's speech),[48] the "Epistle to the King" in Gower's *Vox Clamantis*,[49] and the *Secreta secretorum*, to which Chaucer may have been alluding in lines 379–83 of the F Prologue.[50] Furthermore, the balade *Lak of Stedfastnesse* resembles sections from the Prologue to the *Confessio Amantis*.[51] Its last stanza, the "Lenvoy to King Richard," seems to follow a passage in the "Epistle to the King" in the *Vox* very closely indeed.[52] Still, as moral guide and advisor to the king, Chaucer is less easy to find in his own work than Gower, though some Chaucerians have suggested that one of the themes of the Knight's Tale is the relation between natural (private) passion, human law, and the ruler, and that the Melibee contains ideas about public-spiritedness that Chaucer may have wanted Richard to consider.[53]

Gower clearly presumes to teach Richard II, but Chaucer, if he does so, does so obliquely and at Richard's own pace. Perhaps Chaucer's idea of moral authority found its justification not in the idea of ecclesiastical (hierarchical and didactic) power, but in the notion of judicious and thoughtful independence that entailed a kind of lateral or horizontal allegiance among other civil servants like Chaucer. As R. T. Lenaghan explains:

A chaplain or confessor could lecture a prince because he was in holy orders and the homily directly discharged his duty as a clerk. While any layman, basing his authority on probity and learning, might do the same, a poet's claim to learning would give him special title as a sort of lay clerk, and experience in the household would make him aware of the realities of governmental administration and of values and attitudes in the community of administrators. His roles as poet and civil servant combine to give him some independent standing. That his independence could not have matched a churchman's does not mean that he had none.[54]

Now whether or not Chaucer's lateral kind of moral authority was convincing (Gower never gives up sounding didactic, though *he* is not an ecclesiastic),[55] Chaucer always expects his readers to understand his narratives as fictions that encourage judicious and thoughtful independence of mind. His circle of understanding is not hierarchical; it is communal and, in that sense, public and public-minded. Thus the way Richard II would profit from the lessons in kingship in the Prologue to the *Legend of Good Women* or the Knight's Tale or the Melibee would be to move from fiction to personal application, even if he knew that Alceste in the Prologue to the *Legend* was supposed to be Princess Joan.[56] John H. Fisher's objections to Margaret Galway's conjecture about the identity of Alceste are, I think, convincing.[57] So are Bernard Huppé's.[58] Still, the desire to "make Chaucer historical" is not only understandable; it is really the only way to make him recoverable and valuable. As Lee Patterson reminds us, "The process of historical situating is . . . a discovery not of what the text really means (or meant) but of what it makes history mean. And we perform this situating not to interpret the text, nor even to explain it, but to ground it in the palpable world in which we all live and to locate it within a dialectic that corresponds in some measure to our own historical consciousness."[59] That Galway falls victim to what Patterson calls the "methodology of historicism" is unfortunate, but, if I may say so, altogether laudable. Perhaps Galway has simply done what the best Chaucerians are, by Chaucer himself, invited to do.

Chaucer is difficult to pin down with respect to all his political references. "Jakke Straw and his meynee" are specifically alluded to at one point in the Nun's Priest's Tale, but the allusion literally compares the noise that accompanied the peasants' intention to kill the Flemings to the noise that accompanies the intention of the "sely wydwe and eek hir doghtres two" (3375) to kill the fox:

Ne made nevere shoutes half so shrille
Whan that they wolden any Flemyng kille,
As thilke day was maad upon the fox.

(3395–97)

Now riots are noisy, and although the mob massacred the harmless
Flemings simply because they could better compete in the cloth
trade—a brutal and selfish act in any age—the fox in the story is
not killed. The reference to "Jakke Straw and his meynee" does
not, strictly speaking, tell us where Chaucer stood on the event.
And there is no authorial guidance in the text to help us. In this
instance, I suspect, Chaucer's reticence and modesty, his neutral
attitude on a great public issue like the Peasants' Revolt, was dictated, as Roger Sherman Loomis says, "not by artistic detachment
or cowardice, but by a feeling that right and wrong were so mixed
that to tell the whole truth would merely bring down on his head
the curses of both sides."[60] Besides, the real point of the Nun's
Priest's Tale is Chaucer's invitation to his reader to find the moral of
the story ("Taketh the fruyt, and lat the chaf be stille" [3443]).

The way he anticipates an objection to the silliness of his tale
suggests to me that Chaucer, always less doggedly moral than
Gower, nonetheless shared with him the idea that books are never
pointless and may in fact be edifying. The allusion to St. Paul in the
Nun's Priest's Tale (3441) from Romans 15:4 is surely meant to include Chaucer's tale among books written for our instruction. And
although St. Paul's books are among the Scriptures and Chaucer's
tale lacks that status, the Nun's Priest's Tale may still *teach* its readers something, even if only something about how to manage their
own curiosity.[61] Chaucer's invitation to take the "fruyt" and leave
the "chaf" is, I think, a genuine invitation to look for the moral of
the story—notice that the "chaf" is heard, too, and we are asked to
render it silent ("stille")—but once the members of any audience
begin to participate in the taking of morality, they find that there
are at least three morals that can be taken: Chauntecleer's moral
about flattery and closing his eyes, the storyteller's moral about
flattery, and the fox's moral about talking too much, which the narrator seems to ignore. The real point of the invitation to participate
in the completion of the story seems to be the frustration of the
desire for authorial guidance. As for the reference to what "seint

Paul seith" in Romans 15:4 ("Quaecumque enim scripta sunt, ad nostram doctrinam scripta sunt, ut per patientiam et consolationem Scripturarum, spem habeamus"), Paul most probably had only the Jewish Scriptures in mind. Writing to Timothy (2 Tim. 3:16–17), Paul is equally unambiguous about the kind of written word he considers useful to a perfecting of the faith. Still, according to Robert Burlin, the "liberalization of the Apostle's uncompromising view can be attributed to a long tradition of Christian humanism, apparent as early as Augustine but flowering in the twelfth century."[62] Indeed, theologians and writers throughout the Middle Ages do claim that the books men write, like the books God has written, are written for our enlightenment.[63]

Although Gower in his own work is always a more steadfast and secure moral guide than Chaucer, and thus easier to place in Richard's court, both Chaucer and Gower shared the idea, which Gower gives voice to in the Prologue to the *Confessio Amantis*, that books can teach those who read them because they mirror the world:

> Whan that the bokes weren levere,
> Wrytinge was beloved evere
> Of hem that weren vertuous;
> For hier in erthe amonges ous,
> If noman write hou that it stode,
> The pris of hem that weren goode
> Scholde, as who seith, a gret partie
> Be lost: so for to magnifie
> The worthi princes that tho were,
> The bokes schewen hiere and there,
> Wherof the world ensampled is.
>
> (37–47)

Although Gower restricts his praise of "clerkly" men to those who seek answers for the world in religious books, he, like Chaucer, praises the idea of "bookishness"—serious, studious, truth-seeking through books:

> To thenke upon the daies olde,
> The lif of clerkes to beholde,
> Men sein how that thei weren tho
> Ensample and reule of alle tho
> Whiche of wisdom the vertu soughten.
> Unto the god ferst their besoughten

> As to the substaunce of her Scole,
> That thei ne scholden noght befole
> Her wit upon none erthly wekes.
>
> (193–201)

Gower not only dedicates the *Confessio* to Richard but says that it was written for his "sake," perhaps as part of Richard's education for kingship, which the "moral" Gower had been undertaking for years:

> A bok for king Richardes sake,
> To whom belongeth my ligeance
> With al myn hertes obeissance
> In al that evere a liege man
> Unto his king may doon or can.
>
> (24*–28*)[64]

We cannot say that Chaucer ever undertook the education of his king, although the *Troilus*, which the frontispiece in the Corpus Christi College, Cambridge, MS shows Richard II and others listening to, may have been for Richard a challenging "anatomy of love"—a work that taught him morality as well as natural and speculative philosophy.[65] Margaret Galway assumes that because Richard was a boy king at the time of the *Troilus*, someone other than he must have commanded the social life at court—that Princess Joan "godmothered" Chaucer's genius.[66] Galway, like Aage Brusendorff and George Williams,[67] uses the illumination in the way all Chaucerians do—as evidence of a "Chaucer circle"—in order to suggest what the intellectual as well as political relationship between Chaucer and members of his royal and noble audience may have been. The position of listeners around the pulpit in which Chaucer stands—who is grouped with whom, who is looking, or gesturing, at whom—seems to hint, at least to Galway and Williams, at the pecking order of Richard's court. Each subscribes to a frontispiece theory for delivering up to us the idea of Chaucer as court poet, which the *Troilus* illumination so potently creates. Even A. I. Doyle, in describing the circumstances of Lancastrian patronage responsible for the *Troilus* illumination, seems to subscribe to a frontispiece theory, though it does not so much describe Chaucer's real or imagined historical position at the court of Richard II as the imagined education of a king by elders fostering his learning. In noting that the Corpus Christi MS of the *Troilus* bears the refrain of Lydgate's prayer for king, queen, and people in the hand of John Shirley (who, as secretary to Richard Beauchamp, earl of Warwick, and tutor to the infant Henry VI, had been with Warwick and Henry V in France), Doyle seems to suggest—the queen in Lydgate's poem is Henry VI's mother, Catherine—that this refrain implies that the *Troilus* was regarded as needfully tutorial. Doyle jocularly adds that the infant Henry VI was "surely too young for the *Troilus* [in the later 1420s], and subsequently perhaps too pious."[68] Still, the notion that the Troilus *frontispiece* as a presentation picture illustrates the idea of a young king being groomed for kingship is interesting indeed. Some Chaucerians have argued, convincingly I think, that Chaucer's narrative creates a context for reflection on human problems, a circle of understanding, through which he could exert an educative influence. If extended to social history, whether or not as the historicist idea of the Lancastrians, such a view of the purpose of Chaucer's art, which pins nothing on our knowing what Chaucer himself may have believed in and wanted to teach, yields some engaging theories.

Perhaps—if we can believe for a moment that the *Troilus* illumination is a representation of a scene that *should* have happened, assuming it did not—hearing the *Troilus* performed would have afforded the young king an encounter with the idea of the eventual insufficiency of temporal love without prejudging the philosophical and religious conclusions one ought to come to about that idea. Middleton's suggestion that "the high hopes entertained for the boy king Richard, which soon turned to the pious fiction of a king in need of counsel, [and] may have provided reason" for the "outpouring of large-minded, paternal and heartfelt guidance" of the *Confessio* and of *Piers Plowman*,[69] may apply to the *Troilus*, too. There is, to be sure, an indirection to the counsel Chaucer may be said to be giving the young Richard. Like all readers of the work, Richard had to negotiate its fiction of speaking voices. Furthermore, we cannot know how attentive Richard may have been to the "sentence" of the *Troilus*, if, indeed, he actually heard it. We do know how often some of Chaucer's other readers, including medieval readers like John Gower, seem not to have responded to its complexity. Fisher says that Gower, like Chaucer, knew the story of

Troilus and Criseyde, and not just from Chaucer's version of it, though Fisher reminds us that none of Gower's references to the *Troilus* "betrays real appreciation of Chaucer's elevated treatment."[70] Although Gower refers to the story of Troilus and Criseyde in each of his important works, seven times in all,[71] only the reference in the *Cinkante Balades* betrays any awareness of the overtones of the story; there it is taken simply as an example of the instability of fortune—it is barely a story.

With respect to Chaucer's other readers—Jean of Angoulême, for example—Paul Strohm has made a wonderful case for the "discomfort with the unfamiliar" among Chaucer's late medieval audience:[72]

The reflection that a refined and highly cultivated admirer of Chaucer like Jean could read him so wrongheadedly only a generation after his death causes me to conclude that in Jean we do glimpse the tone and style of some of the more limited and dogmatic members of Chaucer's immediate audience. Certainly, Jean does not represent the taste of the whole of Chaucer's circle. Chaucer needed and had Scogans and Buktons too. But even in his own day Chaucer must have had a mixed audience with mixed reasons for enjoying his work.[73]

Lee Patterson similarly shows that, for the compiler of the *Disce mori*, who brought to Chaucer's text a "preemptive hermeneutic,"[74] the *Troilus* could be used to teach the distinction between *amor* and *amicitia* precisely because the compiler read the *Troilus* at its literal and literary level. In Patterson's view, the compiler is for us one of Chaucer's most instructive medieval readers: "Moral interpretation . . . comes [for the compiler of the *Disce mori*] in the form of literary appreciation. . . . The action of the poem is felt by him as fully *real*, as an accurate (and dangerously imitable) depiction of human conduct. . . . [He] categorized *Troilus and Criseyde* as a text to be read literally, i.e., as an exemplary instance."[75]

Still, despite these two examples from the fifteenth century, and despite his reservations about Gower's capacity for complexity of issue in his little "versions" of the *Troilus*, Fisher makes an admirable case for the morality of *Troilus and Criseyde* by contrasting it with Gower's treatment in his works of the theme of sexual love as a manifestation of the universal creative urge:

For the sophistication of Chaucer's treatment [of love in *Troilus and Criseyde*] grows not out of a moralistic opposition between human and divine love, but rather out of recognition of the essential connection between them. . . . The subtlety and human interest in Chaucer's poem derives from its use of this spiritualized conception of courtly love as the vehicle for its moralization. Gower's works which antedate *Troilus* show no awareness of the literary possibilities of spiritualizing the romantic conventions.[76]

Unlike Gower, Chaucer does not immediately denounce temporal love as degrading. All Chaucer's readers who take on the dual claims of the individual sexual impulse and the divine creative urge—the substance of the *Troilus*—have to struggle with the reconciliation of two kinds of love that can be metaphors for each other. The *Troilus* is educative in this sense; it is neither narrowly didactic nor, as Richard Green implies, given his argument about Chaucer's position as household poet, instructionally elusive.[77] The *Troilus* speaks to the same kind of high-minded secularism that Middleton finds characteristic of Gower's work and William Langland's, where style is both a literary and a social value. Indeed, the literary values Chaucer himself (as storyteller) and some of his pilgrim storytellers seem to possess are both literary and social habits that all of Chaucer's work requires of his audience.

For Middleton, style is not only a feature of literature we can detect, but something we must let literature develop in us in order to describe it fully. Thus Chaucer's characteristic sympathy and speculative turn of mind are stylistic modes through which his stories and values can be said to act in the world—to act not just on us, but through us, as we attend to the "surface of literature." In this sense, we can say that Chaucer "wrote for the king." The *Troilus* has the characteristic Ricardian closure—speculative turns that engage thoughtfulness. Even Strohm's argument, which is altogether convincing, that Chaucer's audience was not solely, or even primarily, the courts of Edward III and Richard II (the monarchs, their queens, and great lords like Richard's uncles) is not the point here.[78] The moral and social value of Chaucer's stories, particularly for those who were, according to Strohm, part of Chaucer's immediate circle, resided precisely in the concern for the kingdom they would want intellectual re-creation to demonstrate and that they found demonstrated in the storytelling, guiding, and listening both of Chaucer himself (as imagined narrator of the *Troilus*, for example) and of certain of his Canterbury pilgrims, whom Middleton has called "new men." For Chaucer and his "new men," the "good of literature lies not only in the exemplary virtues it depicts" but "in the virtues required to derive pleasure from it: the capacity for wonder, sympathy and thoughtful speculation."[79] It seems to me that Middleton means to amplify Strohm's understanding of *how* Chaucer's literature would have engaged Chaucer's audience.[80] I prefer her explanation of why Chaucer's "new men" would value literature that had, in Strohm's words, "the potential to stimulate, to challenge, to annoy,"[81] because these reasons explain literary and social behavior rather than describe a connection between members of Chaucer's socially mobile circle and literature that is itself stylistically and intellectually mobile. Moreover, they explain literary and social behavior not just in late medieval England, but in our time, too.

Wolfgang Iser, for example, has made an admirable case for the idea of the text as mirror:

> The manner in which the reader experiences the text will reflect his own disposition, and in this respect the literary text acts as a kind of mirror; but at the same time, the reality which this process helps to create is one that will be *different* from his own (since, normally, we tend to be bored by texts that present us with things we already know perfectly well ourselves). Thus we have the apparently paradoxical situation in which the reader is forced to reveal aspects of himself in order to experience a reality which is different from his own. The impact this reality makes on him will depend largely on the extent to which he himself actively provides the unwritten part of the text, and yet in supplying all the missing links, he must think in terms of experiences different from his own; indeed, it is only by leaving behind the familiar world of his own experience that the reader can truly participate in the adventure the literary text offers him.[82]

Reading for Iser provides a way for us to play and grow; in this way what is unique in us, personally and socially, will both find expression and be manifest to us. If a text is to be a "real" experience, one analogous to living,[83] it must be "deeper" than either the reader or author expects: "The more a text individualizes or confirms an expectation it has initially aroused, the more aware we become of its didactic purpose, so that at best we can only accept or reject the thesis forced upon us. More often than not, the very clarity of such texts will make us want to free ourselves from their clutches."[84] For Iser, an awareness of richness—surprises, betrayals of expectation—creates a *good* text, both artistically good, because it is not boring, and morally valuable, because it can stand, indeed invite, successively self-revealing interpretations, no one of which is final, since all are contingent on one another. For Iser, and most other phenomenological critics, a predictable text is existentially valueless, for it does not encourage retrospection and projection—remembering what we thought about it and what we now think and project about its direction and meaning. We have seen that Chaucer makes a special point of confounding our expectations of guidance, so that he does not "clutch at us," in Iser's phrase, with inevitable conclusions. He deliberately, consciously, and repeatedly gives up the role of teacher to encourage readers to pursue their own "curious" natures. It is this idea of use—the text as mirror—that Iser and other phenomenological and psychological critics value so highly. Indeed, freedom to remake a text may very well be a faculty of mind that needs cultivating, despite what some readers say about texts that push them in one direction or another; one must learn, perhaps, to acknowledge one's own special bent.[85] For Iser, "indeterminacy" makes a text worth our while,[86] and Chaucer's text, inasmuch as it invites a reader's "choice,"[87] can be accommodated to the reader's needs and limitations.

Edward Said has implicitly suggested why we feel that indeterminacy in a text, and in the world, is a value for us. Indeterminacy, he says, allows us to begin; that is, to assert that we intend to create something else (an other) next to (alongside of) an original.[88] This idea of adjacency is central, I think, to Chaucer's notion of tradition as tidings in a House of Rumor, if you will. Perhaps that is why Chaucer's pluralism as an idea appeals to us, seems so modern, and, as Said shows, seems both moral and good. The idea of adjacency allows us to enter the world, to stand, as it were, on texts (each man on his text) and to assert, not dynastic or lineal descent (father to son) in a world imagined as hierarchical, but rather the idea of inbetweenness (brother to brother). Like the Canterbury pilgrims, we can enter the world by "quiting" one another. Harold Bloom has suggested that poetic self-definition is agonistic—freedom-giving because it creates a certain valuable antagonism.[89] In a way, Chaucer's pilgrims demonstrate such agonistic self-beginning (always with words and in groups) by telling, listening, and answering tales. It is, moreover, attended (for them, if not always for Bloom) by a certain wonderment, despite its aggression, a credulity that surprises them and us and a joyfulness (playfulness) appropriate to their taking on tradition.

If, as most Chaucerians think, the Nun's Priest's Tale is Chaucer's most mature work, it is perhaps because the problem of the efficacy and the value of both texts (the written word) and revelation (the words of God through dreams) is examined there. The Nun's Priest's Tale surrounds us, as it were, with words (from the past and the future) by which, if we can trust them, we ought to understand experience (the now). Of course, it is experience itself, the pressure of the physical present—Chauntecleer's sex organs—that demands the self-gratifying triumphs of textuality:

> Now let us speke of myrthe, and stynte al this.
> Madame Pertelote, so have I blis,
> Of o thyng God hath sent me large grace;
> For whan I se the beautee of youre face,
> Ye been so scarlet reed aboute youre yen,
> It maketh al my drede for to dyen;
> For al so siker as *In principio,*
> *Mulier est hominis confusio,*—
> Madame, the sentence of this Latyn is,
> "Womman is mannes joye and al his blis."
> For whan I feele a-nyght your softe syde,
> Al be it that I may nat on yow ryde,
> For that oure perche is maad so narwe, allas!
> I am so ful of joye and of solas,
> That I diffye bothe sweven and dreem.
>   (3157–71)

In talking to his wife, Chauntecleer misreads and then disregards his own good words—his maxims, his dreams, and his books—and leaps from his beam into the barnyard (into experience), naked of a text, as it were. He has done what other Chaucerian heroes rarely do. He has foregone his words. He has stepped off a text, though words finally save him, when he suggests to the fox how to articulate triumph:

> This cok, that lay upon the foxes bak,
> In al his drede unto the fox he spak,

And seyde, "Sire, if that I were as ye,
Yet sholde I seyn, as wys God helpe me,
'Turneth agayn, ye proude cherles alle!
A verray pestilence upon yow falle!
Now am I come unto the wodes syde;
Maugree youre heed, the cok shal heere abyde.
I wol hym ete, in feith, and that anon!'"
The fox answerde, "In faith, it shal be don."
And as he spak that word, al sodeynly,
This cok brak from his mouth delyverly,
And heighe upon a tree he fleigh anon.

(3405–17)

Chauntecleer's fluency is amusingly human—manipulative, social, and verbal. He masters the present by justifying himself with language, giving the fox a text on which to stand and thereby giving himself his own (another) text. He establishes himself in the world the way a reader might, not by being disinterested, but precisely by being passionate, partial, and sporting. Chauntecleer reads the world and speaks it. He "begins" again, in Said's sense.

I am suggesting here that Chauntecleer is Chaucer's most profound and blatant hermeneutist, not a parody of the real thing. Indeed, it is perhaps Chaucer's fluency with the *idea* of the hermeneutic circle that allows him such amusing play with the idea of the glosser, in this case, a cocky rooster. Moreover, I think Chaucer takes seriously the notion of standing on a text in order to understand the world just *because* such cockiness, such surefire and persistent reading of the world from an appropriated text, generates intellectual life, however misguided, however comic, however wrong. We are most vulnerable and most alive when we affirm our understanding. Indeed, in describing the value we give to fetterless interpretation, to our very prideful mistrust of the institutionalization of interpretation, Frank Kermode proves the best interpreter of Chauntecleer as hermeneutist:

It is of course true that individual acts of interpretation are rarely if ever performed in full consciousness of . . . meta-interpretative considerations. And although we are aware how much any interpretation must depend on a tacit form of knowing acquired from institutional training, we tend to reserve our highest praise for those interpretations that seem most intuitive, most theory-free, seeming to proceed from some untrameled divinatory impulse, having the gratuity, the fortuity of genius. The possibility of such divinations may explain why Hermes once laid claim to a share in the lyre of Apollo. We admire their natural violence or cunning, or their lyric force, and only later do we reason about them, and see how, in spite of everything, the institution helped to shape them.[90]

Now Chauntecleer is no genius, and his intuition is flawed. His "divinatory impulse" is pride and sexuality, the demands of the body and the presentments of the mind. For another author, these might be the enemies of enlightenment. For Chaucer, they are its allies, for they propel to action and quick thinking. For Chauntecleer, as well as for the sober hermeneutist, interpretive vigor wins the day and saves a life. Chaucer's most mature "Canterbury" tale demonstrates the comic triumph of human wit—textuality and lies. Notice the conflation here: scholarship and misunderstanding, the willful and the unconscious. In Chaucer, there is no divine revelation, no verbal intervention. Words, human and Godly, both confound and save because they give us the momentary experience of truth we know through our rival interpretive triumphs. There are no failures of understanding in Chaucer, only vigorous, partial, dangerous, victorious leaps, like Chauntecleer's, of mind and body.

Chapter Four

Who Speaks for the Wife of Bath?

It is unfortunate that we know nothing of actual contemporary oc-casions when the performer of a Chaucerian tale was not Chaucer himself. This possibility, which existed during Chaucer's lifetime when one of his manuscripts circulated privately, raises fascinating questions about the way passages would have been performed by someone pretending to be Chaucer pretending to be someone else. We have trouble enough remembering the idea of double story-tellers in the *Canterbury Tales* as we read the work and, as a con-sequence, tend to see individual tales simply as reflections of their pilgrim narrators. As readers, we may not make Chaucer any clearer to understand, for as interpreters what we often do is formulate theories about the effect of the revelations of character in individ-ual "Canterbury" tales on our idea of the character and psychology of individual storytellers. We remake Chaucer in our own "Gothic" style, reading deeply in our self-revealing way.

There is, of course, no reason to try to reverse our habits of mind—the way we make psychological sense of a piece of writ-ing—although we should understand the sense in which our habits are especially ours. John Speirs, for example, sees the Wife of Bath as compellingly life-affirming. Speirs' view of her, and her trium-phant value for him, is elegant:

[The Wife of Bath] begins by opposing "experience" to "auctoritee." Her own experience, as it is reviewed and assessed throughout her mono-logue, has been stormily rich. The governing motives of her life, as she frankly declares, have been appetite and masterfulness, Venus and Mars. But the pattern of the comedy is by no means simply a morally one-sided sacred-profane opposition. The Wife wins considerable rational sympathy, for she is set in opposition to a meagre and barren, bookish and academic scholasticism that bolsters up age-old theologically sanctioned and authorized male prejudice and tyranny. She is thus not only an object of criticism; she is herself positively a critic, who has nature and sense substantially on her side. Her rebellious excesses—identified by the irony as such—are yet excesses of a joyous spontaneity and fertility essential to the going on and renewal of life. In her own inordinate way she represents life boldly asserted against oppressive forms of death.[1]

As a critic, Speirs is enthusiastic. Like Bertrand Bronson, he hears "the very folds of an individual mind . . . [in the Wife's] windings and doublings."[2] Indeed, he may believe Bronson's theory of the four stages of "Canterbury" influence on stories Chaucer intended for his collection of tales, though Speirs does not, like Bronson, consciously read the Wife of Bath's Prologue and Tale as part of a larger argument about Chaucer's continuous or discontinuous presence in or behind his narratives.[3] Speirs' lively and involved reading of the Wife's character, which constitutes his reading of the Wife of Bath's Prologue and Tale, demonstrates how much her irrepressible female self invites his imaginative penetration. What Speirs responds to in the Wife's "tale" is his own historicist criticism. He sees the Wife of Bath as the best example of Chaucer's maturest art, unfettered by the constraints of a psychologically naïve medieval aesthetic.[4] Speirs sees the Wife's "tale"—her story and her self—as the victory of "rebellious excess" and "joyous spontaneity" over "meagre and barren, bookish and academic scholasticism." For him, the Wife of Bath is a life-affirming heroine, and to the extent that he confuses art and life, and sees good art as good because it depicts the best values of life, Speirs reveals his own place in our cultural history.

Like Bronson, Speirs reads the Wife of Bath's Prologue as a self-revealing dramatic monologue and her tale as a self-revealing fiction made crystalline by her psychological openness.[5] Like Bronson, Speirs "Browning-izes" Chaucer, though that is not my point. It is obvious that no Wife of Bath in costume ever acted on a real stage—a minor point, but nonetheless an important one, because Kittredge's analogy to drama, which Bronson takes seriously, if

not quite literally—has raised vexing questions about the genre
and the reality of Chaucerian narrative. Why are certain characters
in Chaucer more fully "realized" than others? Why do some seem
more "lifelike" than others? What is the appropriateness of tale to
teller in the *Canterbury Tales*, where Chaucer's "dramatic" narrative, as in the Wife of Bath's Prologue and Tale and the Pardoner's Prologue and Tale, seems to have reached its maturity?
Why are only some of the individual tales full dramatic monologues?

Even critics who see Chaucer's work as allegorical or symbolic
read his narratives as if they were, or were about to become, drama,
so influential has Kittredge's theory been in defining the whole
Chaucer canon generically; we perhaps should note that the symbolic, the dramatic, and the realistic are often hopelessly blurred in
such critics. For all that, however, they are not unconvincing, since
what they respond to in Chaucer and what we respond to in them
is their engagement with the text, for which they have no categories of clarifying demarcation.[6] Their failure to explain the text,
even at the level of generic definition, is their triumph as interested, not disinterested, readers—and, of course, the inexhaustible triumph of the text.

As such responses to Chaucer show, reading him engages our
special passions in the circle of interpretation and reflection in
which his text encloses us. Indeed, what all readers from Chaucer's
day to our own have found "real" in him—refreshing and renewing—is the invitation to personal taste and judgment, particularly
when, as we saw with Speirs, a particular critical reading seems to
reveal Chaucer's voice. Who can, on a feeling level, disagree with
Speirs? I would say not even Chaucer's own "medieval" audience.
It is not, of course, the idea that readers can find Chaucer's opinions, or even that their opinions must be Chaucer's. Readers from
Chaucer's day to our own have always found self-affirming values in
him. There is, for Chaucer, no one reading of experience that makes
all experience understandable. As we saw in chapter 3, Chaucer
anticipates in his pluralism "an account of knowing" that does not
"leave *theoria* and *praxis* in a state of estrangement."[7] As Gadamer
explains: "The meaning of application that is involved in all forms of
understanding is . . . not the subsequent applying to a concrete
case of a given universal that we understand first by itself, but . . .
the actual understanding of the universal itself that the given text

constitutes for us. Understanding proves to be a kind of effect and knows itself as such."[8] Speirs' enthusiastic reading of Chaucer's "Human Comedy" (the phrase is Kittredge's too) which "moves within an apprehension of an all-inclusive divine harmony,"[9] reflects an understanding of Chaucer's text Chaucer encourages Speirs to bring to himself. Speirs' performing of the text for himself engages him in a self-affirming account of knowing because he values his ability to read closely and carefully. His sense of the structure and value of the *Canterbury Tales*—his comparison of Chaucer and Dante seems to me facile—tells us, I think, more about Chaucer *in Speirs* than about Chaucer *in himself*, though that is not my point.

Now we cannot really say how Chaucer would have performed the Wife of Bath's Prologue, or how another man or woman might have performed it in Chaucer's day. Were a storyteller present to read it to us, modern listeners might feel it was "dramatic"— that the act of performance by someone would make that part of the text the hearer valued—liked, if we insist on putting it less self-consciously—more accessible. Bronson, for example, has not sufficiently emphasized Chaucer's singularity as "master of ceremonies" of the text; only Chaucer is present before his audience "presenting events."[10] Bronson's phrase "presenting events" is misleading, since there are no events other than one man reading, or declaiming, the text, perhaps from an actual manuscript, perhaps not. Indeed, what calling any of the *Canterbury Tales* "dramatic" has really meant, Kittredge and Bronson notwithstanding, is that we like those parts we can understand. We like those parts that "come to life" from off the page—brought to life by our own values. As such, how we read Chaucer, or how Chaucer actually was read in his own day, is crucial to an understanding of the text if we first grasp how understanding is generated. What we need always to be attentive to, even if we pretend to be someone other than ourselves performing the text, is *how* we read and sort out Chaucer's narrative voices. In this way, we can still talk about the Wife of Bath's Prologue and Tale as "dramatic," meaning that we have found parts of it available to us. Knowing that makes our values and our selves available to us. In this way, too, we do not turn preferences either into theories about Chaucerian genres or historical arguments about Chaucer's maturing art, or both. We can like the Knight's Tale and the Wife of Bath's Prologue and Tale for many reasons and still hear a voice or "voices" in each. Both are tellings we "bring to life." One is not flat and early (or medieval), the other round (psychologically deep, a full dramatic monologue) and mature. Generic distinctions and historical perspectives are self-affirming values too.

We can illustrate the "drama" of hearing, and sorting out, narrative voices or idioms in Chaucer, and so begin to answer the question that is the title of this chapter—who speaks for the Wife of Bath?—by first looking at certain troublesome passages in the Merchant's Tale. First, Justinus's speech, which contains an oddly inappropriate reference to the Wife of Bath and her performance:

> The Wyf of Bathe, if ye han understonde,
> Of mariage, which we have on honde,
> Declared hath ful wel in litel space.
>
> (1685–87)

Justinus's reference to the Wife of Bath's Prologue and Tale, which he could not possibly have read, and to the Wife of Bath's actual presence, which is only true insofar as she is "present" among the Canterbury pilgrims, of whom Justinus is not one, is puzzling. Even if we assume that it is a parenthetical interjection by the Merchant himself, who had "heard" the Wife of Bath's performance and seen her among the Canterbury pilgrims, of whom he was one, the reference is inserted a little strangely before the last line of Justinus's speech. If we insist on disentangling the narrative voices mixed at this single juncture, virtually one line in the Merchant's Tale, in order to hear the Merchant's Tale as a coherently discontinuous performance, we encounter serious difficulties.

Arguing similarly, Robert Jordan suggests that the Merchant's long 126-line "praise-of-marriage" passage at the beginning of the Merchant's Tale, just before Justinus's speech, is not "one of the most amazing instances of sustained irony in all literature,"[11] because the point of view is not solely the Merchant's. Jordan argues on the basis of inconsistent characterization that the passage is an "independently worked-out satire on women," where the "bitter bourgeois husband" has been freely replaced by the "foolish academic debator."[12] Jordan here departs radically from traditional explications of the "praise-of-marriage" passage, even from Muscatine's recourse to the idea of the Gothic monologue in the Merchant's Tale,[13] though Jordan constructs his argument, curiously enough, on a rigorous, and for him genuinely medieval, version of the idea of Gothic juxtaposition.[14]

Although Jordan was among the first to recognize the difficulties in distinguishing narrative voices, and hence point of view, in the *Canterbury Tales*, what he apparently did not see was that to substitute the academic debater, who is not a Canterbury pilgrim, for the Merchant husband, who is, merely compounds the problem. If any "fictional" narrator ought to be the "teller" of the Merchant's Tale, it is the Merchant. If, for example, Chaucer performed the work, the actual narrator would be Chaucer the poet impersonating both the foolish debater, if that is indeed the voice we hear in the "praise-of-marriage" passage, *and* the bitter Merchant husband. In performance, the fiction of the *Canterbury Tales* as stories told by pilgrim travelers easily breaks down. Indeed, it is temporarily abandoned in the discussion of marital views that bears on the narrative when the Merchant's Tale resumes. But this "radical shift" would not have disengaged a medieval audience. Jordan confuses the pleasurable surprises of form with the engaging surprises of content. Medieval readers never required the kind of psychological coherence in art that would have pressed them to appeal to theories of the "inorganic" in quite the way Jordan does. "Inorganic" art, yes, but not *because* dramatic or psychological art breaks down. Gothic juxtaposition is not, for medieval readers, a make-do explanation. Although the strict sorting out of points of view in Chaucer is virtually impossible, that does not make Chaucer less capable of keeping ideas and attitudes straight. It is hard to imagine a bitter Merchant husband becoming the foolish academic debater, but it is important for readers, even if it may be confusing for merchants, or psychologists of merchants, to hear and consider ideas and attitudes about marriage in this opening passage of the Merchant's Tale.

Curiously, Jordan, I think, has missed the point of the "praise-of-marriage" passage *for us*, though he has described its difficulties of voice and attitude remarkably well. Readers need not identify, or try to identify, the voice, or voices, they hear in the passage—

try, that is, to put ideas and ideals about marriage into someone's
head. That kind of dramatizing is dodging the text. They ought
rather to take on, or to try to take on, the ideas themselves *as
ideas*. The fact that the Merchant, the "fictional" narrator of the
"praise-of-marriage" passage, cannot keep his argument *for* marriage from veering off does not make him a foolish thinker. No audience can confidently "Deffie Theofraste, and herke me" (1310).
The Merchant has, I think, a decidedly bookish (clerkly) understanding of marriage that is both true (ideal) and not true. Consider, for example, his argument for the wifely value of women:

> And herke why, I sey nat this for noght,
> That womman is for mannes helpe ywroght.
> The hye God, whan he hadde Adam maked,
> And saugh him al allone, bely-naked,
> God of his grete goodnesse seyde than,
> "Lat us now make an helpe unto this man
> Lyk to hymself"; and thanne he made him Eve.
> Heere may ye se, and heerby may ye preve,
> That wyf is mannes helpe and his confort,
> His paradys terrestre, and his disport.
> So buxom and so vertuous is she,
> They moste nedes lyve in unitee.
> O flessh they been, and o flessh, as I gesse,
> Hath but oon herte, in wele and in distresse.
>
> (1323–36)

This argument gives us both the idea of heavenly marriage (a marriage made on earth by heaven) and the idea of earthly (Edenic)
marriage after the Fall. It is both biblical and blind. No matter who
argues this case as a character in the Merchant's Tale (Jordan's concern), what *we* must do with the argument, such as it is when we
hear it, is take on the implications of the Merchant's attempted rebuttal of Theophrastus—a rebuttal always becoming his defense in
a curious, amusing, and open way. The Merchant's argument for
marriage articulates an ideal (the voice of *doctrina*, as I call it) and
its implicit betrayal.

The two questions posed near the beginning of the "praise-of-
marriage" passage are, for example, without a discernible governing voice—a voice with consistent opinions—and are thus open to

some variety in interpretation, both performative and intellectual. One depends on the other:

> For who kan be so buxom as a wyf?
> Who is so trewe, and eek so ententyf
> To kepe hym, syk and hool, as is his make?
>
> (1287–89)

Because Chaucer's text does not make clear *as drama* the way these questions might be asked, the answers are not roundly self-evident, despite the idea, stated just before these questions, that bachelors live "under noon arreest" (1282) because they are not yet "under this yok of mariage ybounde" (1285). It is possible, for example, to understand from lines 1287–89, usually perceived as mocking in tone, that marital harmony is beautiful rather than ironic. Similarly, the little scene between "he" and "she" later in the "praise-of-marriage" passage may suggest that womanly deference to her husband means ideal marital order and happiness. Indeed, we can read the last line without irony, or at least without the kind of obvious mockery almost everyone since Kittredge seems to hear in it:

> Al that hire housbonde lust, hire liketh weel;
> She seith nat ones "nay," whan he seith "ye."
> "Do this," seith he; "Al redy, sire," seith she.
> O blisful ordre of wedlok precious.
>
> (1344–47)

It is, of course, possible to perform these lines so that the easy mutuality of marriage comes to sound like self-serving duplicity. One need not depend upon knowledge of the story of the marriage of January and May, a blissful marriage of mutual self-interest, to make these lines sound hollow. There might in fact be fully conscious equivocation on a performer's part and quite justified puzzlement on the part of members of his audience about exactly what the lines might mean. They are not, in other words, shaped throughout by one fixed and discernible narrative point of view, and our search for someone to whom we can assign them is part of their meaning, since language gives, and must be given, a context of mind and place. The verse paragraph in F. N. Robinson's edition (1311–18) ends, for example, with the teasing suggestion that

> A wyf wol laste, and in thyn hous endure,
> Wel lenger than thee list, paraventure.
>
> (1317–18)

Is line 1318 meant to sound like a bitter aside or an amused after-thought? If we are looking for hidden communications from the Merchant, say, the line may sound angry. It may, however, sound like a version of the slight usually flung at a mother-in-law: she stays too long. The line is potentially comic. What we hear depends on how it is performed, on how indeed *we* perform it—the line depends on what we already may have in mind, or what we can bring to mind and give voice to.

The idea of marital harmony in the "praise-of-marriage" passage does seem to run aground three lines after the little scene between "he" and "she," when we hear

> That every man that halt hym worth a leek,
> Upon his bare knees oughte al his lyf
> Thanken his God that hym hath sent a wyf,
> Or elles preye to God hym for to sende
> A wyf, to laste unto his lyves ende.
>
> (1350–54)

To get down on one's knees in this context may be excessive and comic. Similarly, the question "For who kan be so buxom as a wyf?" (1287) seems to be turned on its head three lines after it is posed, when a wife's submissiveness seems to harbor dangerous re-sentment and subversion:

> For wele or wo she wole hym nat forsake;
> Shy nys nat wery hym to love and serve,
> Thogh that he lye bedrede, til he sterve.
>
> (1290–93)

The phrase "til he sterve" perhaps ironically suggests that the hus-band may die because of his wife's love and service, or lack of it, though the phrase implies, when performed without Robinson's comma—his directing voice as editor—that the husband is to be loved and served until he dies. Here, as everywhere in the "praise-of-marriage" passage—we have looked at only three examples—ideas are being played with in ways a performer manages handily and an editor necessarily limits. The nuances we hear in the passage cannot be systematically parceled out to individually over-lapping voices—that is what the fiction of the Canterbury "drama," when taken literally, or figuratively (as architecture, a medieval drama of ideas), would compel us to do—because these nuances, which the whole of the Merchant's Tale bears out, occur simultane-ously, or as nearly simultaneously as words and sentences allow.

There is one fact about the difficulty of adequately sorting out "narrators" and narrative points of view we ought to note now: the *Canterbury Tales* is no less clear because there are overlapping points of view. The "I" of the poem, as we have just seen, does not provide readers with a fixed opinion so much as with immediacy of effect. Though Justinus's awkward reference to the Wife of Bath is difficult to attribute to a dramatized viewpoint, it is not hard to understand. The allusion to the Wife of Bath and the Wife of Bath's Prologue and Tale would be clear to anyone who had heard the Wife's words. The allusion does not imply that the prologue and tale were actually declaimed, during the course of an evening, say, before the Merchant's Prologue and Tale; the order of tales within manuscript fragments is no argument for the order of their per-formance. But the allusion to the Wife of Bath does presume that a medieval audience would have been familiar enough with Chaucer's work to permit him to make a disruptive reference not only to the Wife of Bath's Prologue and Tale, but to the Wife of Bath, a fic-tional character he may once have impersonated, who must have been something of a literary legend even in Chaucer's own day.

What we have, of course, in the order of the "Canterbury" tales within manuscript fragments is a "public sequence" for the copies of the work that circulated without Chaucer. But even this order is not final. In the Prologue to the Miller's Tale, we are invited to skip over tales that may offend us morally, to read the tales in an order that accords with our ennobling biases. And Chaucerians have done just that. The "marriage group," for example, is sometimes expanded to include either the Melibee, or the Squire's Tale, or the Second Nun's Tale, or even the Shipman's Tale, or any com-bination of these tales, none of which are in the fragment that be-gins with the Wife of Bath's Prologue and Tale (the first of the three fragments that are supposed to constitute the "marriage group"). Sometimes, however, the "marriage group" is shrunk by passing over the "digressive" Friar's Tale and Summoner's Tale, which are

in fact embedded in fragment 4.[15] And the reasons adduced for
each new grouping, around marriage themes or threads, are never
unsatisfactory; the *Canterbury Tales* always seems richer for it. If
the invitation in the Prologue to the Miller's Tale is not serious, it
has, with good results, been so taken. Insisting on a definitive order
to the *Canterbury Tales* thus seems less important to Chaucer than
prompting his readers to choose how they want to hear the tales.
Chaucer does not require that we understand them in the way they
have been assembled. Even if the order in the Ellesmere manuscript of the *Canterbury Tales* is his,[16] he never uses the fictional
order of their presentation as a vehicle for guiding readers through
them.[17] One can offer reasons for the order of tales within individual manuscript fragments, and even between fragments, but that
order, if followed, does not yield the definitive experience of the
work. It merely constitutes someone's experience, or someone's
suggestion for an experience, whether Chaucer's suggestion, or
someone else's.[18]

Robinson's textual note to line 1686 of the Merchant's Tale explains that W. W. Skeat puts lines 1684–87 in parentheses, taking
them out of Justinus's speech; the majority of the MSS, however,
punctuate the lines so that they are included in the speech. Perhaps Skeat was attempting to edit the Merchant's Tale strictly in
accord with dramatic propriety. J. S. P. Tatlock, defending the
reading of the majority of MSS, suggests that Chaucer adopted the
bold device of making Justinus himself quote the Wife of Bath. Perhaps a simpler explanation for the punctuation as it now stands in
the Robinson edition is that the rather involved distinction between "fictional" characters on the road to Canterbury and the "fictional" characters in the tales of "fictional" pilgrims did not always
matter to manuscript scribes, as it did not to Chaucer or his audience. The reference to the Wife of Bath can be explained on the
grounds that "Chaucer [at the time he was writing the Merchant's
Tale] was still thinking of his own [public] relationship" to his audience—the line is his—and manuscript scribes, still creatures of
live performance, but also private readers too, felt that Chaucer's
reference to the Wife of Bath had to be made, for the sake of *immediate* dramatic coherence, a part of Justinus's speech; they "heard"
it that way.[19] Indeed, the reference to the Wife of Bath in the
Lenvoy de Chaucer a Bukton suggests that the Wife stood for defin-

able attitudes about marriage and would be heard, as in Justinus's speech, at the end of one side of a lengthy debate on marriage in such a way as to cap an argument.[20]

Again, narrative discontinuity only presents an obstacle to sense if a storyteller's voice is not taken to be the only constant in the organization of Chaucerian narrative. That continuous voice always divides the text into its coherently discontinuous parts. The narrator's "intrusions" set the pace for reading and mark off the boundaries between narrative voices in a text *where story and storyteller have literally one voice.* In the *House of Fame,* a narrative that does not present an audience with the problem of fictional narrators, for example, the storyteller clearly marks the exact limits of quoted matter, as in the following passage:

> "Herestow not the grete swogh?"
> "Yis, parde!" quod y, "wel ynogh."
> "And what soun is it lyk," quod hee.
> "Peter! lyk betynge of the see,"
> Quod y, "ayen the roches holowe,
> Whan tempest doth the shippes swalowe."
>
> (2.1031–36)

One voice here *meant* to be different from the storyteller's is, naturally, the Eagle's, and a lucidity of reference ("quod y"; "quod hee") keeps the two unmistakably separate in this example of rapid dialogue. The signaling devices "I said" and "he said" are especially important in declaimed narrative because they keep straight not only who says what but how fast we imagine certain words said. Signaling devices in Chaucer do not slow the narrative. They quicken it, helping an audience identify different voices in succession. In a novel we usually want the storyteller to disappear; in Chaucer he does not, although the more leisurely Chaucer's dialogue is, the less the storyteller seems to switch voices (the less he seems to interrupt a voice he is impersonating in order to impersonate someone else) and the more easily he drifts off into his voice *as storyteller* or into other voices that do not necessarily, as in the "praise-of-marriage" passage in the Merchant's Tale, correspond to actual characters "in the scene."

Although signaling devices never completely disappear in Chaucer, they do become less frequent, and their relative infrequency

in some of the later tales of the *Canterbury Tales* sharpens our
sense that dramatic and psychological appropriateness of speaker
and speech has disappeared. If we can be confused by that disappearance, as the "praise-of-marriage" passage confuses critics who
want to know who in the story says what, we can also be charmed
by the many voices always present in the text. As we have seen,
Chaucerian narrative is not so much additive as simultaneous. It
does consist of "relatively autonomous parts" that are "loosely integrated," although these parts seem to happen at the same time.
Unfortunately, most Chaucerian formalists have not yet given up
the idea that Chaucer is "drama," though they would call Chaucer's
art "non-dramatically" conceived, or inorganic. They usually suggest that Chaucerian narrative is built on the interchange between
characters, but that the text does not always help us identify the
speaking parts; thus we are, as it were, forced to talk about the independently conceived voice of a character replacing *in the text*
the voice of a character actually named, whose voice, like the Merchant's, somehow sounds, or comes to sound after a time, untrue to
itself. In this way, Chaucerian narrative is seen by formalist critics
as incomplete drama *we* can play out by assigning parts to characters and being attentive to ironies of juxtaposition.[21]

In defining Chaucer's "Gothic juxtaposition," Muscatine suggests that Chaucerian narrative is nonlinear. He is right, but not
because Chaucerian narrative is a kind of juxtaposed patchwork—
Muscatine really has not given up the idea of narration through
time. Rather, in a way special to declaimed narrative, Chaucer's
stories seem both to anticipate the direction in which they may be
moving and to catch up with themselves by rehearsing where they
have been. It is really the storyteller's voice in *Troilus and Criseyde*,
for example, creating the illusion of a narrator both telling a story
and listening to it himself—commenting on it and discussing it
with his readers, as if they both were glossing a text—that gives us
the sense of anticipation and retrospection I would call nonlinear.
We can, for example, see the beginnings of the Chaucerian habit of
"drifting off" from a presumably direct narrative line in the *House
of Fame;* there Chaucer seems to abandon his story less freely
than he does in his later works. The formalist phrase "abandon his
story" seems to serve here, although what we are describing is not
formalist segmentation. A developing fluidity of voice in Chaucer
may account for the disappearance of signaling devices ("quod y";

"quod hee") in the text. Such devices are formalized demarcations of voice that an always amusing self-consciousness, implicit in Chaucerian performance, does not require. Perhaps Chaucer saw that. In any case, although signaling devices disappear, a story-teller's voice, marking off the story from his exposition of it, rather than his impersonations, or his commentary on it, never does. Such shifting, which makes it difficult in Chaucer to assign one line to one persona for very long, most likely accompanied Chaucer's increasing confidence in himself as a storyteller, whose charming, dilatory manner, for which he is forever apologizing, his readers must have loved. In the Man of Law's Tale, Chaucer as master of ceremonies making a literary stage appearance is perhaps at his most whimsically slow:

> I wol no lenger tarien in this cas,
> But to kyng Alla, which I spak of yoore,
> That for his wyf wepeth and siketh soore,
> I wool retourne, and lete I wol Custance
> Under the senatoures governance.
>
> (983–87)

Of course, despite what he says here, Chaucer does not rush. His amusingly formal presence occupies five lines of a seven-line stanza. With respect to the impersonations of a performer, Chaucerian narrative is always serialized, though in Chaucer's late work, these voices, like the measured storyteller's voice in the Man of Law's Tale, have no "real place" in the story.

The credibility of the learned Eagle in the *House of Fame*, for example, particularly in his longer speeches, which often echo Boethius or Dante, is never insisted upon, and there is no difficulty in the Eagle's shifting from "egle," a character in the *House of Fame*, to learned Eagle, a Boethian or Dantesque voice, as in the following passage:

> Geffrey, thou wost ryght wel this,
> That every kyndely thyng that is
> Hath a kyndely stede ther he
> May best in hyt conserved be;
> Unto which place every thyng,
> Thorgh his kyndely enclynyng,
> Moveth for to come to,
> What that hyt is away therfro.
>
> (2.729–36)

In the direct reference to "Geffrey" in the first line, we can hear the "voice" of the Eagle, a second voice in the poem (distinct from Chaucer's own) and the one that is, according to the fiction of the poem, talking *to* Chaucer. By the eighth line, however—the above passage continues for another twenty-seven lines—the Eagle comes to sound, with no shock of transition, like a schoolmaster giving Chaucer a soberly condescending lecture on celestial mechanics. Imaginatively we have for the moment moved to the lecturn. Although we can accommodate the idea of an eagle on a mental flight lecturing Chaucer, we would never ask how an eagle comes to know Boethius or Dante. Yet critics persist in asking whether the vitriolic Merchant can "in character" debate so jocularly the question of taking a wife, or how the Wife of Bath can put her special case for sovereignty in marriage in such a clerkly fashion. The answer is that, like the Eagle, they cannot and do not. What has happened in all these "dislocations of character" is that another voice has momentarily emerged, for which there is no "quod he" in the text, since this "he" is an impersonation without a name. Chauntecleer's "psychology"—and indeed the psychology of other animal heroes and heroines in Chaucer, including the "egle"—has not puzzled commentators, for example, and no wonder. Animals—perhaps primates are the exception—only have an inner life to the extent that people do. What Chauntecleer thinks (understands, or does not understand) about his dreams and experience tells us nothing about him as a rooster, but much about ourselves as people. Precisely because Chaucer does *not* alter his mode of characterization—Chauntecleer behaves no less blindly to the truth of his bookish *exempla* of men who have heeded their dreams than the Merchant does—we should, I think, treat all fictional characters in Chaucer similarly; that is, see their humanity as a reflection of our capacity to psychologize—to know something about ourselves and other people.

The passage we were looking at from the *House of Fame* (2.729–36) is part of a longer passage that ends (764) with a reminder that what the audience hears is being taught *to* Chaucer. One line ("Now herke what y wol the lere" [764]) in effect returns us to the scene "in flight" between the Eagle and Chaucer. With a performer's switching of scene through voice, we are brought back "to the story." The passage (2.729–63) beginning with the direct ad-

dress to "Geffrey" has a preamble similar to the line with which
it ends:

> Now herkene wel, for-why I wille
> Tellen the a propre skille
> And a worthy demonstracion
> In myn ymagynacion.
>
> (725–28)

The direct address to "Geffrey" in line 729 comes, I suspect, as a
charming surprise because it places the real Geoffrey in the position of a listener: a storyteller talking to himself. Only the passage
(729–63), marked off as it is by the preamble (725–28) and the
single line (764), contains the Boethian or Dantesque voice, which
is heard, then disappears, then is heard again, in each narrative in-
stallment. Imaginatively we move from a flight in space to a lecture
room and back again several times. But it is always the storyteller's
voice that marks off these segments as he moves from the classroom
voice of *doctrina* to that of the Eagle's on a fanciful flight in space,
the literal level of the poem. The pronoun "the" in line 764 is, for
example, ambiguous, although not unclear, because it is only the
fiction of the Eagle as teacher that makes it seem as if "Geffrey" is
being spoken to.

What is amusing about a "learned" eagle, then, is the idea of its
taking Chaucer on an intellectual flight, not the actual "voice" of
a learned eagle, whatever that would sound like, nor the miming
by the performer of an eagle turned schoolmaster, whatever that
would look like. Though he thinks of his arguments as having
beaks (2.865–69), the Eagle is always schoolmasterly, even self-
congratulatory. The only line in the entire *House of Fame* that
might remotely sound like a bird talking is the Eagle's first "Awak!"
in line 556 of book 2. For the rest, it is the Boethian and Dantesque
voice of the Eagle, broken by the storyteller's charming school-
teacher refrain, spoken to himself ("Now hennesforth y wol the
teche," for example, which begins another independent narrative
segment at line 782), that indicates to readers that an amusingly
textbookish lesson is going on in a series of installments that are
supposed to be grasped one at a time. Indeed, the lesson is amusing precisely because the mode of discourse is decidedly textbookish. Divisions of the text make it easy to follow something pe-

culiarly unsocial, a school lesson, publicly, and to think of such a
performance as play.

As in the *House of Fame*, the storyteller in *Troilus and Criseyde*
handles transitions with obvious care. Consider the following passage from book 1, which gives us Chaucer's *own vocabulary* for the
serialized nature of his narratives:

> But for to tellen forth in special
> As of this kynges sone of which I tolde,
> And leten other thing collateral,
> Of hym thenke I my tale forth to holde,
> Bothe of his joie and of his cares colde;
> And al his werk, as touching this matere,
> For I it gan, I wol therto refere.
>
> (1.260–66)

The "other thing collateral," literally side by side, not digressive or
incidental, to which the narrator refers, is the long passage on the
binding power of Love begun seven stanzas back with the apostrophe "O blynde world, O blynde entencioun!" (211). If Chaucer
meant to imply here any spatial model for the movement of the
Troilus—the word "structure" seems misleading, since the *Troilus*
is a performance—it would be a model that describes the movement of things parallel to, not one that implies digression or veering off from, a central line or point. We are certainly familiar from
modern art with the idea of the flattened picture plane whose objects are intended to be perceived as "side by side." Indeed, that
idea is said to describe Gothic art too.[22] But Chaucer's notion of a
serialized narrative is, as we see here, linked to the idea of a hierarchy of values, neither a Robertsonian hierarchy nor a romantic one
(Robertson's anti-model),[23] but a hierarchy of special cases and generic categories that is neither static nor in the throes of synthesis.
Using the technical phrase "to tellen forth in special" (260) at the
juncture in the *Troilus* we are considering here, Chaucer says that,
having delineated the "other thing collateral," what he will now
narrate will be Troilus's love for Criseyde as a "species" (a special
case) of the generic category "proud men in love."[24] The story of
Troilus, a specific case, though a more elaborately narrated one
than that of "proude Bayard" (218), has temporarily given way to
generalized commentary on proud lovers, though Troilus's story

will be taken up again. Specific cases have to be seen in light of their generalizing categories. Thus the story of Troilus is pushed aside by an equally important and completely independent "collateral" passage of commentary on it, part of which I cite here:

> Forthy ensample taketh of this man,
> Ye wise, proude, and worthi folkes alle,
> To scornen Love, which that so soone kan
> The fredom of youre hertes to hym thralle.
> For evere it was, and evere it shal byfalle,
> That Love is he that alle thing may bynde,
> For may no man fordon the lawe of kynde.
>
> (1.232–38)

There is no "quod I" needed in this passage, for the storyteller is obviously speaking as commenting storyteller. The "wise, proude, and worthi folkes alle" are the audience for whom Troilus has been made an example of love's power. The word "ensample" here suggests, of course, Chaucer's exemplifying mode, which is as much hierarchical in my sense as serialized. Perhaps it has seemed to some static and, therefore, architectural because what is "flat" and serialized about it has not been recognized. Any performer doing the above passage (shifting into the voice of the storyteller) has not so much *displaced* the very story he is declaiming with comments on it as *shifted*, for the moment, that which occupies everyone's attention, including his own. The movement here is not a kind of formalist foregrounding that tells us, or is supposed to tell us, where the significant parts of a text are (for formalists, making a text spatial and judging it go hand in hand, since "space" shades and highlights). Rather the movement here is a shifting between imagined and imaginary mode—the mode of *imaginatio*, mental pictures—and a discursive one, which we call commentary.[25]

For us image and commentary are not, as Chaucer says, "collateral." We prefer the silence of images to the talkiness of commentary, though images for us are still meant to be full of significance—to be, in fact, "talky." What we like are images that "speak for themselves," if that is possible. But Chaucer never sets images before us and leaves. In the *Troilus* the commentary is collateral *with* the story; performance does not encourage us to think that the story exists in the foreground. In the *Troilus* the commentary is set

beside the story (we cannot help sounding spatial), but neither part
in the shifting from generality to specific instances—imagined
cases—is meant to be favored, or rather neither part is slighted. In
the *Troilus* the storyteller puts his story in a context of his own
making and points the direction that thinking about his story ought
to take. Thus when the storyteller in the *Troilus* suggests that his
audience take "ensample" of Troilus, some members may find the
narrative engaging them; for if they are indeed "wise, proude, and
worthi," if they do *not* constitute a special case of the "proud in
love," they ought to know that love cannot be scorned.

In this light, one passage from book 1 of the *Troilus* deserves
comment:

> And wostow why I am the lasse afered
> Of this matere with my nece trete?
> For this have I herd seyd of wyse lered,
> Was nevere man or womman yet bigete
> That was unapt to suffren loves hete,
> Celestial, or elles love of kynde;
> Forthy som grace I hope in hire to fynde.
>
> And for to speke of hire in specyal,
> Hire beaute to bithynken and hire youthe,
> It sit hire naught to ben celestial
> As yet, though that hire liste bothe and kowthe;
> But trewely, it sate hire wel right nowthe
> A worthi knight to loven and cherice,
> And but she do, I holde it for a vice.
>
> (1.974–87)

Even as he is making his special case for Criseyde, Pandarus here
does not specify *when* love is for her, or for Troilus, love "celestial,
or elles love of kynde." The ambiguity intentionally keeps the text
interpretively free and demonstrates that the kind of hierarchy of
generic category and specific cases I have described, which uses
Chaucer's own vocabulary, explains how his text remains open.
The value for us of generalized commentary and specific instances
is that they keep the text accessible, for what we think Pandarus
means by "grace" tells us what we think love is, and when it is what
it is. Though Pandarus makes the distinctions that open the text for
us, the issue here is not how one delimits him from the storyteller
of the *Troilus*, or both from Chaucer the poet as Chaucer's imper-

sonated voices—E. Talbot Donaldson saw that—but in taking on the mixture of narrative and exposition that we hear as authorial deflections to larger contexts and traditions.[26] Unlike Chaucer's "man noght textueel," Pandarus here does not bungle his explanatory gloss, but his commentary invites what Glending Olson calls *confabulatio*, or conversation with the text,[27] as fully as Chaucer's storyteller's awkward glossings do.

As in the *Troilus*, the storyteller in the Knight's Tale also engages his audience's thoughtfulness at crucial junctures:

> Yow loveres axe I now this questioun:
> Who hath the worse, Arcite or Palamoun?
> That oon may seen his lady day by day,
> But in prison he moot dwelle alway;
> That oother wher hym list may ride or go,
> But seen his lady shal he nevere mo.
> Now demeth as yow liste, ye that kan,
> For I wol telle forth as I bigan.
>
> (1347–54)

As we might expect, there is a break in the story here, but not in the performance. What is "collateral" is the response Chaucer's readers (and listeners) make, at varying levels of interest and capacity, to Chaucer's question "Who hath the worse, Arcite or Palamoun?" That question gently forces the specific cases of the narrative onto the reader. Here in the Knight's Tale, the audience provides what I would call the collateral speculatives trips. Indeed, in the last lines of the above passage, the listeners are, as it were, sent home to think ("Now demeth as you liste, ye that kan / For I wol telle forth as I bigan"), though the storyteller, and the story through him, continue.

Now actual members of Chaucer's audience were probably able to tell when Chaucer was pretending to be other than they knew him to be. But the idea of Chaucer playing Chaucer the pilgrim, a storyteller, "rehearsing" the words, say, of the Wife of Bath, which gives to the *Canterbury Tales* its pleasing puzzle-box form, would have been as much an *idea* for a medieval audience as it is for us, and not one, I suspect, that Chaucer would have had to maintain consistently throughout any one performance. At a public reading, Chaucer was either himself or someone else, but only at moments, when he, like his audience, was taking pleasure in the idea of

framed stories, would he pretend to be someone pretending to be
someone else. Of all of Chaucer's work, the *Canterbury Tales* has a
uniquely kinetic form that pleases because it seems to go away and
come back. Then, too, the self-conscious comedy inherent in one
man taking all parts made it unnecessary for Chaucer's audience to
be fooled into preserving the distinction between Chaucer the poet,
Chaucer the pilgrim, and Chaucer "the Wife of Bath."

It is unfortunate that we have no "Canterbury illumination" like the
Troilus frontispiece. We have the Ellesmere portrait of Chaucer
himself, awkwardly astride his horse, pointing to the text of the
Melibee, his "moral tale vertuous" (940); both for readers—Chaucer
is, after all, the author of all the "Canterbury" tales—and for other
pilgrims, Chaucer is one storyteller among many in his own work.[28]
The Ellesmere portrait thus embodies the *idea* of the *Canterbury
Tales* as intellectual play for people, real or fictional, and literally
shows the pictoral emergence in the margin of the idea of voice in
the text; it is an icon of performance. Chaucer might just as well
have pointed to the Wife of Bath's Prologue and Tale as to his "own"
Melibee. This sense of Chaucer "speaking for the Wife of Bath" is
not new. Indeed, it is the theoretical thread for the idea of the *Canterbury Tales* as declamation, enabling us to shift our attention
from delimiting character in Chaucer—who is actually speaking (a
narrow, and narrowing, issue)—to responding to what he or she
says. Moreover, the idea of Chaucer speaking for the Wife of Bath
calls attention to an aspect of voicing that has not, as far as I know,
yet been identified, perhaps because not all "Canterbury" tales
seem to depend on it. But the Wife of Bath's Prologue and Tale certainly does, because the Wife is a woman. As such, sexuality of performance clarifies the Wife's "feminine" tone of voice in ways that
make audible our own voices, male and female, whichever Chaucerian tale we read.

Sexuality of performance makes Chaucer's speaking for the Wife
of Bath a new idea, one that will occupy our attention for the re-
mainder of this chapter. That idea, as we shall see, makes the Wife
of Bath's text accessible to our own speculative trips. It makes the
Wife of Bath's Prologue and Tale include us in Chaucer's circle of
understanding. In this sense, *we* speak for the Wife of Bath *as* we

speak for ourselves. Our own sexual identities, and our imagining of the social and mental predispositions of the opposite sex, make the Wife of Bath's Prologue and Tale a text that mirrors the sexual and intellectual complexities of our nature, no matter what biological gender we are, *because* it permits us to make our moral and social values sexual and self-aware, if they are not already so. I am suggesting, in other words, that the ironies of the Wife's text change surprisingly whether we image a man or a woman performing the Wife of Bath's Prologue and Tale; whether we imagine, say, Chaucer, or any man, declaiming the part, or whether we imagine a woman, one of Criseyde's "folk" (79), say, in book 2 of the *Troilus*—a "mayden" (83)—doing so.

It is, of course, into Criseyde's chambered performance that Pandarus bounds, the *man* to whom Criseyde gives her *woman's* answer when Pandarus asks coyly about the book she is reading *and teasingly assumes he has guessed right:*

> "Is it of love? O, som good ye me leere!"
> "Uncle," quod she, "youre maistresse is nat here."
> (2.97–98)

Pandarus's remarks—his question and his amused request—sound sexually avuncular. They playfully assume that Criseyde is sexually innocent. Pandarus's remarks may sound ulterior if we recall that, in book 1, he has made the lovesick Troilus his charge and is now, in book 2, going to see Criseyde. But for himself *as his own man* his teasing sounds like the nervous appropriations of power men often give in order to introduce themselves to, and into, a circle of women from which they are, for the moment, excluded. Indeed, Criseyde's response to Pandarus may suggest that she has heard his remarks as a kind of wagging finger; she may hear them as mildly condescending, since they assume she needs practice in the art of love. Her reference to Pandarus's mistress knowingly and teasingly (both laugh immediately after Criseyde answers Pandarus [99]) acknowledges his manly appetite and binds together her and her "othere ladys" (81) *as feminine objects* against whom the complaints of men—that women need book learning in the art of love—may indeed seem amusing. For women, I think, such avuncular patronizing from any man has none of the boyish neediness—the

sting of frustration—any man might give these words of encouragement to learn. Criseyde must feel she does not need lessons in the
art of love and that neither does Pandarus's mistress. After all,
Criseyde playfully assumes that Pandarus is coming to visit her (his
mistress) for more love.

Now the book Criseyde and the "othere ladys" are listening to is
not, of course, a story of love, but "the geste / Of the siege of
Thebes" (83–84), a shorter version of this twelve-volume monu-
ment of cultural history, which Pandarus, had he known, might
have found disappointing. For the moment only we know. In this
way, Criseyde's answer to Pandarus's playing picks up *his* sense of
being left out of a circle of women whom he would like to think are
reading a romance, and who therefore—the logic is his—have
a theoretical place for him *as a man*. Pandarus's greeting to his
niece is joyfully sexist. It is situational and appropriative. He notes
what she is doing, calling the book he assumes she and the others
are reading "fayre" (86). Criseyde answers in kind. She says she
dreamed about Pandarus the night before (89–90), a deflectingly
erotic comment from a niece to her uncle. In this way, Criseyde
appropriates *him*, making her uncle *as a man* part of her private
life. We should recall here that the Wife of Bath says her mother
taught her to say she has dreamed about a man as a way of making
herself intriguing to *him* (577–84). Pandarus, of course, excuses
himself for having interrupted Criseyde from a book "ye preysen
thus" (2.95), which, of course, she has not. When he finally encourages her to

> Do wey youre book, rys up, and lat us daunce,
> And lat us don to May some observaunce,
>
> (111–12)

Criseyde replies:

> It sat me wel bet ay in a cave
> To bidde and rede on holy seyntes lyves;
> Lat maydens gon to daunce, and yonge wyves.
>
> (117–19)

Criseyde has a fondness for serious literature that protects her sociability and sexuality precisely because it gives her control over
what stimulates them. Her threat to read "in a cave" is, I think,

both socially and sexually coy. Criseyde is not the passionate exegete that the Wife of Bath is, though she knows how books and
ideas give the self, for as long as one chooses, a textual ground on
which to stand.

Now as a fiction, the scene in Criseyde's "paved parlour" offers
us the social context in which the intimate reading of books by
women occurred in Chaucer's day. Most probably women in the
late Middle Ages only read to other women.[29] We usually assume
that if Chaucer declaimed the *Canterbury Tales*, the Wife of Bath's
Prologue and Tale among them, he read to a mixed audience. But
at least one Chaucerian describes Chaucer's circle as perhaps all
male, and although he acknowledges that "the female presence at
court was becoming more marked throughout the late Middle
Ages,"[30] he does speculate, as I would want to do, about how a
masculine audience would hear and answer Chaucer's *questions
d'amour* in, for example, the Knight's Tale ("Yow loveres axe I
now this questioun: / Who hath the worse, Arcite or Palamoun?"
[1347–48]). We do not have to choose to imagine a man or a
woman declaiming the Wife of Bath's Prologue and Tale to a special audience. We can imagine both, for the issue here rests on
the distinction between imagining and hearing: what we imagine in
narrative declaimed, particularly in narrative we perform ourselves
as men or women, is indeed what we consciously and unconsciously hear. The Wife of Bath's Prologue and Tale yields ironies
sometimes at the expense of woman (the Wife's voice impersonated
by a man may reveal his own misogyny) and sometimes in the defense of women (impersonated by a woman, the Wife's voice reveals a comic masterfulness she, as performer, may ascribe to
Chaucer).

It is, of course, impossible to say how consistently any man, or
any woman, might want to impersonate the Wife of Bath, or imagine her as a fictional character. During performance, for example,
there may be virtually sustained eye contact between performer
and audience. Rather than breaking the dramatic illusion in which
the actor, as in a recitation or a play, is a participant, making eye
contact in performance, where there is only a simulation of drama
(an imaginary drama "in one's head"), implies, as we know, a kind
of understood complicity between the monologuist and the audience, as if he or she and the audience were together creating the

illusion of real-life scenes involving real-life people. Eye contact
with others is, in fact, what divides a performer from himself; looking directly at members of the audience—at one person, then at
another—would tell everyone that the monologuist knows that his
story is not telling itself. For a good monologuist there needs to be
virtually continuous (moving or roving) eye contact. He or she does
not want to single out anyone by staring. A performer always exerts
a mildly hypnotic effect on his audience, whose temporary suspen-
sion of disbelief is as much willed as compelled. Even Geoffrey of
Vinsauf, in the section on delivery in his *Documentum de modo
dictandi et versificandi*, advises that the performer should vary
voice, facial expression, and gesture to fit the material, but that he
or she should be elegant and restrained, not like an actor. His point
is that impersonation of the *confabulator* is to be acknowledged
as self-conscious, not as self-referring like the performance of the
histrio.[31] We are thus not during declamation asked to imagine an
actor's persona.

   The difference is crucial, for what follows any collapse of the
imaginary world of the storyteller is probably best described as a
mild and harmless, but fully conscious, short-circuiting. The collapse of a performance is never really a surprise. We recognize
"collapse" in a comedian's pause for a laugh, which means he expects us to understand not only the incongruity in a comic circumstance he may have just described, but also the idea that the imagining, his and ours, has temporarily ceased. Indeed, the collapse of
fiction, when it occurs, gives a kind of pleasure that comes from a
recognition of the self-consciousness of form. As private readers we
experience collapse when, for example, we read authorial intrusions like "he said," which seem materially different from a text we
read alone and to ourselves. Although we are accustomed to a narrative voice telling us a story when we sit down to read a good
book, we cannot help but be surprised by an intrusion that takes us
back to the *idea* that we are reading. The moment we hear "he
said," we remember that there is an imaginary narrator telling the
story, which, if it so engrossed us, would have taken us "out of ourselves" and our awareness not only of a story being told but also of
the circumstances of our encountering it—in a chair, say, near a
light, imagining a storyteller. Moreover, as private readers we ex-

perience collapse when we intuit intention, when we imagine, in short, a storyteller's roving eye landing on us with a glitter that confirms our assumptions about meaning.

What "wo" (3), for example, does the Wife of Bath suffer in marriage? That depends, I think, on who impersonates her. If a man does, then the Wife's unabashedly heretical exaltation of "experience" as "right ynogh for me / To speke of wo that is in mariage" (1–3) is both dangerous and irresistible.[32] She dismisses male authority with a summary fiat that asks that her "wo"—she means her life—be judged solely *as her experience.* The Wife's forthrightness constitutes an immediate and unstoppable sharing of the secrets of women that engages a male audience and, I suspect, amuses a female one. The Wife is surely less dangerous for women than for men. If we imagine her as the impersonation of a man, then her "take" on tradition, her appropriating glosses of biblical texts, her aligning her life, for example, with Solomon's, become a splendidly imagined masculine wish for a woman of boundless appetite. She says, for example, that she wishes during her life to be "refresshed half so ofte as he" (38), calling his sexual pleasure with "wyves mo than oon" (36)—what understatement!—the "yifte of God" (39). If the Wife's "wo" in marriage is insatiability, her impersonated voice, if a man performs the text, is pure masculine projection: an insatiable woman is the insatiable "fantasye" of a man:

> God woot, this noble king, as to my wit,
> The firste nyght had many a myrie fit
> With ech of hem, so wel was hym on lyve.
> Yblessed be God that I have wedded fyve!
> Welcome the sixte, whan that evere he shal.
>
> (41–45)

Even the Wife's mastery of her first three husbands—merely masterly tricks—constitutes, if we imagine a man impersonating her, masculine play that both implicitly gives men imagined power over woman and takes it away. For a man, the Wife is both potent and frightening:

> The thre were goode men, and riche, and olde;
> Unnethe myghte they the statut holde
> In which that they were bounden unto me.

> Yet woot wel what I meene of this, pardee!
> As help me God, I laughe whan I thynke
> How pitously a-nyght I made hem swynke!
> (197–202)

The idea of old men laboring to perform their sexual obligations—
something they want, but cannot manage—makes the Wife's statement of desire, as the impersonated voice of a man, longingly
tyrannical:

> A wys womman wol bisye hire evere in oon
> To gete hire love, ye, ther as she hath noon.
> (209–10)

It is, indeed, the Wife's insatiability that awakens masculine appetite, over which *she* has negotiating power. If we imagine a man
impersonating the Wife, the description of her sexual orchestrations catches up decidedly mixed and sexist notions of feminine
boundlessness. Her materialism may be a parody of men's own will
to dominate in the real world, which would amuse both men and
women, but her bawdiness, a self-feeding and self-sustaining fe-
cundity—she has no children—awakens what men most desire
and fear. Their potency is challenged by insatiable desire, their
wish for performance by an inexhaustible play.

For this reason, the Wife can awaken in us, men and women,
passing moments of remembrance. These make her insatiability
precious. We lament through her desirous nature the passing of life
for all of us. Here is the Wife's universal voice:

> But, Lord Crist! whan that it remembreth me
> Upon my yowthe, and on my jolitee,
> It tikleth me about myn herte roote.
> Unto this day it dooth myn herte boote
> That I have had my world as in my tyme.
> But age, allas! that al wole envenyme,
> Hath me biraft my beautee and my pith.
> (469–75)

Even her answer to time is generalized enough for us to praise her
victorious practicality:

> Lat go, farewel! the devel go therwith!
> The flour is goon, ther is namoore to telle;

> The bren, as I best kan, now moste I selle;
> But yet to be right myrie wol I fonde.
>
> (476–79)

The Wife's insatiability here is triumphant. It is knowing and thus *feels* unconquerable because she acknowledges the difference between "flour" and "bren" *when it counts*. She makes distinctions of the marketplace the terms of her own gloss on life, for her scholasticism is self-serving and her special reading of tradition, her intellectual enthusiasm, is a species of insatiability. That is perhaps why we love the Wife of Bath for her textuality and forgive her for her textual and human excesses. They constitute an indominable will to live and to think.

The Wife's description of the psychology of desire is, for example, marked by a thoroughgoing commercialism:

> We wommen had, if that I shal nat lye,
> In this matere a queynte fantasye;
> Wayte what thyng we may nat lightly have,
> Therafter wol we crie al day and crave.
> Forbede us thyng, and that desiren we;
> Preesse on us faste, and thanne wol we fle.
> With daunger oute we al oure chaffare;
> Greet prees at market maketh deere ware,
> And to greet cheep is holde at litel prys.
>
> (515–23)

The pun on "queynte" both names the "fantasye"—pudendic—and characterizes it, as if desire itself (what we "crave") were odd or curious, a kind of wonderment. The Wife says that she sells her "chaffare," identified as sex, with "daunger," a coyness that, at the right price, makes her sexuality *seem* scarce. She counterfeits the logic of the marketplace in order to live in it. In this way, the Wife trades in the world. Here is her rationale: desire is a socialized, and socializing, instinct. Her insatiability is not amoral; it has reasons of its own. In this spirit, her promiscuous intellectuality seems very much alive. Precisely because she is in the marketplace, we understand her reasons as necessary, on-going commerce. Moreover, the Wife's description of desire, which is its justification in the world, requires that we do *not* see her values as a kind of feminine bouleversement—a turning of the world upside down to master it. She does not gain freedom, nor does Chaucer gain freedom through her.[33] The Wife's "medieval" values are currency, exchange, and process. She vies for power to strike bargains of mutuality, not to tyrannize.

Like her capacity to awaken our remembrance of life, the Wife's mercantile command of it has a universalizing appeal. We cannot know, of course, how a medieval woman, one of Criseyde's "ladys," say, might have read the Wife of Bath's Prologue and Tale to an audience of women, but I suspect as the impersonated voice of any woman, the Wife of Bath is amusing, not liberating, precisely because she does as a woman what men have always done—justifies herself and strikes bargains.[34] Moreover, what repressive frustrations a medieval woman, or any woman, may feel is released *through* her performance. If the Wife is indeed an embodiment of social and sexual anger, she provides for its socializing expression. Moreover, just as the fear she may embody for a man is caught up in a man's performance of her boundless intellectual and sexual appetite, so the anger she may embody for a woman is caught up in a woman's performance of both the Wife's carping and boundless answers to "auctoritee" and her self-merchandising. For a man perhaps, or rather for the masculine in men and women, the Wife's market analogies describe trading in the world as ascendency and the sharing of power. For a woman, or the feminine in women and men, the Wife's analogies describe trade as play and allurement— as both purely sexual and life-sustaining gratification. What, of course, the Wife never does is consciously and willfully become a mother. Perhaps that is why both men and women feel they can, and do, know her. Chaucer's Wife of Bath seems deeply accessible and awakening. Her sexuality has the kind of androgyny that engages in men and women the constellation of sexual and social signatures we distinguish as masculine and feminine.

For example, throughout the Wife of Bath's Prologue and Tale, we hear a curious mixture of willfulness and sheer power that, once acknowledged, is *given up* in mutually manipulative passivity. The accord of Wife and her fifth husband reach seems to everyone's deepest advantage:

> We fille acorded by us selven two.
> He yaf me al the bridel in myn hond,

To han the governance of hous and lond,
And of his tonge, and of his hond also.

(812–15)

The Wife here says she gained mastery ("governance") because she
was given the "bridel"—management of his property ("hous and
lond"), the articulation of his thoughts ("tonge"), though not perhaps his unspoken thoughts, and his power ("hond"), which accompanied the expression of his and her sexuality. This last reference
echoes the Wife's own description of Jankin's mastery of her, a concatenation that seems to combine brutality with sexual arousal:

Now of my fifthe housbonde wol I telle.
God lete his soule nevere come in helle!
And yet was he to me the mooste shrewe;
That feele I on my ribbes al by rewe,
And evere shal unto myn endyng day.
But in oure bed he was so fressh and gay,
And therwithal so wel koude he me glose,
Whan that he wolde han my *bele chose*,
That thogh he hadde me bete on every bon,
He koude wynne agayn my love anon.

(503–12)

We cannot say, of course, that the Wife links physical abuse with
sexual expression, though she articulates the dynamics of sexuality
broadly enough to engage both men and women. She wins her
"soveraynetee" through "maistrie" (818) *after* a fight provoked by
Jankin's reading to her from his "book of wikked wyves" (685), in
her mind, his on-going intellectual abuse of her:

And whan I saugh he wolde nevere fyne
To reden on this cursed book al nyght,
Al sodeynly thre leves have I plyght
Out of his book, right as he radde, and eke
I with my fest so took hym on the cheke
That in oure fyr he fil bakward adoun.
And he up stirte as dooth a wood leoun,
And with his fest he smoot me on the heed,
That in the floor I lay as I were deed.

(788–96)

Jankin, the Wife says, wanted to flee when he saw what he had done, but he does not. When the Wife awakes from her "swogh" (799), not from her death, she browbeats Jankin by first asking *whether* he had "slayn" (800) her and then whether he wanted to murder (801) her for her wealth ("land"). Her two questions are rhetorical, of course, since she is not dead. Indeed, her very next words to Jankin are not more questions but a single statement of sexual intention ("yet wol I kisse thee") that playfully assumes, I think, that she is *going to die* ("Er I be deed" [802]). Jankin then approaches her—apparently he had *not* backed out of earshot ("tongue shot," one wants to say). He falls to his knees vowing never to "smyte" (805) her *again*, but not admitting he was wrong to have done so now. The Wife then hits *him* again ("And yet eftsoones I hitte hym on the cheke" [808]). Only "atte laste, with muchel care and wo" (811) do the Wife and her fifth husband come to an agreement. Jankin acknowledges the Wife's power in what is clearly the manipulation of his "tonge," but only after what seems like pleasurable fist-to-fist foreplay of indeterminate length:

> And that he seyde, "Myn owene trewe wyf,
> Do as thee lust the terme of al thy lyf;
> Keep thyn honour, and keep eek myn estaat—"
> (819–21)

After that, she says "we hadden never debaat" (822).

Her response to his presumed silence is perfect wifeliness:

> God helpe me so, I was to hym as kynde
> As any wyf from Denmark unto Ynde,
> And also trewe, and so was he to me.
> (823–25)

Like the loathly lady in the Wife of Bath's Tale, the Wife of Bath achieves through mastery a perfect marriage, perhaps as perfect as the Franklin's. Both the Wife and her fifth husband, like the loathly lady and the knight, are kind to each other, and true, presumably sexually true:

> "Kys me," quod she, "we be no lenger wrothe;
> For, by my trouthe, I wol be to yow bothe,
> That is to seyn, ye, bothe fair and good.
> I prey to God that I moote sterven wood,

> But I to yow be also good and trewe
> As evere was wyf, syn that the world was newe.
>   (1239–44)

The Wife pledges geographically universal wifeliness, the loathly lady atemporal wifeliness. If her tale is the Wife's "fantasye," then it catches up the same rounded sexual complexity of her prologue.[35] Indeed, we should note that the knight the loathly lady chooses to master in the Wife of Bath's Tale is a man of proven sexual prowess:

> And so bifel it that this kyng Arthour
> Hadde in his hous a lusty bacheler,
> That on a day cam ridynge fro ryver;
> And happed that, allone as he was born,
> He saugh a mayde walkynge hym biforn,
> Of which mayde anon, maugree hir heed,
> By verray force, ye rafte hire maydenhed.
>   (882–88)

The queen in King Arthur's "hous" (883) does not require that the knight repent with abstinence because he took ("rafte") a maiden-head. Though he rapes the "mayde," I would not call it rape just because the knight's sexual expression is swift and ladies protest. The text says he is "allone as he was born" when he saw her, suggesting that his sexual instincts, when he acts on them, are, in some sense, pure. Happenstance gives him sheer animal—one wants to say "Edenic"—freedom. The knight here, in the Wife's "fantasye," is acting out. For that he must submit to being tamed socially by a woman who *wants* his animality. And the loathly lady acknowledges just that when she shifts the meaning of the word "bothe" (1240) in her declaration of marital conjunction. The knight's choice, which he willingly hands over to her—whether she will be ugly and true or fair and false—is what we at first think she means by "bothe." But she glosses her own word ("this is to seyn" [1241]) and changes its referents, realigning the connections she had made between physicality and values. Her feminine magic turns on this linguistic transformation. Moreover, the Wife's prayer, after she explains that the loathly lady, now a beautiful wife, "obeyed hym in every thyng / That myghte doon hym plesance or likyng" (1255–56) also catches up the complexity of desire for both women and men.

and Jhesu Crist us sende
Housbondes meeke, yonge, and fressh abedde,
And grace t'overbyde hem that we wedde.

(1258–60)

The Wife wants men both submissive and sexual and a kind of mastery of them through time, as if outliving successive husbands could give her continually awakening sexual renewal into old age. For her "housbondes meeke" there is sex without exhausting intellectual management. The Wife, like the loathly lady, wants the *name* of sovereignity.[36] Then there is silence and pleasure. Perhaps even the kind of intellectual negotiation we see occurring mentally and physically between the Wife and Jankin—hitting is token arousal—constitutes renewable and renewing foreplay. For women, the Wife of Bath demonstrates masterful feminine wisdom—coyness and malleability once the idea of sovereignty has been acknowledged. For men, the Wife is infinitely compelling—intellectual, physical, and boundless. She encourages a thrilling abdication of power, which never disappoints. She is for men the woman of their "queynte fantasye" because she never says no when *she* wants to.

The idea of awakening sexual mastery, which the Wife prays for at the end of her tale—outliving her husbands—suggests to me that in the narration of her successive marriages the Wife articulates her own wish for silence for her husbands and herself. Although in her first three marriages, she is irrepressible—she has the "tonge," she says, of a "verray jangleresse" (638), an indefatigible chatterbox, and she cannot abide being lectured—the Wife's actual responses to the three old men she marries and then to Jankin are silencing verbal abuse and sheer rage: for example, she rips a page, or pages, from Jankin's book. *He* does all the talking. She admits on two occasions to having torn one leaf from the book of wicked wives (635, 667), and to three leaves the last time she mentions the incident (790). Jankin must indeed be silenced. But the Wife's emphatic act, not talk, wins her a summary reprieve and, accompanied with a fist, the negotiating power for a mutually happy marriage. Only *we* actually hear the Wife of Bath as a feminine scholastic. With her "clerk of Oxenford" (527), she is sheer rage—hands and fists. Indeed, in a decidedly seductive way, Jankin out-coys her ("he / Was of his love daungerous to me" [513–14]), for which, she says, she

loved him best of all (513). He could "read"—interpret and per-
suade her:

> And therwithal so wel koude he me glose,
> Whan that he wolde han my *bele chose*.
>
> (509–10)

Jankin is smooth. "Daungerous" suggests a manipulative (domi-
nating) coyness,[37] which is, as the Wife admits to us, her counterfeiting salesman's trick (521–23). She adds: "This knoweth every
womman that is wys" (524). This turn to the women in the audience
establishes the idea that the Wife speaks *for* the naturally intimate
circle of women. But what such division of the audience into men
and women creates is an indeterminate text into which we rush,
like a gap in intention, *as men or women*—either left out of the
feminine circle, but privy to it—as men we sense its dangerous invitations—or entirely within such a female circle, like Criseyde
and her "ladys," amused, I suspect, by its forthrightness. The Wife
says she wishes to compete with men for intellectual mastery of the
word and, in this way, the world:

> By God! if wommen hadde writen stories,
> As clerkes han withinne hire oratories,
> They wolde han writen of men moore wikkednesse
> Than al the mark of Adam may redresse.
>
> (693–96)

But *we* never hear her answer Jankin exegetical gloss for gloss. Indeed, all her first three husbands hear are worldly carpings meant
to silence; moreover, *we* never hear the Wife's first three husbands
answer back. For the Wife, despite how *she* explains her victories
of tongue, to "quit" means to harangue:

> For, by my trouthe, I quitte hem word for word.
> As helpe me verray God omnipotent,
> Though I right now sholde make my testament,
> I ne owe hem nat a word that it nys quit.
> I broghte it so aboute by my wit
> That they moste yeve it up, as for the beste,
> Or elles hadde we nevere been in reste.
>
> (422–28)

Indeed, the Wife's sense of her powers of mind ("I broghte it so aboute by my wit") are simply grandiose. She reserves her scholastic exuberance for the Canterbury pilgrims. Her husbands get the haggler's logic she performs for us—her generic abuse of men that has served her profitably for three marriages. She talks to her first husbands ("but herkneth how I sayde" [234]) like a shrew. And she says her performance is an exemplary demonstration of how any wife *should* talk to her husband. The Wife of Bath thus generalizes on two separate occasions her own wifely style (235–378 and 431–50), giving us her sample of intellectual mastery—her woman's story (693).

The Wife begins, as she implies all wives should begin, with an abusive question designed to throw a husband off balance ("Sire olde kaynard, is this thyn array?" [235]). His "array" is a domestic order that means her social poverty:

> Why is my neighebores wyf so gay?
> She is honoured over al ther she gooth;
> I sitte at hoom, I have no thrifty clooth.
>   (236–38)

The Wife here implicitly acknowledges her husband's power over her. She suggests that he is neglecting his duty to "array" her. In upbraiding him, the Wife appeals to his vanity and pride as the man of the house. She can thus blame him for her confinement and then rail at his own neighborly visits (239):

> Is she so fair? artow so amorous?
> What rowne ye with oure mayde? *Benedicite!*
> Sire olde lecchour, lat thy japes be!
>   (240–42)

The Wife simply assumes her husband is sinning with the woman next door *and* with the maid in her own household. Her accusations are unstoppably extravagant. Indeed, she works by cagey shifts of meaning, on the word "array," for example—his arrangements ("array")—and on associative leaps: since she has no suitable clothes to wear, she stays at home; but *he* goes out. Her confinement, which is her husband's fault, reminds her of his freedom and then his liberty. He is now "Sire olde lecchour," jealously guarding his wife's innocent social circle:

> And if I have a gossib or a freend,
> Withouten gilt, thou chidest as a feend,
> If that I walke or pleye unto his hous!
> (243–45)

The Wife has turned the domestic order in which she lives into a
tyranny that makes her the victim of a husband's devilish chiding.
He now becomes the arch misogynist, subjecting her, when he
comes home, to drunken carpings. These she lists (248–302). They
are a collection of misogynistic truisms the Wife puts into her husband's mouth ("thou seyst"). And all the while, as if to answer him,
she punctuates her summary of his preaching with curses. She
brings down upon her husband the wrath of heaven:

> With wilde thonder-dynt and firy levene
> Moote thy welked nekke be tobroke!
> (276–77)

She asks angry rhetorical questions: "What eyleth swich an old
man for to chide?" (281). And she resorts to simple name-calling:

> Thow seyst we wyves wol our vices hide
> Til we be fast, and thanne we wol hem shewe,—
> We may that be a proverbe of a shrewe!
> (282–84)

The Wife in fact never answers her husband's misogyny. She dismisses his arguments for the wickedness of women because they
deserve her outrage. The force of her response is its inexhaustible
righteousness. The Wife here is unabashedly unfair.

She flatly denies that she has any interest in their golden-haired
"apprentice Janekyn" (303), for example, voicing her innocence as a
kind of aside in her generic demonstration of how she talks to a
husband. Once made ("Yet hastow caught a fals suspecioun" [306]),
she changes the subject ("But tel me this" [308]), now charging that
her husband violates marital agreements. She has returned to the
idea of domestic order, but now makes it clear that mastery is nego-
tiable. She asks why he hides the keys to his chest (309), since his
goods are hers, too (310), then threatens not to allow him mastery
of both her body and her goods, making not-so-veiled threats to
withdraw sex (311–15). When she tenders him advice on how to
treat her, she does not display the exegetical intelligence we have

come to love her for, the kind that argues *as if* argument were the
token of shared participation in social arrangements and mental
life; the Wife's words to her husband are given bluntly. She *tells*
her husband what to say:

> Thow sholdest seye, "Wyf, go wher thee liste;
> Taak youre disport, I wol nat leve no talys.
> I knowe yow for a trewe wyf, dame Alys."
>
> (318–20)

Here is her truth about wives—they do not like confinement,
wanting always to be "at oure large" (322):

> He is to greet a nygard that wolde werne
> A man to lighte a candle at his lanterne;
> He shal have never the lasse light, pardee.
> Have thou ynogh, thee thar nat pleyne thee.
>
> (333–36)

The Wife's use of "nygard" not only suggests her husband's misunderstanding of the nature of sex (having more means there is
more to have—it cannot be used up), it tells us that *she* thinks sex
is to be spent, not hoarded. Her implicit analogy is to money. The
wonder of sex is that to spend it is itself good fortune. The more
you spend, the more there is, *mirabile dictu*, to expend—an ap-
pealing, bountiful argument that makes the Wife, for all her carping, seem life-affirming and forgiveable.

The Wife's analogy to money, curiously enough, does not cheapen
sex. Rather, I think, it argues for a mercantile sense of social life
that gives us the theoretical foundation with which to love, not to
condemn her, whatever our own difficulties may be with the idea
of bargaining as a description of human life. The Wife we hear expounding to the Canterbury pilgrims the right way to talk to a husband does not refute authority by glossing it. She simply caps her
assertions of authority by reminding her "olde dotard" (331) that *if*
he does not interfere with her social life, he will have "queynte
right ynogh at eve" (332). The Wife will dispense sex as the autonomous being she insists she is. Her bestowal or withdrawal of sex—
bargaining love for liberty—is a token of her self-sufficiency, a
merchant's material intercourse. The Wife also reminds her husband that there is enough sex for him, and for anyone else she

chooses to give herself to. And about that she is right. This principle of domestic order and marital happiness is non-negotiable. The Wife gets social and, presumably sexual, free rein, and her husband gets sex.

The only "auctoritee" the Wife actually cites in this passage from the Wife of Bath's Prologue (235–378), rarely ever commented on, is "Daun Ptholome" (Ptolemy), whom we heard her cite before (180–83), though neither of the proverbs she ascribes to him are actually found in his *Almageste*. The proverb cited in authority ("Of alle men his wysdom is the hyeste / That rekketh nevere who hath the world in honde" [326–27]), the Wife says, counsels not otherworldliness but minding one's own business—why complain as long as one gets what one needs? The proverb is a merchant's idea of social intercourse—being tolerant of our insatiable desire for bountiful autonomy:

> By this proverbe thou shalt understode,
> Have thou ynogh, what thar thee recche or care
> How myrily that othere folkes fare?
>
> (328–30)

The Wife of Bath does not answer her husband's citation of St. Timothy—that women ought to adorn themselves "with chastitee and shame" (342), and not "in tressed heer and gay perree, / As perles, ne with gold, ne clothes riche" (344–45). She simply dismisses it:

> After thy text, ne after thy rubriche,
> I wol nat wirche as muchel as a gnat.
>
> (346–47)

She is defiant:

> Sire olde fool, what helpeth thee to spyen?
> Thogh thou preye Argus with his hundred yen
> To be my warde-cors, as he kan best,
> In feith, he shal nat kepe me but me lest;
> Yet koude I make his berd, so moot I thee!
>
> (357–61)

Not only does the Wife repeat her husband's charge that she is "lyk a cat" (348) who will "nat dwelle in house half a day, / But forth she wole, er any day be dawed, / To shewe hir skyn, and goon a-caterwawed" (352–54). She embraces it, implying that her cat's skin, like her fine clothes, does give her away. Her nature is visible, not transparent. Thus when the Wife resumes listing her husband's old saws against women (his "parables" [369]), her cataloguing dismisses what is said. The Wife refutes her husband's preacherly "resemblances" (368) with an exhaustive voice. Her intent is to silence by talking. She does not engage him in even the most sophistical kind of argument.

The Wife interrupts her own performance here (379–430) to explain that she has answered *all* her husbands by complaining—she silences them by complaining first:

> I koude pleyne, and yit was in the gilt,
> Or elles often tyme hadde I been split.
> Whoso that first to mille comth, first grynt;
> I pleyned first, so was oure werre ystynt.
> They were ful glade to excuse hem blyve
> Of thyng of which they nevere agilte hir lyve.
>   (387–92)

Grinding grain, like the gnashing of teeth in the Wife's analogy, suggests, I think, that complaining and milling are both profitable if one gets busy doing them right away. Indeed, the Wife's false accusations, she says, flattered her aged husbands (393–96), and when *she* went out at night, presumably to spy on one of them, her "jealousy" was taken as a token of affection (397–99). The Wife calls such nightly excursions ("Under that colour hadde I many a myrthe" [399]) cleverness ("wit" [400]) and boasts that

> Atte ende I hadde the bettre in ech degree,
> By sleighte, or force, or by som maner thyng,
> As by continueel murmur or grucchyng.
>   (404–6)

The point here is that the Wife (and the text) confuse intellectual mastery and intolerable shrewishness. The text is unclear: the Wife is no intellectual, though she is shrewd. When she resumes demonstrating how to talk to husbands (431–50), she counsels patience and silence:

> Thanne wolde I seye, "Goode lief, taak keep
> How mekely looketh Wilkyn, oure sheep!
> Com neer, my spouse, lat me ba thy cheke!"
>
> (431–33)

Her affection here—the Wife calls the husband "lief" and would "ba" his cheek (kiss, as one would kiss a child)—is ironic triumph. Reminding her husband to be as patient as Job, "sith ye so preche of Jobes pacience" (436), she launches into icy logic—the only time, I think, the Wife is genuinely witty:

> And sith a man is moore resonable
> Than womman is, ye moste been suffrable.
>
> (441–42)

And she engages in cruel sexual teasing:

> What eyleth yow to grucche thus and grone?
> Is it for ye wolde have my queynte allone?
> Wy, taak it al! lo, have it every deel!
> Peter! I shrewe yow, but ye love it weel;
> For if I wolde selle my *bele chose*,
> I koude walke as freessh as is a rose;
> But I wol kepe it for youre owene tooth.
> Ye be to blame, by God! I sey yow sooth.
>
> (443–50)

Her power to save or sell her "queynte" is here the threat of complete mastery. Having had all the words, she has the last one too.

The Wife's image of power is, as she says, falconry, where she is falconer and men are falcons:

> And therfore every man this tale I telle,
> Wynne whoso may, for al is for to selle;
> With empty hand men may none haukes lure.
>
> (413–15)

The Wife has characteristically brought this courtly sport to the marketplace where she trades. What she notes about falconry is its "feminine" aspect: that falcons must be lured back to an "empty hand." Power is sexual availability marketed. As a courtly idea of power, falconry is a species of skill and mastered orchestration of

nature.³⁸ Moreover, the Wife's admission that she endured her
aged husband's lust for material gain (416–17) makes her mercan-
tilism, and her sexuality, her triumph. She suffered him, which defines her power. Her admission "And yet in bacon hadde I nevere
delit" (418) is a joke at an old man's expense, full of cruelty and deflected fear, since we all grow old. Such mockery is victory by put-
down, the Wife's manipulative stock-in-trade. It affirms youth and
availability at the expense of age. Indeed, it seeks to silence the
misogynist wisdom of old men with rapacious truth:

> I wolde no lenger in the bed abyde,
> If that I felte his arm over my syde,
> Til he had maad his raunson unto me;
> Thanne wolde I suffre hym do his nycetee.
>
> (409–12)

The Wife's euphemism here ("nycetee") suggests his impotence
and her manipulative coyness. The word is both dark and comic—
cruel and life-demanding.

Now we never hear how the Wife talks to her fourth husband.
We only hear her tell the Canterbury pilgrims how she responded
to his sexual escapades (453–56). He was younger than her first
three husbands, and she made his life a "purgatorie" (489) as an
answer to his vitality:

> I seye, I hadde in herte greet despit
> That he of any oother had delit.
> But he was quit, by God and by Seint Joce!
> I made hym of the same wode a croce;
> Nat of my body, in no foul manere,
> But certeinly, I made folk swich cheere
> That in his owene grece I made hym frye
> For angre, and for verray jalousye.
>
> (481–88)

The Wife "quit" her fourth husband neither with arguments nor
with deeds ("Nat of my body, in no foul manere"), but with tactical
behavior, a kind of gesturing *like* manipulative talk. Only we, and
the Canterbury pilgrims, hear the reference to "the foule cherl,
the swyn" (460) Metellius, who murdered his wife because she was
drunk and, presumably, as a consequence, lecherous (460–62).
The allusion, however, is only a threat to the Wife's fourth husband

alive in memory—he is dead now—because it serves the Wife, before the Canterbury pilgrims, as a self-referring and self-defining point of departure, as a text she can stand on because of her response to it:

> . . . thogh I hadde been his wyf,
> He sholde nat han daunted me fro drynke!
> And after wyn on Venus moste I thynke,
> For al so siker as cold engendreth hayl,
> A likerous mouth moste han a likerous tayl.
> (462–66)

Indeed, as a threat, the Wife's justification by proverb (465–66) of her libertine ways is something we overhear her say—a purely private use of a bookish reference, a buoying psychological gloss—though the boldness of it, had her fourth husband sensed *that* in her behavior, would indeed have made him jealous. For me, that is just the point. The Wife does not admit to the Canterbury pilgrims to having actually committed adultery. She made a show of involvement with other men that made her husband's life, as we might say, pure hell ("But certeinly, I made folk swich cheere" [486]). The text is indeterminate here, and, as usual, readers rush into this gap in specificity with their own manipulative imaginings. Like the triumphant browbeating she subjects her first three husbands to—her old men—and the spontaneous fisticuffs that engage and establish the marital bargain with her fifth husband—her inexhaustible, bold academic—the Wife's coyly blunt response to her fourth is a similar kind of gestural talk, teasing and open. Indeed, the Wife's entire behavior is simulation, or rather dissimulation; in short, lying. And its end is silence that affirms both sexual and mercantile vitality. The engaging combinations here are not simply sex and the marketplace, but silence and power, mutuality and life, all of which make the Wife of Bath catch the feminine and masculine imaginations in both men and women. She can be any reader's social and sexual performance—we speak for the Wife of Bath—and, as we have seen, her rhetoric mirrors the sexual fears and desires of men and the amusing and tantalizingly frank behavior of women like her.

All the Wife's turns to her audience are mixed. Nothing about them clarifies the gender of imagined performer or imagined audi-

ence—whether the Wife is the imagined performance of a man or
woman before a mixed audience or an audience of either men or
women. Sometimes the Wife talks to men about her treatment of
her first husbands:

> Lordynges, right thus, as ye have understonde,
> Baar I stifly myne olde housbondes on honde
> That thus they seyden in hir dronkenesse,
>
> (379–81)

Sometimes she talks only to women:

> Now herkneth hou I baar me proprely,
> Ye wise wyves, that kan understonde.
> Thus shulde ye speke and bere hem wrong on honde;
> For half so boldely kan ther no man
> Swere and lyen, as a womman kan.
> I sey nat this by wyves that been wyse,
> But if it be whan they hem mysavyse.
> A wys wyf shal, if that she kan hir good,
> Bere him on honde that the cow is wood,
> And take witnesse of hir owene mayde
> Of hir assent.
>
> (224–34)

The Wife's "lordynges"—her imagined gentlemen, Canterbury or
courtly—excludes women from her audience, whether or not any
women are to be imagined as present. Moreover, we have heard
her talk to her first three husbands, so that our social and sexually
engaged behavior as either men or women is similarly excluded
or included from the imagined performance of the Wife of Bath's
Prologue and Tale we construct. Likewise, the Wife's "wise wyves"
establishes an audience of women in the imagined presence of men
by simulating the kind of conspiratorial intimacy women may experience—she says she enlists the aid of other women ("hir owene
mayde") to fool her husband or husbands—and men may imagine women experiencing. The Wife tells her "lordynges" that she
spoke to her first husbands boldly ("baar I stifly"); they assailed her
with drunken preaching. She deals thrust for thrust. She tells
her "wise wyves" that women ought to lie to their husbands unequivocally—dissimulate boldly—and she alludes to the point of
the Manciple's Tale, without, of course, invoking for us its moral

complexities—that is, the nature of language and reality.[39] As she has been the *idea* that has capped other arguments about marital behavior—in the Merchant's Tale, for example, in *Bukton* and in the Clerk's Tale—so she uses a gloss of the Manciple's Tale to cap her own. She engages in an exclusive and knowing kind of conspiracy of silence with her "mayde," she says, as a prelude apparently to her bold, dismissing talk. The two passages we have just looked at that address an audience frame the performance she gives of her words to her first three husbands. Her confessional intimacy is thus dangerous, inviting, bold, amusing, and outrageous. The point about its imagined exclusiveness or intimacy is that it engages both the feminine and masculine aspects of all Chaucer's readers. For a man, the Wife's conspiratorial circle may be both frightening and inviting—it is, as a social grouping, frankly sexual. For a woman, the Wife's circle of "wyves" may be amusing. Her bold talk is wonderful and unfair, masterful and sexually rewarding, for both women and men. The kind of androgyny I see in the Wife of Bath as a performance does not, of course, diminish the Wife's unabashed femininity. Rather, it describes the kind of textual indeterminacy that gives readers scope for *their* doubleness, or imagined doubleness, of understanding.

I suggested earlier in this chapter that the idea of a marriage group in the *Canterbury Tales* constitutes an appropriate response in critics to the "tales of Canterbury" precisely because the principal dynamic of the work—spontaneity and self-discovery—welcomes structural dispositions in us as it has welcomed them in the Canterbury storytellers and listeners. In this spirit, then, I would like to add another tale to the "marriage group"—specifically, a discontinuous, but recurring, response to the Wife of Bath's Prologue and Tale. As we have seen, the Wife's "speaking for herself" encourages us also to speak. She can gloss her own story as well as be used to gloss others' stories. In this sense, the *Canterbury Tales* is comprehensive and unfinished. Indeed, its openness of form is its principle, both within tales and between them, for its fictional, historical, and performing audience, not because as Howard has shown, the "tales of Canterbury" are the fragments of a vast, or vaster, design, but because they are as complete as human constructs may be. An important medieval relationship between readers, books, and God lies, I think, at the heart of the difference between medieval and modern literature. Had Chaucer been asked why his narratives are both discontinuous and morally tentative, I suspect he might have replied that since God alone is one, any work of the human intellect must necessarily be incomplete. With its collateral serialization, rather than mirroring the incompleteness of life Chaucerian narrative, by its very incompleteness, mirrors the completeness of God. To rephrase a formula current in modern literary criticism and apply it to medieval literature: art stops; only God finishes. Our obsession with "closure" in literature, with both finding it and creating it, is our own.[40]

In this spirit, then, I would like to add the "Host's Prologue" to the tales of marriage the Wife of Bath encourages us and others to tell. If our own interpretation of the Wife constitutes our reflected stories, so does his. The Host in fact calls his response to the Merchant's Tale his "tale" (2440), and although it is brief, it constitutes a preamble to his life—his prologue, as it were. The Host's commentary on the Merchant's Tale constitutes the revelations the Merchant's Tale encourages from him. Like other pilgrim storytellers, he glosses and applies to his own life the point of the Merchant's Tale, ascribing to a woman's business ("as bisy as bees" [2422]) a perfected sociability for the stinging of husbands. Actually, the Host's "prologue" is a kind of gripe. Harry Bailly claims he is unable to talk about his wife and their life together, though he admits to the same kind of inability to speak we have heard other pilgrims confess. Though the Host is a "man noght textueel," what he says he will *not tell* tells us a good deal about him. In this respect, Harry Bailly is a voluble Chaucerian storyteller:

> But of hir tonge, a labbyng shrewe is she,
> And yet she hath an heep of vices mo;
> Therof no fors! lat alle swiche thynges go.
> But wyte ye what? In conseil be it seyd.
> Me reweth soore I am unto hire teyd.
> For, and I sholde rekenen every vice
> Which that she hath, ywis I were to nyce;
> And cause why, it sholde reported be
> And toold to hire of somme of this meynee,—
> Of whom, it nedeth nat for to declare,
> Syn wommen konnen outen swich chaffare;

And eek my wit suffiseth nat therto,
To tellen al, wherfore my tale is do.

                  (2428–40)

The Host's irritation here is surprising. He rushes over his own
story as if he still hears, on the road to Canterbury, his Wife's "labbyng" tongue. Among the Canterbury pilgrims, Harry Bailly is decidedly social and boisterous. His values are talk—the entertaining
use of time for self-expression—and he is always piqued at those
pilgrims who waste time. He is impatient with the Reeve, for example, ("It were al tyme thy tale to bigynne" [3908]), who has just
finished his sermon on age and desire, partly because the Host believes men should stick to their proper trades ("The devel made
a reve for to preche" [3903]), partly because he sees himself as
the pilgrims' timekeeper ("Sey forth thy tale, and tarie nat the
tyme / Lo Depeford! and it is half-wey pryme" [3905–6]). The
Host, as we know, does not evaluate the tales he hears with a judiciousness that allows right opinion, so much as react to them—that
is judgment, too, perhaps the only kind there is in the *Canterbury
Tales*. But Harry Bailly does assume he has control of the use of
time. In that sense, he is the "governour" (1.813) of the Canterbury pilgrims and the "juge and reportour" (1.814) of their tales. I
would call him a temporal umpire. Indeed, he is, as in the Man of
Law's Prologue, the zodiacal measurer of heaven (1–15). He gives
voice to a kind of hymn on the values of social orchestration. Despite his glossing of Seneca, which lapses into clumsy sexual jokes,
the Host's appeal to hurry shows him to us at his most elegant:

Leseth no tyme, as ferforth as ye may.
Lordynges, the tyme wasteth nyght and day,
And steleth from us, what pryvely slepynge,
And what thurgh necligence in oure wakynge,
As dooth the streem that turneth never agayn,
Descendynge fro the montaigne into playn.
Wel kan Senec and many a philosophre
Biwaillen tyme moore than gold in cofre;
For "los of catel may recovered be,
But los of tyme shendeth us," quod he.
It wol nat come agayn, withouten drede,
Namoore than wole Malkynes maydenhede,

> Whan she hath lost it in hir wantownesse.
> Lat us nat mowlen thus in ydelnesse.
>
> (19–32)

The idea of time as a descending stream is a passing moment of calm philosophic exposition. Malkyn's maidenhead is not. Still, the Host here sermonizes on the value of time, if not on its proper use, and on the loss of virginity, in a generic sense, as the loss of innocence. Harry Bailly does *not*, of course, hear how his own philosophical turns, his judgments of life and value, give expression to his own idea of manly prowess and domination.

We can observe a similarly blind sociability when Harry Bailly encourages the Clerk to talk:

> Ye ryde as coy and stille as dooth a mayde
> Were newe spoused, sittynge at the bord;
> This day ne herde I of youre tonge a word.
> I trowe ye studie aboute som sophyme;
> But Salomon seith "every thyng hath tyme."
>
> (2–6)

The Clerk as bride, looking as if he were thinking up a specious argument, is the Host's perfect object. For him, Harry Bailly would be as sociable as Solomon, who is wise *because*, as the Host implies, he knows the right use of time; it is for storytelling, for participation in social life. For the Host, it is inappropriate to study on a pilgrimage (8). Harry Bailly is indeed the tyrant of social time, controlling others through his regulation and distribution of it. He thus encourages the Clerk to play (10–11) but not sermonize: do not, he says, make us either weep or fall asleep (12–14). The Host encourages the Clerk's "heigh style" (18), but he wants him to "spek-eth so pleyn at this tyme, we yow preye, / That we may under-stonde what ye seye" (19–20). The Host's contradictory requests for a storytelling diction are not the point. What the Host wants from the Clerk is a worldly participatory style. He encourages what he thinks is courtly and learned, but plain enough so that he can understand it. The Host is the great joiner, and the joiner of men. What he wants is not to be left out of a style designed for the court ("as whan that men to kynges write" [18]), from which Harry Bailly is perforce excluded. He is not the great leveler, but a sociable man.

For this reason, then, Harry Bailly's having dismissed his own story, after he hears the Merchant's Tale, being hurried along, as it were, by his wife seems curious and telling. Her "labbyng" tongue, so to speak, keeps him, even on the Canterbury pilgrimage, from participating publicly in his own life. He admits "in conseil" (2431) that he regrets his marriage. Such a moment teases us with an indeterminacy about his domesticity that gives his public, sociable, and philosophic life as keeper of time a private, indeed hidden, turn. The effect is darkening. The Host says that his wife's "heep of vices" (2429)

> sholde reported be
> An toold to hire of somme of this meynee, —
> Of whom, it nedeth nat for to declare,
> Syn wommen konnen outen swich chaffare.
>
> (2435–38)

The Host here makes an anonymous, but not veiled, reference to the Wife of Bath *as if* his "tale," could he tell it ("And eek my wit suffiseth nat therto" [2439]) would "quit" the Wife. The Host's preamble, not told, but implied, has all the participatory features, then, of a "Canterbury" tale. Harry Bailly would pay back in kind the Wife of Bath, who, like his wife, knows how to sell "swich chaffare" (2438). The Host's gloss on "chaffare" implies both the presumed *matere* of his "tale," could he tell it—his wife's vices— and, if the word catches up the sense in which "chaffare" was used in the Wife of Bath's Prologue, the idea of wifely wares, sexuality in a marketplace she trades in. If such a remembered meaning is intended—and this is highly, though appropriately, speculative— then the Host has, like the Wife of Bath's own husbands, something to complain about, and Goodelief's "labbyng" tongue, like the Wife of Bath's—the Host tells us the name of his wife in his response to the Melibee—browbeats him. Indeed, *we hear* what she says to him when she imagines she has not been treated with the deference she demands:

> "Allas!" she seith, "that evere I was shape
> To wedden a milksop, or a coward ape,
> That wol been overlad with every wight!
> Thou darst nat stonden by thy wyves right!"
>
> (1909–12)

Goodelief, of course, has "overlad" (browbeaten) Harry, about which he responds resignedly. We hear the Host's words as comic resignation, an oblique acknowledgment of his dependence, despite his brandishings.

> This is my lif, but if that I wol fighte;
> And out at dore anon I moote me dighte,
> Or elles I am but lost, but if that I
> Be lik a wilde leoun, fool-hardy.
> (1913–16)

Indeed, he says that his wife may make him kill his neighbor, "for I am perilous with knyf in honde" (1919). Mastery is hers, even of *his* martial skill and his symbolic sexual weapon ("By corpus bones, I wol have thy kynf" [1906]).

The difference, however, between the Host's humorous description of his henpecking in his response to Melibee and his threat to repay the Wife of Bath in his response to the Merchant's Tale is that the former is a foursquare revelation occasioned by a "Canterbury" tale. It tells us plainly about the Host's life, his illusions of power. The latter is a participating "tale" in the game of Canterbury "quitting." And presumably Goodelief's vices *are* serious, in any case, more indeterminate at the end of the Merchant's Tale than they are at the end of Melibee, where she seems only a bully ("For she is byg in armes, by my feith" [1921]). The Host's response to the Merchant's Tale and the way he would have his own life framed *in story* for the Wife of Bath, now deeply and teasingly hinted at—the Host has more to complain about than being bullied—shows us a Harry Bailly who values the power of words to embody lives, and the value of stories to give vent to private and perhaps silent ills. The Host, of course, sees storytelling confirming his own view of life, which does not, for him, negate its value. Storytelling is part of a spirited sociability that makes the Host, for all his boisterousness, a marveler at tales. Like us, for whom his responses are encouragement, he can be transported by them and want to use their power to generate involved "quitting." Like the Clerk and the Merchant before him, he caps the "tale he tells" with a reference to the Wife of Bath. For this reason, perhaps, he does not want storytellers whose words do not constitute, through his understanding them, the storial community. Of course, the sequence of references to the

Wife of Bath, who "speaks for herself" as we imagine the per-former who speaks for her, and who can be used by others to speak for them—their kind of "quitting" her—is really *less* important than the idea of engaged tellers and listeners responding personally to storytelling, as the Host does. Harry Bailly, like everyone, loves stories that confirm his view of social and marital life, but his ar-ticulated partialities, even when he says he cannot tell all there is to tell, *unconsciously* praise storytelling and the mirror of the world it gives him. Here is indeed the hermeneutical contradiction with which we began this chapter—the psychological and social effects of taking on tradition: we always generalize our views, and in that way constitute the public world. The Host is uncritical, but his enthusiasms and his silences make him deeply social. We like his forthrightness, his piety, his silly, frail, and precious mascu-linity. We can feel tender about him in his willful nonresponse to the Wife of Bath, who, even when she has finished speaking, con-stitutes his talk and his silence.

Chapter Five

Voices and Books

Chapter 5, divided into two parts, considers aspects of two "Canterbury" tales—the Pardoner's and the Knight's—as examples of a storytelling continuum in Chaucer that includes tales usually seen as pure voiced performances (as species of drama, with varying degrees of deep or rounded characterization) and tales usually seen as purely voiceless juxtapositions of style or idiom (as species of narrative, with allegorical or emblematic, flat or idealized characters). The Pardoner's Prologue and Tale—which I have called the "Pardoner's 'Prologue,'" for reasons that should be clear shortly— and the Knight's Tale are not usually grouped together. They seem conceptually different. But I have taken them together to illustrate a Chaucerian wholeness that is the idea of this book: that all of Chaucer, imagined as voiced or voiceless, always demands hermeneutic recovery—interpretive penetration and application— that "brings to life" by mirroring for our use both "dramatic monologues" and purely bookish stories. Chaucerian narratives are not complete, not told unless we tell them to ourselves. My aim in considering the "Pardoner's 'Prologue'" and the Knight's Tale together is not polemical, but heuristic. Just because these two tales seem at conceptual extremes—one is thought to be pure voice, the other all style—taking the "Pardoner's 'Prologue'" and the Knight's Tale together demonstrates how I think Chaucer works everywhere.

Perhaps the first place readers look to find an author in his text are the junctures where characterization calls attention to itself. As Germaine Dempster uses the term, *dramatic irony* describes an unexpected moment of insight into the psychology of a character in literature ("a strong contrast unperceived by the character") that changes both what an audience thought it understood about human nature and what it can expect to understand about people and circumstances.[1] Whatever the nature of the incongruity between character and setting, dramatic irony gives an audience a sense of "seeing more" than a character sees. It presents a sudden, perhaps startling, always arresting and important, revelation of knowledge. As a critical term, dramatic irony has been used rather loosely and been applied to literature of all kinds, not merely drama, although it always defines irony in terms of the irony in drama, as if character, in all genres of literature, were "center-stage."

Though the idea of a dramatic irony need not be restricted to drama proper, because it describes the fact, not in itself untrue, that an audience can be given changes of perspective, talking about dramatic irony (or ironies) in Chaucer usually confuses two issues about authorial intention *by not raising either one*. First, the fact that Chaucer sees more than his characters *and* may see more than members of his audience makes any statement about dramatic ironies that depend on Chaucer's role as artist incomplete if Chaucer is not said to see dramatic ironies along with us. The issue of authorial intention is peculiarly important in declaimed narrative, especially for private readers (especially for us), since a narrative read aloud once had a performer pretending to be one or several storytellers. Second, because it is impossible to know how Chaucer intends us to judge people and events, his mastery of the illusion of scenes between people and his elusiveness as a guide should be understood as part of the aesthetic and moral complexity of his tales. Thus a dramatic irony, if it does not lose its power to surprise, does lose its power to surprise just for the sake of the character being revealed to us. Dramatic irony again and again draws us closer to an author and performer only to disappoint us with hidden communications we may have thought (and wanted) to be there. Dramatic irony makes a play more lifelike, serving to diminish a sense of the author's presence. In narrative repeatedly performed, dramatic irony reminds the audience that a storyteller is present everywhere—that what it is "seeing" is being told to it, but that it is not being told how to take sides on complexity meant to engage it. Responding to dramatic ironies in performed narrative

makes it apparent that declaimed narrative is generically *nothing
but* declaimed narrative—that it is not to be imagined as a play
whose author continually fades as the story unfolds and the audience is transported ("carried to the other side") emotionally. Dramatic ironies in public performance repeatedly set the performing
storyteller before members of an audience who would understand
that declaimed narrative is a one-man show.

Critics have never confined dramatic irony to drama, and I do
not imagine that they will start now. But talking about dramatic
ironies in performed narrative should entail the idea of authorial
presence, not the idea of the illusion of a self-revealing character.
Declaimed narrative moves in a direction opposite to that of a play:
at a performance, we imagine scenes between people, but see an
impersonator on stage; at a play, we see actors on stage and clamor
for the author after the curtain falls. Indeed, we "see double" at
a public reading, or rather "imagine" and "see" at the same time,
so that dramatic ironies serve content, the revelation of character,
and form, the calling up of the live narrator, simultaneously. Re-
gardless of the insights into character being expressed, a dramatist
always uses the freedom of his or her own absence to make them,
deliberately letting characters "become deep" on their own. We
never forget that a play is artifice, but we are usually encouraged
to. In narrative performed we are never rid of an impersonator,
commentator, and guide, however elusive, who *intends* to lead us
from scene to scene, making us "see more."

We can illustrate the performative idea of dramatic irony in
Chaucer by looking at the Pardoner's Prologue and Tale, usually
assumed to be a kind of continuous prologue to (and revelation of)
the Pardoner himself, because the tale is virtually embedded in the
prologue—the Pardoner's voice at line 915, some fifty lines before
the end of fragment 6, returns us to the Canterbury pilgrimage.
Indeed, because the Pardoner *seems* a fully dramatized character
giving a full dramatic monologue (a "Pardoner's 'Prologue'"), the
Pardoner's Prologue and Tale, taken together as a character's (an
actor's) performance, is the best example in Chaucer of how the
performative idea of dramatic irony renders even the "Pardoner's
'Prologue'" as much a storyteller's (as opposed to an actor's) performance as any other pilgrim narrative in the *Canterbury Tales*.

The Pardoner has, of course, long been thought one of Chaucer's fully self-portraying characters, perhaps his most mature and believably lifelike pilgrim. In any case, it is often said, the Pardoner is his most atypically medieval characterization.[2] Even Derek Pearsall's astute observation that the Pardoner exists only "as a creature of naked will, unaware of its existence but in the act of will" is, as Pearsall uses it, a psychological reading of the Pardoner's "atrophied" state.[3] "[The Pardoner] never talks about his motives, except to reiterate monotonously that his purpose is ever one. He never once says 'I think' or 'I feel,' but only describes what he has done or what he will do."[4] Pearsall is right, I think, that the Pardoner is *not* psychologically like the Wife of Bath, though whatever "interest in the workings of the individual consciousness" Chaucer's portrait of her shows,[5] she, too, is a performance: a figure of performative androgyny. Still, even with Pearsall's sense of the "horror of vacuity" that is for Pearsall the Pardoner's self,[6] the Pardoner seems to a great many critics to have, as a fictional character, some kind of life of his own—a credible, albeit repulsive, psychological core, if not a "roundness," that happily—and here is the point—associates Chaucer's best narratives with more mature and less "medieval," or flat and lifeless, kinds of fiction. Other critics see the Pardoner not as a fully dramatized character in a genre of narrative fiction that is simultaneously approaching both the drama and the novel, but as a character who is as distinctly medieval as the Knight or the Parson—not cardboardlike, but idealized. The Pardoner is said to draw his vitality, which is not necessarily his lifelikeness, from the powerful concepts he represents and not from Chaucer's mature and successful attempt at psychological realism. These ideas are "painted"—the word is used figuratively—with a good deal of psychological truth, but not with the idea of psychological depth as an end in itself.[7] The Pardoner is, in short, an emblem. Rather than the roundness associated with characters in psychological drama or the novel, he possesses the intellectual fullness associated with an allegorical picture. The Pardoner is False-Seeming as a psychological type, a version of *Faux-Semblant* his literary antecedent in the *Roman de la Rose*.[8]

Aside from the fact that both views employ the Pardoner as part of a larger thesis about Chaucer's growth as a medieval poet, either

as a premodern or a late medieval, the distinction between purely
psychological and purely moral, or allegorical, description, usually
drawn too sharply with respect to Chaucer's work,[9] does not essentially change the nature of the argument that the "Pardoner's 'Prologue'" is the final (and convincing, because it is a late) example of
Chaucer's intentional self-effacement as a storyteller. In my view,
talking about the Pardoner's Prologue and Tale ought not depend
on whether or not the Pardoner is a fully dramatized character or a
fully conceptualized and graspable emblem. It should depend on
what an audience would make of the Pardoner's self-revelation perceived as the progressive performative illusion of the Pardoner's
self-portrayal. It is perhaps the *convincing* illusion of the Pardoner's self-portrayal that has led so many Chaucerians to assume that
the Pardoner is "real" in a sense other than one a performance
can create. Because he is so interesting a phenomenon, he seems
less an impersonation than a character in drama proper or a "dramatic" novel, a view of the Pardoner that only tells us something
about our notions of "true art" since Henry James. But despite his
fictive power, the Pardoner, in a strict and important, though by
no means diminished, sense, is the impersonation of whoever performs him.

Although as a character the Pardoner gives believable reasons
for the things he does—credible in psychological terms, Augustinian or Freudian, medieval or "modern"[10]—why he does them is
not, I believe, the concern of the Pardoner's Prologue and Tale.
The Pardoner is a bad man who can, ostensibly, do good things.
Such a formulation seems more moral than psychological; indeed,
it may even seem psychologically absentminded. But the Pardoner
is *not* in some ways surprising, though he is altogether compelling. Donald Howard has caught very acutely what it is about the
Pardoner's sexuality that so draws an audience to him, just because
Howard sees the Pardoner at an appropriate distance. "If the Pardoner is not drunk, not a dead give-away, and not the modern
stereotype of a homosexual, what is he? My answer is that he is a
mystery, an enigma—sexually anomalous, hermaphroditic, menacing, contradictory. He has a magnetic power of attraction partly because he is frightening and loathsome."[11] Howard's discussion of
the Pardoner is perhaps the most thoroughgoing I know of, and
what Howard has shown, and what I think he would readily admit

to, is how good a reader Chaucer has *in him.* He has taken on the moral and philosophical concern Chaucer explores through the Pardoner—what a certain psychological type can do with language.[12]

Lesser studies of the Pardoner's psychology than Howard's have often made what was intended to be self-evident in the Pardoner's character and behavior seem like the revelation of what was intended to be kept hidden. Thus the revelation of the Pardoner's "real" nature has been said to provide an audience with a dramatic irony—"dramatic" in the sense that it is all absorbing since the sudden and surprising revelation of the Pardoner's psychology affords an audience a greater perspective on the Pardoner than he has on himself. Kittredge, for example, has surely offered the most ingenious and probably the most influential explanation for what is called the Pardoner's Benediction, an invocation so blatantly "out of character" that some comment on it seemed necessary to him in 1893. The so-called Benediction occurs in a scene at the end of the Pardoner's sermon, where, after offering the Canterbury pilgrims his "forgiveness," the Pardoner offers them Christ's:

> . . . And lo, sires, thus I preche.
> And Jhesu Crist, that is oure soules leche,
> So graunte yow his pardoun to receyve,
> For that is best; I wol yow nat deceyve.
>
> (915–18)

Kittredge's reasoning for the violent change in the Pardoner's character runs roughly as follows: proud of his successful villainy, which his superb histrionic talent always supports, the Pardoner suffers a revulsion of feeling at the end of his sermon. His better nature, always kept hidden, finally asserts itself, and he speaks in earnest when he invokes the true pardon of Christ. But his holy mood is momentary; he catches himself and relapses into a wild orgy of reckless jesting, then sudden wrathful silence after the Host's counterattack. The Pardoner's moment of spiritual truthfulness has thrown him off balance, and he is reduced to paralysis because of the moral struggle within him. How much of his own psychology the Pardoner understands is unclear, but all of it, for Kittredge, is apparent to any attentive reader.[13]

Although Kittredge's gloss seems quite unacceptable today, the Pardoner's sincerity or insincerity, his self-consciousness or lack of it, in the Benediction seems an appropriate concern. We may feel Kittredge has overread—the Pardoner's "paroxysm of angonized sincerity" is in him, not in the text.[14] But the text invites such interpretive opening up, as Howard says. His explanation for the Pardoner's Benediction is no less psychological than Kittredge's, though because it is grounded on the idea of performance, Howard's explanation is easily recognized as being made *for us*:

A blessing is conventional at the end of a tale, but the phrase he [the Pardoner] chooses is scarcely formulaic or perfunctory ["I wol yow nat deceyve"]. He has made no effort to deceive the company, so that there is nothing outrageous in his saying this unless he had already planned the unsuccessful trick which follows. We do not know whether his utterance is sincere or part of his game. . . . Since the Pardoner is an ironist, it is in character that, having said "I wol yow nat deceyve," he should proceed to deceive them. What does it matter? If they only laugh, he can shrug it off as a joke. Yet he thinks like enough of them to suppose (perhaps rightly) that some at least would be taken in; and he is impudent, dares to confront and challenge them to be his dupes, either by buying his pardons like fools or joining him in an intimate joke against the fools who buy. It is a perfect piece of bravado, for he can pretty well count on the one or the other response.[15]

Because the Pardoner is an ironist and his performance is self-parody, as Howard says, the Benediction pins nothing on him. About that I agree. The Pardoner "with his own irony challenges us to take an ironic view of him, and scarcely anyone has met the challenge."[16]

In Chaucer's day, the Pardoner's Benediction would itself have been performed, and impersonations, as we know, are not *dramatis personae*. As a self-parodying ironist, the Pardoner is supposed to come undone. Thus the Pardoner as impersonation is believable *not* because he makes us forget that someone is doing an impersonation. Rather, he derives his fictive power, his effect on us, because "he knows" that he is feigned—we are expected, indeed invited, to see through him. Thus dramatic irony serves form and the experience of reading. Everyone, including a performer, enjoys the performance—the more histrionic, the more demonic the better. Like Howard's Pardoner, mine is also compelling and playful, perhaps, even as Howard suggests, playful because he is compelled to play. I can certainly imagine the Pardoner's performance, as Howard describes it, actually done. Indeed, the Pardoner's challenging virtuosity and what an audience hears of his performance allow the Pardoner to say what is, after all, only the simple truth, as everyone knows—that Christ's pardon is best.

There was probably no general agreement, even among members of the medieval audience who first heard the Pardoner's Prologue and Tale, about when the storyteller, perhaps Chaucer himself, was reading *in his voice as storyteller* and when he was impersonating the Pardoner. Extra-verbal devices, such as eye movement or hand gestures, as we know, enable a performer to dissimulate almost hypnotically. Confusion of voice is inherently part of any performance. Thus the Pardoner's Benediction is as much a performer's as it is the Pardoner's. Insofar as it is the Pardoner's, the Benediction may sound like something else—a parody of doctrine, a mockery of it, or even a curse. Insofar as it is a performer's, it is a statement of doctrine, obviously true. Confusion of person may be an obstacle in assigning, or attempting to assign, lines to any one character, the storyteller included, though it is not a serious handicap in following a text. Forgetting and remembering in performance presents no real confusion to an audience, though it is an engaging difficulty. The imaginary drama that takes place in the minds of those who read is always breaking down and beginning again. Even a single line can have two speakers, for all the lines the performer declaims have an abstract and independent existence before they have a "real voice." It is as if they are uttered first and then assigned to a speaker both by the storyteller and by anyone who hears or imagines him. The problem of the relationship between language and speaker is itself one of the concerns of the Pardoner's Prologue and Tale—that is, how can a good sermon, when delivered as a put-on, do good?[17] In general we are perhaps unaccustomed to thinking of language as having an existence in the world of ideas apart from men, so that an evil man is assumed to be able to say only evil things. With our antimetaphysical bias, we immediately put language into someone's head. We do not usually imagine language looking for a speaker, but rather as already having one. The Pardoner's Prologue and Tale, however, keeps a distinction between language and speaker that we may have lost.[18]

That Christ's pardon is best is not a lie. The Pardoner is not deceiving the pilgrims when he points out the difference between it and his own pardon. His insisting on this distinction is, of course, what confuses those who would read all of the Pardoner's Prologue and Tale (the "Pardoner's 'Prologue'") in light of what they hypothesize about the Pardoner's psychology apart from "his performance," because it seems to be a distinction which the Pardoner, if he were "true" to his psychological nature, could not make, unless it were a ploy (which it is not).[19] The Pardoner has, moreover, told all the pilgrims that his pardon, unlike Christ's, is false (which is true). In this respect he has not deceived the pilgrims either. He is, it appears, perfectly honest.

There is, moreover, a suggestion of intentional verbal play in a section of the Pardoner's Tale preceding the Benediction, and anticipating it, that asks audiences to distinguish between kinds of curing. Because the Pardoner is a feigned preacher through whom Chaucer, I believe, is examining the nature of performance, religious and artistic, the Pardoner can equivocate without our imagining any psychological trauma on his part. Thus while the Pardoner claims his "pardoun may yow alle warice" (906), he affirms that only Christ is "oure soules leche" (916). The Pardoner can, he says, "cure" men of avarice by tricking them into giving him money, but the use of the word "warice" is purposefully misleading. It demands that audiences struggle with the Pardoner's equivocation. He goes free. The Pardoner does not cure or heal men of sin, like Christ—he admits as much—although he can give a type of cure to those who, in all innocence, believe him. He is a false physician—he admits that—but those he "cures" are not less healed because their piety has in fact duped them. They are not cured by the Pardoner—he is a charlatan—but their impulse to be cured may have been real and, as such, they are on their way to being cured. To be tricked into doing good—the Pardoner's language is good—is still perhaps to have done good.

Although the Pardoner cannot distinguish the actual spiritual state of a penitent who might accept his pardon—perhaps he would not want to if he could; he only sees the act—it is reasonable to assume that a penitent's intention to accept a pardon may be genuine; in any case, it would not depend on the Pardoner's judgment. The Pardoner reveals his confidence game only to the Canterbury pilgrims and Chaucer's readers, so that when he finally outrageously

offers the pilgrims *his* pardon, he presents them and Chaucer's audience with the full scope of their moral dilemma—to accept or reject on theological grounds what he so confidently tenders. To be
angered at the Pardoner because he has attempted to fool those
who may be true believers is praiseworthy, but it betrays self-
righteousness, a kind of narcissistic rage, that short-circuits the exercise of judgment.

The Pardoner as preacher is clearly duplicitous: he can say one
thing and believe something else. Moreover, he explicitly says as
much about himself at least three times. His preaching, he says, at
the outset of the Prologue, is merely rhetorical:

> "Lordynges," quod he, "in chirches whan I preche,
> I peyne me to han an hauteyn speche,
> And rynge it out as round as gooth a belle,
> For I kan al by rote that I telle."
>
> (329–32)

The verb phrase "I peyne me" is the giveaway. The Pardoner's sermon is "hauteyn"—loud, lofty, and arrogant. "Hauteyn" probably
refers both to the kind of speech the Pardoner would take pains to
make as well as to his manner in making it. Style and delivery are
bound up together in a performance that is never "from the heart,"
but mechanical or given "by heart." Moreover, the Pardoner inter-
mingles, as he says later, a few Latin words

> To saffron with my predicacioun,
> And for to stire hem to devocioun.
>
> (345–46)

"To saffron" suggests the idea that the Pardoner's performance is
cookery, and that what he prepares for his guests is a kind of food
they order for themselves; they are "stired" by what they get. In a
way the Pardoner's mechanistic performance—his rhetoric is masterful—is at the heart of, perhaps even the creator of, sociability
itself; his performance engages men in spiritually profound and public matters, though he is not, as he admits, a disinterested host. He
sees himself in his performance, religious and social, as both dove-
like and snakelike, calling, like the Holy Spirit from atop a barn (a
homely, even innocent, turn of phrase), with a serpent's tongue:

Thanne peyne I me to strecche forth the nekke,
And est and west upon the peple I bekke,
As dooth a dowve sittynge on a berne.
Myne handes and my tongue goon so yerne
That is it joye to se my bisynesse.

(395–99)

The idea of a busy tongue suggests both a facile and sinister performance; the idea of busy hands, like the idea of the Pardoner's sermon as a church bell (331), suggests an obviously ironic one. But as a prepared performance, the Pardoner's sermon *is* a summons to an action. The Pardoner claims that it can "stire" to devotion, and, to the extent that his performance is believable, perhaps to pious listeners, he may be right.[20] As John Halverson remarks, the Pardoner, "by virtue of his extraordinary histrionic powers, may well induce genuine contrition, however fake his relics and however bad his motives."[21] Even in light of his own moral depravity, which he admits, the Pardoner's conclusion

But though myself be gilty in that synne,
Yet kan I maken oother folk to twynne
From avarice, and soore to repente

(429–31)

is potentially true.

The Pardoner may not be evil so much as bold—bold with language because he is bold with the idea of language as skill, and performance as making. He distinguishes motive from deed and forthrightly raises the question of the moral efficacy of language considered as technique pure and simple. In this respect, he is no psychological puzzle. He affords an audience the occasion to consider whether feelings about a man who admittedly misuses words—good words at that—can be squared with what is a religious and, as it turns out, plausible argument about rhetoric— whether genuine contrition effected by powerful language is necessarily qualified by the morality of the rhetorician who "moves with words." Chaucer has in the Pardoner's Prologue and Tale raised the question of the morality of poetry, a question as old as Plato and St. Augustine, and seems to suggest that the morality of performance, religious and aesthetic, depends *not* on the morality of the performer, which would make us respond in light of our judgment of him, but on the use to which we put the affective power of a performance for the sake of our own transformation.

It is disappointing that some literary historians have not posed the question of the morality of language with respect to Chaucer's debt to the rhetoricians. A curious concern with art for art's sake has perhaps encouraged these historians to discuss Chaucer's rhetorical poetic simply as technique, neglecting an important issue about the value of human skill, and thus leaving the impression that the real question in the discussion of rhetoric in Chaucer is a rather trivial one: how is such and such a figure used? Robert O. Payne has explained this narrowness of inquiry as in part due to the weakness of the medieval rhetorical handbooks themselves, which modern critics, perhaps wanting to be authentically medieval in the issues they raise about Chaucer, have let guide them. "The analysis made in the rhetorical treatises is an analysis of causes in the structure of poetry, rather than of effects in the reader. Its ultimate aim was, of course, to instruct in the art of producing a poetry which *would* move its readers, and it is no doubt a limitation in the instruction that it has so little to say about how those effects follow from the causes listed, or what effects may follow." [22] Still the issue of the morality of rhetoric, its social as well as individual effects, is raised in the Pardoner's Prologue and Tale, whether or not Chaucer learned about them, or could have learned about them, from the twelfth-century handbooks. Moreover, as Paul Beckman Taylor suggests, the "Pardoner's insistence that public word and deed are not reflections of private intent"—his thoroughgoing nominalism—was an epistemological and moral topic in the Middle Ages (the "discontinuity of mental concept and its physical expression") neither confined to nor clearly addressed by the rhetorical handbooks. [23] St. Augustine is the standard medieval authority for ideas on words and intention. [24]

Not referring to his own sermon directly, though he explicitly implicates himself later in the passage (432–33), the Pardoner concludes:

> For certes, many a predicacioun
> Comth ofte tyme of yvel entencioun.
>
> (407–8)

The Pardoner's "predicacioun" confirms that a sermon of this kind can be good—that is, effective. Although his reasoning may "feel sinister," because he judges the effectiveness of his sermon by his purse, we can only assume that true believers may judge according to their faith. There is, moreover, nothing explicit in lines 407–8 to suggest that because the intention behind a sermon is evil, the sermon is, as a consequence, evil. An audience may feel not only that such an implication is to be presupposed, but that it is justified in doing so. The Host, after all, says he will have "Cristes curs" (946) if he buys the Pardoner's "relikes" (944), offered first to his dupes, if there are any, and then to the Host, whom he bates. To pay for absolution, in the Host's mind, consciously mocks Christ's Benediction (916–18), which the Pardoner invokes immediately before he offers his goods to the Canterbury pilgrims. And the Host's anger, a kind of Kohutian narcissistic rage, is, in one sense, admirable— simple piety that sees the truth distorted.[25] In Kohutian terms, the Pardoner has outraged the Host's grandiose sense that, as a pious man, he cannot be tricked into piety, that his omnipotent goodness can manage the impious. Indeed *for us* that piety *is* admirable, for our own healthy narcissism may also be endangered by the Pardoner's unabashed attempt at mastering our righteousness.[26] Like the Host, we, too, may suddenly erupt out of a need for revenge against someone who has injured our sense of wholeness. We are the "deep" psychological focus of the "Pardoner's 'Prologue.'"

Aggressions employed in the pursuit of maturely experienced causes are not limitless. However, vigorously mobilized, their aim is definite: the defeat of the enemy who blocks the way to a cherished goal. The narcissistically injured, on the other hand, cannot rest until he has blotted out a vaguely experienced offender who dared to oppose him, to disagree with him, or to outshine him. "Mirror, mirror, on the wall, who is the fairest of them all?" the grandiose-exhibitionistic self is asking. And when it is told that there is someone fairer, cleverer, or stronger, then, like the evil stepmother in "Snow White," it can never find rest because it can never wipe out the evidence that has contradicted its conviction that it is unique and perfect.[27]

In Kohut's view, narcissistic rage can be turned in psychoanalysis into ego dominance.[28] But what the Host may immediately arouse in us as we read the "Pardoner's 'Prologue'" not only guides but reinforces feelings of outrage we share with him, a self-affirming combination of thoughts and prejudices. We should observe here that Harry Bailly has not experienced any sanguine psychoanalytic transformation, however incomplete. His narcissistic rage merely happens and then disappears. But Chaucer has *not* made the issues go away just because he had given the Host a psychological volte face that happens in fiction. Chaucer's text demands we take on the mixture of rage and play in our reactions to the Host. That is just the point. The Host's irresistible righteousness, his passing Lollardry, is made all the more reasonable and difficult for us by the unabashed context out of which lines 407–8 come:

> For myn entente is nat but for to wynne,
> And nothyng for correccioun of synne.
> I rekke nevere, whan that they been beryed,
> Though that hir soules goon a-blakeberyed!
>
> (403–6)

Letting a soul "pick blackberries"—go on a wild-goose chase—is the Pardoner's idiomatic way of saying that he does not care if the buried souls he has saved are finally damned for having, as he mockingly sees it, sold their faith to fill his pockets. How right it is to feel, after these lines of colloquial sneering, that the Pardoner deserves, indeed invites, our anger. His "predicacioun," born out of "yvel intencioun," cannot be good in any sense because he himself is not.

But with respect to his preaching, the Pardoner is "both worthy and orthodox. To accuse him of false preaching is to take a heretical Donatistic position, for there is nothing false about it except that it comes from a 'ful vicious man.'"[29] Although John Halverson is correct on this one point, he has not put the case as fully as he might. His argument seems theologically narrow and ahistorical. For any audience the issue is not siding with the Pardoner, which is difficult, or against him, which is easy. To be angered at the Pardoner for having fooled true believers may be naïve, since the contrition he induced in them may be genuine, despite what he thinks. Nonetheless, anger at the Pardoner may be deeply felt because to be tricked into doing good is still to be tricked.[30]

Although the Pardoner and the Host literally kiss at the end of the tale (the "courtly gesture" of the Knight who likes "smooth surfaces"), their kiss is symbolic, too, of the "kiss of peace," signifying

Christian charity and brotherhood—moral and emotional judgment does not go away.[31] The Host's rage is stilled as suddenly as it happened, but a reader's rage may not be. The Pardoner seems not so much silenced by the Host, as silent and angry, willfully silent—sulky, really—not because his trick did not work—he never said he was not a trickster—but because the Host will not play by his rules, will not knowingly participate in his performance:

> This Pardoner answerde nat a word;
> So wrooth he was, no word ne wolde he seye.
>
> (956–57)

But the Host, who apparently takes the Pardoner's silence as a sign of his own victory—the Host "quits" the Pardoner both abusively and righteously—then says he was only playing:

> "Now," quod oure Hoost, "I wol no lenger pleye
> With thee, ne with noon oother angry man."
>
> (958–59)

Perhaps we are meant to imagine that Harry Bailly is as surprised by his outburst (946–55) as the Pardoner is by his own bold, reckless, and ineffective taunting of the Host a moment before:

> I rede that oure Hoost heere shal bigynne,
> For he is moost envoluped in synne.
> Com forth, sire Hoost, and offre first anon,
> And thou shalt kisse the relikes everychon,
> Ye, for a grote! Unbokele anon thy purs.
>
> (941–45)

The Pardoner seems to have offered Harry Bailly a chance to "kisse the relikes everychon"—there is a sexual innuendo here the Host picks up later—indeed, to kiss the Pardoner's relics at a reduced price ("Ye, for a grote!"). He even seems to command Harry Bailly to take the offer. Both men seem out of control in this exchange. Unfortunately for the audience, neither man helps anyone judge the case either for the Pardoner—apparently his expert rhetorical machinery cannot stir *all* men to devotion—or for the Host—his indignation, he says, was only play.

To my knowledge, it has virtually gone unnoticed that the Pardoner's Tale, unlike any other, ends not with a pilgrim's voice, but with Chaucer's.[32] The uniqueness of the ending shifts the Pardoner's

Tale, first, from the Pardoner's sermon to Chaucer's recollection (as a fictional pilgrim) of the interchange between the Pardoner and the Host and, then, because of its performative mode, which a medieval audience would experience firsthand, but which we only grasp as an idea, from Chaucer's recollection to Chaucer's performance now. With fascinating disregard for any idea of discrete voices, Chaucer presents himself *before* the end of the Pardoner's Tale to give us, with his wide-eyed and curious neutrality, two views of a single issue. The rubric "Heere is ended the Pardoners Tale" is in all manuscripts of the Pardoner's Prologue and Tale inserted *after* Chaucer enters. The effect on a medieval audience of the transition from "Pardoner's sermon" to Chaucerian performance is analogous, I think, to the surprise anyone reading a novel feels when he senses that he has caught a glimpse of his author and looks up from the book that has been absorbing him to reflect on the idea of his reading words on a page and imagining scenes in his head. It is a moment of consciousness we have all experienced and which we have all been delighted by, for it gives us a sense of omniscience and power.

By drawing away from the events of the narrative at the very end of the Pardoner's Tale, Chaucer thus moves us away from an easy judgment about either the Pardoner or the Host. He does not ask that we routinely judge language and speaker separately. Rather, he expects us to keep the distinction between language and speaker in mind as we judge both the Pardoner and responses to him, like the Host's response. Surely what matters for Chaucer in the Pardoner's Prologue and Tale are the values that determine the use and abuse of sympathy and antipathy, not the encouragement of either sympathy or anger for its own sake. The distancing at the end of the Pardoner's Tale is an example of a characteristically Chaucerian technique, giving us something of Chaucer's intention about the way we are to *use* his text. Whatever he is—philosophical, humane—Chaucer is not a sensationalist. He can create rhetorical exuberance, like the ending of the Pardoner's Tale from line 915 on, when the Pardoner plainly says that Christ's forgiveness, not his own, is best. But then Chaucer anticipates that the intellect will not so much check as augment by tempering—by being itself— whatever responses are necessarily felt, whatever responses are left to us only after the narrative "has happened." In this way, an

audience is drawn into the story to finish it—to mirror, as Howard
suggests, the "funny charade of charity" that we see embodied in
the narrator's "puppyish enthusiasms for everybody, good and bad
alike."[33] If we begin to grasp something of the idea of wide-eyed
neutrality at the end of the Pardoner's Tale, we come to it through
the exercise of judgment about an evil man and his "good" sermon.
We perhaps learn, in St. Augustine's dictum, to love the man
but hate his evil, no easy kind of lesson in charity that makes the
Chaucerian text a mirror for us. Thus Chaucer helps us turn the
Pardoner's Prologue and Tale away from the Pardoner and onto
ourselves, despite the compelling ironies we may feel we see at
the Pardoner's expense. What is special about the way we handle
Chaucer's Pardoner is how fully we intuit the degree to which the
Pardoner is reflected in Chaucer as his storytelling counterpart in
the *Canterbury Tales*, not the degree to which the Pardoner turns
art on himself in his desperate "bid for existence."[34]

In a way, the Pardoner is perhaps Chaucer's *only* storytelling
counterpart in his work.[35] The Pardoner's performance is not merely
feigned; it is acknowledged publicly as feigned. As such, it is not
an illusion that makes us merely theater spectators, inattentive or
transported. The Host's abusive response to the Pardoner's playing
(946–55) does not spring from moral or aesthetic distance. "It tum-
bles out," as Howard says, "in images of excrement and castration,
a possible response whether the Pardoner were a eunuch or not."[36]
In one sense, the Host's rage is his triumph. He hears the Pardoner's performance as if it mattered. He is not alienated from a
performance he regards as an object of aesthetic pleasure—his
judgments, vividly aesthetic, are his own. And that is finally what
is always at issue in Chaucer. The Pardoner's performance turns
performance itself, mirrorlike, on the Host. His self-congratulatory
piety is served by it because it confirms what Harry Bailly always
knew about himself.

In this way, then, Pardoner is a kind of "open" performer. His
silence ("This Pardoner answerede nat a word" [956]) is not a sign
of his vulnerability to an audience who will not knowingly play
his performance, for the Host has responded fully. As a performer
the Pardoner is finished, since his performance has been evalu-
ated (valued) and judged (used for the Host's self-affirmation). The
Pardoner's anger ("So wrooth he was, no word ne wolde he seye"

[957]), given as a reason for his silence, may be as much feigned as his whole psychological performance was. It may even be imagined as giving the Host a cue to say that his abusive response, a true one, was also only play, an admission that, whether we think of it as true or not, renews the sociability among the Canterbury company ("al the peple lough" [961]), which the Pardoner's performance had momentarily made self-reflecting. Men who consciously turn their work on others as a mirror are not so much performing in the world as showing it, and ourselves, to us. Like Chaucer's "elvishness" in the Prologue to Sir Thopas, the Pardoner's playing is seen by the Host as antisocial—distant, observing, not playful. Though it is finally valuable and useful, it is, in a way, valuable *because* it is useful. The Pardoner is more thoroughly terrifying than Chaucer; our salvation, who we are, is wrapped up with our judgment of the Pardoner, our response to his words and our capacity, inherent or developed, to separate the two. The Pardoner and Chaucer both have marginal status in their work—the one menacing and parasitic, the other bemused and endearing. We hear no dramatic ironies at the Pardoner's psychological or artistic expense. His Prologue and Tale is pure self-unmaking, art through which we see ourselves. What is complex about the Pardoner's Prologue and Tale from this point of view is that Chaucer has chosen to explore the nature of art in a performance that matters. I can think of no other *ars poetica* that links art and its use, its social value and its morality, as engagingly as the Pardoner's Prologue and Tale. We can hardly avoid the concern of the tale—the condition of our souls. We are galvanized into response, but if we side blindly with the Host against the Pardoner, without seeing what our responses to the Pardoner's art, his *technē*, tell us about our faith and our theory of knowledge, we have not let the Pardoner's performance, Chaucer's performance as a storyteller, act in and for us.

Most stylistic studies of Chaucer, in particular the Knight's Tale, assume that because a style is conventionalized meaning, relatively stable over a period of time, it need not be governed by the context in which it may happen to be found or put. As Charles Muscatine observes, a style in Chaucer carries with it "an element of independence and integrity." It carries a meaning, or rather "an area of meaning" in the sense that it is made up of particular configurations of "literary traits, large or small," the meaning of which is not only understood, but understood over a period of time; a style possesses "an inherent fitness-to-mean." It can both give meaning and accept it and still remain relatively coherent. "A convention in poetic style, like other conventions, acts as a kind of orientation for parties to the convention, limiting and even defining an area of expectation or reference or meaning with security and consistency. It can be widely used and understood."[37] Moreover, because a style carries a conventional meaning that can be identified by a poet and be valuable to him as a tool, it can easily be put side by side with another style that carries an alternate and contrasting meaning.

Although the "mixed style" in Chaucer, as Muscatine defines it, is made up of the juxtaposition of the Bourgeois and the Courtly conventions inherited from twelfth-century French literature, a "mixed style" of any kind, not necessarily one that employs historical styles, can yield a structural irony: the perspective supported in the minds of an audience by conventional styles and conventionalized meanings juxtaposed "to give each other point and clarity" and "help define each other."[38] Philosophic irony is another kind of structural irony (the term *structural irony* has come to be identified with Muscatine's mixed style), which juxtaposes not the Bourgeois and the Courtly conventions but two philosophical perspectives, one earthly, time-bound, and limited, the other celestial, timeless, and limitless. To the extent that the Bourgeois convention expresses, among other things, a worldly perspective and the Courtly convention an otherworldly one, philosophic irony may be equated with structural irony and Muscatine's mixed style, although it need not be.

While the words *juxtaposition* and *perspective* are general enough, they are troublesome in a way. Stylistic studies of Chaucer assume that juxtaposition for the sake of perspective, no matter which conventional styles are being juxtaposed, is the distinguishing feature of Chaucer's Gothic art and, moreover, that that art is performative in an intellectual or mentalistic sense only. Structural irony in Chaucer is said to describe irony that results from the simple arrangement of parts of the narrative, whether or not those parts were read aloud by a performer or could be. Indeed, a private reader might even imagine the arrangement of the parts of the narrative as a drama, thinking of them as stylistic and conceptual (but sayable) idioms.

Although juxtaposition is probably too broad a definition of the Gothic style,[39] juxtaposition for the sake of perspective arguably enough characterizes Chaucer's Gothic art. Nonetheless, focusing on perspective and juxtaposition in Chaucer's poetry somehow leaves Chaucer without a subject other than perspective and juxtaposition, often of obviously opposing points of view—the worldly and the otherworldly, the realistic and the idealized, the particular and the general, all vying for intellectual ascendancy in a pure structuralist drama. Moreover, it is usually only assumed, and not argued, that juxtaposition for perspective is not only the *subject*, but also the *reason* for Chaucer's poetry: that the general structural irony that results is the aim of the narrative.

Muscatine is not, unfortunately, altogether clear about what Chaucer intended his audience to understand, assuming it perceived the mixed style. He seems to imply that the perception of a mixed style was, for Chaucer, an end in itself and suggests that because it was how Chaucer went about constructing his poetry, it can tell us why he did it, or what he did. Muscatine uneasily combines the romantic notion of style as the "organic" relationship between words and meaning—where style is content—and the Renaissance and neoclassical notion of style as initially dependent on subject matter, but independent of the context in which it may be found or put. Chaucer's writing of verse narrative, as Muscatine describes it, sounds like the "mechanical" placement side by side of styles that *have become* their meaning and not merely the expression of it. Muscatine insists, for example, that the Bourgeois style *is* the bourgeois point of view and not merely Chaucer's "dressing up" of thoughts anyone might have in the language of the bourgeoisie. Muscatine has a curious tendency to make it sound as if Chaucer's narratives, built out of Bourgeois and Courtly "blocks," are writing themselves.

Furthermore, Muscatine argues that there is, paradoxically, no resolution to the structural irony a reader perceives in Chaucerian narrative: the juxtaposed meaning supported by two conventional styles contributes "to the creation of new, compound meaning" and "an unresolved dialectic" is established, both in the work and in the reader's perception of the work, in which the mind, the scene of a pure drama of ideas, delights, with a kind of pure perception.[40] Muscatine claims that Chaucer is being ironic about his ironies, and that there may be an infinite resonance to his seemingly rather simple juxtapositions. For Muscatine, mixedness in Chaucer is a mechanical way to achieve organic capaciousness, the quality Chaucer is admired for.

Even if we accept the assumption that conventional style not only gives meaning but is, at least partly, the meaning, there is perhaps another way to look at the idea of dramalike mixedness in Chaucer. What may be juxtaposed in a mixed style may not be opposites, but inclusives. The fact that an audience may perceive first the worldly perspective in Chaucer and then the otherworldly is not ironic, for example, except in the sense that the word *irony* is used to describe what may be surprise at recognizing that perspectives not only can be altered, but ought to be, because they are limited. To characterize a reaction to a change in perspective—a perception of incongruity—as irony is only human. Irony is the condition of men in a world they imagine ruled only by fortune, or the habit of mind of readers who do not acknowledge that an otherworldly perspective incorporates a worldly one. *Irony* is a word in fortune's vocabulary. It is not an appropriate word to describe the perception of what are, in fact, two perspectives, one of which comprehends the other, unless irony means the enlargement of perception. In short, to perceive an irony in Chaucer is to correct for it automatically. It surely represents a failure of vision on the part of any critic to dwell on the ironic juxtaposition of double perspectives in Chaucer, to assume that Chaucer meant his audience to be content with only half the truth—simply the perception of two points of view. It is only the modern amusement with the idea of precariousness that limits Chaucerians from acknowledging that incongruity resolves itself. Ironies, for whatever they are worth in Chaucer, are temporary.[41] And their resolution, or completion, makes of the drama of mixedness a drama in which *it matters* to the reader and to Chaucer that ironies are resolved. It is in fact *between* a text and a reader that a Chaucerian tale occurs, even a tale that looks like a drama of pure styles or idioms or ideas—a structuralist's game.

The Knight's Tale, in particular Theseus's First Mover speech (2987–3074), illustrates some of the challenges of pursuing a study of structural irony, as I understand it, in Chaucer, since it does not seem at first glance to be a performance—for example, unlike the Pardoner's Tale, the Knight's Tale has no elaborate and elaborating prologue. Indeed, no summary statement about the tale can be made in terms of the static juxtaposition of two opposing points of view. The contradictions in the Knight's Tale cannot be isolated—put poles apart—in order to show how two points of view are juxtaposed in an ironic—a precarious, though never collapsing—balance. The Knight's Tale is not "'a philosophical romance' which raises the problem of an apparently unjust and disorderly universe,"[42] because with its insistence on resolution, it does not rest merely on the statement of a problem. Even where, as in Theseus's speech, the Knight's Tale is supposed to show that what "appeared to be the operation of blind Fortune is . . . the working of Providence,"[43] it does not altogether succeed. The audience is left with inconclusive "proof." Theseus's speech, far from being a simple and plain exposition of Boethian consolation—it begins confidently enough—eventually moves from a just restatement of Boethius to a statement of practical Stoic wisdom about how we ought to live in this world, but the "move backwards" is an obvious retreat from Christian consolation *for which an audience would consciously correct.* The retreat in the Knight's Tale is countered by readers who amend it, resolve the imbalance or irony of it—that is, "complete" it.

Boethius is clearly the source both for the opening reference to

> The Firste Moevere of the cause above,
> Whan he first made the faire cheyne of love,
> (2987–88)

and the repetition of that same idea some six lines later:

> "That same Prince and that Moevere," quod he, [Theseus],
> "Hath stablissed in this wrecched world adoun
> Certeyne dayes and duracioun
> To al that is engendred in this place,
> Over the whiche day they may nat pace,
> Al mowe they yet tho dayes wel abregge."
>
> (2994–99)

The stable and eternal chain of love comprehends death, which is as necessary to the stability and eternality of the chain as God's love is. If men simply look at the natural world, Theseus says, it will be evident that the universe is a "cheyne of love." No philosophical authorities are needed; no book learning is required as proof:

> Ther nedeth noght noon auctoritee t'allegge,
> For it is preeved by experience.
>
> (3000–3001)

Theseus's speech not only argues for the naturalness and rationality of the way things seem, but also for the stability and eternality of the First Mover who made things the way they are. In both cases, the argument is the same; all men need do is look at the world in which they live, "read" it, like a book, and gather its *exempla*, which teach the truth so plainly. The analogy between reading a book, or an authority who has written a book, and "reading" nature, as if it were a book, and therefore God who wrote the book of nature, is not meant to confuse what are two very different kinds of appeals to authority. The analogy, common enough in medieval thinking, is not helpful. Proof, as Theseus understands it, is a two-part self-evident analogy in the form "as below, so above"; a survey of the world leads, first, to a conclusion about its natural and rational order and then to a conclusion about the stability of the Creator who, in so loving a fashion, set the world "moving" coherently. The argument may be circular, but that is not the point. Whatever is circular about such an argument—it postulates a closed universe whose Creator cares about what He has created—is exactly the kind of consolation one wants to derive from it.

Although Theseus retreats in crucial ways from his happy conclusion, it is not because it is illogical, which it is, but because it becomes for him emotionally untenable, something altogether different. The naturalness and rationality of life and death become for Theseus a necessity men must endure. What has changed is Theseus's attitude toward naturalness and rationality, not the idea of nature and reason:

> Thanne is it wysdom, as it thynketh me,
> To maken vertu of necessitee,
> And take it weel that we may nat eschue,
> And namely that to us alle is due.
>
> (3041–44)

Theseus admits that men "grucchen" about this wretched world and in fact uses the verb twice in elaborate and specific rhetorical questions that imply that men are naturally anxious about the fact

of death. Still, he confidently asserts—perhaps too confidently—
that men ought not be anxious, since it is both folly to doubt the
truth (3045) and willfulness to rebel against "hym that al may gye"
(3046).

The change in Theseus's view of his own argument has never,
so far as I am aware, been ascribed to a change in Theseus's nature, psychological or otherwise. Indeed, the problem of coherent
psychological characterization is usually not raised either for the
Knight or for any of the characters in the Knight's Tale.[44] To say
"Theseus says" or "Theseus argues" is natural enough, but using
such locutions should not imply that what Theseus says or argues
reflects what he is or is not. The shift in Theseus's view of Boethian
consolation is emotional and not logical, but it affords the audience,
not Theseus, an opportunity to gauge responses to both the logic
and emotion of Boethian consolation, which may convince on one
level but not on another. Thus the place in the Knight's Tale where
a resolution of the philosophical themes occurs is the intellectual "space" between the tale and the audience. Theseus's retreat
leaves the Knight's Tale philosophically unfinished but for the cooperation of an audience.

Theseus's speech offers two kinds of consolation. It asserts both
the happy orderliness of the universe, which is self-evident, and the
sad inevitability of universal order: the best way to live in a world
where change and death are unavoidable is to bear up bravely. The
chain of love is both a chain of order and a chain of necessity. Moreover, because of its emotional context, Theseus's speech seems to
suggest that although the universe is rational in the abstract, the
closer death comes, either to oneself or to someone one knows,
the harder it becomes to make death seem rational; not that the
universe is, in fact, irrational, but that we are perhaps less clear-
headed about our reasoning (which is sound) the closer we look.
Thus the psychological retreat from the consolation of a logical and
necessary world entails a call for practical wisdom, the poignant
language of heroism that Theseus employs everywhere. In eulogiz-
ing Arcite, for example, Theseus explains:

> And certeinly a man hath moost honour
> To dyen in his excellence and flour,
> Whan he is siker of his goode name;

> Thanne hath he doon his freend, ne hym, no shame.
> And gladder oghte his freend been of his deeth,
> Whan with honour up yolden is his breeth,
> Than whan his name apalled is for age,
> For al forgeten is his vassellage.
>
> (3047–54)

Although Theseus's speech is not a direct answer to Palamon's arraignment of Divine Providence at the end of book 1, it nevertheless attempts to console us in answer to a similar kind of complaint against nature. It seems, moreover, at least at the end, to put the question of making a virtue of necessity in language that Palamon used when he, both literally and figuratively, found himself imprisoned and began reasoning, not altogether successfully, on the problem of God's foreknowledge and man's free will:

> The answere of this lete I to dyvynys,
> But wel I woot that in this world greet pyne ys.
>
> (1323–24)

Stoically, and perhaps bitterly, Palamon retreats to the sombre, generalized, and matter-of-fact pessimism that Theseus, no theologian himself, expresses in the face of Arcite's death.

Of all the characters in the Knight's Tale, only Egeus

> That knew this worldes transmutacioun,
> As he hadde seyn it chaunge bothe up and doun,
> Joye after wo, and wo after gladnesse
>
> (2839–41)

can comfort Theseus when he sees Arcite's cold body. What Egeus does is show Theseus "ensamples and liknesse" (2842) similar to the examples of mutability that Theseus, at Arcite's funeral, will draw upon from his reading of the book of nature. Although Egeus's consolation is in substance Boethian, its cast is Stoic. We can perhaps hear a modified two-part retreat in Egeus's consolation from the logical and rational exposition

> "Right so ther lyvede never man," he seyde,
> "In al this world, that som tyme he ne deyde"
>
> (2845–46)

to the darker recognition that inexorable logic is not necessarily a support:

> "This world nys but a thurghfare ful of wo,
> And we been pilgrymes, passynge to and fro.
> Deeth is an ende of every worldly soore."
>
> (2847–49)

What is surprising to critics who have taken their surprise as evidence that the Knight's Tale is "problematic" is that Boethian consolation in the tale finally sounds more like Stoicism, with which it has logical, historical, and perhaps emotional affinities, than like Christianity, with which it is usually associated in Chaucer. Theseus appears to take Boethian consolation in the wrong direction: back to the pessimism, albeit dignified, ceremonial, and even chivalric, that seeks consolation in a violent world, rather than in the happy and prophetic anticipation of a revelation that will make "classic" Boethian equilibrium a psychological truth.

The difficulties of Theseus's speech as I have sketched them should not lead to a statement about structural ironies in the Knight's Tale. Even if we assume that Theseus's retreat from Boethian equilibrium is ironic, we should not also assume that the perception of disequilibrium defines what the narrative is about. The resolution of the Knight's Tale requires the natural cooperation of an audience that hears the insufficiency of Theseus's consolation. The Knight's Tale affords Chaucer an occasion to explore a non-Christian view of the world and to allow an audience the possibility of amending it. Among critics, C. David Benson, in an early article, has perhaps come closest to my view of the Knight's Tale as a narrative whose explicit philosophy is completed by Chaucer's audience pursuing the implicit logic of the tale—that Boethian consolation should necessarily foreshadow Christianity. Although Benson does not discuss the Knight's Tale as a performance, he does conclude that even a private reader will recognize that "the poem raises more questions about the meaning of human life than it is capable of solving; its ideal of chivalry is not begun but fulfilled by Christianity. The First Mover speech does not itself transcend the poem's pagan tragic view of life, yet it points in the direction from which this change is to come." [45]

If the Knight's Tale encourages conversion, it requires the intellectual cooperation of an audience to change perspectives.[46] A medieval reader may not have heard the Knight's Tale as problematic,
though he might anticipate imaginatively the direction in which
Theseus's speech should move. After all, such a reader might know,
if not believe, how Christianity "consoles" Boethian consolation.
Not that a medieval reader would condemn the Knight's Tale; its
heroic appraisal of this world is not wrong. Any reader might, however, fulfill the promise of the tale's philosophical consolation by
pursuing the implications and retreats of Theseus's speech. As an
imaginative experience, pursuing philosophical half-truths in the
Knight's Tale does in fact bring about Boethian consolation. It
would be wrong to see the Knight's Tale as a test of the orthodoxy of
anyone in Chaucer's audience. But to see only the way in which the
Knight's Tale is philosophically limited is to stress it as a work of
irony, for it is to divide the tale into its philosophical parts in the
interests of analysis. In this case, however, to dissect is to murder
it. The Knight's Tale is not problematic. It is only incomplete.

Although the retreat from Boethian consolation is a move any
virtuous pagan might make, the benefit of Christianity, which we
possess, would surely render the choice of a retreat from Boethian
poise to Stoic practical wisdom—a makeshift pessimism—the less
happy and the less "truthful" consolation. Chaucer's audience could
naturally correct the pagan half-truths of the Knight's Tale from
its own "historically advantageous" position. There is one minor,
but telling, passage in the tale, not a part of Theseus's speech,
which demonstrates specifically how an audience might amend the
Knight's Tale. The passage, an observation on the destination of Arcite's soul, has always been considered contextually problematic.
Arcite's last words, just before he dies ("Mercy, Emelye!" [2808]),
are followed immediately by the narrator's ingenious explanation:

> His spirit chaunged hous and wente ther,
> As I cam nevere, I kan nat tellen wher.
> Therfore I stynte, I nam no divinistre;
> Of soules fynde I nat in this registre,
> Ne me ne list thilke opinions to telle
> Of hem, though that they writen wher they dwelle.
> Arcite is coold, ther Mars his soule gye!
>
> (2809–15)

But the narrator's caution has explained nothing; in fact it has made something more difficult to explain than it presumably should be. Robinson's note to these lines warns that "the flippancy of the remark about Arcite's soul should not be taken as evidence that Chaucer was doubtful either about human immortality in general or . . . about the destiny of virtuous pagans. It was characteristic of Chaucer, as of Horace, to seek in a jest relief from the strain of pathos."[47]

Although Robinson misreads lines 2809–15 in a way characteristic of all those who find Chaucer philosophically dark—he sees Chaucer's lightness of tone as a needful mask lest Chaucer openly wail—Robinson has rightly noted that Chaucer's hesitancy to commit himself in no way reflects religious doubt or heresy on his part. There may in fact be something deliberate in Chaucer's arguing that those who claim knowledge about the afterlife are necessarily speaking without direct experience. Perhaps the flippancy of the argument seems openly callous, but Chaucer must have understood that the narrator's coyness in refusing to commit himself as to the destiny of Arcite's soul puts the problem squarely before the audience. Some members of Chaucer's audience would certainly "feel" they knew where Arcite's virtuous and heroic soul had gone—a Hall of Worthies?—even if no one in the audience knows for sure, as Chaucer reasonably and amusingly points out (though that hardly matters since our imagination has already been engaged).[48] Chaucer's literalism is no accident. The audience is made to face a problem of interpretation the narrator says he is incapable of settling logically. The narrator's retreat into sophistics, of course, precludes anyone from assuming too much too soon, but it consciously opens for the audience the question of how one may intelligibly think about the tenets of orthodoxy.

Besides being a telling retreat, the narrator's ratiocinative move is also amusing. Before an attentive audience that may be looking for him to guide better than he does, a bemused storyteller reasons himself out of his reason. It thus requires the cooperation of Chaucer's "abandoned" audience to amend the Knight's Tale at this point in the narrative by filling in what the narrator has consciously avoided saying. Although some might see the expectation of cooperative reading as irony—Chaucer covering his atheism, which he reluctantly admits, in a passage of fastidiously logical burlesque—

other readers will, I hope, understand it as counterpoint—an opportunity to supply meaningful and truthful alternatives to a position only half articulated. Arguments for the reasonableness of life after death belong to the narrator; feelings for the truth about the eternal soul to the audience. Between them, the tale is told completely.

Chapter Six

Franklins, Nuns, and Jews

We saw in chapter 5 how Chaucerian narrative engages its readers to complete it—to realize its form and value by using it in self-revealing ways. We need, however, to argue for the historicizing of Chaucer's reader, a theme that emerged at the very end of the discussion of the way the Knight's Tale is realized by readers on the other side of an intellectual and historical divide. Indeed, the "otherness" of the Knight's Tale, its alterity even to readers in Chaucer's own day, makes Chaucer's readers of any day his engaged audience precisely because such readers know how removed they are historically from the Boethian consolation, partial and temporary, of the Knight's Tale. Terry Eagleton, whose sharp and stinging indictment of modern literary theory implicitly argues for a historicized criticism, can help us here. "Even in the act of fleeing modern ideologies," Eagleton writes,

literary theory reveals its often unconscious complicity with them, betraying its elitism, sexism or individualism in the very "aesthetic" or "unpolitical" language it finds natural to use of the literary text. It assumes, in the main, that at the centre of the world is the contemplative individual self, bowed over its book, striving to gain touch with experience, truth, reality, history or tradition. Other things matter too, of course—this individual is in personal relationship with others, and we are always much more than readers—but it is notable how often such individual consciousness, set in its small circle of relationships, ends up as the touchstone of all else.[1]

Notice the telling shift of pronouns in Eagleton's mordant description of the ahistorical apotheosis of the self as the "touchstone" of literary meaning and value. The "contemplative individual self" is an *it*, "bowed over its book" in solitary acts of connection with itself and the world it constitutes. I am sure Eagleton meant the ironic Arnoldian ripple in his use of "touchstone"; the modern literary self represents, for him, an image of ideological solipsism, however far into the world the self thinks it goes. One is reminded of the medieval definition of God as a circle whose infinite radius is merely the center of yet another infinitely radiating circle.[2] This medieval idea of "all there is" is precisely Eagleton's implicit emblem of the self-valuating self that embraces the world it really knows only *as the self.* For Eagleton, such an emblem defines the speculative sphere—phenomenological, structuralist, and psychoanalytic (all Cartesian)—into which literary criticism has withdrawn, becoming "a symptom, in its solitary, alienated brooding, of the very crisis [the retreat from history] it offered to overcome."[3]

Michael Ryan has shown, I believe, that deconstruction, which for American Derridaeans characterizes the infinite labyrinth of text and world, a kind of endless apotheosis of the self as text reading the world as text, where mind and world are self-referring commentary,[4] and Marxism both "point out that supposedly ahistorical ideas must take place in concrete history." In this light, Eagleton's idea of the state of the reader should itself be historicized. It represents our historical wish for a powerful, encompassing isolation. Eagleton's crystalline and biting commentary makes clear our alienated, essentially frightened, confrontation with the world we can only *want* to master. Our speculative isolation is thus a kind of intellectual domination of the world, an impossible bourgeois wish to exploit. Even criticisms of our supposed ahistoricity reveal their own historicalness and our own historical flight from history.[5]

Our own linguistic and conceptual practice is historical, and therefore, heterogeneous, unavailable to the idealizing desire of a supposedly sovereign subject to decide absolute truth as valid meaning and to direct action solely as conscious intention. For marxist dialectics as well as for deconstruction, the historical moment is the only absolute, which is to say that there are no idealist absolutes outside of the differential movement of history. The differentiation of historical situations does not allow a concept of truth which claims transcendent or absolute validity. Nor does it allow a concept of action which delivers the complex of conditions and effects of action into the control of a single subject. One can make one's own history only through history. Similarly, one's systems and methods are equally out of one's control. The mind is too much in history ever to master it absolutely through ahistoric taxonomies or nomenclatures.[6]

Perhaps Michael Ryan is right. Perhaps American Derridaeans have *not* appropriated the political Derrida for the reasons Frank Lentricchia suggests: that for American Derridaeans, and other post-structuralists, who have not broken (how could they?) with their Anglo-American formalism (an essentially bourgeois and elitist tradition), criticism is still "something like an ultimate mode of interior decoration whose chief value lies in its power to trigger our pleasures and whose chief measure of success lies in its capacity to keep pleasure going in a potentially infinite variety of ways."[7] Perhaps, too, it is a curiously impossible mode of self-understanding, because it confuses self-expression, which it sees as critical thinking, with understanding. In any case, Ryan's bridging these ideological rifts or pseudo-rifts leads to sure and certain ground: that there is no value-free, historically transcendent criticism.

Of course, Ryan's connecting polemics, and I think he is correct, do not *show us how we read as historicized selves*, how indeed the "prestructuring propensity of human understanding"—Eagleton's representation of the state of reading—offers us a model that at once respects "the radical alterity of the text while not ignoring the historicized consciousness of the interpreter."[8] Now such an overwhelming enterprise of mind does not, to be sure, soar or collapse with any sort of historicized reading of Chaucer. Nevertheless, I hope my explication of the Franklin's Tale and the Prioress's Prologue and Tale, two works usually read "historically"—as texts that illuminate, or that should illuminate, their own time—will be clarifying examples of the kind of historicized reading I see Chaucer encouraging: one that gives his texts a place in our history, as well as their own, and that sees such use of them as implicit acknowledgment of their value. For Chaucer, reading is grounded in history because we are, and historically engaged readings of texts implicitly show us how and why they matter. The Franklin's Tale is a case in point, in particular Arveragus's responses to Dorigen's confession. There are several responses, and all require a kind of speculation, at once personal and historicized, about Arveragus's motives—who he is as a fictional character and as a historical type—

and about our own projected and reflected motives, which Chaucer's indeterminate text engages. Psychological and historical speculation about ourselves and about Chaucer's Franklin's Tale demonstrates how meaning and value, as they emerge from reading, inform and confirm one another.

> Hoom cam Arveragus, this worthy knyght,
> And asked hire why that she weep so soore;
> And she gan wepen ever lenger the moore.
> "Allas," quod she, "that evere was I born!
> Thus have I seyd," quod she, "thus have I sworn"—
> And toold hym al as ye han herd bifore;
> It nedeth nat reherce it yow namoore.
> This housbonde, with glad chiere, in freendly wyse
> Answerde and seyde as I shal yow devyse:
> "Is ther oght elles, Dorigen, but this?"
>
> (1460–69)

When Chaucer's "worthy knight" (1460), Arveragus, returns home from "Engelond" (810), he finds his wife, Dorigen, as the text says, weeping, and, though only *we* know this, "purposynge evere that she wolde deye" (1458). Her first response to what must have been his puzzled and altogether innocent question "why that she weep so soore" (1461) is more weeping. The text (1457–59) says she had cried for three days and that Arveragus returned home on the third night. The text also abbreviates her answer (1464), perhaps to suggest she told her story amid tears so that the fullness of her difficulty—she promised to marry the squire Aurelius—might emerge. In any case, the textual abbreviation allows us to rehearse to ourselves the circumstances of Dorigen's fate and, in this way, to hear, or imagine hearing, the Franklin's Tale to this juncture a second time through as a kind of reprise before Arveragus responds to his wife's explanations (1465–66).

Arveragus's first response to Dorigen (1469) is not moral or virtuous anger at an outrage to his ethical or social code. He dismisses the dilemma with a question that diminishes Dorigen's concern for the truth of her word. Arveragus masters the circumstances Dorigen lays before him by dismissing them. His "glad chiere" and his tone ("freendly wyse") *may* belie other more personal or sensitive responses, but the text, perhaps by omission, only teases us into imaging them. Perhaps, too, Dorigen's response to him, which does not pick up his nonchalance ("Is ther oght elles . . . but this?"), makes us uneasy with Arveragus's prepossessing values.

> "Nay, nay," quod she, "God helpe me so as wys!
> This is to muche, and it werre Goddes wille."
>
> (1470–71)

Dorigen's playfully rash (988) promise to marry the squire Aurelius, if he removes the rocks along the coast of Brittany, is not, of course, God's will, but obliging grandiosity she thinks is courtly. Dorigen never imagined Aurelius would manage what she "complains" about:

> That swich a monstre or merveille myghte be!
> It is agayns the proces of nature.
>
> (1344–45)

Aurelius's power to remove the "grisly rokkes blake" (859) is, of course, magical, but it has the appearance of omnipotence. That, I think, constitutes the source of Dorigen's "noble" conclusion that she has but two choices: "Save oonly deeth or elles dishonour" (1358). Her complaint to fortune (1355–1456) thus rehearses, in her mind, examples of womanly honour meant to prove her distressed self-congratulatory reasoning.

> yet have I levere to lese
> My lif than of my body to have a shame,
> Or knowe myselven false, or lese my name;
> And with my deth I may be quyt, ywis.
> Hath ther nat many a noble wyf er this,
> And many a mayde, yslayn hirself, allas!
> Rather than with hir body doon trespas?
>
> (1360–66)

Although Dorigen's exemplary allusions—she answers her own question—do not in fact make her specific point, they do illustrate in a three-part pattern virtuous feminine conduct: feminine chastity (1364–1423), feminine fidelity (1424–41), and feminine fame (1422–56).[9] The pattern does not, I think, decenter Dorigen's argument that suicide is preferable to sexual dishonor ("I wol conclude that it is bet for me / To sleen myself than been defouled thus" [1422–23]). The pattern amplifies it by giving Dorigen's case for her own virtue a context, partial and staged, in which *she* can see

herself as a moral heroine and in which we are invited to see her.
Dorigen's complaint is a characteristically Chaucerian example of
collateral statement, where the voice of *doctrina*, precisely because it is partial and staged, encourages our assessment of speaker
and action. Dorigen's complaint enriches our assessment of her; it
does not make Dorigen herself a psychological knot. That would be
reading Chaucer for Dorigen's sake, not ours. I do not, for example,
hear Dorigen's complaint as either tonally disjunct or inconsistent,
as satiric, or even dreary. Indeed, even one of the most thoroughly
engaged responses to the Franklin's Tale is disappointingly narrow
in its manner of argument, though not in its illuminating conclusions, precisely *because* it takes Dorigen as the psychological center of the tale. Anne Thompson Lee makes a fascinating case for
Dorigen's wifely virtues, "her commitment, loyalty and deference
to her husband," her Eriksonian emptiness and her Beauvoirian
powerlessness. What Dorigen wants, Lee says, "is to have her
husband at her side, and without him she is lost." But Lee finds
Dorigen's complaint false—empty and misleading—because, for
Lee, "the Franklin's own middle class values prevail for the portrayal of his heroine," but fail when he "tries to model Dorigen
along the lines of certain classical heroines of antiquity in order
to give her a kind of class distinction which, in his sincere but
misguided notion, he thinks she should have."[10] Lee amplifies
Dorigen's visceral case-putting: now Erik Erikson and Simone de
Beauvoir, not just St. Jerome or her, and perhaps the Franklin's,
courtly concepts like "trouthe" (Lee's phrase for such concepts
is "shadowy chimaeras"). Because Chaucer encourages our historicized reading (reading and interpreting from our own time and
place), Erikson and de Beauvoir can be part of our intellectual context for Dorigen's speech. We should, however, question Lee's dis-
trust of abstract medieval formulations like "trouthe"—not because Lee ought to believe the medieval abstractions we know
Chaucer believed (I would not make Lee a historicist), but because
Lee simply assumes Chaucer and his middle-class Franklin would
not have believed them. Lee assumes too much. Dorigen's complaint puts her in a context that is intentionally multiple. Her case
for her own virtue, which Lee finds intellectually and emotionally
false, is both like and unlike the cases for the virtue of the classical
heroines she herself articulates. Her act of intertextuality is neither

presumptuous nor blind; it is provoking, and its broad and comprehensive amplification—it is intentionally a kind of grab bag—has encouraged Lee to reject it. Moreover, whatever we assume Chaucer's intentions were as a middle-class courtier of, as Lee and others assume, irrepressibly real and rising middle-class values, we can really only say this: that Chaucer encourages us to read the Franklin's Tale with values that must necessarily be our own, but that do justice to and account for the tale's, and Chaucer's, perceptions of the difficulties of breaking into and sustaining the concepts that explain it fully. That is precisely what language for Chaucer cannot do.

Lee's reading of the Franklin's Tale is thus not wrong. It takes the concerns of the tale seriously and amply demonstrates our antispeculative turn of mind: for us as historicized readers, the doctrinal abstraction of the Franklin's Tale is empty:

In the end, then, the Franklin leaves the stage once more to the shadowy chimaeras of generosity, sovereignty, equality, gentilesse and "trouthe," abstractions which he admires without completely understanding. We know, and Chaucer knows too, that Dorigen's truth lies elsewhere. In the solid workaday world she inhabits, marriage is not an idea but a living reality, where perhaps the most important home truth of all has turned out to be, not that marriage partners should have equal rights, but that marriage would be better all round if wives could count on their husbands not spending too many years away at the wars.[11]

If Lee's reading is correct, then Arveragus's quick response (1472) to Dorigen's distress at having betrayed the exemplary context in which she has placed her life is essentially a kind of welcome and renewing chauvinism. Arveragus retakes the marital command he never should have abandoned:[12]

> "Ye, wyf," quod he, "lat slepen that is stille.
> It may be wel, paraventure, yet to day.
> Ye shul youre trouthe holden, by my fay!
> For God so wisly have mercy upon me,
> I hadde wel levere ystiked for to be
> For verray love which that I to yow have,
> But if ye sholde youre trouthe kepe and save.
> Trouthe is the hyeste thyng that man may kepe"—
> But with that word he brast anon to wepe,
> And seyde, "I yow forbede, up peyne of deeth,

That nevere, whil thee lasteth lyf ne breeth,
To no wight telle thou of this aventure, —
As I may best, I wol my wo endure, —
Ne make no contenance of hevynesse,
That folk of yow may demen harm or gesse."
                                        (1472–86)

But Arveragus's responses are complex, not simply husbandly.
He reassures his wife with a performative bravery ("I hadde wel
levere ystiked for to be") and intellectual idealism ("Trouthe is the
hyeste thyng") that undoes him ("But with that word he brast anon
to wepe"). The text here juxtaposes the difficulties of Arveragus's
double response. It does not invalidate one by showing us both.
Arveragus is initially commanding—he leads with words that, I
imagine, he hopes will lead him, since they define his initial social
and moral code. But what he gives voice to after he weeps—for
having to send Dorigen to keep her word?—is not an idealism that
rends, but imagined shame at having the neighbors know about
"this aventure." The text here is teasingly oblique. "Aventure"
means "misfortune," though one hears "adultery." This implicates Arveragus in his wife's behavior since, by confidently enunci-
ating his own code of truth—more like a code of freedom—he
gives Dorigen liberty to live by *her words*. That is perhaps what
Arveragus weeps at. The text does not say. Thus we can imagine
that Arveragus is both unhappy because he *will* be cuckolded,
and because he *must* be, if he is to be true to his idealism and let
Dorigen keep her word (her "trouthe"). The dissolution of his perfect marital circle (no children, just the two of them) is the consequence of his own perfectly harmonious concepts.

The complexity of this passage in the Franklin's Tale (1472–86),
where we expect psychological reasons for ideological and rhetorical behavior (behavior that defines how the characters will act, that
defines the self as it defines the future), springs not from what the
text says specifically, but from what it does not say. There is nothing
in the passage that suggests we should think Arveragus is giving
voice to rhetorically empty ideas of truth and independence. Indeed, it is because we can take them seriously that Arveragus
seems complex. Moreover, social shame, to which Arveragus reminds his wife not to make him victim, is shame at having his personal marital code violated if others ("folk") find out. Perhaps it

seems as if Arveragus here is being purely social: that his values are bourgeois respectability and not a personal and aristocratic code of honor that would set Arveragus knightlike against a morally fallen world. But Arveragus, who only here gives Dorigen specifically threatening orders ("I yow forbede, up peyne of deeth / That nevere, whil thee lasteth lyf ne breeth"), wants more than middle-class respectability. Most readings of the Franklin's Tale that see its aristocratic values deflated by irrepressibly bourgeois ones take this passage as a proof text. The Franklin's Tale thus becomes Chaucer's commentary, sometimes ironic, sometimes nostalgic, on the middle-class use, narrow and naïve, of aristocratic forms— Chaucer's "irony" or "nostalogia" depends, of course, on the historicism of Chaucer's particular reader.[13] But although Arveragus wants the kind of social counterfeiting that betrays "no contenance of hevynesse" (1485), he says he "wol my wo endure" (1484) in private. He will thus not be comforted with social cosmetics, though veneers should comfort if Dorigen sees to it that no one guesses what she has to do. Arveragus should, in fact, have nothing to fear from Dorigen, who would want her to keep her word. What clearly constitutes Arveragus's "wo" is the necessity his intellectual coherence—his liberality ("trouthe")—requires of him: that Dorigen *must keep her word.* Thus what Arveragus feels as shame, and what has narrowly been taken for bourgeois values masquerading as aristocratic truth, is also genuine intellectual discomfort. Arveragus's ideas of personal freedom and social autonomy are for him, and perhaps for us, emotionally distressing. Arveragus cannot require Dorigen to break her word. That would destroy him, because he takes his idea of truth seriously. Dorigen's word guarantees his conceptual world. *Her not committing adultery* would constitute (be the sign of) his self-betrayal.

What looks like interdependence in the Franklin's Tale is really autonomy. The only value here is a personal freedom that depends on intellectual coherence. In effect, there is no social fabric in the Franklin's Tale other than the grand pursuit of ideals. Everyone is his or her own freedom-giving law, which seems both perfect and, as in Arveragus's responses to Dorigen, where ideal behavior has personal consequences, flawed. Adultery is emotionally serious, not simply morally wrong. In this way, the Franklin's Tale is complex. We take on both Arveragus's shame and his distress, since the

moral betrayal of love is as significant for him as the verbal betrayal, or possible betrayal, of ideals. We should dismiss neither
Arveragus's rhetoric nor Dorigen's exemplary complaint as manipulative examples of social climbing, as courtly lies in middle-class
mouths. Both are conceptual reflections of the ideals of social independence and personal autonomy that ideally constitute "harmonious" society. If, moreover, the Franklin's Tale is Chaucer's
commentary on the Franklin's appropriation of aristocratic values,
what the tale illuminates are values that describe emotionally
unworkable ideals, except in a world of happy endings. Indeed,
Chaucer himself encourages us to note Arveragus's emotional dilemma and intellectual trauma, if we have not already done so,
with his characteristic turn to us:

> Paraventure an heep of yow, ywis,
> Wol holden hym a lewed man in this
> That he wol putte his wyf in jupartie.
> Herkneth the tale er ye upon hire crie.
> She may have bettre fortune than yow semeth;
> And whan that ye han herd the tale, demeth.
>
> (1493–98)

Chaucer here acknowledges our difficulties with Arveragus. He is
"lewed," both wicked and foolish, and our "crie" may constitute a
range of distress—anger at his moral turpitude, sympathy, reverence, even wonderment at his idealistic purity, laughter at his
foolish knightly honor, and knowingness about its possible harm.
All such responses assume, of course, that Chaucer and Chaucer's
text (that is, the voice we hear reading, which is our own) confirm
these assumptions. The text itself does not, of course, confirm any
of our possible responses. It both asks us to hold off judgment
and hints that "bettre fortune" will befall Dorigen, and hence
Arveragus. We are asked to read on, anticipating the kind of wonderment that has initially lead us to distinguish, as best we can,
Arveragus's "wo" from his idealism—his private sorrow, of which
we see one manifested sign ("But with that word he brast anon to
wepe"), and his public action ("'Gooth forth anon with Dorigen',
he sayde, / 'And bryngeth hire to swich a place anon'" [1488–89]).

  It is, of course, Arveragus's complexity that transforms Aurelius.
Like us, he finds Arveragus a wonder just because Arveragus em-

bodies irreconcilable difficulties in a world that, thanks to Aurelius, will need to entertain such difficulties only momentarily:

> Aurelius gan wondren on this cas,
> And in his herte hadde greet compassioun
> Of hire and of hire lamentacioun,
> And of Arveragus, the worthy knyght,
> That bad hire holden al that she had hight,
> So looth hym was his wyf sholde breke hir trouthe;
> And in his herte he caughte of this greet routhe,
> Considerynge the beste on every syde,
> That fro his lust yet were hym levere abyde
> Than doon so heigh a cherlyssh wrecchednesse
> Agayns franchise and alle gentillesse.
>
> (1514–24)

Moral values are radically transformed here. Aurelius is moved to have "greet compassioun" for Dorigen and for her "lamentacioun," though all she says when he greets her on her way to the garden, where they were to meet, is that she is, unfortunately, going to keep her promise:

> And he saleweth hire with glad entente,
> And asked of hire whiderward she wente;
> And she answerde, half as she were mad,
> "Unto the gardyn, as myn housbonde bad,
> My trouthe for to holde, allas! allas!"
>
> (1509–13)

One can imagine Aurelius happy ("with glad entente"), though Dorigen seems not to recognize him. Despite Arveragus's words, Dorigen does make a "contenance of hevynesse" (1485). She laments her husband's forcing her to meet Aurelius. She is half-crazed ("as she were mad"). But if Aurelius is moved "of hire lamentacioun," it must surely be because he also responds to what he (Aurelius), and we, imagine is Arveragus's agonizing idealism. For Dorigen's "cas" is after all Arveragus's truth. For Aurelius, Arveragus is "the worthy knyght." Moreover, if we fear, as Arveragus seems to, that Dorigen's revelation of their unfortunate "aventure" (1483) will rain down bourgeois scandal upon him, we are wrong. Dorigen gives voice both to her husband's unwavering idealism and, curiously enough, to her own dismay. Her exclamations ("allas!

allas!") reinforce at least one of our responses to Arveragus's idealism: its compromising inflexibility. Arveragus's idealism causes
pain, and Dorigen is the voice of his harmful intellectual folly—his
truth. In exercising the idealism he thought would guarantee both
his and Dorigen's autonomy—Arveragus is the guardian of Dorigen's
"trouthe"—Arveragus has bidden Dorigen compromise what she
now feels is her sexuality. Dorigen's "lamentacioun" is surprising
because she seems not to acknowledge the freedom that Arveragus's
idealism ensures for her, the reason the Franklin gave at the beginning of his tale for Dorigen's and Arveragus's marital bliss:

> Love is a thyng as any spirit free.
> Wommen, of kynde, desiren libertee,
> And nat to been constreyned as a thral;
> And so doon men, if I sooth seyen shal.
>   (767–70)

She is presumably not moved by Arveragus's ideals. Aurelius is, or
rather he is moved to "greet routhe" by Arveragus's unswerving
truth. This transforms him, and he refuses to do "so heigh a cher-
lyssh wrecchednesse" (1523)—love Dorigen—when Arveragus
displays both "franchise" and "gentillesse" (1524).

"Franchise" here, I think, means "frankness" of an intellectual
kind. What Aurelius understands about Arveragus is his devotion
to the pledged word. "Gentillesse" means something more courtly
than "franchise," so that the two words together, as a description of
Arveragus, require adjustment. "Gentillesse" describes a nobility
of birth one associates with those of aristocratic lineage. To possess
"gentillesse" implies good breeding. "Franchise" describes an intellectual honesty that proclaims social autonomy, the complexity
of which Aurelius feels. If having "franchise" is an aristocratic virtue, Arveragus means something we would call being libertarian. It
is only because critics see the Franklin as *nouveau riche* that his
"gentillesse" is taken to be aristocratic veneer for his Epicureanism,
as described in the General Prologue ("For he was Epicurus owene
sone" [336]), and his hospitable landed self-sufficiency ("Seint Julian
he was in his contree" [340]).[14] But the Franklin's household is a
kindgom unto itself. Hence his "franchise" is a kind of privilege his
landed autonomy confers on him (*Oxford English Dictionary*, s.v.
"franchise," 2.6). In this sense, his "franchise" is aristocratic; we

would call it his inalienable freedom. "Franchise" also describes
the values of idealism that torment Arveragus the knight and enno-
ble Aurelius the squire (1543–44), for Aurelius out-knights Arveragus. Aurelius releases Dorigen from her pledge in the legal
language of a medieval quitclaim (1533–36), which suggests the seriousness of Dorigen's promise for Aurelius and implicitly acknowledges Aurelius's understanding of Arveragus's "trouthe." But the
emotional reasons for his releasing Dorigen from her pledge are
complex for us:

> Madame, seyth to youre lord Arveragus,
> That sith I se his grete gentillesse
> To yow, and eek I se wel youre distresse,
> That him were levere han shame (and that were routhe)
> Than ye to me sholde breke thus youre trouthe,
> I have wel levere evere to suffre wo
> Than I departe the love bitwix yow two.
>
> (1526–32)

Aurelius acknowledges *both* Arveragus's "gentillesse" to Dorigen
and Dorigen's "distresse." He acknowledges in effect our several
responses to idealism, the kind of freedom-giving social autonomy
Arveragus would preserve—his "franchise," not his middle-class
shame—*and* Dorigen's second thoughts about her verbal and legal
autonomy—she made the promise to Aurelius "in pley" (988) with
a kind of aristocratic abandon she never imagined the magic and
magicians of the Franklin's Tale would force her to keep. Indeed,
Aurelius mentions Arveragus's "shame" and the pity of it (1529).
But what he means is an aristocratic "gentillesse" that includes
"franchise" and that defines for Aurelius the love between Arveragus and Dorigen. We should note, too, that Dorigen thanked
Aurelius for having released her from her pledge ("a gentil dede"
[1543]) upon "hir knees al bare" (1545), hardly the position of sovereignty that Arveragus's nobility would guarantee for her at home.

My reading of the Franklin's Tale is, of course, of its own time, at
least I hope it is. I have responded, I believe, to the openness of
the text, its indeterminacy in any age; for my reading both acknowledges the otherness of the text—the conflation in the Franklin's
Tale of aristocratic values with an intellectual idealism perhaps inherent in that tradition, but in any case one that causes emotional

pain, or possible pain (the Franklin's Tale is all impossibility, all happy endings) in such a world—and the text's accessibility. The Franklin's Tale feels familiar, and I can appropriate it. Indeed, the one assumption I do make is that Chaucer intends to make it available to me as a constellation of invitations to reflect, not a constellation alien to me because it is of Chaucer's time. I can recover his "medieval" text, which surely was his hope.

I believe Henrik Specht is correct in showing that the Franklin is not a *parvenu* and that readings of the tale that see it as either an ironic or nostalgic commentary on social change are historical readings in a bad sense—that is, historicist.[15] Such readings tell us more about our sense of middle-class ascendency than about Chaucer's. Moreover, they are not attentive to Chaucer's social description of the Franklin in the General Prologue. He was often, Chaucer says, "knyght of the shire" (356)—a member of parliament for the county. Many franklins were knights in Chaucer's day and some were little less than magnates; all were wealthy and influential members of their local communities. The Franklin, Chaucer says, was "a worthy vavasour" (360), a feudal landowner below the rank of baron. As applied to the Franklin, the term reflects Chaucer's sense of the Franklin's "gentle" status, not his middle-class ascendency. Indeed, as Anne Middleton points out, the Franklin's Tale is not even an example of bourgeois nostalgia for a heroic ideal.[16] Rather, the tale imagines medieval life as the extravagant spectacle of personal magic. According to Aurelius's brother:

> For ofte at feestes have I wel herd seye
> That tregetours, withinne an halle large,
> Have maad come in a water and a barge,
> And in the halle rowen up and doun,
> Sometyme hath semed come a grym leoun;
> And sometyme floures sprynge as in a mede;
> Somtyme a vyne, and grapes white and rede;
> Somtyme a castel, al of lym and stoon;
> And whan hem liked, voyded it anon.
> Thus semed it to every mannes sighte.
>
> (1142–51)

The "barge" referred to here is a reference to part of an entertainment at a banquet for Emperor Charles IV arranged by his nephew, Charles V of France, in January 1378, part of an impressive theatrical illusion dramatizing the First Crusade.[17] The "grim leoun" and the "floures" and the "castel" are also illusions. Conjuring in the Franklin's Tale is the prerogative of princes; it represents power that displays itself as alternate creation. It neither changes reality nor dominates it. Rather, it is the exercise of absolute self-sufficiency that belongs to the Franklin's grandiose imagination. Like his brother's magician, the "tregetour" Aurelius meets in Orleans is also a self-sustaining magnate:

> Doun of his hors Aurelius lighte anon,
> And with this magicien forth is he gon
> Hoom to his hous, and maden hem wel at ese.
> Hem lakked no vitaille that myghte hem plese.
> So wel arrayed hous as ther was oon
> Aurelius in his lyf saugh nevere noon.
> He shewed hym, er he wente to sopeer,
> Forestes, parkes ful of wilde deer;
> Ther saugh he hertes with his hornes hye,
> The gretteste that evere were seyn with ye.
> He saugh of hem an hondred slayn with houndes,
> And somme with arwes blede of bittre woundes.
> He saugh, whan voyded were thise wilde deer,
> Thise fauconers upon a fair ryver,
> That with hir haukes han the heron slayn.
> Tho saugh he knyghtes justying in a playn;
> And after this he dide him swich plesaunce
> That he hym shewed his lady on a daunce,
> On which hymself he daunced, as hym thoughte.
> And whan this maister that this magyk wroghte
> Saugh it was tyme, he clapte his handes two,
> And farewel! al oure revel was ago.
> And yet remoeved they nevere out of the hous,
> Whil they saugh al this sighte merveillous,
> But in his studie, ther as his bookes be,
> They seten stille, and no wight but they thre.
>
> (1183–1208)

The magician here, I think, with his Epicurean hospitality and self-possession, is a kind of Franklin; his "hous" is his kingdom. Aurelius and Aurelius's brother, who disappears nameless from the Franklin's Tale after he and Aurelius journey to Orleans, lack "no vitaille that myghte hem plese" (1186), in settings the magician, Prospero-like, can summon and dismiss. We observe medieval life here as if it were a series of wall hangings, a universal backdrop, changeable at will, against which Aurelius finds himself ("he clapte his handes two, / And farewel! al oure revel was ago"). Moreover, the magician's images of life are really decorative ideas from books. The "forestes" and "deer" and "houndes" and "fauconers" and "knyghtes justyng in a playn" are aristocratic visions of the magician's private library: from his self, his hand, and his head. The magician appropriates images of history *from history* for his own self-enclosed kingdom, not to hoard his aristocratic panorama, but to share it on his own spectacular terms. In this competitive sense, the magician encompasses the courtly world in order to be its master. The Franklin's Tale represents medieval life as manorial decor: the allusions of power.

The medievalism of the Franklin's Tale is not unlike that of the Knight's Tale, although in that tale the heroic pageantry of "knyghtes justying" is performed—that is, described *as if* it were real. To imagine it is to deny it as a private illusion. What we notice in the Knight's Tale is chivalric spectacle that embodies, or tries to embody, civic game. The Great Tournament of the Knight's Tale is described in a style meant neither to mask military cruelty nor to transform it, but to stage it:

> The heraudes lefte hir prikyng up and doun;
> Now ryngen trompes loude and clarioun.
> Ther is namoore to seyn, but west and est
> In goon the speres ful sadly in arrest;
> In gooth the sharpe spore into the syde.
> Ther seen men who kan juste and who kan ryde;
> Ther shyveren shaftes upon sheeldes thikke;
> He feeleth thurgh the herte-spoon the prikke.
> Up spryngen speres twenty foot on highte;
> Out goon the swerdes as the silver brighte;
> The helmes they tohewen and toshrede;
> Out brest the blood with stierne stremes rede;
> With myghty maces the bones they tobreste.
> He thurgh the thikkeste of the throng gan threste;
> Ther stomblen steedes stronge and doun gooth al;
> He rolleth under foot as dooth a bal;
> He foyneth on his feet with his tronchoun,
> And he hym hurtleth with his hors adoun;

He thurgh the body is hurt and sithen take,
Maugree his heed, and broght unto the stake;
As forward was, right there he moste abyde.

(2599–2619)

What is described here is a spectacle of violence, a bloody melee, not a tournament. Medieval battle in the Knight's Tale is imperfectly assimilated to courtly circumstance. But such imperfections show us the telling illusions of a warrior knight whose brutalities of battle have no coherent form of public display *other than* the appropriated and misappropriated language of the chivalric tournament. Notice, for example, that King Emetreus attacks Palamon while the latter is fighting someone else:

Som tyme an ende ther is of every dede.
For er the sonne unto the reste wente,
The stronge kyng Emetreus gan hente
This Palamon, as he faught with Arcite,
And made his swerd depe in his flessh to byte.

(2636–40)

Emetreus, who may be attacking Palamon from behind, has grabbed ("gan hente") him—that is, surprised him—while Palamon is already preoccupied, which is no doubt appropriate in actual battle, but inappropriate to a tournament—the staged *idea* of battle meant as a ceremony of life, a kind of ideological acting out. In the Knight's Tale, however, such ceremonial idealizations are not an ironic mask for another reality. Although they cannot describe it truthfully or transform it, these idealizations are powerfully explanatory. What they leave us with is complexity of description (verbal decor) we must take on and disentangle. The medievalism of the Knight's Tale, like that of the Franklin's Tale, is magic—a construct of mind.

Now the Host's interruption of the Franklin is, I think, essentially rude, spoiling the Franklin's willful and coherent verbal surface, his illusions of power. It is in sharp contrast to the Franklin's diplomatic praise of the Squire's Tale and his response to the Host. Chaucer's text sets Harry Bailly's indiscriminate mixing of polite ("Straw for *youre* gentillesse!" [695]) and familiar ("What, Frankeleyn! pardee, sire, wel *thou* woost" [696]) forms of address against the Franklin's consistent politeness (my emphasis). I take the indiscriminate mixing as designed to exhibit the Franklin's command of the linguistic forms of aristocracy, his mastery of appropriate social performance. I hear no authorial irony here, no implicit social criticism, no revelation of the Franklin's social climbing.[18] The text describes the Franklin's poise and the Host's imbalance. Perhaps Harry Bailly's response to the Franklin only betrays the Host's characteristic impatience with others, including the Franklin—an example of the kind of narcissistic anger the Host always reveals when pilgrims on the Canterbury road, who do not share his canonical expectations of storytelling, do not respond to what a tale evokes in him. The Squire's Tale reminds the Franklin of the waywardness of his son and of his own aristocratic disappointment with the latter's ungentle behavior—his son is a wastrel; he gambles (690–91) and keeps company with those beneath him ("a page" [692]). The Franklin would have liked his son to have heard the Squire's Tale. Indeed, if the Host's dismissive response to the Franklin's wish for the moral use of the Squire's Tale ("Straw for youre gentillesse!") is a personalized social attack on the Franklin, the Host has surely sensed the misapplication of the Franklin's moral outburst ("Fy on possessioun, / But if a man be vertuous withal!" [686–87]), since it is his son's mishandling of his possessions that the Franklin finds distressing, not his son's refusal to be solely gentle—that is, otherworldly and aristocratic. The Franklin's distinctions are not clear, but that in no way makes him *nouveau riche*. Indeed, he betrays the disappointment with the worldly behavior of his son that someone with money and position might express.

Although Morton Bloomfield's reading of the Franklin's Tale is not historicist, but initially and perhaps finally aesthetic, it is curiously narrow; it does not acknowledge its own timely wisdom. Bloomfield does not pose any overtly historical questions to help him establish either tone of voice or Chaucer's social or historical intention in the Franklin's Tale, conscious or unconscious. But the unresolved current in Dorigen's indictment of God's power, a dark moment for her (865–93), represents for Bloomfield an instance of Chaucer's philosophical darkness, the "first example in Western literature of which I know where the horrible and frightening aspects of nature lead a spectator to question God's goodness." Moreover, the happy ending, "part of the great pleasure of the tale," clashes with "the fundamental quality of the first question it raises" in Dorigen's complaint against God; the clash "makes problematic the whole of creation, or rather emphasizes the problematic in creation." Bloomfield is clearly uneasy with the indeterminacy of the Franklin's Tale, though that, as I see it, is its point of engagement. Its ending, which resolves nothing ("Lordynges, this question, thanne, wol I aske now, / Which was the mooste fre, as thynketh yow?" [1621–22], a question Bloomfield finds "finally not very troubling"), awakens in us our often unarticulated need for happy endings. Bloomfield himself makes this point: "The plot of *The Franklin's Tale* satisfies our need for order in a rock-strewn world, for decency in a world dominated by sin and self-interest, and at the same time it reminds us by its questions that there are no simple answers."

Bloomfield's reading of the Franklin's Tale thus represents the kind of ahistorical criticism that, despite itself, gives us speculative, metaphysical connections: our own wished-for ahistorical brooding, which is in effect our history. Curiously enough, Bloomfield makes the Franklin's Tale matter precisely because he shows us how it presents us with our dilemma—philosophic, speculative, and moral (though Bloomfield does not seem to acknowledge the hermeneutical value of its indeterminacy). Bloomfield has explained the value of the Franklin's Tale for us—why we like coherent endings, the sense in which we are indeed unwitting historicists—but he is disappointed with the tale because it lacks majesty and seems to forget itself. Despite himself, however, Bloomfield has appropriated the Franklin's Tale for his and our metaphysical needs. He has appropriated it "from" history *for our use;* he has, in other words, made it historical again. Even his explanation of the resolution of the plot would make Chaucer's concern human rather than narrowly historical: "Chaucer may wish," Bloomfield says of the final question of the tale, "to convey to us the depth of human decency when faced with difficult dilemmas."[19] Here Bloomfield sees the Franklin's aristocratic play, his *demande d'amour* ("Which was the mooste fre, as thynketh yow"), as Chaucer's humanity, which only deepens the Franklin's Tale for him and puts it back in history for us. Bloomfield's view of the Franklin's Tale is finally illuminating because those who have read the tale "historically" have been preoccupied with narrow and difficult answers to historicist questions about the social status of Chaucer's fictional Franklin rather than

with Bloomfield's speculative questions. Even Specht's clarification
of the status of franklins in Chaucer's day, a welcome antidote to
our blind historicism, seems, curiously enough, much less engaged, much less central to our historical concerns and much more
thesis-ridden and sobering than we like our history to be. Specht is
no doubt correct, though his judicious scholarship will not, nor
should it, change the kind of questions about the past our imagination will always ask, since we are in history too.

The Prioress's Tale has not been read ahistorically. Unlike the
Franklin's Tale, it has not itself suggested speculative or philosophical readings—it seems completely of its time and place. Its treatment of Jews, however, causes sufficient psychological and moral
difficulty for us to have reread it—I should not say distorted it—to
accommodate both its values and ours. The Prioress's Tale thus
demonstrates how we have read a text alien enough to engage our
historicized consciousness. Now no one doubts that the tale expresses some anti-Jewish sentiments, though Chaucerians seem
obliged to identify whose sentiments these are (Chaucer's or the
Prioress's), not to deny them, but to explain them. Indeed, that
critical task has framed the context in which the general discussion
of the Prioress's Tale has taken place.[20] No critic, as far as I know,
has asked what we are to do with such anti-Jewish platitudes—that
is, no critic has asked what the value of the tale may be for us. Generally, critics have asked and answered questions of intention. They
have dodged questions of use and value in order to establish the
dramatic integrity of the Prioress's Tale. Even those who argue that
Chaucer is attacking anti-Semitism in the tale argue for the appropriateness of the tale to the Prioress.

The tale, so the argument runs, is the Prioress's psychologically
appropriate utterance, whether she knows it or not (usually not).
There is a persistent assumption in the argument for the appropriateness of the Prioress and her tale that her anti-Jewishness is unconscious—simply an unexamined part of her piety. It is implicit in
this assumption that Chaucer's anti-Jewishness is conventional.
"Unconscious" in the case of the Prioress means "natural," so that
the Prioress's blindness is forgiveable. We see what she is and can
exercise our understanding, certainly broader than hers, as benevo-
lent judges. As Florence Ridley explains, "Only from the Prioress

of the 'General Prologue' could we expect a humorless display of naivete, ignorance, blind, vehement devotion, and suppressed maternal longing; and that is precisely what we get."[21] Moreover, "in the context of his time and place . . . Geoffrey Chaucer . . . could not have had extensive contact with Jews, or have been taught particular tolerance of them by the English church, or have formed an impression of them from popular literature which was anything but damning."[22] For Ridley, the "social and intellectual milieu of a poem's origin often has a direct bearing upon its meaning; and when it does, responsible critics cannot ignore the milieu, but must consider it."[23] For Ridley, Chaucer's anti-Semitism is unexceptional.

Notice how establishing the appropriateness of the Prioress to her tale—that is, verifying the appropriateness of language to speaker—is seen as giving us a kind of artistic potency and moral clarity we imagine we derive from knowing, or intuiting, Chaucer's intention. We establish the congruity of character and text, which is said to establish the Prioress's, and perhaps Chaucer's, appropriateness to history. Her anti-Jewishness, and perhaps his, is of their time and place, and she, and perhaps he, cannot feel otherwise. What such assumptions do, of course, is give a kind of formalist and historical integrity to the Prioress's Tale, as if establishing who tells the tale psychologically implicitly makes clear why the Prioress tells it (how could she do otherwise?) and thus makes what she says a perfect utterance in the pure historical past. Again, even those who argue that Chaucer is *attacking* anti-Semitism in the Prioress's Tale, those who hear Chaucer's moral and artistic irony, argue that the Prioress's Tale is appropriately hers: her own "naivete, ignorance, blind, vehement devotion and suppressed maternal longing" now argue *against* her. Thus the tale's anti-Jewishness, seen as one of the telling attitudes of its certain historicalness, whatever we may think Chaucer intends, makes the Prioress's Tale an impregnable and imperishable medieval gem, a rhetorical object, and gives it an aesthetic radiance we should not seek to diminish. What Ridley and others want to establish, in accounting for the psychological complexity of the Prioress and the psychological wholeness of her tale, whatever they may think Chaucer intends, is the coherence of the text, its determinacy. They assume the tale is clear, and that its available clarity gives us Chaucer's intention. Even those who argue that he is attacking anti-Semitism through the tale make

its use for us aesthetic, or at least makes our historicist use of it
depend on its aesthetic integrity. We are asked to marvel in the
Prioress's Tale at Chaucer's humanity, his gentle vision, and his incipient moral grandeur. "But how great a thing it was in such a
complex social and cultural environment," R. J. Schoeck says, "for
a poet to insist that anti-Semitism could be viewed through the recognizable frame of such a woman as the Prioress, one who suc-
cumbed too easily to the worldly concern with things and manners,
and whose charity was too much of this world."[24] Thus Chaucer's
moral irony is seen as both unmistakably gentle and unmistakably
exceptional. If the Prioress's Tale makes Chaucer's art a praiseworthy adumbration of our own tolerant ideals, a historicist view of
the tale as an artistic whole that confirms our values, it does so at
the expense of the tale's artistic and evaluative complexity. The indeterminacy I observe in the Prioress's Tale makes it less clear that
a statement for or against anti-Semitism or anti-Judaism (there is a
difference) is implicit in the tale than has been assumed. There are
indeed indeterminacies of style, event, setting, and doctrine in the
tale, and in the reception of the tale, that invite the kind of engaged reflection on intention and engaging self-reflection we have
noticed everywhere in Chaucer.

We should observe, to begin with, that the first responses to the
Prioress's Tale within the *Canterbury Tales* are puzzling:

> Whan seyd was al this miracle, every man
> As sobre was that wonder was to se,
> Til that oure Hooste japen tho bigan,
> And thanne at erst he looked upon me,
> And seyde thus, "What man artow?" quod he;
> "Thou lookest as thou woldest fynde an hare,
> For evere upon the ground I se thee stare."
>
> (691–97)

Rather than simply describing the effect of the Prioress's Tale, the
text here describes Chaucer's incredulity at its effect. "Wonder"
suggests surprise, perhaps astonishment at the seeming transformation of the Canterbury pilgrims. "Sobre" suggests attentiveness,
perhaps reverential awe, a kind of hush that descends over the pilgrims who have listened and heard, though it is not clear, I think,
in what sense the tale is believed as a miracle of the Virgin. It is

certainly not stated that anyone's faith was affirmed or renewed or
even, for that matter, found after hearing the tale. Rather, an effect
is noted *from without* as a description of signs (theirs and Chaucer's)
rather than a revelation of meaning. The description makes it impossible to know whether irony is intended here, or if the miraculous
has happened. Chaucer's response is, I think, characteristically
bookish and betrays a tentativeness that encourages more sure-
footed responses than he has given. Only *after* whatever we imagine transpires during the pilgrim's thoughtful stillness does the
Host respond. He jokes, perhaps uncomfortable with the hushing
and, in his mind, antisocial effect of the tale. This seems to lead
him to notice "at erst" Chaucer the pilgrim staring at the ground.
The text is tentative about time: "til that oure Hooste" and "thanne
at erst." We are not told how long the pilgrims remained "sobre"
before Harry Bailly began joking, his response to the pilgrims' absorbing silence. Nor are we told when he finally noticed Chaucer
absorbed, according to the Host, in another and, for the Host, trivial and antisocial world ("as thou woldest fynde an hare"). As the
pilgrims' responses to the Prioress's Tale are opaque to Chaucer
(only signs), Chaucer's own inwardness is opaque to the Host. That
inwardness may tease us with explanations held back, but as a dis-
position of character, Harry Bailly finds inwardness annoyingly
comic. Nowhere does Chaucer make explicit how we are to understand the miraculous point of the Prioress's Tale, though he says it
is the tale of a "miracle." Schoeck's notion of Chaucer's satiric intention is, as noted, speculative and historicist. For Schoeck, and
other good men who abhor anti-Semitism, Chaucer's attack on
pious bigotry is crystalline.

But the images of Jews in the Prioress's Tale are not clear. They
are seen as both real and typological, having an existence in real
time and in Christian time. Indeed, the Prioress sees the Jews as
living witness to a schematized eternal moral opposition working
itself out in the world, as if history were a stage for revealed meaning if only we could see it. In this sense, the Jews are ideas. Like a
moral enemy, they menace the "litel clergeon" (503) who, singing
his *Alma redemptoris*, passes through the Jewish quarter of the city:

> Oure firste foo, the serpent Sathanas,
> That hath in Jues herte his waspes nest,

> Up swal, and seide, "O Hebrayk peple, allas!
> Is this to yow a thyng that is honest,
> That swich a boy shal walken as hym lest
> In youre despit, and synge of swich sentence,
> Which is agayn youre lawes reverence?"
>
> (558–64)

Robinson notes there is "strong manuscript support for 'oure lawes reverence,'" suggesting that "Chaucer may have intended to make Satan identify himself with the Jews."[25] Whether or not we accept this reading, Satan's identification as our serpent foe who has his "waspes nest" in Jewish hearts makes Jews Satanic. Chaucer's mixed metaphor—Satan as serpent and as wasp—is infelicitous only if we do not see it as an example of an emotionalism that disregards literal meaning for effect. The Prioress's style here is precious and aureate; her purity of concept gaudy, even violent. The Parson, too, sees the Jews as agents in Christian moral experience, which is always happening, always "now," but his tone is decidedly clinical. Compared to the Prioress, the Parson is matter-of-fact. What he says about the Jews does charge us emotionally. He uses them, for example, to reinforce his lesson on swearing: "For certes, it semeth that ye thynke that the cursede Jewes ne dismembred nat ynough the preciouse persone of Crist, but ye dismembre hym moore [by swearing]. . . . Thanne semeth it that men that sweren so horribly by his blessed name, that they despise it moore booldely than dide the cursede Jewes, or elles the devel, that trembleth whan he heereth his name" (591–99). The Pardoner, too, another sermonizer among the Canterbury pilgrims, and a far more vibrant one than the Parson, whose "sermon" is in fact a treatise on the Seven Deadly Sins, not a performance at all, mentions the Jews in passing to reinforce his vivid description of the tavern rioters at the very beginning of his tale:

> They daunce and pleyen at dees bothe day and nyght,
> And eten also and drynken over hir myght,
> Thurgh which they doon the devel sacrifise
> Withinne that develes temple, in cursed wise,
> By superfluytee abhomynable.
> Hir othes been so grete and so dampnable
> That it is grisly for to heere hem swere.

Oure blissed Lordes body they totere,—
Hem thoughte that Jewes rente hym noght ynough.

(467–75)

The Pardoner uses the same analogy as the Parson: swearing rends
the body of Christ, as the Jews rent it—by swearing one becomes
morally a Jew, figuratively crucifying Him. But the Pardoner, whom
we might imagine embellishing such a moral analogy, simply uses
it as if it were a moral and anagogical commonplace from a manual
on how to write sermons. The analogy thus amplifies the Pardoner's
sermon as it should be amplified. The reference to the Jews serves
the Pardoner's own demonstration of skill, not to mark him as anti-
Semitic in our highly charged sense, though he is histrionic as a
performer of sermons. The point is not that the Parson, as well
as the Pardoner, and Prioress are being anti-Semitic,[26] but that
the Parson's anti-Semitism, like the Pardoner's, is formulaic. The
Prioress's is emotional. The difference is telling. Like the Parson
and the Pardoner, the Prioress sees the Jews as the Devil's people,
and as such she acknowledges their necessary place in Christian
salvific history. Indeed, as Jeremy Cohen has pointed out, the Jews
as Hebrews—biblical Jews—were thought to be preserved "for
the sake of the Church, so that in adhering to the Old Testament
they might witness the truth of and historical basis for christo-
logical prophecy, and so that they might ultimately accept the implications of this prophecy by converting to Christianity at the end
of days. Although they now remain blind to this truth, their biblical
tradition offers cogent proof of Christian doctrine, enabling the
Church to respond effectively to its enemies."[27] The anti-Judaism
of the Middle Ages, distinct in Cohen's view from anti-Semitism,
only emerged in the thirteenth century, when the Church,

with the friars at the forefront, [made] a systematic study of contemporary
Judaism and Jewish literature and endeavor[ed] to demonstrate in public,
officially conducted disputations with real Jews that the rabbinic tradition
of medieval European Jewry could not be tolerated in Christendom. No
longer did Christian anti-Jewish polemic aim primarily at fortifying popular Christian belief, simply portraying the Jew as one whose obstinate ad-
herence to a literalist interpretation of the Old Testament prevented his
acceptance of Jesus as messiah and God. . . . The Church now depicted
the "living" Judaism of its own day as a heresy and perversion, a per-

nicious oral tradition of religious law and doctrine, a gross deviation from
the religion of the Old Testament. The Talmud not only, in the words of
Gregory IX, held "the Jews obstinate in their perfity" but also, with the
equation of the talmudic *goy* and the medieval Christian, proffered a real
threat to Latin Christendom. Toleration consequently gave way to the ha-
rassment of daily Jewish life, and the Jew in Christian theology, formerly a
relic or artifact, at once became real and incurred immediate and direct
suspicion and hatred.[28]

Augustinian tolerance for the Jews,[29] who were to be preserved in
Christian lands as proof of revealed truth, gave way to the assertion
that Jews were no longer biblical Jews since they had abandoned
the Hebrew Scriptures for the Talmud. Having rejected the Bible,
they could not be expected to provide evidence for Christian truth
as the morally fossilized, holy remnant in Christian history who
would finally convert.

   Cohen points out that only from the thirteenth century "were
Jews portrayed as real, active agents of Satan, charged with innumerable forms of hostility toward Christianity, Christendom, and individual Christians."[30] These, I think, are in part the Jews of the
Prioress's Tale. They have neither lost their typological place in
Christian history—the Prioress links them with the serpent, Satan,
"oure firste foo" (558)—nor their present and active evil—they are
Satan's murderous agents, his wasps. One can only make artistic
sense of such an aureate conflation of metaphors intellectually, not
visually (one reads allegory this way too), since the mix of reptiles
and insects is jarring. As serpents, the Jews are Hebrews and the
Prioress's view of them, like the Parson's and the Pardoner's, is
formulaically anti-Semitic. As wasps, the Jews are "Jews" and the
Prioress's view of them is, in Cohen's sense, anti-Jewish. Indeed, it
is the Prioress's emotionalism that makes clear her double view.
The Jews never lose their necessary theological place in Christian
history, though conceptions of them change—one cannot really say
"deepen," since the Jew as Hebrew always elicits more emotional
grace than the Jew as heretic and human. Even today, pious Christians can see Jews as the biblical people who deny the Savior and
bear witness to the truth of God's plan. They can, at the same time,
see Jews as willful outsiders refusing to be enfolded within a Christian kinship. In describing the difference between the Christian
and the Jewish views of pets, Marc Shell explains, I think, the

Prioress's seeming misextension of charity to diminutive animals, who are, unlike the Jews, within her kingdom of kindness. The Prioress can weep, for example, at the death or injury of a mouse caught in a trap (1.144–45) or the death or beating of "smale houndes" (1.146–49) that she feeds not with dog food but with food from her table ("With rosted flessh, or milk and wastel-breed" [1.147]). These demonstrations of the Prioress's "tendre herte" (1.150), if they in fact constitute her moral portrait in the General Prologue, are usually heard as if her exercise of conscience betrays lavish misdirection of feeling. Lavish, yes, not just because the objects of feeling seem inappropriate, but because the idea of injury to a mouse or to dogs evokes as much feeling as the idea of death. Lavish, indeed, but not in a special sense that seems to justify and support her misdirected piety, since the Prioress would extend "kinship to all extraspecies beings," as well as to all "extratribal human beings in such a way that all human beings become brethren in a single group." What is surely as interesting as the Prioress's emotional piety is her "disturbing slide from the extension of kinship to others" to "the denial of kindness to others." Unlike Judaism, where "there are human beings both within and without the Jewish tribe," Christianity "does not allow either for extratribal human beings or for extraspecies sentient beings protected by the rule of the covenant. If one is not essentially akin to a Christian, one is not humankind; and, as an animal, one has no *legal* right to be treated kindly; one is exploitable along with vegetables and stones."[31] If the Prioress's mouse and small dogs and "litel clergeon" are her kin, the Prioress's Jews are not. The way her piety creates pets is, of course, psychologically engaging for us; we can comfortably talk about irrepressible and insistent motherhood denied. But boundless piety can also create anti-pets who are, because they are *willfully* their own species and harmful to hers, deservingly outside a circle of care she would aggressively extend to them. They are no longer the *idea* of Jews who retain a significant place in her theology as witness to the eventual triumph of a universal family. They are actively their own kind.

Satan's speech to his Jews in the Prioress's Tale also betrays this double view. The Jews are "Hebrayk peple" (560) for whom the "litel clergeon" (503), walking among them and signing "of swich sentence, / Which is agayn youre lawes reverence" (563–64), is an affront ("in youre despit" [563]). Satan's speech as a rallying cry has a measure of nobility. Satan acknowledges the integrity of the Jewish community ("Is this to yow a thyng that is honest?" [561]), which, in the Prioress's Tale, is a "Jewerye" at the "ferther ende" (496) of which "A litel scole of Cristen folk ther stood" (495). Moreover, we should note that the "lord of that contree" (490) and his "provost" (616) are not Christian governors of a Christian land. The "greet citee" (488), in which both Jewish and Christian communities live, is "in Asye" (488). The Jews live "amonges Cristene folk" (489) but the "litel scole" borders the Jewish community. It is diminutive compared to the Jewish quarter next to it. In this Asian city, pagan authority rules.[32] We have thus three communities, each of whom has its own law, though Jews and Christians, minorities both, are allowed to exist and are governed in non-religious matters by secular law. As Cohen points out, Jews before the thirteenth century enjoyed a "measure of religious and civil autonomy," even in Europe. "Their theoretical right to live in Christendom as Jews—to regulate their own religious affairs, to solve their own doctrinal and philosophical disputes, and to determine their own cultural priorities—had not been questioned."[33]

The Prioress's Tale is set in Asia, where Jews certainly enjoyed communal autonomy. Moreover, their "Jewerye" in the Prioress's Tale is not a ghetto ("And thurgh this strete men myghte ride or wende / For it was free and open at eyther ende" [493–94]). Jews are not walled into it, and Christians and others can, and do, pass through it. It is, as it were, alimentary, snakelike, a kind of aesthetic and moral emblem of the Jewish entrails through which, as the Prioress says, the "litel clergeon" passed on his way to his murder by a hired "homycide" (567), a type of Judas—his death and his figurative entombment in the Jewish "privee" (568). The "homycide" stands for the entire community of Jews:

> I seye that in a wardrobe they hym threwe
> Where as thise Jewes purgen hire entraille.
> O cursed folk of Herodes al newe,
> What may youre yvel entente yow availle?
> Mordre wol out, certeyn, it wol nat faille,
> And namely ther th'onour of God shal sprede;
> The blood out crieth on youre cursed dede.
>
> (572–78)

The emotionally charged scatological imagery, interlaced here in an engaging display of aestheticized piety, describes the Prioress's own religious emotionalism. John Archer has rightly pointed out the typological treatment of Jews in the very setting of the tale. For him, the tale describes the theological battle between old and new law in a more neutral and conceptual way than has hitherto been seen in criticism.[34] The anti-Semitism of the tale guarantees the Jews a self-governing Satanic community against which the new law can battle. Indeed, for such a battle, autonomous communities are required. In this way, the Prioress's Tale can demonstrate the triumph of Christian theological history. The Jews of that "greet citee" in Asia are, for example,

> Sustened by a lord of that contree
> For foule usure and lucre of vileynye,
> Hateful to Christ and to his compaignye.
>
> (490–92)

Nevertheless, they are sustained, until, of course, the murder of the "litel clergeon" brings down upon the Jewish community the wrath of the "lord of that contree" through his "provost." For the Prioress, the punishment of the Jews confirms their hatefulness, and in this way the death and figurative resurrection of the "litel clergeon" transforms the world.[35] His murder, as Archer explains, is also a sacrifice, like the Crucifixion:[36]

> With torment and with shameful deeth echon
> This provost dooth thise Jewes for to sterve
> That of this mordre wiste, and that anon.
> He nolde no swich cursednesse observe.
> "Yvele shal have that yvele wol deserve";
> Therfore with wilde hors he dide hem drawe,
> And after that he heng hem by the lawe.
>
> (628–34)

The Jews are beyond the Prioress's narrow community of mercy, the "synful folk unstable" (687) for whom she asks Hugh of Lincoln to pray at the end of her miraculous tale. For the Prioress, the sinful do not equal the murderous. The death and resurrection of the "litel clergeon" are, to be sure, necessary for the Prioress's theological history. Her piety is historicized. Perhaps that accounts for the Prioress's highly charged description of the treatment of the

Jews. They are dragged about, bleeding and mutilated, but still alive, and then hung. Here is the sensationalist triumph of Christianity, for which violent religiosity is the transforming, outer sign. As John Archer explains,

Chaucer emphasizes the non-religious nature of the positive law [which condemns the Jews for the murder of the Christian boy] by placing it between Christians and Jews as the battle ground for the struggle of the Old and New Laws. Early in the poem the Jews are protected by the secular law, which as a set of external ordinances is more susceptible to the Old Law than to the rather ephemeral Golden Rule. By the tale's conclusion, however, the murderers have been hanged "by the lawe" (634) and the Jewish community has structurally lost the protection of the prince, even though this is not directly portrayed in the narrative. An old society has been completely replaced by a new society through a secular legal system that can either conform to the Old Law or be informed by the New Law.[37]

The full victory of the New Law is, of course, only apparent to us in the Prioress's double view of the Jews as hateful Hebrews. The actual setting of the Prioress's Tale works against her own pious affirmations of Christian triumph. In this sense, she is blind because her tale gives to the Jews, for a time at least (before the murder of the Christian boy), their own world. Chaucer's Prioress's Tale, in other words, shows us a militant piety in a setting that does not altogether support it.

We should note that the murder of the "litel clergeon" elicits from the Prioress a second, but related, typological view of the Jews: "O cursed folk of Herodes al newe" (574). Their murder of the Christian boy thus reenacts, in the Prioress's mind, the murder of the Innocents, celebrated on 28 December. "Al newe" is the Prioress's shorthand for the idea that present events are past history. The Jews are Herod's agents, again murdering an innocent, though his death, like the death of the Innocents, is always a sacrifice so that Christ might live to die. Jewish violence is theologically necessary, their evil appropriate, to an aestheticized piety. Archer suggests that the Jews' "cursed dede" is also Cain's murder of Abel, whose "blood out crieth" (578). Archer is right in establishing an adumbrating series of murders and sacrifices in the Prioress's Tale, for that series reflects the anti-Semitism of the Prioress's typological imagination that gives Jews their necessary place in the plan of salvation. Her religiosity, of course, gives her little celestial grace, little clinical transcendence through which to view the Jews. We should note, too, that the Jews in the Prioress's Tale do not kill the "litel clergeon" in mockery of the Crucifixion. His blood is not used for magical purposes at Passover. His death is, as we have seen, also a crucifixion, not a ritual murder. The story of Hugh of Lincoln, who was supposed to have been killed for ritual sacrifice, and who is invoked at the end of the Prioress's Tale, only shows us how the Prioress's piety has in effect warped her theological rigor and, of course, invites us to consider the effect of religious affect:

> O yonge Hugh of Lyncoln, slayn also
> With cursed Jewes, as it is notable,
> For it is but a litel while ago,
> Preye eek for us, we synful folk unstable,
> That, of his mercy, God so merciable
> On us his grete mercy multiplie,
> For reverence of his mooder Marie. Amen.
>
> (684–90)

Whether or not the Prioress's Tale is a study of the religious character of the Prioress,[38] the tale affords us the occasion to puzzle out with Chaucer something of the religious piety of his own day, perhaps something of the nature of piety in general—its immediate emotional needs and aesthetic forms—and the shape, perhaps distorted, but always powerful, into which it casts pure theological explanation, which may not move people without sufficient coloration. St. Augustine's theological tolerance of the Jews was no doubt not easily sustainable in men and women less thorough-mindedly Christian than Augustine himself, though vestiges of that theological conception of the Jews, *that* anti-Semitism—typological, necessary, and redemptive—give the Prioress's Tale the subtext on which emotion and conviction shape a tale whose effect is, as Chaucer's says, astonishing (a "wonder").

In one significant way, I think, the reference to Hugh of Lincoln has astonished Chaucerians, too, because the reference makes the tale the kind of rallying call to anti-Judaism, which from the Middle Ages to our own day has resulted in religious persecution. The Blood Libel was seen as a reason to murder Jews. Only Alfred David, as far as I know, has posed the essential historical question about the anti-Judaism of the Prioress's Tale.

To dismiss the anti-Semitism [he means "anti-Judaism"] in the tale as "conventional" is to beg the real question why it should have become conventional, for the Jews were not always so despised in the Middle Ages. The persecution of the Jews and the proliferation of legends of ritual murder that accompanies it begins to accelerate in the course of the twelfth century and leads finally to the expulsion of the Jews from France and England in the thirteenth century. A century later literary anti-Semitism is still flourishing in the drama and in the miracles of the Virgin. Why should this be?[39]

David suggests that the Prioress's Tale is historically an example of "sentimentalized" religion that "worships beauty as a version of truth," characteristic of the "new and fashionable religiosity" of Chaucer's day that "combines gentility with emotion, decorousness with enthusiasm" and anticipates the aureate style of the fifteenth century.[40] Even the triumphant power of the miraculous Second Nun's Tale is given to us in the exaggerated context of sexual melodrama, summary martyrdom (for Valerian and Tiburce) and final rhetorical victory of an emotionalized faith (at Cecile's trial and at her death as a saint—she still preaches after her neck is severed), all driven by divine fiat.[41] David's point is that the literary anti-Judaism of the Prioress's Tale, as an example of sentimentalized religion, tells us less about what we imagine was the incitement to violence against Jews the reference to Hugh of Lincoln in the Tale reminds us of, and more about the artistic and literary form of fourteenth-century English piety—its violent yoking of opposites such as good and evil, innocence and cruelty, which seem conceptually clear but represent the pervasive emotional and formulaic religious style of the period. No actual Jews lived as a community in Chaucer's England whom an aroused audience might have injured—can we seriously imagine Chaucer's listeners, at court or at home, running frenzied into London's "Jewerye"? The reference to Hugh of Lincoln in the Prioress's Tale seems to make the tale dangerous and reprehensible to us. We should note that the only response to the Prioress's Tale Spurgeon lists that comments on its "fierce bigotry" dates from the nineteenth century.[42] Brewer lists one reference in an anonymous literary history of England dating from the 1820s.[43] Perhaps only well after the general emancipation of Jews in Europe were references to them in literature seen as needing commentary. Perhaps because Jews were in

real life accused of ritual murder, the passing reference to Hugh
of Lincoln, only sentimentally appropriate to the Prioress's Tale,
which is not about ritual murder at all, seems to make the Prioress's Tale a work that cries out for moral salvaging. But the
extravagant word play and imagery of the piece, its fourteenth-
century religious mannerism, particularly in its treatment of Jews,
invites us to observe in the tale both religious piety beautified
and beauty worshipped. The Prioress's Tale invites us to use it to
recover fourteenth-century religiosity and to anatomize piety in
general.

The following stanza from the Prologue to the Prioress's Tale is, I
think, a miraculous example of sexualized religious devotion, a
style Chaucer masters in the Prioress's Tale and in *An ABC:*

> O mooder Mayde! o mayde Mooder free!
> O bussh unbrent, brennynge in Moyses sighte,
> That ravyshedest doun fro the Deitee,
> Thurgh thyn humblesse, the Goost that in th'alighte,
> Of whos vertu, whan he thyn herte lighte,
> Conceyved was the Fadres sapience,
> Help me to tell it in thy reverence!
>
> (467–73)

The stanza is the Prioress's apostrophe to the Virgin, whose contradictory miraculous aspects ("mooder" and "mayde") are both invoked with an unembarrassed clarity and then compared typologi-
cally to the same kind of wondrous yoking of impossible opposites
("O bussh unbrent"). The reference to the biblical burning bush
(Exodus 3:2–4) is also found in *An ABC*. But there the reference is
explained rather than invoked.

> Moises, that saugh the bush with flawmes rede
> Brenninge, of which ther never a stikke brende,
> Was signe of thin unwemmed maidenhede.
>
> (89–91)

The reference to the "bussh unbrent" in the Prologue to the Prioress's Tale is glorious identifying song. Its miraculousness is
offered as unexplained proof that it is a foreshadowing reference to
the Virgin Mother's nature. Her humility is said to have drawn
from God Himself ("ravyshedest down") the Holy Spirit ("Goost")
that settled in her. Her impregnation with spirit is seen as an illu-

mination of her being. The rhyme of "alighte" and "light" suggests
that the "settling" Holy Spirit resides like a child in the Virgin
Mother as light. At the same time, her impregnation is a sexual rav-
ishing, a taking possession that is powerful, wondrous, and immediate. It can only be described in the language of orgasm, our experience of Divine infusion. One thinks here of the opening lines of
the *Canterbury Tales* itself for a parallel kind of language of renewal from on high *down to us:*

> Whan that Aprill with his shoures soote
> The droghte of March hath perced to the roote,
> And bathed every veyne in swich licour
> Of which vertu engendred is the flour;
> Whan Zephirus eek with his sweete breeth
> Inspired hath in every holt and heeth
> The tendre croppes, and the yonge sonne
> Hath in the Ram his halve cours yronne,
> And smale foweles maken melodye,
> That slepen al the nyght with open ye
> (So priketh hem nature in hir corages);
> Thanne longen folk to goon on pilgrimages.
>
> (1–12)

Sexual rain ("perced to the roote") and the divine breath in the
zodiacal cycle of eternal renewal awaken flowers, crops, birds, and
human reverential sociability. Nature "priketh hem"—the reference is literally only to the birds—and people go on pilgrimages.
Here we have human renewal through purposive social celebration, a journey with a healing purpose, a pilgrimage, during which
renewing social impulses are engaged. The light the Virgin Mother
carries in the Prologue to the Prioress's Tale is "the Fadres sapience"
thought of as "conceyved" (472). For the Prioress, renewal is a
decidedly more narrow transformation of the world than the full-
bodied renewal of the opening of the General Prologue to the
Canterbury Tales. Moreover, the Prioress's religious language uses
sexualized devotion for an emotionality of expression that directs
all feeling to transcendent understanding.

   As she has a typology for the Jews, so the Prioress has a typology
for the mother of the "litel clergeon." The description of the little
Christian boy being removed from the "Jewerye" is both dramatic
and conceptual. Indeed, the emotionality of the immediate scene
informs the typological reference to the "newe Rachel":

This child with pitous lamentacioun
Up taken was, syngynge his song alway,
And with honour of greet processioun
They carien hym unto the nexte abbay.
His mooder swownynge by the beere lay;
Unnethe myghte the peple that was theere
This newe Rachel brynge fro his beere.

(621–27)

The "newe Rachel" here is an allusion to Rachel in Jeremiah 31:15 weeping for her children, refusing to be comforted "because they were not," and to Matthew 2:18, where Herod slays the Innocents. What the swooning mother in the Prioress's Tale does not yet understand, of course, is that her son ("syngynge his song alway") still lives as a martyr. Here religious theatricality amplifies biblical allusions, not simply to the Slaughter of the Innocents, but, in Jeremiah, to the God's promised joy. The verse that follows the reference to Rachel weeping in Ramah anticipates the astonishing joy with which the "litel clergeon" infuses the Christian community in the "greet citee" of the Prioress's Tale:

Thus saith the Lord, Restrain thy voice from weeping, and thine eyes from tears; for thy work shall be rewarded, saith the Lord, and they shall come again from the land of the enemy. (Jeremiah 31:16)

The mother as the "newe Rachel" and the "litel clergeon" as the "martir" laid "in a tombe of marbul stones cleere" (680–81)—a kind of visible relic—are icons of the triumph of Christianity. The setting of the Prioress's Tale "in Asye" gives an appropriate historical frame, with an allusion to the return of the children of Israel to Israel, in which to observe Christian theological descriptions of their own Divine victory.

What may finally be alien to the Prioress's Tale is the Prioress's emotional piety, of which her anti-Judaism is but one example. The Prioress's Tale engages our need to understand. We begin with our alienation. How, indeed, can we do otherwise? But we always assume common human experience. Hermeneutics cannot reveal the utterly alien, so that as we read we come to understand both ourselves as readers and believers and the texts and traditions that enfold us.[44] Chaucer's hermeneutic circle engages the historicized consciousness with itself and with the text it reads. Moreover, Chaucer anticipates in the indeterminacy of meaning and intention the rejection of one explanatory method implicit in the idea of the hermeneutic circle. For Chaucer, there is no one mediating model that makes experience explainable, understandable, and true. We know the world *through a text* and we know ourselves *as we read other texts*. Hence Chaucer's world is a world of stories, including our own as readers. Reading assumes an otherness, a recoverable alterity. Moreover, we have seen in our discussion of the Prioress's Tale and the Franklin's Tale how an indeterminate text gives us a pluralism of value and intent as a kind of hermeneutic manifestation of being: every man or woman speaks his or her own text; every reader is that reader's text. That, to be sure, does not close out readers of Chaucer's text in any age or make us objective observers of a text whose conceptual distance from us constitutes an awe we would not violate and cannot penetrate. Rather, pluralism as a manifestation of being creates readers—the possibility that we can appropriate texts in ways telling for us. What the Franklin, the aristocratic characters in his tale, and the devotional Prioress *mean* constitutes the point of engagement and value for own own reading and meaning.

We can perhaps conclude this chapter by recalling Gadamer's concept of language as the medium of experience ("Being that can be understood is language"), not a kind of oblique, tyrannizing authority:[45]

Language . . . is not the finally found anonymous subject of all social-historical processes and action, which presents the whole of its activities as objectivations to our observing gaze; rather, it is by itself the game of interpretation that we all are engaged in every day. In this game nobody is above and before all the others; everybody is at the center, is "it" in this game. Thus it is always his turn to be interpreting. This process of interpreting takes place whenever we "understand." . . . This idea recalls what we said about the *atopon*, the strange, for in it we have "seen through" something that appeared odd and unintelligible: we have brought it into our linguistic world.[46]

In this light, Chaucer's indeterminacy, his making available to us texts as worlds, is a source of understanding, affirmation, and renewal for us. "Reality does not happen 'behind the back' of language; it happens rather behind the backs of those who live in the subjective opinion that they have understood 'the world' (or can no longer understand it); that is, reality happens precisely *within* language."[47]

•　　•　　•

In the final chapter of this study, I shall examine Chaucer's last demonstrated retreat as guide to his stories, his "leave-taking" after the Parson's Tale. Even there Chaucer will not let us affirm a tyranny of explanation. His giving up of authorial power, refusing a textual closure that excludes us, gives us, or any reader, being.

Chapter Seven

Chaucerian "Leave-Taking"

Because a number of passages in Boccaccio's *Decameron* define an idea of a circle of reading similar enough to Chaucer's, looking at Boccaccio makes it clear how Chaucer expects readers to use his stories. In the preface to his *Decameron*, Boccaccio explains that

in these tales will be found a variety of love adventures, bitter as well as pleasing, and other exciting incidents, which took place in both ancient and modern times. In reading them, the aforesaid ladies will be able to derive, not only pleasure from entertaining matters therein set forth, but also some useful advice. For they will learn to recognize what should be avoided and likewise what should be pursued, and these things can only lead, in my opinion, to the removal of their affliction.[1]

Boccaccio here seems to be answering what might have been allegations that his *Decameron* was not edifying. Unfortunately, Boccaccio's argument sounds like a ploy, although in theory it is not. The *Decameron* always seems on the verge of openly undercutting its own idealism, and Boccaccio's justifications in the work seem wholly self-serving. They have a mocking tone that Chaucer, who takes justifications of this kind seriously, would need to amend—if he in fact borrowed them from the *Decameron*—for Boccaccio has a sophistication and a cynicism that makes the very apparatus of justification for ribaldry itself obscene.

Although Boccaccio's reasoning sounds specious, it defines an altogether sound principle of rhetorical theory: morality is in the eyes of moral beings. As Boccaccio puts it, "Like all other things in this world, stories, whatever their nature, may be harmful or useful, depending upon the listener." Boccaccio's argument comes directly out of St. Augustine. As Boccaccio explains, "No word, however pure, was ever wholesomely construed by a mind that was corrupt. And just as seemly language leaves no mark upon a mind that is corrupt, language that is less than seemly cannot sully a mind that is well ordered, any more than mud will contaminate the rays of the sun, or earthly filth the beauties of the heavens."[2] What Boccaccio is here asserting is the notion that man has the capacity to judge the value of a work of art and to see judgment as a sign of human worth rather than artistic merit. This notion, despite the Augustinian echoes, is actually not a sign of Boccaccio's medievalness. Rather, it is a sign of the falling apart of a consensus about literary value, a "vernacularizing" of stories in Boccaccio's day, which Boccaccio reflects in seeing the reader as the focus of his stories. In general, the modern aesthetic has turned medieval rhetorical theory on its head: the response of a reader to a story is taken as an index of the "wholeness" of a work of art, and any defect in the work of art, as the reader perceives it, is said to be a sign that the author has failed in his actual "vision," and necessarily in the execution of it. Focus here is on either the work or the author's conception of the work—for Benedetto Croce they are in theory the same—rather than on the reader and what the reader's judgment may say about his moral condition. Perhaps this is why the Horatian dictum "teach and delight," a rhetorical commonplace in the Middle Ages, is thought to be applicable solely to the author as the standard by which he is judged to have succeeded or failed *as an artist* (has he "taught"? has he "delighted"? both? neither?), rather than to the reader as the ground on which he judges himself by judging what is presented to him (why do I think I am being "taught"? or "delighted"? or both? or neither?). My thinking I am being taught something tells me what constitutes my category of "things-needed-to-be-taught." "Why do I think I am being taught something?" should, moreover, not be equated with "Did the author teach me something?" To answer the second question, I must know or ascertain an author's intention, and even if I am able to conclude that an author did *not* intend to teach me the thing I have learned, I have still been taught something. Thus we can praise an author "incorrectly" for his teaching—he may not understand what we are saying about him—though we cannot praise him "falsely," if indeed we have learned something from his work.[3]

Boccaccio assumes that the will of the reader can make of a work of art anything it pleases:

All things have their own special purpose, but when they are wrongly used a great deal of harm may result, and the same applies to my stories. If anyone should want to extract evil counsel from these tales, or fashion an evil design, there is nothing to prevent him, provided he twists and distorts them sufficiently to find the thing he is seeking. And if anyone should study them for the usefulness and profit they may bring him, he will not be disappointed. Nor will they ever be thought of or described as anything but useful and seemly, if they are read at the proper time by the people for whom they were written.[4]

Boccaccio has put the case in terms of the usefulness of a work of art to a mind that wishes to read idiosyncratically. In this sense, Boccaccio cannot teach anything that is not already in the reader, for the way in which the reader learns—interprets what he reads— is, as we know, evidence for the kind of reader he is. Perhaps what sounds rigged about this argument is that Boccaccio seems to imply that he is teaching the reader, by a kind of rhetorical duplicity, who the reader is: Boccaccio presents tales that turn interpretation over to readers themselves. In theory, he teaches them nothing, though they may learn much, particularly about their values.

In at least one passage in the *Canterbury Tales*, Chaucer seems to assume that the story he tells will draw conclusions from readers they already know. In the Prologue to the Nun's Priest's Tale, Harry Bailly, speaking as a member of the fictional audience of a fictional tale-telling, remarks:

> And wel I woot the substance is in me,
> If any thyng shal wel reported be.
>
> (2803–4)

If Harry Bailly has the makings of an attentive listener, it is because, as we know, a story told well touches something already in the Host ("substance is in me"). A story is a kind of flint that makes intelligible to the reader—awakens ("lights up")—whatever substance, in a figurative sense, is already in him. Harry Bailly cannot help but read subjectively; that is the point. Preferences are personal and telling and are, as we have seen, the only basis on which, and from which, anyone can read. The Host's response to the stories he hears does not, of course, constitute the kind of self-awareness that we value in readers and literary critics. His literary criticism is not a "rational enterprise" whose "tests for validity act as constraints on its proceedings" and whose "critical commitments can be analyzed and debated."[5] His telling preferences define him as a reader whose values produce interpretations rather than reveal them. But if he is not self-aware, he is self-conscious, and what his blind and interested, not disinterested, reading gives us is the legitimate ground of our own values for becoming good readers.[6] As Walter Benn Michaels puts it, reading is constitutive because "readers have themselves been constituted."[7] The scientistic model of the autonomous—context-free and neutral—reader confronting an autonomous text with determinate meaning is a fiction: "There are no text-derived canons of interpretation which prevent the self from doing what it wants; there is only our conviction that what the self wants has already been constituted by canons of interpretation."[8] Thus while Harry Bailly does not display the judicious interpretive behavior we value, he seems to know that literature does not teach by giving the readers "substance" with which they are unfamiliar. He knows, as it were, that interpretation does not operate "in the empty moment before constitution or in the reified world after but in the act of constitution itself."[9] He is neither an autonomous victim nor a tyrant of reading and the sociability it creates and recreates. Indeed, his interpretive zeal, his play of power in the *Canterbury Tales*, is not so much challenged as skirted. His vehemence does not silence others. Rather, it gives encouragement to the sure and certain volubility of the Canterbury pilgrims, and to our own breaking into language, that reveals to us our context-bound values, our immediate and historical canons of interpretations. As Robert Payne puts it, Chaucerian narrative is for us the "keye of remembraunce," the key to historical meaning and self-awareness.[10] Chaucer does not teach readers something new, but articulates something recognized as already in them as constitutive kinds of self-texts.

Like the epilogue to Boccaccio's *Decameron*, the *Canterbury Tales* also concludes with a passage in which the author "taketh . . . his leve." The passage is not itself a retraction of anything, although it contains a list of books that the author withdraws. The entire passage (1081–92), which follows the Parsons' Tale and may refer to it, presents both an account of the author's judgment of himself—

what the author, in the sight of God, wishes to have taken out of his canon—and, by implication, an invitation to the reader to make an account of his own tastes. Whatever else it may tell us, Chaucer's "leave-taking" encourages us to assume that, however obviously unfinished the *Canterbury Tales* is, Chaucer *was finished with it,* at least when he took "his leve." Hence Chaucer's judgment is usually taken to be the guideline for the reader's own judgment of Chaucer—like author, like reader—so that what Chaucer values is assumed by critics to be what the reader should value. But such an authoritarian reading of the epilogue to the *Canterbury Tales* is troublesome.[11] As I read it, the epilogue is divided into two parts: the first (1081–83) states the principle that forming a judgment about the moral value of "this litel tretys" is the need and responsibility of each reader. It makes explicit an assumption behind the first reference in the General Prologue to the limitations of the narrator and the implicit invitation to Chaucer's audience to read cooperatively: "If ther be any thyng in it that liketh him, that therof they thanken oure Lord Jhesu Crist, of whom precedeth al wit and al goodnesse. / And if ther by any thyng that displese hem, I preye hem also that they arrette it to the defaute of myn unkonnynge, and nat to my wyl, that wolde ful fayn have seyd bettre if I hadde had konnynge" (1081–82).

Although the logic here may be puzzling, the passage is not unclear. First, Chaucer explains that if the reader likes something in the "tretys" (1081) he has just finished reading—reasons for liking it would be telling of the reader's moral capacity—he ought to "thanken oure Lord Jhesu Crist," from whom "al wit" and "al goodnesse" flow; that is, he ought to thank Jesus Christ not only for the capacity Christ has given him to understand, but also for the poet's wit to communicate so readily, and he ought to thank Christ for the wisdom to make a choice that is morally sound. Both "wit" and "goodnesse" are gifts of God—capacities, really—that define the humanity of the reader. The key to these lines is the medieval commonplace—it may be surprising to some—that to thank Jesus Christ for what we like is equivalent to thanking God for His gift of free will. Fundamentally, cooperative reading of the kind we have been describing in Chaucer assumes the freedom of readers to read personally and to be judged accordingly. The role of the storyteller in Chaucer, which a performer—a private reader is a performer—

ought not to, and really cannot, obscure, is to let the text speak for itself through him. A storyteller's rhetoric of limitations—disavowal of his skill in guiding—ensures, as we know, that the omniscience any reader imputes to him as a matter of course is deflected. At those moments when the Chaucerian storyteller "backs away," the reader "emerges" to interpret for him. I am characterizing the activity with verbs that describe complementary action, for it is in this sense that a storyteller and an audience share the public reading of the story, even if Chaucer is read at home. Any fear of subjectivism, again as Walter Benn Michaels explains, stems from a misconception—the Cartesian inheritance of much of modern literary criticism—about the reader's neutrality—the notion of the self "free to assert its subjectivity without constraint" and the notion of the self "wiped clean of prejudice and ready to accept determinate meaning."[12] At any actual performance of Chaucer in his own day, the man reading aloud never stops reading or sits down, and the listeners never actually speak. But an analogous sharing of the text occurs, no less "in the mind" because the occasion is public. In both instances, reading Chaucer at home and in public, the members of his audience are free to judge not only what they like but what they dislike. Nor can they blame Chaucer's storyteller, however they see the fiction of Chaucer the poet and Chaucer the pilgrim-storyteller. He has done his best.

The "litel tretys" mentioned in line 1081 probably refers to the Parson's Tale.[13] It may, moreover, be a "convention of authorial modesty, which bears no relation to the actual length of the work."[14] That Chaucer should invite the cooperation of his audience in reading what is an unequivocally "moral" treatise on the Seven Deadly Sins—hardly a tale at all—is startling. But Chaucer does not expect his readers to decide the morality or immorality of the Parson's Tale; that would be presumptuous. Rather, he expects them to take from it what they can—to read it in the light of their personal preferences.[15] Moreover, even the Parson's Tale invites what I have called cooperative reading. Although he does not speak for highminded secularism, the Parson offers his text on penitence as mediating and meliorative and gives to the *Canterbury Tales*, immediately before Chaucer's "leave-taking," that same closure. It is easy, Middleton argues, to create an ending to a work designed to illuminate the truth: "Present your speaker with an ultimate vision or revelation which will make intellectual and emotional coherence of all that has led to it." But the *Canterbury Tales* is not the *Divine Comedy.* "[Then] what end is there," Middleton asks, "to a worldly voice, except death, either of the speaker or of the world itself? . . . There can be no end to the human voice's testimony to its own experience before the end of time."[16]

Now the Parson suggests that the "olde pathes" (77) of that "parfit glorious pilgrymage" (50) on which the Canterbury company are embarked are "olde sentences" (77); *for him* that means penitence, though for others, readers as well as pilgrims, participants both, it has meant a figurative voyage among books—the mental journey of tale-telling, the remembered and imaginary experience of "sentence" as well as "solas." The Parson's text in lines 77–78 cites Jeremiah 6:16:

State super via, et videte, et interrogate de viis antiquis que sit via bona, et ambulate in ea; et inuenietis refrigerium animabus vestris, etc.

[Stondeth upon the weyes, and seeth and axeth of olde pathes (that is to seyn, of olde sentences) which is the goode wey, / and walketh in that wey, and ye shal fynde refresshynge for youre soules, etc.]

But the Parson glosses "viis antiquis" as "olde sentences" as a preparation for *his* spiritual path.[17] "Manye been the weyes espirituels that leden folk to oure Lord Jhesu Crist, and to the regne of glorie. / Of whiche weyes, ther is a ful noble wey and a ful convenable, which may nay fayle to man ne to womman that thurgh synne hath mysgoon fro the righte wey of Jerusalem celestial; / and this wey is cleped Penitence" (79–81). Christian Zacher reads the Parson's allusion to Jeremiah 6:16, which, he notes, neglects the people's response to Jeremiah's call in the same verse ("But they said, We will not walk"), as a rebuke of the "literal, imperfect, earthly pilgrimage" of the Canterbury company, with its "pervasive noise and dissension," its wayward descent into curiosity.[18] But if the Parson's treatise is compelling as spiritual truth and as a statement about the pilgrimage we, as well as the Canterbury pilgrims, ought to embark on, it is *not* because we can hear in the Parson's voice some final authority, either the word of God or Chaucer's sober tone—the voices of *doctrina* and morality, now one. What is compelling about the Parson's "myrie tale in prose"

(46)—it may have been called a tale just *because* it is the Parson's "goode wey"—is the seriousness of its conception of conduct in this world and the means it affords us for righting our errors here on earth.[19] In this sense, the Parson's "tale"—he himself calls it a "meditacioun" (55)—indeed works "To knytte up al this feeste, and make an ende" (47), not the kind of end that gives final answers— makes the pilgrimage to Canterbury come to an end by scolding the participants—but the kind that provides morality against which to judge, as we remember them, the tales of Canterbury, including the Parson's Tale itself,[20] or the "tales" we ourselves may tell, as we continue our "curious" journey. Hannah Arendt makes this last connection, too, between storytelling and history. It is for her the way we enter history.[21]

We would be misunderstanding the nature of penance, I think, if we were to compare it to judgment. Penance does not fix our na- ture; rather it requires both a healthy and dignifying measure of self-knowledge—we must recognize our sins of conduct and in- tention—*and* an overriding and directing faith in God and in our capacity, with God's help, to remake ourselves. For all its rigor, penitence is the welcome sign of our better self; it is a willing and conscious effort to be better. Indeed, the Parson reminds us that "verray perfit Penitence" stands on three things: "Contricioun of herte, Confessioun of Mouth, and Satisfaccioun" (107–8). Notice that whether sin be "delit in thynkynge" or "reccheleesnesse in spekynge" or "wikked . . . werkynge" (111), penitence is a public act for both private and public behavior. It is essentially a social act and does not distinguish insight from behavior, as some of us may be prone to do. For the Parson, penitence rectifies both men and the body social. It does not restore order and holiness at the end of the *Canterbury Tales* by fiat; rather it directs us to restoring them along a path that links thought and behavior with the socially good.

We cannot, moreover, take the Parson's treatise on the Seven Deadly Sins as an example of the kind of sermon Zacher suggests pilgrims actually heard when they arrived at Jerusalem.[22] If any- thing, the Parson's "tale" is an example of the kind of "humanistic" text scholars like R. W. Southern see the "literary humanists" of the Renaissance mistaking for formalism and hostility to human experience:

As the residuary legatee of the scientific and systematic humanism of the twelfth and thirteenth centuries, a new kind of humanism came into existence. It was the product of disillusion with the great projects of the recent past. When the hope of universal order faded, the cultivation of sensibility and personal virtue, and the nostalgic vision of an ancient utopia revealed in classical literature, remained as the chief supports of humane values. Instead of the confident and progressive humanism of the central Middle Ages, the new humanism retreated into the individual and the past; it saw the aristocracy rather than the clergy as the guardians of culture; it sought inspiration in literature rather than theology and science; its ideal was a group of friends rather than a universal system; and the nobility of man was expressed in his struggle with an unintelligible world rather than in his capacity to know all things.[23]

But the Parson commends what is best in us by showing us what *may* be worst in us; it is optimistic in this way, and intellectual. We are dignified by system and by a universal treatment of our nature; there are Seven Deadly Sins we *may* be victims of and there is a private and public mode of self-understanding, acknowledgment, and rectification.[24] If the Parson's "myrie tale in prose" knits up the *Canterbury Tales,* it does not do so by making the work cease to be art because it has become, with the Parson's treatise, pure spirit. Rather, as we shall see, the Parson's treatise gives vent in Chaucer's "leave-taking" to Chaucer's act of acknowledgment and penance and, in our lives as readers, to an accounting of taste. If the Parson's Tale "puts secular values in perspective . . . [and] recommends moral values which would be productive in making a better world,"[25] Chaucer's "retractions," where "the author appears *in propria persona* without irony,"[26] can be seen as Chaucer's "own act of penance."[27] If Chaucer the man appears somewhere between the end of the Parson's Tale and the end of the *Canterbury Tales,* he appears with the word "wherfore" at the beginning of line 1084. At this point, as I read the text, Chaucer is taking his cue from the Parson and judging his own work, hence the reference to tales in the *Canterbury Tales* that "sownen into synne" (1086). The rubric that announces the author's "leave-taking" probably should have been inserted just *before* line 1084, not where it presently stands in the Robinson edition. It is clearly scribal and, I think, misplaced.[28]

Now whether or not a reader likes what he reads, Chaucer insists on the general dictum that books are for enlightenment—a mirror for the reader—although he nowhere suggests (as Boccaccio does) that the reader who fails to appreciate them is thereby found wanting or insufficiently pure of mind: "For oure book seith, 'Al that is writen is writen for oure doctrine,' and that is myn entente" (1083). The implicit comparison between the book that Chaucer has written and the book in which the words of St. Paul are written is only made to establish the value of all books for all readers.[29] "Doctrine" here does not mean moral doctrine defined in a strictly patristic sense. It has been interpreted so narrowly perhaps only because Robertsonians seem to take seriously the notion of Chaucer as a "moral" artist and have offered an explanation of him as a "medieval" moralist, which anti-Robertsonians not so much challenge as modify (or, as they usually see it, humanize or universalize).

Ironically, the Robertsonians, who see in the "retractions" a full-blown statement of an Augustinian aesthetic, have not, I think, understood an essential principle of Augustinianism—that in life each man must freely choose from among moral possibilities that the world and books present to him, and that the choice defines his spiritual state. Of all the Church Fathers, St. Augustine is the least doctrinaire. Even if we restrict ourselves to *On Christian Doctrine*—the text at the heart of Robertsonianism—the argument involving "Egyptian Gold" (2.40.60–61) is Augustine's principle of conversion that must be enacted in each individual life. According to it, Christians are supposed to adapt whatever pagan ideas and institutions they find suitable to their purposes and thereby demonstrate that they know intrinsic value when they see it: "The whole temporal dispensation was made by divine Providence for our salvation. We should use it, not with an abiding but with a transitory love and delight like that in a road or in vehicles or in other instruments, or, if it may be expressed more accurately, so that we love those things by which we are carried along for the sake of that toward which we are carried."[30] To understand the difference between "enjoying" something and "using" something is a condition of spiritual awareness that, for Augustine, always precedes understanding, because understanding is predicated upon God's grace.[31] Each individual act of judgment is therefore a conditional sign of blessedness and each act of choice, with God requires of all men, is an act that must be risked, because by that act we signify who we are.[32]

The second part of the epilogue begins, as we have said, with the word "wherfore"—Chaucer's own voice—at line 1084. The word is pivotal to the entire passage and in fact renders what would take us an entire clause to say. Let me suggest a paraphrase: taking into account the principle of individual responsibility that has just been stated (1081–83), what follows (1084–89) will be my (Chaucer's) acknowledgment of my responsibilities—the choices, as it were, of a "pilgrim" who—the fiction of the narrative collapses just at this point—has told the tales of other storytellers as he has heard them:

Wherfore I biseke yow mekely, for the mercy of God, that ye preye for me that Crist have mercy on me and foryeve my my gildes; / and namely of my translacions and enditynges of worldly vanitees, the whiche I revoke in my retracciouns: / as is the book of Troilus; the book also of Fame; the book of the xxv. Ladies; the book of the Duchesse; the book of Seint Valentynes day of the Parlement of Briddes; the tales of Caunterbury, thilke that sownen into synne; / the book of the Leoun; and many another book, if they were in my remembrance, and many a song and many a leccherous lay; that Crist for his grete mercy foryeve me the synne. (1084–87)

What follows this list of works Chaucer names as writings ("translacions and enditynges") of worldly vanity (1086–87) is a list he calls books of "moralitee, and devocioun" (1088). This second group is, I think, apart from the reference to "the translacion of Boece de Consolacione" (1088), strikingly vague, as are in fact the references to "the tales of Caunterbury, thilke that sownen into synne" (1086) and "many another book, if they were in my remembrance, and many a song and many a leccherous lay" (1087). The point of this imprecision for Chaucer's readers is that any attempt at specifying, say, the sinful tales of Canterbury, or the books of morality and devotion—this category is virtually empty—will in fact begin to establish Chaucer's canon.[33] Chaucer's *not* being precise about most of his "good" works and some of his "bad" ones calls on readers both to name and evaluate his work—to constitute it both for themselves and for him. Chaucer seems concerned in his "leave-taking," not inappropriately I think, with the establishment of his corpus through readerly blame and praise, and I suspect our judgment will be far less one-sided than Chaucer's. We want to accept, not revoke, Chaucer's work and to fill his category of good books.

Actually the idea of retraction for Chaucer implies both a withdrawal of something because a judgment about it has been made—it is good or harmful—and a withdrawal of something *in order to make* a judgment about it. Moreover, Chaucer uses the word "retraction" as a plural noun ("my retracciouns"), which suggests individual reexamination of individual works.[34] For Chaucer to "revoke in my retracciouns" (1085) is to invite readers to review his work *with him*—to revoke, as it were, after retraction. Chaucer's retraction constitutes the beginnings of evaluation, so that having divided his work into two general and generalizing classes, he asks forgiveness for his sinful writings, taking the Parson's wholesome advice: "And he that synneth and verraily repenteth hym in his laste, hooly chirche yet hopeth his savacioun, by the grete mercy of oure Lord Jhesu Crist, for his repentaunce; but taak the siker wey" (94). Chaucer has made rather broad distinctions between the good and the harmful, but the conventionality of his choices—their incompleteness and one-sidedness—sets readers to evaluating what he in effect has left undone. Perhaps the ordinariness of Chaucer's repentance, the routineness of his "retracciouns"—as the Parson suggests, he takes the "siker wey"—is disturbing because we imagine Chaucer less orthodox than he seems to be here. We are disappointed at Chaucer's conventional choices, given, for example, the latitude, the range of moralities, he seems to have allowed readers of the *Canterbury Tales*, and the Canterbury storytellers, from the beginning. But Chaucer's way is strictly in keeping with the moral limitations he has for the moment imposed on himself in his "art of dying."[35] Chaucer's own moral choices, so sweeping and incomplete, encourage initiative in his readers. His frankness, wholesomeness *and* imprecision work against rote response. In the epilogue to the *Canterbury Tales*, Chaucer demands not unconventional choices but personal ones from his readers.

Chaucer in his "leave-taking" at the end of the *Canterbury Tales* is doing seriously what he invites his readers at the end of the Nun's Priest's Tale to do comically—to choose:

And ye that holden this tale a folye,
As of a fox, or of a cok and hen,
Taketh the moralite, goode men.
(3438–40)

Through an analogous kind of separation, not so much a falling
away of the "fruyt" from the "chaf" as a rethinking of what *is*
"fruyt" and "chaf," the Parson's Tale provides a way through the
world—a "ful noble wey"—Chaucer *and* his readers take. Penance
leads to what the Parson calls "satisfaccione," a condition that has
about it a kind of transcendence, though it never leads out "of the
world." It does not separate body and spirit, the way death does.
Rather, it gives a figurative separation, an awareness about what
men do *in the world* and what they should do, which reading fiction, as a mirror of the world, lets us demonstrate and exercise:

Thanne shal men understonde what is the fruyt of penaunce; and, after
the word of Jhesu Crist, it is the endelees blisse of hevene, / ther joye
hath no contrarioustee of wo ne grevaunce, ther alle harmes been passed
of this present lyf, ther as is the sikernesse fro the peyne of helle; ther as is
the blisful compaignye that rejoysen him everemo, everich of otheres
joye; / ther as the body of man, that whilom was foul and derk, is moore
cleer than the sonne; ther as the body, that whilom was syk, freele, and
fieble, and mortal, is inmortal, and so strong and so hool that ther may no
thyng apeyren it, / ther as ne is neither hunger, thurst, ne coold, but
every soule replenyssed with the sighte of the parfit knowynge of God. /
This blisful regne may men purchace by poverte espiritueel, and the
glorie of lowenesse, the plentee of joye by hunger and thurst, and the
reste by travaille, and the lyf by deeth and mortificacioun of synne.
(1076–80)

This "blisful regne" sounds rather like the "eighthe spere" (1809)
of book 5 of the *Troilus*. Indeed, it is perhaps a clearer vision of
heaven than Troilus seems to have, just because it is, in its generalized and conventional way, more schematic. After he dies, Troilus
merely sees

with ful avysement,
The erratik sterres, herkenyng armonye
With sownes ful of hevenyssh melodie.
(1811–13)[36]

Moreover, the epilogue to the *Canterbury Tales*, Chaucer's "leave-taking," resembles Troilus's "seeing after death" (1814–25), when Troilus "held al vanite / To respect of the pleyn felicite / That is in hevene above" (1817–19). Chaucer in his "dying" in the *Canterbury Tales* makes distinctions similar to Troilus's about the "blynde lust, the which that may nat laste" (1824), by retracting his "translacions and enditynges of worldly vanitees" and "the tales of Caunterbury, thilke that sownen into synne"—works that may not be unambiguously pious because they are of this world. If Chaucer has retracted his "worldly vanitees" in *imitatio mortis*, he lives, at least imaginatively, in a separation of worlds, so that his judgment now of the things of this world need not make accommodation for the way people and ideas have always to wrestle with a certain mixedness of nature: an urge to transcendence that can only be hinted at in our language, where human and divine love are usually metaphors for each other. Troilus, too, from our point of view—we are still alive—makes a rather easy judgment of things, though "on earth" he had to struggle with the language of love that seemed to mean one thing to him and something else to everyone else.

When the Parson tells us how we may "purchace" the "blisful regne," he links our getting it in a kind of metaphysical irony, purely conventional in religious language, though nonetheless meaningful, with the words "poverete espiritueel" and the "glorie" of "lowenesse." Our "plentee of joye" is obtained through "hunger and thurst"; our "reste" through "travaille"; our "lyf" through "deeth and mortificacioun of synne." Practical steps, it seems, bring us to the "blisful regne," a foretaste of which we have negatively in its opposite here on earth. Thus we need the death of the old self in this life through judgment—a separation of self, an act of self-consciousness, self-transcendence, and "seeing" while alive, an *imitatio mortis* that the reader performs every time he turns Chaucer's text on himself. Chaucer's performance of dying makes out of him another reader—not one with culminating judgment, but one who seems to step out of the reader's way into otherworldly, unambiguous, and perhaps disappointing, judgments. Dante, I think, would not have understood Chaucer's "leave-taking"—leaving his fictional world to the reader for the reader to leave it too—as an ending for a work about human pilgrimage.

Chaucer never directs his readers, though he shows them, by judging what he has done, how to direct themselves.

The prayer with which Chaucer invokes God's insight on his own behalf and invites us to do the same is thus an altogether fitting end to the making of choices—to being a reader: "Lord Jhesu Crist, and his blisful Mooder, and alle the seintes of hevene, / bisekynge hem that they from hennes forth unto my lyves ende sende me grace to biwayle my giltes, and to studie to the salvacioun of my soule, and graunte me grace of verray penitence, confessioun and satisfaccioun to doon in this present lyf" (1089–90). Chaucer has, of course, already made his reckoning with God—his choices—so that, in a literal sense, he cannot pray for the wisdom to choose what, in God's eyes, is good about his earthly work—his writings. Chaucer's prayer is thus not a petition for understanding in order to choose so much as it is an expression of hope that what he has understood about his work—its truth and usefulness—is indeed sound. Chaucer's prayer for grace may pull the reader up short, but for Chaucer it signifies the kind of humility—a dependence on God—that prevents him from making his choice arrogantly. The prayer is also an invitation to the reader to check his own intellectual arrogance lest he believe that the judgments he has made—his interpretations of the stories he has heard—are infallible. Prayers for grace are prayers for help and compel the petitioner to acknowledge his dependence on God, not necessarily in order to retract judgment—that would be difficult after one has read something— but to stem arrogance and dogmatism about judgment, the very things that the cooperative reading of a story in Chaucer consciously works against. That kind of sharing puts a reader at the focus of storytelling, and Chaucer, who is magically center-stage at the public performance of his work, or the imagined performance for the private reader, can consciously withdraw. He can retreat before the stories he makes accessible, valuable, and true to our capacity for articulating a self that always participates, even in private, in the social and historical world reading creates. Chaucer's "leave-taking" leaves us worlds, the web of talk that knits us up. This is closure that encourages us to begin again, Chaucerian closure that renews.

Abbreviations

ABR	*American Benedictine Review*
CE	*College English*
ChauR	*Chaucer Review*
CL	*Comparative Literature*
CLAJ	*College Language Association Journal*
EETS	*Early English Text Society*
ELH	*English Literary History*
EM	*English Miscellany*
ES	*English Studies*
GaR	*Georgia Review*
JEGP	*Journal of English and Germanic Philology*
MÆ	*Medium Ævum*
MLN	*Modern Language Notes*
MLQ	*Modern Language Quarterly*
MLR	*Modern Language Review*
MS	*Mediaeval Studies*
MP	*Modern Philology*
NLH	*New Literary History*
NM	*Neuphilologische Mitteilungen*

PLL	*Papers on Language and Literature*
PMLA	*Publications of the Modern Language Association of America*
RES	*Review of English Studies*
RR	*Romanic Review*
SAC	*Studies in the Age of Chaucer*
SAQ	*South Atlantic Quarterly*
UTQ	*University of Toronto Quarterly*
YES	*Yearbook of English Studies*
YFS	*Yale French Studies*

Notes

1. Irony, Declamation, and Chaucer's Presence in His Own Work

1. Charles A. Owen, Jr., "The Crucial Passage in Five of the *Canterbury Tales:* A Study in Irony and Symbol," *JEGP* 52 (1953): 294.

2. *Boccaccio on Poetry, Being the Preface and the Fourteenth and Fifteenth Books of Boccaccio's "Genealogia deorum gentilium,"* trans. C. G. Osgood, 2d ed. (Indianapolis: Bobbs-Merrill, 1956), p. 62.

3. Ibid., p. 48. See also St. Augustine, *On Christian Doctrine* 2.6.8: "No one doubts that things are perceived more readily through similitudes and that which is sought with difficulty is discovered with more pleasure" (trans. D. W. Robertson, Jr., [New York: Liberal Arts Press, 1958], p. 38).

4. Raymond Preston, *Chaucer* (New York: Sheed and Ward, 1952), p. 104.

5. Ibid., pp. 56, 65.

6. Charles Muscatine, *Chaucer and the French Tradition* (Berkeley and Los Angeles: Univ. of California Press, 1957). For Muscatine, the juxtaposition of idioms, initially a sequential experience, is finally not an experience of linear (progressive) contradiction—Muscatine's spatial analogies to architecture are misleading—but an experience of multiplicity (mixedness, as Muscatine would say). *We* bring juxtaposed styles into play *everywhere* in Chaucer. The action occurs "in our heads"; the text informs our thinking by teaching us how to read (or hear) contrasting styles. Muscatine's notion of Chaucer as a "complex ironic whole" suggests that whatever perspective his Gothic style affords, it always holds out the prospect of greater perspectives and new "wholes" that the reader can discover as he weighs possible attitudes toward the narrative.

7. Ibid., p. 153. Muscatine's emphasis.

8. G. L. Kittredge, *Chaucer and His Poetry* (Cambridge, Mass.: Harvard Univ. Press, 1915), p. 115. Kittredge's analogy is suggestive, a first-rate *obiter dictum* about the breadth and comprehensiveness of the work, much like Dryden's apt, but casual, phrase "that here is God's plenty." Kittredge's description of the *Canterbury Tales* as a "Human Comedy"—the words recall the title Balzac gave his series of novels— praises rather than categorizes the *Canterbury Tales* as drama and implies in late-nineteenth-century fashion that drama and the novel are "true to life" in the same way—both are psychological and panoramic.

9. See Muscatine's uneasy explanation of the way the dramatic principle in Chaucer explains Chaucer's poetry as a philosophical and stylistic series of contrasts: "Chaucer . . . often follows the first procedure, ignoring dramatic consistency in a whole class of situations in which philosophical expansion is called for. But he rarely, if ever, reverses the meaning of a character without grounding the inconsistency in the characterization itself" (*Chaucer and the French Tradition*, p. 94). The patterns of philosophical contrast Muscatine gives us with one hand, he takes back with the other—dramatic consistency of the kind celebrated in the nineteenth-century dramatic monologue: thoughts best grasped as personal and perhaps conventionalized style.

10. See Paul Ricoeur, "Biblical Hermeneutics," *Semeia* 4 (1975): 65: "Structuralism as ideology starts with the reversal in the relation between code and message which makes the code essential and the message unessential. And it is because this step is taken that the text is killed as message . . . that no existential interpretation seems appropriate for a message which has been reduced to a pure epiphenomenon of the 'codes'."

11. Robert O. Payne, *The Key of Remembrance: A Study of Chaucer's Poetics* (New Haven: Yale Univ. Press for the Univ. of Cincinnati, 1963), argues that nearly all of Chaucer's critical and theoretical vocabulary either derives from the school rhetoricians of the twelfth century or expresses ways of thinking closely similar to those of the rhetoricians. James J. Murphy has questioned the specific sources of influence on Chaucer and his English contemporaries, arguing that the teaching of rhetoric as defined by the rhetorical handbooks never took a very strong hold in the English universities and certainly had not done so by the time of Chaucer and Gower; for Murphy any "rhetorical" influence on Chaucer was indirect, the result of the influence of the rhetorical poetic everywhere in Western Europe. See esp. James J. Murphy, "A New Look at Chaucer and the Rhetoricians," *RES* 15 (1964): 1–20. For Payne's answer, see Payne, "Chaucer and the Art of Rhetoric," in *Companion to Chaucer Studies*, ed. Beryl Rowland (New York: Oxford Univ. Press, 1968), pp. 54–55.

12. Medieval theories about literature encourage the coherence of

parts; a "discontinuous" and juxtaposed unity was possible. Payne, *Key of Remembrance*, pp. 42–51, suggests that because medieval writers were habituated to using preexisting texts, medieval literary theorists lacked concern for *inventio* and *dispositio;* medieval rhetoric books focused on *elocutio*, the adornment of parts (the labor of style), in a narrative that had already been composed. J. W. H. Atkins, *English Literary Criticism: The Medieval Phase* (Gloucester, Mass.: Peter Smith, 1961), p. 99, suggests that medieval compositions lacked unity and proportion because of "the influence of oral traditions, according to which poems were recited episode by episode, instead of being written for readers capable of forming judgments with the whole work before them." Both Payne's textual explanation and Atkins' rhetorical one are probably correct.

13. See Robert M. Jordan, *Chaucer and the Shape of Creation: The Aesthetic Possibilities of Inorganic Structure* (Cambridge, Mass.: Harvard Univ. Press, 1967), esp. pp. 8, 129–31, "The Compositional Structure of the Book of the Duchess," *ChauR* 9 (1974): 99–117 (esp. pp. 102–3, 114–15), and "Chaucerian Romance?" *YFS* 51 (1974): 223–34 (esp. pp. 229, 232–33). Jordan's argument throughout is that Chaucerian narrative is digressive and dilatory in movement, made up of relatively autonomous parts. These parts, brought together in a loosely integrated, additive manner, do not amplify the basic narrative line since they are often thematically remote, if not irrelevant.

14. Walter Benjamin, "The Storyteller," in *Illuminations*, ed. Hannah Arendt, trans. Harry Zohn (New York: Schocken Books, 1969), pp. 91–92.

15. Ibid., p. 97.

16. Elizabeth Salter and Derek Pearsall, introduction to *Piers Plowman*, York Medieval Texts (Evanston, Ill.: Northwestern Univ. Press, 1967), p. 3. See also Priscilla Martin, *Piers Plowman: The Field and the Tower* (London: Macmillan, 1979), pp. 9–10.

17. Hugh Kenner, *The Stoic Comedians: Flaubert, Joyce, and Beckett* (Berkeley and Los Angeles: Univ. of California Press, 1962), pp. 35, 41.

18. See Muscatine's discussion of the ending of the *Troilus* (*Chaucer and the French Tradition*, p. 165). For Muscatine our recognition of mixedness (juxtaposition) as a feature of style *is* the recognition of mixedness in the world; a poetry of juxtaposition is, as it were, the window on which, like paneled stained glass, the pictures of ideas are drawn. One observes each panel in sequence (as if on a journey); the combined effect is a comprehensiveness that is distancing, like a view from above. For Muscatine's visual and architectural analogies, see esp. ibid., pp. 167–68. My analogy to paneled stained glass is meant to combine Muscatine's idea of the panoramic survey (seeing all) and the journey (seeing stage by stage—learning to see).

19. H. W. Fowler, *Modern English Usage*, 2d ed. (New York: Oxford

Univ. Press, 1965), p. 305. For a tabular comparison of *irony* and other words (e.g., *humour, wit, satire, sarcasm, invective,* and *cynicism*), see p. 253.

20. Elizabeth Eisenstein, *The Printing Press as an Agent of Change* (Cambridge: Cambridge Univ. Press, 1979), pp. 92–94.

21. Ibid., p. 57 n. 52. Eisenstein's emphasis.

22. Benjamin, "The Storyteller," pp. 97–101.

23. See M. B. Parkes, "The Influence of the Concepts of *Ordinatio* and *Compilatio* on the Development of the Book," in *Medieval Learning and Literature: Essays Presented to Richard William Hunt* (Oxford: Clarendon Press, 1976), p. 135–36.

24. See Parkes, "Influence of the Concepts of *Ordinatio* and *Compilatio*," p. 134, on the *Canterbury Tales* as a compilation. On the *ordinatio*, such as it is, of the Corpus Christi College MS of the *Troilus*, see M. B. Parkes, "Palaeographical Description and Commentary," in Geoffrey Chaucer, *Troilus and Criseyde, A Facsimile of the Corpus Christi College Cambridge MS 61*, intro. M. B. Parkes and Elizabeth Salter (Cambridge: D. S. Brewer, 1978), pp. 4–5. Parkes notes (p. 4) that the "emphatic indication of the division of the work into books" is clearly Chaucer's (see in evidence *Troilus and Criseyde* 3.1818 and 4.26). The quotation in the text is from Parkes, "Influence of the Concepts of *Ordinatio* and *Compilatio*," p. 115.

25. The evidence Paul Strohm has assembled ("Chaucer's Fifteenth-Century Audience and the Narrowing of the 'Chaucer Tradition,'" *SAC* 4 [1982]: 3–32) suggests to me a distinction between private performance among those in Chaucer's fourteenth-century audience and private performance among those in Chaucer's fourteenth- and fifteenth-century audience who could (and would) imagine Chaucer performing, and who did, according to Strohm, read him selectively. Private performance as the re-creation (imitation) at home of the performance of literature was common in Chaucer's day and beyond. See ibid., p. 15, on the dispersion of what Strohm calls Chaucer's "primary audience," and pp. 16–17 on the implications of the shift from an intimate Chaucer circle to a geographically wider, though morally narrower, one. See also ibid., pp. 19–20, for Strohm's account of Derek Pearsall's distinction "between 'court poetry' produced in and for a court environment and 'courtly poetry' reflecting its values but disseminated among an enlarged public." On Chaucer's "secondary audience," Strohm observes: "Paradoxically, for all their increased geographical and social latitude, the members of this new audience seem to have inclined strongly toward works which they perceived in some usually nebulous sense as 'courtly' or 'of the court'" (p. 18). On the general, and clearly recognizable, shift in literary taste (expectation) among those in the fifteenth century who read Chaucer, see esp. pp. 25–27.

26. Citations of Chaucer in my text are from *The Works of Geoffrey Chaucer*, ed. F. N. Robinson, 2d ed. (Boston: Houghton Mifflin, 1957).

27. On texts as figuratively the "material" of speaking pictures, see Richard Firth Green, *Poets and Princepleasers: Literature and the English Court in the Late Middle Ages* (Toronto: Univ. of Toronto Press, 1980), p. 62. The analogy Green draws between tapestries ('picture stories') and verse narratives ('story pictures') is a good one; as art, both tapestries and court narratives speak as visualizations in and for the *camera regis*.

28. For an influential reading of Chaucer that is an example of just such a disassociation of publicness, see H. Marshall Leicester, Jr., "The Art of Impersonation: A General Prologue to the *Canterbury Tales*," *PMLA* 95 (1980), esp. p. 217. My reservation (about Leicester's argument) is that even if he is correct theoretically (that "the speaker is created by the text itself as a structure of linguistic relationships, and the character of the speaker is a function of the specific deployment of those relationships in a particular case to produce the voice of the text"), readers *do* imagine a person talking. One rarely hears "language" speaking, except in linguistic models or real-life vacuums. For modern private readers, that *imagined* person (voice equals person, which is consonant with our experience of language) is usually and profitably thought of, when thought of at all, as an actual (or imagined actual) speaker in an actual (or possible) performance. For a medieval reader, say, at home, that person was a voice and a presence imitated, not constructed through a kind of leap to analogy. The idea of imitation (mimicry) has historical and social implications, not only for the idea of reading, but also for the idea of replication—re-creating privately a real communal performance. The purity of Leicester's thinking—his seeming refusal to recognize our very human impulse to think and explain according to referential analogies (voice in the text becomes voice in the world, and that too is a theory)—makes his argument true, but narrow. Curiously enough, Leicester has recently been criticized for not making a thoroughgoing enough distinction between voice and presence in Chaucer. See Jesse M. Gellrich, *The Idea of the Book in the Middle Ages: Language Theory, Mythology, and Fiction* (Ithaca: N.Y. Cornell Univ. Press, 1985), p. 234 n. 21. See also Robert M. Jordan, *Chaucer's Poetics and the Modern Reader* (Berkeley and Los Angeles: Univ. of California Press, 1987), p. 121 n. 5. Such criticism implicitly argues for a disassociation of publicness that leaves a "postmodern" Chaucer lost in the house of language. Gellrich argues that Chaucer's idea of voice as the wholly fictive construct of the text leads us, because voice cannot be construed as a sign of presence and hence authority, into interpretive indeterminacy unique in medieval literature. On Chaucer's unprecedented departure from, according to Gellrich, medieval theories

of the perfect embodiment of voice in text, see esp. chap. 5 (on the *House of Fame*). Jordan argues for a "virtuoso Chaucerian voice" that gives us, because Chaucer as "artificer" is "absent and unembodied" enjoying a "privileged status outside the language of the text," a "sequence of discourses whose presentational voices are always subject to nominal displacement" (p. 148). For Jordan, Chaucer's rhetorical poetic leaves him free to "contemplate language itself" (p. 169). In such a poetic, "meaning dances elusively among the interstices of discourse and the spaces between his own mind, the text he is composing, and the illusion his text creates" (p. 170).

29. Charles Koban, "Hearing Chaucer Out: The Art of Persuasion in the *Wife of Bath's Tale*," *ChauR* 5 (1971): 225–39. The phrase "pervasive structure" is Koban's (p. 226).

30. On the medieval idea of circumstance as the context for making and exercising moral judgments about stories, see Glending Olson, "Rhetorical Circumstances and the Canterbury Storytelling," *SAC Proceedings* 1 (1984): 211–18.

31. Bertrand H. Bronson, *In Search of Chaucer* (Toronto: Univ. of Toronto Press, 1960), p. 30. See also p. 66.

32. Ibid., p. 67.

33. A. C. Baugh, "Chaucer the Man," in *Companion to Chaucer Studies*, ed. Rowland, rev. ed., 1979, p. 14.

34. Neither Bronson's view that Chaucer as narrator was present everywhere for a medieval audience and thus ought to be imagined as the "consistent" narrator in the written text as we have it and read it (see *In Search of Chaucer*, pp. 25–32) nor E. Talbot Donaldson's view that Chaucer's manuscript narrative is similar enough to a modern work of fiction that its "rhetor" can be said to have been consciously built into the text as the author's persona (see "Chaucer the Pilgrim," *PMLA* 69 [1954]: 928–36) tells the whole story. Donaldson knows that Chaucer performed his own verse narratives (see esp. pp. 935–36), and Bronson knows that Chaucer made it possible for others to perform them.

35. See R. W. Chambers, "Robert or William Langland?" *London Mediaeval Studies* 1 (1948, for 1939): 443. See also George Kane, *The Autobiographical Fallacy in Chaucer and Langland Studies*, Chambers Memorial Lecture, 1965 (London: H. K. Lewis for University College, 1965), p. 15.

36. Kane makes this point too. See *Autobiographical Fallacy*, p. 14. See also Anne Middleton, "The Idea of Public Poetry in the Reign of Richard II," *Speculum* 53 (1978): 108–9.

37. James Winny, "Chaucer Himself," in Maurice Hussey, A. C. Spearing, and James Winny, *An Introduction to Chaucer* (Cambridge: Cambridge Univ. Press, 1965), p. 17.

38. See Alfred L. Kellogg, "Chaucer's Self-Portrait and Dante's," in *Chaucer, Langland, Arthur: Essays in Middle English Literature* (New Brunswick, N.J.: Rutgers Univ. Press, 1972), p. 354. See also Stanley Fish, "The *Nun's Priest's Tale* and Its Analogues," *CLAJ* 5 (1962): 227.

39. See Alan Gaylord, "Chaucer's Dainty 'Dogerel': The 'Elvyssh' Prosody of *Sir Thopas*," in *SAC* 1 (1979): 83–104, on Sir Thopas as "rym," not just parody. See also Gaylord, "The Moment of *Sir Thopas:* Towards a New Look at Chaucer's Language," *ChauR* 16 (1982): 311–29.

40. Alfred David, "The Man of Law vs. Chaucer," *PMLA* 82 (1967): 219.

41. Ibid., p. 220 n. 8. For John H. Fisher's suggestion, see his *John Gower: Moral Philosopher and Friend of Chaucer* (New York: New York Univ. Press, 1964), pp. 286–92.

42. See the Manciple's Tale 235–36 and 316 for the phrase "noght textueel." For a similar phrase, see the Manciple's Tale 211 ("I am a boystous man, right thus seye I"); in context this phrase implies the inability to make interpretative distinctions. See the Manciple's Tale 207–10 and the Prologue to the Miller's Tale 3170–75 for the same kind of apology (and justification) for being literal by a "man noght textueel" as General Prologue 725–46.

43. Barbara Nolan, "'A Poet Ther Was': Chaucer's Voices in the General Prologue to *The Canterbury Tales*," *PMLA* 101 (1986): 159.

44. Perhaps Paul Strohm, "The Social and Literary Scene in England," in *The Cambridge Chaucer Companion*, ed. Piero Boitani and Jill Mann (Cambridge: Cambridge Univ. Press, 1986), p. 12, should have drawn a more sociable conclusion than he does about the "absence or near-absence of manuscripts from Chaucer's lifetime." If such evidence does suggest that Chaucer "prepared only a limited number of copies" of his work and "used them mainly as texts for oral delivery," it is likely that others in Chaucer's circle declaimed his work too—to themselves, having heard Chaucer read, and perhaps to Chaucer who, no doubt, would want, as any medieval author might, to hear his own work read to him as a kind of public proofreading.

45. See Donald R. Howard, *The Idea of the Canterbury Tales* (Berkeley and Los Angeles: Univ. of California Press, 1976), p. 119. See also Betsey Bowden, *Chaucer Aloud: The Varieties of Textual Interpretation* (Philadelphia: Univ. of Pennsylvania Press, 1987), p. 6, on the awkwardness of late-twentieth-century academics in performing the "critical crux" in Chaucer. Perhaps what Bowden has found is an impingement of critical reverence on an otherwise expressive appropriation of the text by Chaucerians who, when they can impersonate Chaucer, do so.

46. See Parkes, "Influence of the Concepts of *Ordinatio* and *Compilatio*," p. 115, on monastic and scholastic *lectio*. See also ibid., pp. 130–31, on the parallel between Chaucer and Vincent of Beauvais.

47. On Chaucer as "outsider," inexperienced in worldly matters, particularly in the relationship between men and women, see, for example, the Legend of Dido 1166–67 in the *Legend of Good Women*, where he says he has only heard about love, or the *Parliament of Fowls* 8–11, where he says he has only read about it.

48. See, for example, the Nun's Priest's Tale 3050–57.

49. See J. Leslie Hotson, "Colfox vs. Chauntecleer," *PMLA* 39 (1924): 762–81.

50. Ibid., p. 780.

51. Anne Middleton, "The Clerk and His Tale: Some Literary Contexts," in *SAC* 2 (1980): 149. See Middleton's discussion of the Clerk's Tale as a performance, not a "dramatic experience" but a "textual one" (p. 147), though a no less public one because it is an "act of literary-critical wit" (p. 148).

52. Howard, *Idea of the Canterbury Tales*, p. 48.

53. Ernst Robert Curtius, *European Literature and the Latin Middle Ages*, trans. Willard R. Trask, Bollingen Series 36 (1953; reprint, New York: Harper and Row, 1963), pp. 83–85, groups under the heading "Affected Modesty"—he means self-conscious modesty—those versions of the humility topos commonly intended to put hearers (p. 83) "in a favorable, attentive, and tractable state of mind," e.g., statements of submissiveness, humility, feebleness, inadequate preparation and devotion (on the so-called "devotional formula," see esp. ibid., pp. 407–13).

54. Alfred David, *The Strumpet Muse: Art and Morals in Chaucer's Poetry* (Bloomington: Indiana Univ. Press, 1976), pp. 57–58.

55. See my review of David's book in *University Publishing* 9 (1980): 21. See also Lee Patterson, "Writing about Writing: The Case for Chaucer," *UTQ* 48 (1979), esp. pp. 278–80.

56. David, *Strumpet Muse*, p. 58. On the tension between moral judgment and instinctive emotional reaction as a central feature of the General Prologue, see Jill Mann, *Chaucer and Medieval Estates Satire: The Literature of Social Classes and the General Prologue to the Canterbury Tales* (Cambridge: Cambridge Univ. Press, 1973), esp. her conclusions, pp. 187–202.

57. Patricia J. Eberle, "Commercial Language and the Commercial Outlook in the *General Prologue*," *ChauR* 18 (1983): 166.

58. Ibid. See also Paul Strohm, "Chaucer's Audience: Discussion," *ChauR* 18 (1983): 179–80.

59. There is no evidence that the merchant class was a part of Chaucer's audience, or that they read vernacular literature. See V. J. Scattergood, "Literary Culture at the Court of Richard II," in *English Court Culture in the Later Middle Ages*, ed. V. J. Scattergood and J. W. Sher-

borne (London: Duckworth, 1983), pp. 42–43 (appendix B), on the literary taste of late-fourteenth-century merchants. On Chaucer's bourgeois ethos, see, for example, V. J. Scattergood, "The Originality of the *Shipman's Tale*," *ChauR* 11 (1974): 210–31. On misleading class distinctions in Chaucer, see Strohm, "Social and Literary Scene in England," pp. 14–15: "While contemporary evidence *does* suggest a split in literary taste between *gentils* and others in the middle strata, that split was . . . probably actually grounded more on the inclination of the *gentils* toward both secular and devotional literature versus the inclination of the others toward devotional literature alone, rather than (as Chaucer seems to suggest) a clash between the *gentils'* taste for hagiographical and other elevated genres on the one hand and the taste of the non-*gentils* for fabliaux or other 'ribaudye' (6.324) on the other" (Strohm's emphasis).

60. Eberle, "Commercial Language," p. 163.

61. See Britton J. Harwood, "Chaucer and the Silence of History: Situating the Canon's Yeoman's Tale," *PMLA* 102 (1987): 338–42. For Gratian's distinction between productive and commercial capitalism, see ibid., p. 339: "Whoever buys a thing, not that he may sell it whole and unchanged, but that it may be a material for fashioning something, he is not a merchant. But the man who buys it in order that he may gain by selling it again unchanged and as he bought it, that man is of the buyers and sellers who are cast forth from God's temple" (Harwood's translation). For Marx's distinction between commercial capitalism that does not "overthrow . . . the old mode of production" (Harwood notes that Chaucer will describe what we call capitalistic feudalism) and productive capitalism that is truly "revolutionary," see ibid., p. 347 n. 4.

62. See Howard, *Idea of the Canterbury Tales*, esp. pp. 45–56, 130.

2. Medieval Storytelling

1. On medieval libraries, see Paul Saenger, "Silent Reading: Its Impact on Late Medieval Script and Society," *Viator* 13 (1982): 396–98 and 408.

2. We perhaps should imagine Chaucer saying the words of his own verse narratives aloud to himself as he wrote them, visualizing his audience at a public reading of his works. *Legere* meant *audire*, even though in the fourteenth century *inspixere* and *videre* were employed to denote silent private reading. See Saenger, "Silent Reading," p. 384. Composition for Chaucer was as much an acoustical (a social and preparatory) experience as the actual presentation of a narrative publicly. He is clearly looking forward to a formal presentation when, in the F Prologue to the *Legend of Good Women*, Alceste gives her command to the poet: "And

whan this book ys maad, yive it the quene, / On my byhalf, at Eltham or at Sheene" (496–97). Chaucer, as we know, also read his manuscripts to a circle of listeners that may have included the king, but probably did not always include him, to revise his work perhaps as well as to entertain. For Chaucer, given the fluid nature of the written manuscript in medieval times, reading aloud at court or at the home of a nobleman may easily have become a kind of dress rehearsal. See Derek Pearsall, "The Troilus Frontispiece and Chaucer's Audience," *YES* 7 (1977): 70, on the *idea* of the frontispiece: "[It] represents as a reality the myth of delivery that Chaucer cultivates so assiduously in the poem." Cf. Elizabeth Salter, "The 'Troilus Frontispiece'," in *Troilus and Criseyde, A Facsimile of Corpus Christi College Cambridge MS 61*, intro. Parkes and Salter, p. 22, on the frontispiece as a reflection of the poem it introduces. For a reference in Chaucer to reading in a "chambre," see *Anelida and Arcite* 165–66; also the legend of Hypsipyle and Medea, 1554–55, in the *Legend of Good Women*. On Chaucer's reading before John of Gaunt, see Edward I. Condren, "The Historical Context of the *Book of the Duchess:* A New Hypothesis," *ChauR* 5 (1971), esp. p. 196. Until John of Gaunt's own death in 1399, an elaborate anniversary ceremony kept alive Blanche's memory. It is not unlikely that the performance of the *Book of the Duchess*—a public reading of it, not necessarily by Chaucer—would have been appropriate for one of these annual events. See Sidney Armitage-Smith, *John of Gaunt* (New York: Barnes and Noble, 1964), p. 77. See also N. B. Lewis, "The Anniversary Service for Blanche, Duchess of Lancaster, 12th September, 1374," *Bulletin of the John Rylands Library* 21 (1937): 176, and Rossell Hope Robbins, "Geoffroi Chaucier, Poéte Français, Father of English Poetry," *ChauR* 13 (1978): 101. Robbins thinks that the *Book of the Duchess* may have been "composed for public recital at a small house gathering following" the funeral mass for Blanche—a gathering of "sixty or seventy persons" who comprised the duke's personal household in residence at the Savoy Palace. Condren, "Historical Context," p. 211 n. 21, even speculates that an original version of the *Book of the Duchess* may have eulogized Edward III's wife, Queen Philippa. See Condren's response to John N. Palmer, "The Historical Context of the Book of the Duchess: A Revision," *ChauR* 8 (1974): 253–61, on this point in Condren, "Of Deaths and Duchesses and Scholars Coughing in Ink," *ChauR* 10 (1976): 90–91.

    3. Walter Benjamin, "The Work of Art in the Age of Mechanical Reproduction," in *Illuminations*, ed. Arendt, trans. Zohn, pp. 220–23.

    4. Benjamin, "The Storyteller," p. 98.

    5. See Howard, *Idea of the Canterbury Tales*, pp. 60–67. Howard's three terms—*bookness, voiceness,* and *paperness*—nicely catch the sense

of my argument about Chaucer's storytelling: that Chaucer's manuscript narratives, objects of veneration intended for a reader's edification (Howard's idea of the "bookness" of the *Canterbury Tales*), declaimed aloud by Chaucer himself from a pulpit at public performances (Howard's idea of "voiceness"), *could* be used at the discrimination of any performer and *his* listeners, or the private reader performing for himself (Howard's idea of the "paperness" of the *Canterbury Tales*). I particularly like Howard's notion of reading as a voyage of exploration (see ibid., pp. 66–67).

6. For a comic version of this same problem about what Chaucer can or does tell us about the behavior of a character, see Derek S. Brewer, "Towards a Chaucerian Poetic," *Proceedings of the British Academy* 60 (1974): 241, on Pandarus's location, and the larger issue of verisimilitude, or the lack of it, in Chaucer.

7. See *The Works of Geoffrey Chaucer*, ed. Robinson, p. 814, line 15.

8. Robert Worth Frank, Jr., *Chaucer and The Legend of Good Women* (Cambridge, Mass.: Harvard Univ. Press, 1972), p. 186. But see, too, V. A. Kolve, "From Cleopatra to Alceste: An Iconographic Study of *The Legend of Good Women*," in *Signs and Symbols in Chaucer's Poetry*, ed. John P. Hermann and John J. Burke, Jr. (University, Ala.: Univ. of Alabama Press, 1981), pp. 130–78, who argues that the idea of the *Legend of Good Women*, unfinished, not conceptually incomplete, was to demonstrate the insufficiency of the ideas of noble love the pagan world provided Chaucer by showing in the final legend of Alceste, not of course written, the story of a lover willing to die so that another might live ("the legend of a death that had served an end beyond its own fame" [p. 171]), a story adumbrating the central motif of Christianity ("a typological adumbration of transcendence" [p. 174]). For Kolve, the *Legend of Good Women* does not anticipate the plurality of voice and text of the *Canterbury Tales*. The *exempla* of the *Legend* are "moral" lives for the God of Love. Since they witness their own insufficiency, they are incomplete (ironic) and demand Christian completion of their pagan narrowness of vision. Even if Kolve is correct, Chaucer did not, to my mind, move in the sure and certain direction in which Kolve sees the *Legend* taking him. Rather than fulfilling the demand of the *Legend's* castigating voice as Kolve describes it (p. 178), Chaucer found a pluralist way to transcendence that celebrates the entanglement of spirit in matter.

9. Only Robertsonians claim that Chaucer is avowedly patristic. See, for example, D. W. Robertson, Jr., *A Preface to Chaucer: Studies in Medieval Perspectives* (Princeton, N.J.: Princeton Univ. Press, 1962), esp. pp. 65–137, on the use and abuse of beauty. But even those who argue that Chaucer is moral to the extent that he is *human* have accepted a kind

of Horatian distinction between Chaucer the moralist and Chaucer the entertainer that dates from the sixteenth century (see Caroline Spurgeon, *Five Hundred Years of Chaucer Criticism and Allusion*, vol. 1 [Cambridge: Cambridge Univ. Press, 1925], pp. xvii–xxi) and that Robertsonians, who believe that medieval literature is essentially moralistic, have adopted too. See, for example, Charles Muscatine, *Poetry and Crisis in the Age of Chaucer* (Notre Dame, Ind.: Univ. of Notre Dame Press, 1972), p. 144: "Apart from his perception and sympathy with life, Chaucer's great virtue is morale. It is a morale that is based, not on a doctrinaire conservatism, but on a felt acquaintance with all the alternatives."

10. C. H. Dodd, *The Parables of the Kingdom*, rev. ed. (New York: Charles Scribner's Sons, 1961), p. 5. See Robert W. Funk, *Language, Hermeneutic, and Word of God* (New York: Harper and Row, 1966), chap. 5 ("The Parable as Metaphor"), on Dodd and the linguistic nature (and phenomenology) of the parable.

11. Edgar de Bruyne, *The Esthetics of the Middle Ages*, trans. Eileen B. Hennessy (New York: Frederick Ungar, 1969), esp. pp. 73–78.

12. Ibid., pp. 75, 76.

13. Ibid., pp. 77, 78.

14. Ibid., pp. 75, 78.

15. Ibid., p. 77.

16. Joseph Mazzeo, "Dante's Conception of Poetic Expression," *RR* 47 (1956): 241–58.

17. Howard, *Idea of the Canterbury Tales*, p. 174.

18. Donald R. Howard, *Writers & Pilgrims: Medieval Pilgrimage Narratives and Their Posterity* (Berkeley and Los Angeles: Univ. of California Press, 1980), p. 102.

19. Ibid. Howard's emphases.

20. See de Bruyne, *Esthetics of the Middle Ages*, p. 78: "The medieval thinkers were not content to create allegories, whether literary or plastic; they attempted to discover in story and fiction hidden meanings which cannot be perceived at first reading. If the hidden meaning is concealed within a true story to such a point that one reality transports the reader into another, profane reality, we must speak of allegory. If the hidden meaning is merely suggested by a fable, to the point where the reader feels himself being transported from an imaginary world into a world which is true only in a moral sense, we must speak of an integument." See also ibid., p. 162.

21. Dodd, *Parables of the Kingdom*, p. 5.

22. Ibid., p. 7.

23. Ibid., p. 9. Dodd's emphasis.

24. Ibid., p. 10. Dodd's emphasis.

25. Ibid., p. 35.

26. Ibid., p. 159.

27. Ibid., p. 12.

28. Ibid., p. 11.

29. Funk, *Language, Hermeneutic, and Word of God*, p. 162.

30. St. Augustine, *On Christian Doctrine* 2.6.7 (trans. Robertson, p. 37). Biblical citations are from the King James version, except where noted.

31. Ibid., 2.6.8 (p. 38).

32. See Frank Kermode, *The Genesis of Secrecy: On the Interpretation of Narrative* (Cambridge, Mass.: Harvard Univ. Press, 1979), p. 5, on the idea of the "secular canon"—the authoritative list of books that are "guaranteed to be of such value that every effort of exegesis is justified without argument."

33. Until fairly recently, the parables of Jesus were grouped with the illustrative tale. For a medieval example, see *Boccaccio on Poetry*, trans. Osgood, pp. 47–51. Boccaccio argues (p. 51) that "the power of fiction" is that "it pleases the unlearned by its external appearance, and exercises the minds of the learned with its hidden truth; and thus both are edified and delighted with one and the same perusal." On the allegorizing of the parables of Jesus, see Dodd, *Parables of the Kingdom*, pp. 4–5. His distinction between rabbinic parables and Hellenistic myths, "allegorically interpreted, as vehicles of esoteric doctrine" (p. 4), would make no real difference to a defense, like Boccaccio's, of the veil of fiction.

34. J. A. Mosher, *The Exemplum in Early Religious and Didactic Literature in England* (New York: Columbia Univ. Press, 1911), uses *exemplum* broadly, like others since him, to mean a consciously and obviously moralized tale. Mosher makes, I think, an untenable distinction between *exempla* and "secular" tales, sometimes in the guise of *exempla* (Gower's *Confessio* is his example). Cf. Charles Runacres, "Art and Ethics in the 'Exempla' of 'Confessio Amantis,'" in *Gower's Confessio Amantis: Responses and Reassessments*, ed. A. J. Minnis (Cambridge: D. S. Brewer, 1983), esp. pp. 107–11. Like Mosher, Runacres does not distinguish between *Exempla* and parables, though he sees Gower's requiring a reader's attention to storial particulars as Gower's way of being engagingly moral. See ibid., pp. 128–29.

35. See T. D. Kelly and John T. Irwin, "The Meaning of *Cleanness*: Parable as Effective Sign," *MS* 35 (1973): 232–60; and John T. Irwin and T. D. Kelly, "The Way and the End Are One: *Patience* as a Parable of the Contemplative Life," *ABR* 25 (1974): 33–55.

36. Irwin and Kelly, "The Way and the End Are One," p. 54.

37. Ibid., p. 53: "Indeed, Christ tells his disciples that the meaning of

the parables is specifically reserved for those who have been given the knowledge of the kingdom of heaven." On the parable as a "communicative situation," see Hans Robert Jauss, "The Alterity and Modernity of Medieval Literature," *NLH* 10 (1979): 228–29. Unfortunately, Jauss's historical discussion of parables in the Middle Ages is less satisfactory than his understanding of them as modes of speaking and teaching (see pp. 218–19), perhaps because Jauss, oddly enough, does not really see the connection between biblical parables and the generalizably parabolic. Similarly, Kermode's notion (*Genesis of Secrecy*, p. 45) that "the apparently perspicuous narrative yields up latent sense to interpretation" so that "we are never inside it" and "from the outside may never experience anything more than some radiant intimation of the source of all these senses" does not tell the whole story. See *Genesis of Secrecy*, esp. pp. 125–26, for Kermode's own brand of unconsolable (Kafkaean) hermeneutics.

38. See Joachim Jeremias, *The Parables of Jesus*, trans. S. H. Hooke, 2d rev. ed. (1954; reprint, New York: Charles Scribner's Sons, 1972), esp. chap. 3. Jeremias concludes (p. 230) that "all the parables of Jesus compel his hearers to come to a decision about his person and mission."

39. Paul Ricoeur, "Biblical Hermeneutics," pp. 99–100: "My suggestion is that the trait which invites us to *transgress* the narrative structures is the same as that which *specifies* the parable as a 'religious' kind of 'poetic' discourse. This trait is, to my mind, the element of extravagance which makes 'oddness' of the narrative, by mixing the 'extraordinary' with the 'ordinary'. Could we not say that this dimension of extravagance delivers the *openness* of the metaphorical process from the *closure* of the narrative form? . . . The parabolic message proceeds from this *tension* between a form which circumscribes it and a process which transgresses the narrative boundaries and points to an 'other', to a 'beyond'. . . . it is not utterly useless to consider a while the narrative pattern of the parables as *unstable*, as polarized between the 'closed' and the 'open', and to look at the dimension of extravagance as the kind of narrative *impertinence* (or irrelevance, or inconsistency), which 'winks' (as Heidegger would say!) in the direction of a metaphorical interpretation, echoing in that way the warning 'Let those who have ears hear!'" Ricoeur's emphasis. See also ibid., pp. 114–18.

40. *The Didascalicon of Hugh of St. Victor: A Medieval Guide to the Arts*, trans. Jerome Taylor (New York: Columbia Univ. Press, 1961), p. 143 and p. 137.

41. Ibid., p. 144.

42. Ibid., pp. 135–36.

43. Ibid., p. 150.

44. Beryl Smalley, *The Study of the Bible in the Middle Ages* (Notre

Dame, Ind.: Univ. of Notre Dame Press, 1964), p. 95. On "hasty allegory" that "must fail if it lacks a basis in historical exegesis," see Peter Classen, "*Res Gestae,* Universal History, Apocalypse: Visions of Past and Future," in *Renaissance and Renewal in the Twelfth Century,* ed. Robert L. Benson and Giles Constable, with Carol D. Lanham (Cambridge, Mass.: Harvard Univ. Press, 1982), p. 406.

45. Smalley, *Study of the Bible in the Middle Ages,* pp. 96–97.

46. *Didascalicon of Hugh of St. Victor,* trans. Taylor, p. 88.

47. Ibid., pp. 88–89.

48. Ibid., p. 102.

49. See ibid., p. 92: "Exposition includes three things: the letter, the sense, and the inner meaning. The letter is the fit arrangement of words, which we also call construction; the sense is a certain ready and obvious meaning which the letter presents on the surface; the inner meaning is the deeper understanding which can be found only through interpretation and commentary. Among these, the order of inquiry is first the letter, then the sense, and finally the inner meaning. And when this is done, the exposition is complete." Hugh's method for explicating the Scriptures follows this same three-level process. Although he acknowledges that the letter of a sacred text may be "imperfect" (p. 147) and that the sense may be "incredible" or "impossible" or "absurd" or "false" (p. 148), Hugh expects us to proceed in an orderly fashion, from letter to sense, if possible, and not to rush to expound what he calls, for a sacred text, its "deeper meaning" (p. 147) (*sententia*), which "can never be absurd, never false" (p. 149). Hugh notes (p. 147) that "some discourses contain only the letter and sense, some only the letter and a deeper meaning, some all three together. But every discourse ought to contain at least two." We should note, too, that when Hugh describes interpreting the deeper meaning of a sacred text he is as thorough an allegorist as any: "Although . . . many things are found to disagree, the deeper meaning admits no contradiction, is always harmonious, always true" (pp. 149–50).

50. Ibid., p. 96.

51. Ibid., p. 95.

52. Smalley, *Study of the Bible in the Middle Ages,* pp. 105–6.

53. But see Nikolaus M. Häring, "Commentary and Hermeneutics," in *Renaissance and Renewal,* ed. Benson and Constable, pp. 190–99, on the influence of the Abbey of St. Victor on biblical hermeneutics in the twelfth century. On the idea of "a school of St. Victor," see Jean Leclercq, "The Renewal of Theology," in *Renaissance and Renewal,* pp. 73 and 75.

54. Jeremias, *Parables of Jesus,* p. 13.

55. See Hans W. Frei, *The Eclipse of Biblical Narrative: A Study in Eighteenth and Nineteenth Century Hermeneutics* (New Haven: Yale

Univ. Press, 1974): "Clearly, if figural or typological interpretation was to be successful, it required a delicate balance between the temporally separated occasions, a firm connection with literal or realistic procedure, and a clear rooting in the order of temporal sequence" (p. 29). On allegory: "The attachment of a temporally free-floating meaning pattern to any temporal occasion whatever, without any intrinsic connection between sensuous time-bound picture and the meaning represented by it" (p. 29). On the rooting nature of figural interpretation: "Figuration made sense of the general extra-biblical structure of human experience, and of one's own experience, as well as of general concepts of good and evil drawn from experience" (p. 3).

56. See Erich Auerbach, *Mimesis: The Representation of Reality in Western Literature* (Garden City, N.Y.: Doubleday, Anchor Books, 1953): "The total content of the sacred writings was placed in an exegetic context which often removed the thing told very far from its sensory base, in that the reader or listener was forced to turn his attention away from the sensory occurrence and toward its meaning. This implied the danger that the visual element of the occurrences might succumb under the dense texture of meanings" (p. 42). On the origin of figural interpretation and the difference between it and allegorizing on the one hand and symbolic or mythical and magical interpretation on the other, see Auerbach, "'Figura,'" in *Scenes from the Drama of European Literature* (New York: Meridian Books, 1959), esp. pp. 49–50. On the capacity of figural prophecy to connect the time-bound and the timeless, see esp. pp. 58–60.

57. Brian Stock, *The Implications of Literacy: Written Language and Models of Interpretation in the Eleventh and Twelfth Centuries* (Princeton, N.J.: Princeton Univ. Press, 1983), p. 87.

58. See ibid., pp. 90–92. See also Janet Coleman, *English Literature in History, 1350–1400: Medieval Readers and Writers* (London: Hutchinson, 1981), pp. 157–60 for a historical argument similar to Stock's that textual communities make earlier oral communities self-conscious. The distinction Coleman would keep between the mythical and the logico-empirical modes of thought seems to me misleading. For a slight modification of Stock's earlier position, see his "Medieval Literacy, Linguistic Theory, and Social Organization," *NLH* 16 (1984), esp. pp. 17–20.

59. See Eric A. Havelock, *The Muse Learns to Write: Reflections on Orality and Literacy from Antiquity to the Present* (New Haven: Yale Univ. Press, 1986), esp. pp. 36 and 50. For Havelock, literacy, which should be opposed historically and theoretically to nonliteracy, not illiteracy, shows "a continuing commemoration of the orally transmitted [and controlling] tradition" (p. 89). Moreover, "all reasonable considerations point not to a ready acceptance of the alphabet but to a resistance to it" (pp. 87–88). On the value of alphabetic efficiency for a continuing orality

on paper, see pp. 90–91: "[The alphabet's] initial advantage . . . was to provide a script which could fluently and unambiguously transcribe the full gamut of orally preserved speech. Anything, any meaning acoustically framed and spoken, any emotion or expression, could after being heard now be written down, as we say, 'in full'." Writing was thus not the immediate condition of our terrifying solipsism, the traces of a self-affirming, isolating, and powerful subjectivity, but the phonetic record of an authentic context of communicative presence, the sound of the visible and the sociable that performance (reading) makes audible.

60. *Oeuvres de Froissart, Poésies*, ed. Auguste Schéler, vol. 1, (Brussels: Devaux, 1870), p. 108 (11.724–27): "Et la damoiselle s'embat / En un lieu qui adonnoit rire. / Or ne vous saroi je pas dire / Le doulc mouvement de sa bouche."

61. See St. Augustine, *Confessions* 6.3: "When he read, his eyes scanned the page and his heart explored the meaning, but his voice was silent and his tongue was still" (trans. R. S. Pine-Coffin [New York: Penguin Books, 1961], p. 114).

62. See Saenger, "Silent Reading," esp. p. 384. Saenger's argument is that there existed from classical times both silent and oral reading (see p. 370). The important difference between oral reading, essentially communal and social, within monasteries and without, and silent reading, essentially devotional, was the context of real or imagined (wished-for) reception. Saenger's thesis is that "in a curious fashion, recent scholars, inspired by McLuhan, have substituted an oral Middle Ages terminating in a silent Renaissance for the more traditional view of a Middle Ages of silent prayer and a Renaissance characterized by a revival of the antique passion for eloquent public discourse" (pp. 369–70).

63. The phrase is George Wilson's. See his "Chaucer and Oral Reading," *SAQ* 25 (1926): 296.

64. Daniel Poirion, *Le Poète et le prince: L'Evolution du lyrisme courtois de Guillaume de Machaut à Charles d'Orléans* (Paris: Presses Universitaires de France, 1965), p. 232. Poirion's emphasis. Poirion describes Deschamps' idea of poetic performance in very much the same way I would describe Chaucer's, for Deschamps' self-presentation as a poet *in* his poems is as pleasing and useful a fiction for him and his court audience as is Chaucer's presence as story maker and storyteller in his own narratives. The distinction we might make between self-presentation in poetry and telling a story was not sharp in the fourteenth century, where performance is the medium of a literary text. Poirion thinks of literary performance as a kind of magical miming.

65. *Oeuvres complètes d'Eustache Deschamps*, ed. Gaston Raynaud, vol. 7 (Paris: Firmin Didot, 1891), p. 270.

66. Poirion, *Le Poète et le prince*, p. 232. Poirion says that the poet

himself, through his voice and his body, his physical presence, and his meaning ("la dance du corps"), gives ideas their presence: "body" accompanies literary imagination in the way a musical instrument might. He calls Deschamps' art "la musique naturelle." It is highly doubtful that Chaucer sang his poetry like a minstrel, though his reading aloud would probably have been thought of as "musique naturelle." Indeed, what has been taken as the traditional and, for Chaucer, empty association of the words *read* and *sing* in the *Troilus* ("And red wherso thow be, or elles songe" [5.1797]) probably indicates, in a formula to be sure, just how declamation was, in Chaucer's mind, *like* the older art of the medieval "mynstralles and gestiours"—both are music; his "naturelle." Moreover, see Barry Windeatt, "Gesture in Chaucer," *Medievalia et Humanistica: Studies in Medieval & Renaissance Culture*, n.s., 9, ed. Paul Clogan (Cambridge: Cambridge Univ. Press, 1979), 143–61. Because "Chaucer's most persistent interest in gesture . . . centers on the eyes and faces of his characters and their acts of looking, which are expressive outwardly of the inner life—not necessarily of a cognitive self-analytical activity, but often of a force of feeling or a strength of will, a capacity to appreciate the full difficulty of their situation" (p. 143), Chaucerian gestures are easily simulated in a one-man show.

67. Medieval reading was simply performance, and with respect to Chaucer, as far as we know, even a simpler kind of live performance than Roman drama as it was understood in the Middle Ages to have been performed—no one mimed while Chaucer read. A few scholars in the Middle Ages seem to have realized that the persons who spoke in a Roman play were also the persons who mimed. See Mary H. Marshall, "Boethius' Definition of *Persona* and Mediaeval Understanding of the Roman Theatre," *Speculum* 25 (1950): 471–82. On the classical concept of the "three voices" in poetry, see V. A. Kolve, *The Play Called Corpus Christi* (Stanford, Calif.: Stanford Univ. Press, 1966), p. 27. See also P. B. Salmon, "The 'Three Voices' in Poetry in Mediaeval Literary Theory," *MÆ* 30 (1961): 1–18. Yet there was no continuing classical tradition of dramatic (mimed) performance in the Middle Ages. Cf. Laura Kendrick, "The *Troilus* Frontispiece and the Dramatization of Chaucer's *Troilus*," *ChauR* 22 (1987): 81–93, on the frontispiece as an imagined dramatization of the poem, where the audience mimes while the poet declaims, and the reader, who is holding the book not pictured on Chaucer's pulpit, is invited to participate.

68. The distinctly medieval idea of the theater *as game* (see Kolve, *Play Called Corpus Christi*, esp. pp. 13–19) is similar to the idea of Chaucer's declamation as imagined visualization. Public reading and medieval drama both share a common theory about the exemplary nature of the visual. "The need to instruct in doctrinal truth, to clarify and make visual certain important meanings that were spiritual and mysterious in

nature, undoubtedly played its part in shaping the medieval conception of theatre: it had to be a medium in which these things could 'happen'" (ibid., p. 27). Medieval theater was thus neither a medium in which things were simply shown nor a theater of illusion. John Edgar Stevens even argues that sound in the medieval theater was not used "to increase dramatic tension" or to "soften up" the audience—that is, to aid in the imagining of an illusion. Because "'heaven is music', so at the crises in the drama when heaven actively intervenes, music too intervenes" ("Music in Mediaeval Drama," *Proceedings of the Royal Musical Association* 84 [1958]: 83).

69. St. Augustine, *Confessions* 10.17 (trans. Pine-Coffin, pp. 223–24).

70. Ibid. 10.8 (p. 214).

71. See, for example, ibid. 10.25 (pp. 230–31) on God and memory.

72. Frances A. Yates, *The Art of Memory* (Chicago: Univ. of Chicago Press, 1966), p. 81.

73. Ibid., p. 104.

74. For a discussion of images and image-making in Chaucer, see V. A. Kolve, "Chaucer and the Visual Arts," in *Writers and their Background: Geoffrey Chaucer*, ed. D. S. Brewer (Athens: Ohio Univ. Press, 1975), pp. 290–320. See esp. his discussion of book 1 of the *House of Fame*, which offers, Kolve says, "the most interesting evidence concerning the way in which the verbal, the visual, and the memorial were linked in Chaucer's mind" (p. 304). In book 1 "we are shown a poet remembering a poem [the *Aeneid*] he has read *as a series of pictures*, by way of creating a new poem that describes those pictures as though they were real" (pp. 305–6). Kolve's emphasis. In this way the narrator's experience of the *Aeneid* in book 1 of the *House of Fame* "offers a medieval paradigm of how narrative poems are made, responded to, and remembered" (p. 305). See also Kolve, *Chaucer and the Imagery of Narrative: The First Five Canterbury Tales* (Stanford, Calif.: Stanford Univ. Press, 1984), esp. pp. 8–58, on mental images as a means of knowing, of poetic making, and of Christian remembering.

75. For a discussion of medieval psychology, see Kolve, "Chaucer and the Visual Arts," pp. 298–304.

76. Guillaume de Deguileville, *The Pilgrimage of the Life of Man*, trans. John Lydgate, ed. Frederick J. Furnivall, EETS, e.s., 77, 83, 92 (1899, 1901, 1904), lines 6253–56.

3. Chaucer's Circle of Understanding

1. See Sidney's *Apologie for Poetrie* (1583) in *English Literary Criticism: The Renaissance*, ed. O. B. Hardison, Jr. (New York: Appleton-Century-Crofts, 1963), p. 128.

2. Donald M. Lowe, *History of Bourgeois Perception* (Chicago: Univ. of Chicago Press, 1982), pp. 6–7.

3. See Lennard J. Davis, *Factual Fictions: The Origins of the English Novel* (New York: Columbia Univ. Press, 1983). But see William Nelson, *Fact or Fiction: The Dilemma of the Renaissance Storyteller* (Cambridge, Mass.: Harvard Univ. Press, 1973), who sees as characteristic of Renaissance storytelling the need to establish the play between a story's factual and figurative truth.

4. Davis, *Factual Fictions*, p. 73.

5. Ibid., pp. 82–83.

6. Ibid., pp. 82–83.

7. See Edmond Faral, *Les Arts poétiques du XIIe et du XIIIe siècle* (Paris: Edouard Champion, 1924), p. 198:

> Si quis habet fundare domum, non currit ad actum
> Impetuosa manus: intrinseca linea cordis
> Praemetitur opus, seriemque sub ordine certo
> Interior praescribit homo. . . .

8. Ibid., p. 198. According to the medieval view, Erwin Panofsky suggests, a work of art "does not arise by man coming to terms with nature, as the terminology of the nineteenth century puts it, but rather by the projection of an inner image into matter." Dante summarizes the medieval view "in a single lapidary sentence," Panofsky says. "'Art is found on three levels: in the mind of the artist, in the tool, and in the material that receives its form from art'" (Panofsky, *Idea: A Concept in Art Theory,* trans. Joseph J. S. Peake [New York: Harper and Row, 1968], p. 43).

9. See Howard, *Idea of the Canterbury Tales*, pp. 135–37, on the phrase ("but he wol bide a stounde") that Chaucer adds to his translation, and on the substitution of "send out" for "measure" (see *Works of Geoffrey Chaucer*, ed. Robinson, p. 818, on lines 1065–69), which results in a switch of metaphor.

10. See Martin Irvine, "Medieval Grammatical Theory and Chaucer's *House of Fame*," *Speculum* 60 (1985): 850–76, on the medieval sources for Chaucer's examination of the nature of traditional texts ("that literary discourse is reducible to a form of speech, spoken sounds inscribed in texts as a form of written memory perpetuated by the arbitrary institution of tradition" [p. 850]).

11. On "pointing" as "describing in detail" in Chaucer and elsewhere, see J. A. Burrow, *Ricardian Poetry: Chaucer, Gower, Langland and the "Gawain" Poet* (London: Routledge and Kegan Paul, 1971), pp. 69–78.

12. On the use of punctuation (pointing) to *prevent* misunderstanding, see M. B. Parkes, "Punctuation, or Pause and Effect," in *Medieval Elo-*

quence: Studies in the Theory and Practice of Medieval Rhetoric, ed. James J. Murphy (Berkeley and Los Angeles: Univ. of California Press, 1978), esp. pp. 133–39. Parkes's examples are all drawn from medieval manuscripts of the same biblical text. On the prophylactic nature of punctuation and on the misunderstanding of medieval punctuation as "irregular," see Parkes's conclusion: "I suggest that the key to the understanding of medieval punctuation lies not in grammatical theory, nor in the analysis of syntactical or intonation patterns, but in the concern of the scribe or corrector to elucidate the text transmitted to him according to the needs of his audience. He seems to have realized that he could achieve the desired effect by means of punctuation: that the adroit use of pauses would ensure that his readers followed what the punctuator regarded as his own correct interpretation of the text" (p. 139).

13. George Steiner, "'Critic'/'Reader,'" *NLH* 10 (1979): 440 (Steiner's emphasis). See esp. pp. 439–51 (on readers) and pp. 451–52 (on the need for readers).

14. Glending Olson, *Literature as Recreation in the Later Middle Ages* (Ithaca, N.Y.: Cornell Univ. Press, 1982), esp. chaps. 2 and 3.

15. Ibid., p. 37.

16. See Howard, *Idea of the Canterbury Tales*, pp. 279–82, on the idea of the Monk's tales as "a study in the psychology of powerlessness" (p. 281).

17. See William C. Strange, "The *Monk's Tale*: A Generous View," *ChauR* 1 (1966): 176–77. On the Monk's sexual infractions, if any, see Robert M. Lumiansky, *Of Sundry Folk: The Dramatic Principle in the Canterbury Tales* (Austin: Univ. of Texas Press, 1955), pp. 97–101. On the particular worldliness of the Monk of the General Prologue, see Paul E. Beichner, "Daun Piers, Monk and Business Administrator," *Speculum* 34 (1959): 611–19, reprinted in *Chaucer Criticism: The Canterbury Tales*, ed. Richard Schoeck and Jerome Taylor, vol. 1 (Notre Dame, Ind.: Univ. of Notre Dame Press, 1960), pp. 52–62. See esp. p. 62 n. 19. For the Monk's mismanaged distinction between Fortune's justice and *Fortuna's* cruel chance, see Strange, "*Monk's Tale*," pp. 170–76. The Monk's "confusion," Strange says, "is our clear drama" (p. 170). See also Jill Mann, *Chaucer and Medieval Estates Satire*, pp. 17–34, on the misreading of the portrait of the Monk in the General Prologue as monastic satire.

18. The phrase is Norman N. Holland's. See his *5 Readers Reading* (New Haven: Yale Univ. Press, 1975), esp. pp. 113–29, for what he calls the way "we meet ourselves in the books we read" (p. 113). On the idiosyncrasies that make the Host the arch-critic, see Walter Scheps, "'Up Roos Oure Hoost, and Was Oure Aller Cok': Harry Bailly's Tale-Telling Competition," *ChauR* 10 (1975): 113–28. See also Norman Holland,

"UNITY IDENTITY TEXT SELF," *PMLA* 90 (1975): 820, on the idea of reading as creation and recreation of identity. For a critical discussion of Norman Holland, see Marshall W. Alcorn, Jr., and Mark Bracher, "Literature, Psychoanalysis and the Re-Formation of the Self: A New Direction for Reader-Response Theory," *PMLA* 100 (1985): 342–54. On Chaucer's notion of poetic tradition, see Donald R. Howard, "Chaucer's Idea of an Idea," *Essays & Studies*, n.s., 29 (1976), esp. pp. 42–50 (on the *House of Fame* as an *ars poetica*). Howard argues that Chaucer's work has interest and value for us precisely because it acknowledges the way individual readers create tradition "in their heads." This last phrase (or a variation of it) was Chaucer's too. See *House of Fame* 3.1101–5 and 2.523–26.

19. Burrow, *Ricardian Poetry*, p. 88. Although he nowhere mentions parables or parablelike stories, Burrow has anticipated my argument: "The prevailing *modus significandi* in Ricardian narrative is not allegorical but literal" (p. 82). See ibid., pp. 82–83, on the exemplary mode.

20. Ibid., p. 90. On the idea of group dynamics in the *Canterbury Tales*, see Howard, *Idea of the Canterbury Tales*, esp. pp. 154–55.

21. Middleton, "Idea of Public Poetry," p. 98. Middleton does not include *Sir Gawain and the Green Knight* and the other poems in the manuscript Cotton Nero A.x in her assessment of Ricardian literary values. See also "Chaucer's 'New Men' and the Good of Literature in the *Canterbury Tales*," in *Literature and Society: Selected Papers from the English Institute, 1978*, n.s., no. 3, ed. Edward W. Said (Baltimore: Johns Hopkins Univ. Press, 1980), pp. 15–56, where Middleton has begun to explore Chaucerian "indirect discourse"—her examples are not confined to the *Canterbury Tales*—and suggested how literary style is the mode and mold of our sociability. She has defined what she calls "enditing" in Chaucer, his idea of "high vernacular eloquence," the end of which is "the celebration not of the court to the court, but of the human world and condition to the whole commonwealth" (p. 39).

22. Middleton, "Idea of Public Poetry," p. 94. See also n. 2 on that page.

23. See Howard, *Idea of the Canterbury Tales*, p. 189.

24. Middleton, "Idea of Public Poetry," p. 112. See also p. 95.

25. See Morton Bloomfield, "Allegory as Interpretation," *NLH* 3 (1972), esp. p. 302.

26. Hans-Georg Gadamer, "The Universality of the Hermeneutical Problem," in *Philosophical Hermeneutics*, ed. and trans. David E. Linge (Berkeley and Los Angeles: Univ. of California Press, 1976), p. 9.

27. For these distinctions, see Paul Strohm, "Chaucer's Audience(s): Fictional, Implied, Intended, Actual," *ChauR* 18 (1983): 137–45.

28. Edith Rickert, "King Richard II's Books," *The Library*, 4th ser., 13 (1932–33): 144–45.

29. V. J. Scattergood, "Literary Culture at the Court of Richard II," in *English Court Culture*, ed. Scattergood and Sherborne, p. 34.

30. Richard Firth Green, "King Richard II's Books Revisited," *The Library* 31 (1976): 237.

31. Ibid., p. 238.

32. V. J. Scattergood, "Two Medieval Booklists," *The Library* 23 (1968): 237.

33. See Scattergood, "Literary Culture at the Court of Richard II," in *English Court Culture*, ed. Scattergood and Sherborne, pp. 34–36, for a list of books appearing among the possessions of Thomas Woodstock, duke of Gloucester, books bequeathed by noble ladies, and books belonging to non-aristocratic courtiers.

34. Gervase Mathew, *The Court of Richard II* (London: John Murray, 1968), p. 22.

35. "Omerus" is not used to praise Chaucer or Gower, but the idea of a first or founding poet is explicit in the self-positioning of those who see themselves as successors to either Chaucer or Gower, or both. See, for example, John Lydgate, *Curia sapiencie* (1403), cited in Spurgeon, *Five Hundred Years of Chaucer Criticism and Allusion*, vol. 1, pp. 16–17, who calls Chaucer and Gower "erthy goddes two / Of thyrste of eloquent delycacye / With all your successours few or moo."

36. Elizabeth Salter, "Chaucer and Internationalism," *SAC* 2 (1980), pp. 76–77.

37. The phrases "triumph of internationalism" and "high-prestige vernacular literature" are Salter's. See "Chaucer and Internationalism," pp. 79 and 71 respectively. For Salter's argument, see esp. pp. 72–77.

38. See, for example, J. W. Sherborne, "Aspects of English Court Culture," in *English Court Culture*, ed. Scattergood and Sherborne, pp. 20–21.

39. Scattergood, "Literary Culture at the Court of Richard II," in *English Court Culture*, ed. Scattergood and Sherborne, p. 36.

40. See G. E. Woodbine, "The Language of English Law," *Speculum* 18 (1943): 395–436. On the official and unofficial use of English in Parliament, see John H. Fisher, "Chancery and the Emergence of Standard Written English in the Fifteenth Century," *Speculum* 52 (1977): 879–80.

41. Scattergood, "Literary Culture at the Court of Richard II," p. 37.

42. See David Wallace, "Chaucer's Continental Inheritance: The Early Poems and *Troilus and Criseyde*," in *The Cambridge Chaucer Companion*, ed. Boitani and Mann, p. 33: "Boccaccio shares Chaucer's ambition of establishing himself as a poet of European stature who, in company with a few Continental contemporaries, joins hands across the centuries with the great authors of antiquity. See Paul A. Olson, *The Canterbury Tales and the Good of Society* (Princeton, N.J.: Princeton Univ. Press, 1986), pp. 111–13, on the general literary movement, also re-

flected in Chaucer, toward classical and Latinate literature and serious works about government.

43. Translation of the Latin is by Fisher, *John Gower*, p. 89. The reference to Richard's commission appears in at least fifteen manuscripts of the earliest versions of the *Confessio;* there is a later form of the colophon replacing the statement I quote with "which was made in honor of his most valorous lordship, Henry of Lancaster, then count of Derby" (Fisher's translation, p. 90). This second colophon, which dedicates the *Confessio* to the new king, perhaps in an official version, actually softens the whole initial sense that the work is a "presentation" or occasional piece, though it does not, of course, change the sense in which the *Confessio* is dedicated to the common good of the king's domain.

44. See Scattergood, "Literary Culture at the Court of Richard II," in *English Court Culture*, ed. Scattergood and Sherborne, pp. 33 and 41–42 (appendix A), on the *Libellus geomancie*, a book Richard II probably commissioned. As for Richard II's receiving presentation volumes, Jean Froissart tells us that when he came to England for a brief visit in 1395, he brought with him and presented to Richard II an illuminated book of his love poems. According to Froissart (*Oeuvres de Froissart, Chroniques*, ed. Kervyn de Lettenhoven, vol. 15 [Brussels: Devaux, 1871], pp. 167–68), Richard took an active interest in the handsome French volume he was given; he opened it there and then and read aloud from it. See Scattergood, p. 33, on another presentation volume, specifically addressed to Richard II—Philippe de Mézières's *Epistre d'un viele solitaire des Celestins de Paris* (1395–96), a propagandist work urging the Christian princes of Europe, especially Charles VI and Richard II, to forget their differences and combine in a crusade against the infidel. There is no evidence that Richard II asked for this book, though the frontispiece to the manuscript depicts the author presenting the volume to the king.

45. In the revised Prologue, whose text lines are not marked by asterisks in G. C. Macaulay, ed., *Works of John Gower*, 4 vols. (Oxford: Clarendon Press, 1899, 1901, 1902), the account of Gower's meeting with the king is omitted; in that Prologue there is simply a statement that Gower is going to write a book (52–60) so that "The wyse man mai ben avised" (65) and send it (perhaps give it as a presentation copy) "unto myn oghne lord, / Which of Lancastre is Henri named" (86–87).

46. See Fisher, *John Gower*, pp. 187–203. Fisher argues that "the familiar theme of national peace and unity promoted by love under the leadership of the king is the real conclusion of the *Confessio Amantis*, not the withdrawal from romantic love" (p. 192).

47. Ibid., p. 236.

48. Cf. F Prologue to the *Legend of Good Women* 373–78 and *Mirour*

de l'omme 23233–78. In the G Prologue to the *Legend*, the advice to the king is extended to forty-three lines (353–96).

49. Cf. F Prologue to the *Legend of Good Women* 379–83 and *Vox Clamantis* 6.581–86; F Prologue 384–90 and *Vox* 6.741–47. The reference to the "gentil knyde of the lyoun" that will not "hurt a fly" (F Prologue 391–96) is not found in the *Vox*, although, as Fisher, *John Gower*, says, *Vox* 6.791 ("Musca nocet modica, modicis sis prouidus ergo") provides "at least the fly" (p. 246). F Prologue 397–408 repeats motifs already expressed; lines 397–98 resemble *Vox* 6.801–2. Fisher notes that none of the parallels suggest that Chaucer was quoting Gower. "At most, Chaucer's lines are a distillation from, and commentary upon, Gower's more diffuse generalizations; and both passages grow out of traditional *speculum regale* material and the popular unrest surrounding the Parliament of 1386" (pp. 246–47). He then goes on to point out the differences in emphasis between Alceste's speech and the Epistle in the *Vox*.

50. Cf. *Three Prose Versions of the Secreta Secretorum*, ed. Robert Steele, EETS, e.s., 74 (1898), p. 36. In *The Works of Geoffrey Chaucer*, ed. Robinson, p. 845, on line 381, Robinson suggests that the "philosophre" is probably Aristotle, whose advice to Alexander on liberality is cited at length by Gower (*Confessio Amantis* 7.2031–57, 2149–2216).

51. See Fisher, *John Gower*, pp. 247–49, where the two texts are set against each other.

52. Cf. ll.26–28 ("Shew forth thy swerd of castigacioun, / Dred God, do law, love trouthe and worthinesse, / And wed thy folk agein to stedfastnesse") and *Vox Clamantis* 6.709–12.

53. On the Knight's Tale, see, for example, Robert S. Haller, "The *Knight's Tale* and the Epic Tradition," *ChauR* 1 (1966), esp. p. 83, and Fisher, *John Gower*, pp. 220–24: "Theseus throughout exhibits the traditional virtues of kingship that Gower detailed in the 'Epistle to the King' in the *Vox Clamantis*, which dates from the same period as the *Knight's Tale* (i.e., between 1382 and 1386)" (p. 221). On the Melibee, see Howard, *Idea of the Canterbury Tales*, pp. 309–15; Green, *Poets and Princepleasers*, p. 142; and Gardiner Stillwell, "The Political Meaning of Chaucer's Tale of *Melibee*," *Speculum* 19 (1944): 440. See also J. Burke Severs, "The Source of Chaucer's *Melibeus*," *PMLA* 50 (1935): 99 n. 14. On Hoccleve's purposeful misreading of the Melibee—he sees Chaucer as a royal counselor—see James H. McGregor, "The Iconography of Chaucer in Hoccleve's *De Regimine Principum* and in the *Troilus* Frontispiece," *ChauR* 11 (1977): 343.

54. R. T. Lenaghan, "Chaucer's Circle of Gentlemen and Clerks," *ChauR* 18 (1983): 158.

55. But see C. David Benson, "Incest and Moral Poetry in Gower's

Confessio Amantis," *ChauR* 19 (1984), for the argument that "Gower has no simple cures for the sexual passions he so effectively portrays; the result, as the Man of Law has helped us to see, is that the *Confessio Amantis* is less rigidly prescriptive and a more complex literary achievement than we might expect from 'moral' Gower" (p. 108).

56. See Margaret Galway, "The 'Troilus' Frontispiece," *MLR* 44 (1949): 173–74, who holds that Alceste's addresses to the God of Love in the Prologue to the *Legend of Good Women* paraphrases the lecture Joan gave Richard after he quarreled with John of Gaunt in January 1385.

57. See Fisher, *John Gower*, p. 243.

58. See Bernard F. Huppé, "Historical Allegory in the *Prologue to the Legend of Good Women*," *MLR* 43 (1948): 393–99, for the case against Galway's first article, "Chaucer's Sovereign Lady: A Study of the *Prologue to the Legend* and Related Poems," *MLR* 33 (1938): 145–99.

59. Patterson, "Writing about Writing," p. 281.

60. Roger Sherman Loomis, "Was Chaucer a Laodicean?" in *Essays and Studies in Honor of Carleton Brown* (New York: New York Univ. Press, 1940), reprinted in *Chaucer Criticism*, ed. Schoeck and Taylor, vol. 1., p. 296. We can perhaps detect Chaucer's view of mob rule in the Clerk's Tale 995 and *Troilus* 4.183–4 (there may be a reference to "Jakke Straw" in the description of the "noyse of peple" starting up "As breme as blase of straw iset on-fire"). Paul Olson's view of Chaucer's Lollardry (see *Canterbury Tales and the Good Society* for example, pp. 297–98) reflects what the Robertsonian historical ideal shares with the ahistoricity of New Criticism (see Lee Patterson, *Negotiating the Past: The Historical Understanding of Medieval Literature* [Madison: Univ. of Wisconsin Press, 1987], pp. 36–37).

61. For an interpretation of the Nun's Priest's Tale as Chaucer's reworking of a common schoolboy fable, now directed to adults, see R. T. Lenaghan, "The Nun's Priest's Fable," *PMLA* 78 (1963): 300–307.

62. Robert Burlin, *Chaucerian Fiction* (Princeton, N.J.: Princeton Univ. Press, 1977), p. 236.

63. See, for example, St. Thomas Aquinas, *Summa theologiae* 1a.1.9–10, ed. Thomas Gilby, O.P. (Garden City, N.Y.: Doubleday Image Books, 1969); *Boccaccio on Poetry*, trans. Osgood, esp. pp. 39–54. See also Edgar de Bruyne, *Esthetics of the Middle Ages*, esp. pp. 160–62.

64. The change from a book "for the King Richardes sake" (24*) to a "bok for Engelondes sake" (24), later "commended in general terms to Henry of Lancaster" (see Fisher, *John Gower*, pp. 116–24), was not, for Gower, "a matter of deferential politeness to a ruler, but of rising to sufficient largeness of mind and of reference for a public occasion, and a broad common appeal," Middleton notes ("Idea of Public Poetry," p. 107). That consideration dictated Gower's tone in the *Confessio* from the beginning.

For Gower in any of the versions of the *Confessio*, the king "is not the main imagined audience, but an occasion for gathering and formulating what is on the common mind."

65. I do not, however, contend as Nevill Coghill does ("Chaucer's Narrative Art in *The Canterbury Tales*," in *Chaucer and Chaucerians: Critical Studies in Middle English Literature*, ed. D. S. Brewer [University, Ala.: Univ. of Alabama Press, 1966], pp. 135–36), that the *Troilus* illumination shows us the historical Richard and his newly married wife, both nineteen, listening to Chaucer recite *in order to argue* that "it can be dangerous to lecture a king" (Coghill, p. 135) and that Chaucer, however wide his circle of listeners (see Pearsall, "Troilus Frontispiece and Chaucer's Audience," pp. 73–74), hoped that his narrative would be thought serious, engaging, and transforming (see Middleton, "Idea of Public Poetry," p. 107). See Fisher, *John Gower*, pp. 225–27, on the distinction between moral virtue and intellectual and speculative excellence and his explanation of the double dedication in book 5 of the *Troilus* to "moral Gower" (1856) and "philosophical Strode" (1857). Fisher argues that "the most important evidence the double dedication provides is that Chaucer was as conscious of the moral dimension of the *Troilus* as he was of its learning" (pp. 226–27).

66. See Galway, "'Troilus' Frontispiece," pp. 161–62. She concludes that the foreground of the illumination "was designed to commemorate the author's recitals of the poem in the eventful months preceding the death of Princess Joan, to recall the wedding of Richard and Anne, which had occasioned" the *Troilus*, and to depict "its presentation to the queen and king under the aegis of the princess, to honour her as its sponsor" (p. 176). Galway even suggests that Chaucer and Sir Guichard d'Angle, one of Richard's boyhood tutors, may be seen standing together among the small-scale figures in the upper right of the illumination, part of a kind of educational setting in Aquitaine with Richard, Princess Joan, and her two sons by Sir Thomas Holland (pp. 167–68).

67. Aage Brusendorff, *The Chaucer Tradition* (London: Oxford Univ. Press, 1925), p. 23 n. 2, argues that the *Troilus* manuscript "was ordered from a firm of publishing copyists by the Duke [of Lancaster] himself, who had his own likeness inserted—in a comparatively humble place—in the splendid frontispiece of what must have been one of his favourite books." George Williams, "The *Troilus and Criseyde* Frontispiece Again," *MLR* 57 (1962): 174–75, takes a similar view, though he would put the Duke of Lancaster in a more prominent place than would Brusendorff. Like Galway's theory of the "argument" of the illumination, Williams' is equally speculative and perhaps also too ingenious. He suggests that "the chief purpose of the frontispiece seems to be to emphasize the relationship of Chaucer and the *Troilus* to the family of John of Gaunt. King Richard and

his family appear in the picture as (literally) a side issue whose function is merely to add lustre to Chaucer and the Gaunt family" (p. 178).

68. A. I. Doyle, "English Books in and out of Court from Edward III to Henry VII," *English Court Culture*, ed. Scattergood and Sherborne, p. 175.

69. Middleton, "Idea of Public Poetry," p. 112.

70. Fisher, *John Gower*, p. 235.

71. See *Cinkante Balades* 20.19–22; *Mirour de l'omne* 5251–55; *Vox Clamantis* 6.1325; *Confessio Amantis* 2.2456–58; 4.2795; 5.7597–7602; 8.2531–35.

72. Paul Strohm, "Jean of Angoulême: A Fifteenth Century Reader of Chaucer," *NM* 72 (1971): 73.

73. Ibid., p. 76. See id., pp. 74–76 on John Shirley, another fifteenth-century admirer of Chaucer. See also Michael Olmert, "Troilus in Piers Plowman: A Contemporary View of Chaucer's *Troilus and Criseyde*," *Chaucer Newsletter* 2 (1980): 13–14; B. A. Windeatt, "The Scribes as Chaucer's Early Critics," *SAC* 1 (Norman: Univ. of Oklahoma Press, 1979), pp. 119–41.

74. Lee Patterson, "Ambiguity and Interpretation: A Fifteenth-Century Reading of *Troilus and Criseyde*," *Speculum* 54 (1979): 319.

75. Ibid., pp. 327, 324. Patterson's emphasis.

76. Fisher, *John Gower*, p. 228.

77. See Green, *Poets and Princepleasers*, pp. 110–12. But see Scattergood, "Literary Culture at the Court of Richard II," in *English Court Culture*, ed. Scattergood and Sherborne, p. 40, on Ricardian audiences: "From the evidence of books owned by the aristocracy it appears they preferred literature in Latin and French on a variety of serious subjects, but that for entertainment they relied almost exclusively on romances; the career diplomats, civil servants, officials and administrators . . . appear to have been open to the new, serious-minded poetry dealing with philosophy and love, often written in the vernacular." Although Scattergood argues (p. 38) that Chaucer's "more significant readers" appear to have been such career diplomats and civil servants, he does acknowledge (p. 37) that "Chaucer found some of his early readers [for such works as the *Troilus* and the F Prologue to the *Legend of Good Women*] among courtly ladies—perhaps including the queen [Anne of Bohemia]."

78. See Strohm, "Chaucer's Audience," *Literature & History* 5 (1977): 30–34.

79. Middleton, "Chaucer's 'New Men' and the Good of Literature," p. 16.

80. See Strohm, "Chaucer's Audience," p. 39. See also id., "Chaucer's Fifteenth-Century Audience," p. 31.

81. Strohm, "Chaucer's Fifteenth-Century Audience," p. 26.

82. Wolfgang Iser, *The Implied Reader* (Baltimore: Johns Hopkins Univ. Press, 1974), p. 281. Iser's emphasis.

83. The analogy is Iser's. See ibid., pp. 290–91: "Any 'living event' must, to a greater or lesser degree, remain open. In reading, this obliges the reader to seek continually for consistency, because only then can he close up situations and comprehend the unfamiliar. But consistency-building is itself a living process in which one is constantly forced to make selected decisions—these decisions in their own turn give a reality to the possibilities which they exclude, insofar as they may take effect as a latent disturbance of the consistency established. This is what causes the reader to be entangled in the text-'gestalt' that he himself has produced."

84. Ibid., p. 278.

85. D. W. Harding, "Psychological Processes in the Reading of Fiction," in *Aesthetics in the Modern World*, ed. Harold Osborne (London: Thames and Hudson, 1968), pp. 313–14, argues against the idea of simple identification with what is read.

86. Iser, *Implied Reader*, p. 283. See also Iser, "Indeterminacy and the Reader's Response in Prose Fiction," in *Aspects of Narrative*, English Institute Essays, ed. J. Hillis Miller (New York: Columbia Univ. Press, 1971), pp. 1–45, and *The Act of Reading: A Theory of Aesthetic Response* (Baltimore: Johns Hopkins Univ. Press, 1978), esp. chaps. 7 and 8.

87. Howard, *Idea of the Canterbury Tales*, esp. pp. 182–85.

88. See Edward W. Said, *Beginnings: Intention and Method* (Baltimore: Johns Hopkins Univ. Press, 1975), p. 66.

89. See Harold Bloom, "The Breaking of Form," in *Deconstruction and Criticism*, ed. Harold Bloom et al. (New York: Seabury Press, 1979), p. 9: "There is always and only bias, inclination, pre-judgment, swerve; only and always the verbal agon for freedom, and the agon is carried on not by truth-telling, but by words lying against time."

90. Kermode, *Genesis of Secrecy*, pp. 4–5.

4. Who Speaks for the Wife of Bath?

1. John Speirs, *Chaucer the Maker* (London: Faber and Faber, 1951), p. 137. For a nice summary of the range of critical appraisal the Wife of Bath as character has been subject to ("a picaresque shrew, a farcical buffoon, a female Falstaff"), see Robert J. Meyer, "Chaucer's Tandem Romances: A Generic Approach to the *Wife of Bath's Tale* as Palinode," *ChauR* 18 (1984): 221, 236–37 nn. 1 and 4. Meyer's characterizations are accurate, though he has perhaps not seen the hermeneutical value of what he calls "the affective blather about her warmth, charm, and humanity

which had dominated earlier criticism" (p. 221). What the Wife of Bath has occasioned in critics are, as Meyer knows, responses that matter, and indeed such critical partiality is preferable to either the exegetical or the formalist argument that understanding begins with textual objectivity. That argument *as an argument* begs the question. For a discussion of the limitations of both the comic (Falstaffian) and tragic views of the Wife of Bath, see Donald B. Sands, "The Non-Comic, Non-Tragic Wife: Chaucer's Dame Alys as Sociopath," *ChauR* 12 (1978): 171–82. Sands' transactional perspective is engaging—it feels new—precisely *because* it touches the special value we give psychological analysis as a species of caring. See Susan Crane, "Alison's Incapacity and Poetic Instability in the Wife of Bath's Tale," *PMLA* 102 (1987): 20–27, for a feminist deconstruction of the idea of coherent female presence in the Wife of Bath's Prologue and Tale. For Crane, the Wife of Bath is finally "inarticulate, even about the meaning of the sovereignty she imagines. She desires to validate the forbidden but can hardly formulate what it is" (p. 25). There are, for Crane, no contexts for the Wife's conception of gender and power: "Her insatiable desire is more forceful and preoccupying than any of her illusory conclusions" (p. 27).

2. Bronson, "Chaucer's Art in Relation to His Audience," p. 47. See also Bronson, *In Search of Chaucer*, pp. 71–72.

3. See Bronson, "Chaucer's Art in Relation to His Audience," pp. 42–49, for the idea that the imaginary drama of pilgrims and stories in the *Canterbury Tales* was a slow and incomplete awakening in Chaucer of imaginary storytelling as the fiction of his narrative. See also Bronson, *In Search of Chaucer*, pp. 31–32.

4. Speirs, *Chaucer the Maker*, pp. 97–98.

5. See ibid., pp. 148–49.

6. See, for example, Ralph Baldwin, *The Unity of the Canterbury Tales*, Anglistica 5 (Copenhagen: Rosenkilde and Bagger, 1955), who rejects the view of the *Canterbury Tales* as an "additive and tell-as-you-go composition . . . [which] springs from the medieval *artes poeticae* and the medieval mind in general." For Baldwin the *Canterbury Tales* has an architectonic structure, albeit not "a shaded and circular or global composition" (p. 15) because it is incomplete, that coalesces into a roadside drama, so that the abstract frame supports the realism of the work. He argues that "the tales actually are performances incorporated into the frame story; they are the subjects of conversation [and] they are, in a sense, the converse of the pilgrims themselves" (p. 78).

7. Roy J. Howard, *Three Faces of Hermeneutics: An Introduction to Current Theories of Understanding* (Berkeley and Los Angeles: Univ. of California Press, 1982), p. 130.

8. Hans-Georg Gadamer, *Truth and Method* (New York: Crossroad, 1975), p. 305.

9. Speirs, *Chaucer the Maker*, p. 99.

10. Bronson, *In Search of Chaucer*, p. 31.

11. G. L. Kittredge, "Chaucer's Discussion of Marriage," *MP* 9 (1912): 436.

12. Robert M. Jordan, "The Non-Dramatic Disunity of the *Merchant's Tale*," *PMLA* 78 (1963): 295. See id., *Chaucer and the Shape of Creation*, pp. 132–51, for a restatement of Jordan's case for the disunity of the *Merchant's Tale*. See Donald R. Benson, "The Marriage 'Encomium' in the *Merchant's Tale*: A Chaucerian Crux," *ChauR* 14 (1979), esp. pp. 48–51, for a nice survey of scholarship on the question of the voice, or voices, of the marriage passage.

13. Muscatine, *Chaucer and the French Tradition*, pp. 230–32.

14. Jordan, *Chaucer and the Shape of Creation*, esp. pp. 46–47 and 60.

15. Eleanor Prescott Hammond, *Chaucer: A Bibliographical Manual* (New York: Macmillan, 1908), p. 256, first suggested that the tales of fragments 3, 4, and 5 constituted the "marriage group"; Kittredge, "Chaucer's Discussion of Marriage," pp. 435–67, saw the group as a discussion of marriage among the Canterbury pilgrims themselves—a self-contained dramatic unit treating a common theme. On the subsequent treatments of the idea of the "marriage group" since Kittredge, see the note appended to p. 158 of the reprint of Kittredge's essay in *Chaucer Criticism*, ed. Schoeck and Taylor, vol. 1.

16. See Larry D. Benson, "The Order of *The Canterbury Tales*," *SAC* 3 (1981): 77–120. See esp. pp. 110–12 (arguments for Chaucer's ordering, rather than for the ordering of an anonymous scribal genius), p. 112 (the reference to Chaucer as compiler of the *Canterbury Tales*), pp. 113–14 (arguments for Chaucer's carelessness over inconsistencies of time in the *Canterbury Tales*), pp. 114–15 (arguments for disregarding the one geographical reference supporting the "Bradshaw shift" and the implicit argument that geographical consistency is a narrowing nineteenth-century concern), and pp. 115–16 (on other "minor errors" in the *Canterbury Tales*). For Benson's summary, see pp. 116–17.

17. See, for example, Carol V. Kaske, "Getting around the Parson's Tale: An Alternative to Allegory and Irony," in *Chaucer at Albany*, ed. Rossell Hope Robbins (New York: Burt Franklin, 1975), pp. 147–77, who has identified what she calls the "misfortune group" in the *Canterbury Tales* (p. 149). See also James Dean, "Dismantling the Canterbury Book," *PMLA* 100 (1985): 746–62, on the "closure group" in the *Canterbury Tales*.

18. See, for example, David Lawton, "Chaucer's Two Ways: The Pil-

grimage Frame of *The Canterbury Tales*," *SAC* 9 (1987): 3–40, for the argument that the placement of fragment 10 at the end of the *Canterbury Tales*, as the judgment of a compiler who "need not have been Chaucer" but who "might just as well have been" (p. 40), makes a predictable moral closure to the work because it makes explicit a "moral dichotomy between tale-telling and virtuoso pilgrimage" implicit in the General Prologue (p. 28). My only reservation about Lawton's argument is that I think Chaucer's sense of stories as entanglements works against what Lawton argues is the anxiety of narrative deferment (see pp. 17–19) that the *Canterbury Tales*, as a framed narrative, creates—that error wants correction from one story to the next. See Howard, *Idea of the Canterbury Tales*, esp. chap. 5, for a theory of the structure of the *Canterbury Tales* that has, among its other virtues, the fact that it maintains the distinction between the idea of the form of a literary work and the idea of its structure, so that what is in fact "unfinished" about the *Canterbury Tales* is not confused with what may have been "complete" about it in Chaucer's mind. On the sequential order of the "Canterbury" tales, a problem that "has loomed larger than it deserves to" (p. 212), and the idea of junctures between tales, see Howard, pp. 211–16.

19. Bronson, "Chaucer's Art in Relation to His Audience," p. 48. See Robinson, ed., *Works of Geoffrey Chaucer*, p. 893, for his textual note to line 1686 of the Merchant's Tale. See J. S. P. Tatlock, *Development and Chronology of Chaucer's Works* (Gloucester, Mass.: Peter Smith, 1964), p. 204.

20. See *Lenvoy de Chaucer a Bukton* 29: "The Wyf of Bathe I pray yow that ye rede." See also the Clerk's Tale 1170–72.

21. On the problem of punctuating Chaucer, see E. Talbot Donaldson, "The Manuscripts of Chaucer's Works and Their Use," in *Writers and Their Background: Geoffrey Chaucer*, ed. D. S. Brewer, esp. pp. 87–89. What Donaldson shows is that the "punctuation" in Chaucer manuscripts—there is virtually none, unless the caesura is to be considered punctuation—allows for a doublessness, or simultaneity, of meaning as one reads, or as the text is performed, which modern punctuation of Chaucer (that of the Robinson edition, for example), tries to iron out.

22. See Jordan, *Chaucer and the Shape of Creation*, pp. 130–31.

23. See Robertson, *Preface to Chaucer*, pp. 3–51 ("Introduction: Medieval and Modern Art").

24. For similar uses of the phrase "in special" to mean a specific case, a species, see for example, Melibee 1355 and Merchant's Tale 1221–22. For a variant ("in especial"), see Melibee 1233–35 and *Romaunt* 6715. For a looser use of "in special," see *Troilus and Criseyde* 1.896–903 and *Truth* 24–27. Although in both these examples the phrase "in special" is op-

posed to "in general," the idea of categories is there by implication. Elsewhere in Chaucer "in special" means "in particular" or "especially."

25. See Douglas Kelly, *Medieval Imagination: Rhetoric and the Poetry of Courtly Love* (Madison: Univ. of Wisconsin Press, 1978), chap. 3, esp. pp. 29–45. What Kelly's discussion shows is that because "the Imaginative process" uses "metaphor to make incorporeal and abstract sentiments and qualities visible and thus comprehensible," images are thoughts—the eye and the mind are not theoretically separable in medieval aesthetics (p. 34).

26. "Much of Chaucer's irony in the *Canterbury Tales* becomes operative in the no man's land that exists between the poet Chaucer—who if he read his poem aloud must have been a very personal fact to his own audience—and the assigned teller of the tale, whether the Miller, the Knight, or, in *Sir Thopas*, Chaucer the pilgrim" (E. Talbot Donaldson, "Idiom of Popular Poetry in the Miller's Tale," *English Institute Essays, 1950*, reprinted in *Speaking of Chaucer* [New York: Norton, 1970], pp. 28–29). Id., "Chaucer the Pilgrim," reprinted in *Speaking of Chaucer*, pp. 1–12, published four years after Donaldson's piece on the Miller's Tale cited above, also makes this point (p. 10). See also John Major, "The Personality of Chaucer the Pilgrim," *PMLA* 75 (1960): 160–62, and Donald R. Howard, "Chaucer the Man," *PMLA* 80 (1965): 337–43. Howard writes that "the narrating persona and all the devices associated with him [Chaucer the Pilgrim] are of interest to us precisely because everywhere *in* and *behind* them lies Chaucer the Man" (p. 337). Howard's emphasis.

27. See Olson, *Literature as Recreation*, pp. 82–89, on the art of the *confabulator*. I am using *confabulatio* in a sense implicit in Olson's argument for the hygienic justification of literature in the Middle Ages. Olson shows that as a critical term *confabulatio* sees the intellectual play of literature as literature's therapeutic value. Because storytelling engages the mind, it comforts.

28. See Howard, *Idea of the Canterbury Tales*, pp. 13–15, for his explanation of the Ellesmere portrait.

29. See, for example, Green, *Poets and Princepleasers*, pp. 65–66, on the miniature showing Christine de Pisan offering a work to Isabel of Bavaria.

30. Richard Firth Green, "Women in Chaucer's Audience," *ChauR* 18 (1983): 152.

31. Faral, *Les Arts poétiques du XIIᵉ et du XIIIᵉ siècle*, p. 318.

32. See R. A. Shoaf, *Dante, Chaucer, and the Currency of the Word: Money, Images, and Reference in Late Medieval Poetry* (Norman, Okla.: Pilgrim Books, 1983), pp. 175–76, on the Wife as heretic in the Isidorean

sense: from the Greek *haeresis*, meaning "choice." She "chooses willfully to disobey orthodoxy or to supplant orthodoxy or to set [herself] up as an independent orthodoxy" (p. 176). On the Wife's discussion of marriage versus virginity as a *sermon joyeux*, see Lee Patterson "'For the Wyves love of Bath': Feminine Rhetoric and Poetic Resolution in the *Roman de la Rose* and the *Canterbury Tales*," *Speculum* 58 (1983): 677 n. 42. See also Howard, *Idea of the Canterbury Tales*, p. 250.

33. See David, *Strumpet Muse*, pp. 135–36, 157–58.

34. See Shoaf, *Dante, Chaucer, and the Currency of the Word*, pp. 183–84, who sees in the Wife of Bath's Prologue and Tale an example of the linguistic blindness of the modern feminist movement. See Susan Crane, "Alison's Incapacity," p. 26, for a distinction between wielding power and having it that seems to inform her understanding of the Wife as an insatiable non-participant: "If I were attempting to wrest coherence from the Wife's preoccupation with women's sovereignty, I would argue that sovereignty's associations with and dissociations from financial gain, domestic control, sexual aggressiveness, and love are all informed by a conviction that women should not strive for equality in marriage but should, rather, refuse to wield power that they have securely won."

35. See T. L. Burton, "The Wife of Bath's Fourth and Fifth Husbands and Her Ideal Sixth: The Growth of a Marital Philosophy," *ChauR* 13 (1978): 44–47.

36. See Howard, *Idea of the Canterbury Tales*, pp. 253–55. See also Anne Kernan, "The Archwife and the Eunuch," *ELH* 41 (1974): 1–25.

37. See Burton, "The Wife of Bath's Fourth and Fifth Husbands," pp. 41–43.

38. See Constance B. Hieatt, "Stooping at a Simile: Some Literary Uses of Falconry," *PLL* 19 (1983): 339–60, for other literary ideas of falconry.

39. See Leonard Michael Koff, "Wordsworth and the *Manciple's Tale*," *ChauR* 19 (1985), esp. pp. 341–46.

40. See, for example, Barbara Hernstein Smith, *Poetic Closure: A Study of How Poems End* (Chicago: Univ. of Chicago Press, 1968), p. 1: "There are few things, good or evil, of which we can say without some emotion of uneasiness, 'the end will never come'. Haunted, perhaps, by the particular delight, not in all endings, but in those that are designed, our most gratifying experiences tend to be not the interminable ones but rather those that conclude." See also Barry Windeatt, "Literary Structures in Chaucer," in *The Cambridge Chaucer Companion*, ed. Boitani and Mann, pp. 195–212, for whom the range of incomplete closure in Chaucer's work is *for us* a managing feature of its structure.

5. Voices and Books

1. Germaine Dempster, *Dramatic Irony in Chaucer*, Stanford University Publications in Language and Literature 4 (Stanford, Calif., 1932), p. 7.

2. See, for example, Speirs, *Chaucer the Maker*, p. 169.

3. "Chaucer's Pardoner: The Death of a Salesman," *ChauR* 17 (1983): p. 361.

4. Ibid.

5. Ibid.

6. Ibid.

7. Rosemond Tuve, *Allegorical Imagery* (Princeton, N.J.: Princeton Univ. Press, 1966), p. 26, describes how an emblem should be read: "Instead of personality giving the abstraction life, the figure often works the other way around; the excitement comes when we 'conceive' the idea, the person suddenly then becoming charged with meaning of very great depth and extension." See also Robertson, *Preface to Chaucer*, p. 248, who generalizes about Chaucer's method of delineating character: "*Characterization* is . . . somewhat misleading since the aim is not to delineate character in a psychological sense, but to call attention to abstractions which may manifest themselves in human thought and action."

8. See Germaine Dempster, "The Pardoner's Prologue," in *Sources and Analogues of Chaucer's Canterbury Tales*, ed. W. F. Bryan and Germaine Dempster (Chicago: Univ. of Chicago Press, 1941), pp. 409–11.

9. See Howard, *Idea of the Canterbury Tales*, pp. 355–56.

10. See ibid., pp. 355–57, for a description of the Augustinian pattern in the Pardoner's "progressive sinning." See also Alfred L. Kellogg, "An Augustinian Interpretation of Chaucer's Pardoner," *Speculum* 26 (1951): 465–81.

11. Howard, *Idea of the Canterbury Tales*, p. 345. See also Howard's entire discussion of the Pardoner's sexuality (pp. 343–45) and theory of the Pardoner as a "grotesque" (pp. 339–57). Cf. Monica E. McAlpine, "The Pardoner's Homosexuality and How It Matters," *PMLA* 95 (1980): 8–22. McAlpine has rightly noticed that the narrator in the General Prologue offers a reader little help in determining the sexual status of the Pardoner: "I trowe he were a geldyng or a mare" (691). The phrase "I trowe" may denote speculation or certainty. Thus McAlpine's argument for the Pardoner's homosexuality and his covert "plea for the redemptive kiss" (p. 17) is grounded, like Howard's interpretation of the Pardoner, on the Pardoner's disturbing sexuality, which Chaucer's narrator does not make less shadowy ("we initially encounter the Pardoner as a kind of puzzle to be solved rather than as a pilgrim to be judged" [p. 14]).

12. See Howard, *Idea of the Canterbury Tales*, pp. 349–56, on the

Pardoner's performance and psychology, the performer's psychology. See also Lumiansky, *Of Sundry Folk*, pp. 210–11; James L. Calderwood, "Parody in *The Pardoner's Tale*," *ES* 45 (1964): 302–9; and Paul E. Beichner, "Chaucer's Pardoner as Entertainer," *MS* 25 (1963): 160–72, all of whom anticipate Howard. See Howard, p. 346 n. 17, for Howard's comments on each. See, too, Edmund Reiss, "The Final Irony of the Pardoner's Tale," *CE* 25 (1964): 260–66, who has anticipated me on a number of points.

13. See G. L. Kittredge, "Chaucer's Pardoner," *Atlantic* 72 (1893): 829–33, and id., *Chaucer and His Poetry*, pp. 211–18. See also G. G. Sedgewick, "The Progress of Chaucer's Pardoner, 1880–1940," *MLQ* 1 (1940), reprinted in *Chaucer Criticism*, vol. 1, ed. Schoeck and Taylor, pp. 213–20. Sedgewick rejects Kittredge's reading, though his own, as he admits, involves imputing motives too. He imagines, for example, that "a hush has fallen over the pilgrims as the Pardoner brings his 'sermon' to a close" and that because the hush flatters "the preacher's vanity," it "leads to his undoing. Tempted beyond measure, he lets fling at the Pilgrims with his impudently ironic joke, all guards down" (pp. 217–18).

14. Kittredge, *Chaucer and His Poetry*, p. 217.

15. Howard, *Idea of the Canterbury Tales*, pp. 363–64.

16. Ibid., p. 376.

17. On Chaucer's "rediscovery" (as a practical issue—he performed his work) of the ethical problem of bad men (e.g., the Pardoner) giving good speeches and good men (e.g., the Parson) giving poor or (ineffectual) ones, see Robert O. Payne, "Chaucer's Realization of Himself as Rhetor," in *Medieval Eloquence*, ed. Murphy, esp. pp. 273–76. See pp. 276–81 for Payne's convincing view that the "possibilities and hazards of the deliberate creation of a *persona* by the orator or poet" (p. 278)—the "question of impersonation" (p. 279) and the "ethical pressure" (p. 278) of the appeal from ethos—in fact survived into the Middle Ages as a rhetorical, and hence poetic, concern.

18. See Paul Beekman Taylor, "*Peynted Confessiouns:* Boccaccio and Chaucer," *CL* 34 (1982): 116–29, on language and intention as a recurring epistemological issue Chaucer knew. See esp. p. 124.

19. McAlpine, "Pardoner's Homosexuality," argues (p. 16) that the Pardoner can make the distinction between his pardon and Christ's and that he believes that Christ's pardon is best because he desires the redemptive gesture of those who, in good faith, buy his "forgiveness and satisfaction."

20. See Reiss, "Final Irony," p. 264: "Certainly the Pardoner's way of life deserves condemnation, but at the same time there is no denying that the man, whatever his motives, excels as a teacher. His sermon is power-

ful and, if we may believe him, usually well received. While the good words he speaks may not, because of his sinful state, help him unless he repents [cf. Parson's Tale, 231–54], the words are still good."

21. John Halverson, "Chaucer's Pardoner and the Progress of Criticism," *ChauR* 4 (1970): 191. See Stephen A. Barney, "An Evaluation of the *Pardoner's Tale*," in *Twentieth-Century Interpretations of the Pardoner's Tale*, ed. Dewey R. Faulkner (Englewood Cliffs, N.J.: Prentice-Hall, 1973), esp. pp. 84–90, for a convincing case for the Pardoner's eloquence.

22. Payne, *Key of Remembrance*, p. 50. Payne's emphasis.

23. Taylor, "*Peynted Confessiouns*," p. 116. See also ibid., pp. 125–26, on the nominalist irony of the Pardoner's pronouncements an audience must struggle with. The Pardoner "gives his audience a living example of current abuses of ecclesiastical powers as well as insights into current theological speculations about the qualifications for granting and receiving grace" (p. 125).

24. See ibid., pp. 117–19, on St. Augustine's reflections on lying.

25. For a view of the "bout" between the Pardoner and the Host as a Chaucerian "happening," see Howard, *Idea of the Canterbury Tales*, p. 367.

26. See Heinz Kohut, "Thoughts on Narcissism and Narcissistic Rage," in *The Search for the Self: Selected Writings of Heinz Kohut: 1950–1978*, ed. Paul H. Ornstein, vol. 2 (New York: International Universities Press, 1978), pp. 618–20.

27. Ibid., pp. 643–44.

28. Ibid., pp. 646–54. See also Heinz Kohut, *How Does Analysis Cure?* (Chicago: Univ. of Chicago Press, 1984), esp. pp. 47–63.

29. Halverson, "Chaucer's Pardoner," p. 191. See also Reiss, "Final Irony," p. 263. On the forensic problem of an immoral man preaching morality, see St. Augustine, *On Christian Doctrine* 4.27.59: "For he who speaks wisely and eloquently, but lives wickedly, may benefit many students, although, as it is written, he 'is unprofitable to his own soul'. Whence the Apostle also said, 'Whether as a pretext or in truth [let] Christ be preached'. For Christ is the Truth, and, moreover, the truth may be announced but not in truth, that is, evil and fallacious hearts may preach what is right and true. Thus indeed is Jesus Christ announced by those who 'seek the things that are their own, not the things that are Jesus Christ's'" (trans. Robertson, p. 164).

30. See Charles Mitchell, "The Moral Superiority of Chaucer's Pardoner," *CE* 27 (1966): 437–44, who remarks that Chaucer "uses impiety to unmask simulated piety and holds up the Pardoner's evil as a gauge of the evil in others" (p. 438). See also Barney, "Evaluation of the *Pardoner's*

Tale," pp. 90–92, on the biblical echoes in the Pardoner's Tale that put us in a position "to see things substantially while the rioters see accident only" (p. 91).

31. See Howard, *Idea of the Canterbury Tales*, p. 368.

32. Howard, who is the notable exception, has anticipated my argument here. See ibid., pp. 370–71.

33. Ibid., p. 371.

34. The phrase is Edward I. Condren's, used to describe the Pardoner's "effort to replace . . . [his] nothingness with stylistic brilliance" ("The Pardoner's Bid for Existence," *Viator* 4 [1973]: 201). But it might apply to McAlpine's Pardoner who, unlike Condren's, bids successfully for his existence through our redemption of him. Both Condren and McAlpine have understood the Pardoner's playing, a symptom of his emptiness, as a call make *him* whole. Cf. Shoaf, *Dante, Chaucer, and the Currency of the Word*: "[The Pardoner] lets the seed of language (or the seed of the signs which are his relics) inseminate others with conversion, but he charges them for it so that, as language converts them, they convert language or seed into money which then 'inseminates' and 'fertilizes' as it 'redeems' the Pardoner and his 'dead' body" (p. 217).

35. Cf. H. Marshall Leicester, Jr., "'Synne Horrible': The Pardoner's Exegesis of His Tale, and Chaucer's," in *Acts of Interpretation: The Text in its Context, 700–1600, Essays on Medieval and Renaissance Literature in Honor of E. Talbot Donaldson*, ed. Mary J. Carruthers and Elizabeth D. Kirk (Norman, Okla.: Pilgrim Books, 1982), esp. pp. 47–50, on what Leicester calls Chaucer's critique of typology. For Leicester, the Pardoner's performance is an example of "the temptation to pride and illusion of power that typological thinking encourages" (p. 48). In Leicester's view, the Pardoner reveals a Kierkegaardian psychology of despair Chaucer intends to show the dangers of. Leicester argues that the Pardoner has a demonic self-consciousness (p. 43) and that the Pardoner's performance entails an implicit Chaucerian critique of artistic megalomania—an alienated irrationality that consciously and willfully separates words and things and remakes things into one's own words (and world). Leicester, I think, rightly identifies a Chaucerian response to medieval nominalism, but what he sees it implying is, I believe, a rather modern, really modernist, psychology of artistic creation, where verbal self-consciousness is akin to a kind of artistic solipsism, imagined as madness.

36. Howard, *Idea of the Canterbury Tales*, p. 367.

37. Muscatine, *Chaucer and the French Tradition*, p. 2.

38. Ibid., p. 8.

39. See Arnold Hauser, *The Social History of Art*, trans. Stanley God-

man, vol. 1 (New York: Knopf, 1952), 272–73, cited by Muscatine, *Chaucer and the French Tradition*, pp. 167–68. Hauser's notion of Gothic juxtaposition ("expansion," "coordination," and "open sequence") seems to me equally applicable to Cubism. He argues that "Gothic art leads the onlooker from one detail to another and causes him . . . to 'unravel' the successive parts of the work one after the other" (p. 168). Cf. E. H. Gombrich, *Art and Illusion: A Study in the Psychology of Pictorial Representation*, Bollingen Series, 35.5, 2d ed., rev. (Princeton, N.J.: Princeton Univ. Press, 1961), pp. 282–83. Although Cubism does not lead the viewer through space, through "the stages and stations of a journey" (Hauser, in Muscatine, p. 167), there is a kind of mental "unraveling," a making extensive, of the parts of a Cubist work (intentionally confined to a single picture plane) that is attempted by anyone who looks at a Braque or a Picasso. Superimposition is surely a kind of juxtaposition.

40. Muscatine, *Chaucer and the French Tradition*, pp. 8–10.

41. In the ballad *Fortune*, Chaucer observes that

> This wrecched worldes transmutacion,
> As wele or wo, now povre and now honour
> (1–2)

is actually, rightly understood,

> . . . th'execucion of the majestee
> That al purveyeth of his rightwysnesse.
> (65–66)

The world only *seems* "up-do-doun." It is surely helpful to explain irony in Chaucer in a way that returns it to God, but does not allow men to thrust it desperately, as it were, into the heavens. For Chaucer, God has created the world as much to have us free of it as to have us see it clearly. Perhaps that is the same thing for Chaucer, who does not soar, as Howard says (see "Flying through Space: Chaucer and Milton," in *Milton and the Line of Vision*, ed. Joseph Anthony Wittreich, Jr. [Madison: Univ. of Wisconsin Press, 1975], p. 5), "into space—into the Ptolemaic sky, into eschatological realms, into chaos and old night or the limbo of vanities." Managing incongruities is hard for anyone and to the extent that Chaucer succeeds, he produces great art; his work becomes eminently human, a genuine mirror for us who are in the world: we see; we laugh; we forgive.

42. Richard Neuse, "The Knight: The First Mover in Chaucer's Human Comedy," *UTQ* 31 (1962): 299.

43. A. C. Spearing, ed., *The Knight's Tale* (London: Cambridge Univ. Press, 1966), p. 75.

44. Critics will talk, however, about "the imaginative act of the Knight-narrator" (Neuse, "The Knight," p. 300). See also T. K. Meier, "Chaucer's Knight as 'Persona': Narration as Control," *EM* 20 (1969): 11–21. But psychological interest in the Knight is usually seen as a reflection of the themes of chivalry and obsolescence in the Knight's Tale. See, for example, Judith Shere Herz, "Chaucer's Elegiac Knight," *Criticism* 6 (1964): 212–24; Edward E. Foster, "Humor in the *Knight's Tale*," *ChauR* 3 (1968), esp. p. 93; and Howard, *Idea of the Canterbury Tales*, esp. p. 237: "It is hard to say whether Chaucer viewed the Knight's tale, despite its mannerisms, sympathetically. The Knight himself was presented in the General Prologue as a noble, indeed ideal figure, though from an older order that no longer examined its assumptions. In the tale, civil virtues give the characters and their actions dignity. But this civility is, as perhaps with all imposed codes, an artifice." On the "I" of the *Knight's Tale*, see Howard, pp. 230–34. For a reading of the Knight's Tale that sees exemplified in Theseus's imperial self Chaucer's interest in hermeneutics, see Judith Ferster, *Chaucer on Interpretation* (Cambridge: Cambridge Univ. Press, 1985), pp. 23–45. For Ferster, the "First Mover speech is not an attempt to describe the design *of* the world but an indication of Theseus's design *on* the world. It may be a shrewd argument from a ruler whose aim is to secure his city against enemies, but it is not good-faith interpretation. Its aim is not truth but domination of Emily in order to dominate Thebes. Theseus is seeking not to describe or imitate reality, but to control it. The imperial self we see here is neither solipsistic nor fully engaged in knowing the world. Rather, it combines selfishness and interaction with the world" (p. 35). Ferster's emphasis.

45. C. David Benson, "The *Knight's Tale* as History," *ChauR* 3 (1968): 123. Benson's recent book, *Chaucer's Drama of Style: Poetic Variety and Contrast in the Canterbury Tales* (Chapel Hill: University of North Carolina Press, 1986), pp. 64–88, treats the Knight's Tale with the Miller's Tale as a "dynamic literary contrast" (p. 66). On the Knight's Tale as intentionally limited, see Kolve, *Chaucer and the Imagery of Narrative*, p. 149: "*The Knight's Tale* never breaks free of its historical moment in order to name, in the manner of palinode, an ultimate truth whose authority is derived from outside the narrative itself, and which can measure, judge, and remedy the partial truth of the poem." But Kolve argues—I disagree—that "its usefulness to the larger fiction depends upon a scrupulous respect for the integrity and limitations of the pagan experience within the tale itself, and upon those limitations being remarked by the tale's audience in turn." On Chaucer's noble pagans, see A. J. Minnis, *Chaucer and Pagan Antiquity* (Cambridge: D. S. Brewer, 1982), pp. 108–43.

46. See Morton W. Bloomfield, "Chaucer's Sense of History," *JEGP*

51 (1952): 311–12: "The sense of the historic serves Chaucer in his satire and in his humor. It is one view which enables him to place the world in its right perspective for him—and for us. It is basic to the particular type of tragic objectivity which he often manifests. . . . It serves his artistic power of restraint. A sense of history is one of the ways Chaucer follows to enable attitudes to say themselves, to be objectified."

47. Robinson, ed., *Works of Geoffrey Chaucer*, p. 682.

48. Kaske, "Getting around the Parson's Tale," in *Chaucer at Albany*, ed. Robbins, p. 158, reminds us that what "Chaucer's rejected from his real source [of the Knight's Tale], Boccaccio's *Teseide*, at this point, is a picture of Arcite's soul in the eighth sphere, presumably the equivalent of heaven." On Arcite's death, see Edward Schweitzer, "Fate and Freedom in *The Knight's Tale*," SAC 3 (1981): 13–45.

6. Franklins, Nuns, and Jews

1. Terry Eagleton, *Literary Theory: An Introduction* (Minneapolis: Univ. of Minnesota Press, 1983), p. 196.

2. My image of medieval spiritual geometry is adapted from Nicholas of Cusa's *De docta ignorantia* 2.11, trans. Germain Heron (London: Routledge and Kegan Paul, 1954) to suggest the Cartesian isolation and omniscience that I think is an illusion of power and knowledge.

3. Eagleton, *Literary Theory*, p. 61.

4. See Frank Lentricchia, *After the New Criticism* (Chicago: Univ. of Chicago Press, 1980), p. 179: "The text, at any rate, as reified locus of determinacy, is replaced by textuality, a putative nonconcept, often figured in American Derridean commentary with much enthusiasm by the metaphor of the labyrinth. As it incorporates decentering, difference, differance and other grammatological moves, the labyrinth places writing before us as the setting of the abyss. *Mise en abyme* . . . has become a battle cry, along with two corollary themes: that reading is no mimesis but a violence of mastery and substitution, and that history . . . is a chimera."

5. Terry Eagleton, *The Function of Criticism: From the Spectator to Post-Structuralism* (London: Verso/NLB, 1984), does make this last point. Indeed, he argues that the historical change in the social place of criticism as an expression of cultural and political self-awareness (criticism began as a sign and symptom of bourgeois rationalized, i.e., "commoditized," self-sufficiency) amounts to an unfortunate loss of criticism's valued function as a general critique of the forms of power and performance. On rhetoric as critical analysis, see also id., *Literary Theory*, esp. pp. 205–7, 210–11, and *Walter Benjamin, or, Towards a Revolutionary Criticism* (London: NLB, 1981), pp. 101–13.

6. Michael Ryan, *Marxism and Deconstruction: A Critical Articulation* (Baltimore: Johns Hopkins Univ. Press, 1982), p. 81.

7. Lentricchia, *After the New Criticism*, p. 186. On American deconstructionists, see Vincent B. Leitch, *Deconstructive Criticism: An Advanced Introduction* (New York: Columbia Univ. Press, 1983), esp. pp. 100–102.

8. Lentricchia, *After the New Criticism*, p. 187.

9. Gerald Morgan, "A Defence of Dorigen's Complaint," *MÆ* 46 (1977): 77–97. See also Morgan, ed., *Franklin's Tale*, London Medieval and Renaissance Series (London: Hodder and Stoughton, 1980), pp. 40–43.

10. See Anne Thompson Lee, "'A Woman True and Fair': Chaucer's Portrayal of Dorigen in the *Franklin's Tale*," *ChauR* 19 (1984): 169–75. Lee makes a rather fine argument that the Franklin's Tale is not an "abstract formulation about sovereignty in marriage" but a "study" of "one marriage relationship in some depth, particularly from a woman's perspective" (p. 170).

11. Ibid., p. 177.

12. See ibid., p. 175.

13. See Henrik Specht, *Chaucer's Franklin in the Canterbury Tales: The Social and Literary Background of a Chaucerian Character* (Copenhagen: Akademisk Forlag, 1981), esp. pp. 142–46, for his criticism of the Lumiansky "school": "Chaucer's Franklin, in their view, emerges as a *parvenu* and a show-off, a social climber who, uneasy about his own social status, is eager to ingratiate himself with the 'gentils'. He, allegedly, imitates their ways without mastering them, and crawls to the Host when this worthy has sharply snubbed him for his presumptuous preoccupation with *gentilesse*. The Franklin emerges, moreover, as a person of shallow materialistic instincts, who, unable to penetrate to the essence of such concepts as *gentilesse, franchise*, and *trouthe*, is incapable of grasping the implications of his own Tale, contenting himself with the mere appearance of nobility of character and behaviour" (p. 144). See also Mary Carruthers, "The Gentilesse of Chaucer's Franklin," *Criticism* 23 (1981): 283–300, Howard, *Idea of the Canterbury Tales*, esp. pp. 270–71, and G. H. Gerould, "The Social Status of Chaucer's Franklin," *PMLA* 41 (1926): 262–79.

14. See, for example, R. S. Haller, "Chaucer's *Squire's Tale* and the Uses of Rhetoric," *MP* 62 (1965): the Franklin, "a self-indulgent country gentlemen who has been a knight of the shire, would like to think of himself as a 'gentil wight'" (p. 294). Haller assumes our distaste for the clumsy rhetorical excesses of the middle class and our remembered regret for the poise and restraint of the aristocracy, embodied in the knight. For

Haller, the present is always at the bottom of the hill. He hears irony and nostalgia everywhere.

15. Specht, *Chaucer's Franklin*, pp. 179–82. See esp. p. 181: "His [Chaucer's] intention seems . . . to have been to portray the Franklin so as to make him a worthy and fairly unexceptional representative of the class of untitled gentlemen, who formed an important element in the country gentry of late medieval England."

16. Anne Middleton, "War by Other Means: Marriage and Chivalry in Chaucer," *SAC Proceedings* 1 (1984): 119–31.

17. Laura Hibbard Loomis, "Secular Dramatics in the Royal Palace, Paris, 1378, 1379, 1389, and Chaucer's 'Tregetours,'" *Speculum* 33 (1958): 242–55.

18. See David, *Strumpet Muse*, p. 186, who reads the distinction in forms of address as the Host's "abrupt put-down" of the Franklin, whom he thinks "is putting on airs," and the Franklin's refusal "to get down to the Host's level of discourse" so that he replies with "*ironic* courtesy" (my emphasis). Although David says (p. 184) that the Franklin "is not a social-climber," he does think "he has social aspirations that are clearly evidenced in this scene." David's historicism, like the historicism of other critics, makes, rather than finds, its buttressing arguments in a close and descriptively accurate reading of the text—there are indeed polite and familiar forms of address in Chaucer's English, though what these linguistic forms signify historically is not self-evident without a historically informing intellect.

19. Morton W. Bloomfield, "The *Franklin's Tale:* A Story of Unanswered Questions," in *Acts of Interpretation*, ed. Carruthers and Kirk, pp. 189–98.

20. R. J. Schoeck, "Chaucer's Prioress: Mercy and Tender Heart," in *The Bridge: A Yearbook of Judaeo-Christian Studies*, vol. 2, ed. John M. Oesterreicher (New York: Pantheon Books, 1956), pp. 239–55, rev. and reprinted in *Chaucer Criticism*, vol. 1, ed. Schoeck and Taylor, pp. 245–58, argues that Chaucer is attacking anti-Semitism through the Prioress. See also E. Talbot Donaldson, *Chaucer's Poetry: An Anthology for the Modern Reader*, 2d ed. (New York: Ronald Press, 1975), pp. 1096–98. Florence Ridley, *The Prioress and the Critics*, Univ. of California Publications, English Studies 30 (Berkeley and Los Angeles: Univ. of California Press, 1965), pp. 16–26, argues that the anti-Semitism of the tale is a reflection of the age and of Chaucer's own beliefs. See also Albert Friedman, "The *Prioress's Tale* and Chaucer's Anti-Semitism," *ChauR* 9 (1974): 118–29.

21. Ridley, *Prioress*, p. 29. Cf. John C. Hirsh, "Reopening the *Prioress's Tale*," *ChauR* 10 (1975): 30–45.

22. Ridley, *Prioress*, p. 14. Cf. Howard, *Idea of the Canterbury Tales*, esp. p. 277 n. 69: "Since some people were indignant toward the persecution of Jews the point of view was not entirely impossible to the Middle Ages; and even if it was, it does not follow that it was impossible to Chaucer who was in other respects an exceptional man." Howard also argues that the Prioress's naïveté, ignorance, blindness and vehement devotion were not "lost on Chaucer, on whom very little was lost" (p. 278 and n. 72).

23. Ridley, *Prioress*, p. 4.

24. Schoeck, "Chaucer's Prioress," p. 257.

25. Robinson, ed., *Works of Geoffrey Chaucer*, p. 735.

26. That is Ridley's point. She rightly notes that "in the light of sentiments like these, it is very difficult to see why critics condemn the Prioress for religious prejudice, but not the Parson" (*Prioress*, p. 8). For the two other references to Jews in the Parson's Tale, see 663 and 889.

27. Jeremy Cohen, *The Friars and the Jews: The Evolution of Medieval Anti-Judaism* (Ithaca, N.Y.: Cornell Univ. Press, 1982), p. 20.

28. Ibid., p. 76.

29. See ibid., pp. 19–32.

30. Ibid., p. 244. For the distinction between anti-Semitism and anti-Judaism that continued to inform intellectual life in the Christian West, see Shimon Markish, *Erasmus and the Jews* (Chicago: Univ. of Chicago Press, 1986).

31. Marc Shell, "The Family Pet," *Representations* 15 (1986): 137–38. Shell's distinctions are, I think, subtle and true with respect to Judaism "under Christianity," Mosaic intolerance (see esp. Num. 25:6–8) notwithstanding. His point is that although the Jewish covenant with God is special—it singles out Jews for responsibility—it does not leave non-Jews without a relation with God. Judaism comes in its own way to humanitarianism—some beings are finally more humane than others. Christianity, as Shell describes it and as it appears in the Prioress's Tale, is both more pious and violent than the religion with which it shares a biblical tradition.

32. Edward H. Kelley, "By Mouth of Innocentz: The Prioress Vindicated," *PLL* 5 (1969): 368.

33. Cohen, *Friars and the Jews*, p. 52.

34. John Archer, "The Structure of Anti-Semitism in the *Prioress's Tale*," *ChauR* 19 (1984): 50–52.

35. See Sister Nicholas Maltman, O.P., "The Divine Granary, or The End of the Prioress's 'Greyn,'" *ChauR* 17 (1982), on the "greyn" the Virgin Mother placed on the tongue of the "litel clergeon" as a symbol of "the martyr's soul purged from the body and transported to the divine granary" (p. 166). The little boy's continued singing with the grain on his tongue describes his miraculous incarnation, his presence in the world as

a martyr, *before* his death ("And he yaf up the goost ful softely" [672]), when the monk took the grain away. Thus the Prioress's wish is fulfilled that the "litel clergeon" be with the "white Lamb celestial" (581), as described in Revelation 14:3. Indeed, she invokes his presence there in the stanza (579–85) that immediately follows his being thrown in the Jewish "privee," his figurative entombment.

36. John Archer, "The Structure of Anti-Semitism in the *Prioress's Tale*," pp. 47–49.

37. Ibid., p. 52.

38. See Bronson, *In Search of Chaucer*, p. 78: "And can we assume that Chaucer chose this story in order to develop a hypothesis about the Prioress's unconscious psychic needs or desires? To ask the question is not to impugn Chaucer's judgment in assigning the tale to its teller. Appropriate we must all feel it to be, for more reasons than one—not the least perhaps being the overt streak of cruelty masked as pious hatred which is the visible obverse of the rather shallow sensibility that marks this nun's temperament. But she could have cited all-too ample sanctions for her anti-Semitism; and neither have we here licence to infer an intention on Chaucer's part to trace the anfractuosities of a psyche." On the Prioress as a cockney nun, see Charles Moorman, "The Prioress as Pearly Queen," *ChauR* 13 (1978): 25–33.

39. Alfred David, "An ABC to the Style of the Prioress," in *Acts of Interpretation*, ed. Carruthers and Kirk, p. 156.

40. Ibid., p. 157.

41. On the pictoral context of the Second Nun's Tale, see V. A. Kolve, "Chaucer's *Second Nun's Tale* and the Iconography of Saint Cecilia," in *New Perspectives in Chaucer Criticism*, ed. Donald M. Rose (Norman, Okla.: Pilgrim Books, 1981), pp. 137–74. Kolve does not suggest that the iconographic representations of Saint Cecilia roughly contemporary with Chaucer constitute a specifically emotionalized version of representations of the legend of Saint Cecilia, though he does note in some of the representations he examines an intellectual yoking of the visual symbols that depict Saint Cecilia's place of martyrdom ("in a bath of flambes rede" [515]) and the condition of her blessed chastity ("For al the fyr, and eek the bathes heete, / She sat al coold, and feelede no wo" [520–21]).

42. See Spurgeon, *Five Hundred Years of Chaucer Criticism and Allusion*, vol. 3, p. 3. The phrase "fierce bigotry" is from Wordsworth's headnote to his own modernization (1801) of the Prioress's Tale, where he notes the violent concatenation of cruelty and tenderness in the Prioress's Tale.

43. D. S. Brewer, *Chaucer: The Critical Heritage, 1385–1837*, vol. 1 (London: Routledge and Kegan Paul, 1978), p. 304: "When lady prior-

esses talked after this fashion, and other ladies and gentlemen too agreed with her in opinion; when the Jews were every where persecuted, despised, or hated—spit on, trampled on, and bearded;—their sufferings made a jest, and the law made an instrument of infliction; was it not in human nature that 'the serpent, Sathanas' should dwell in their hearts? But the progress of knowledge has been accompanied with progressive liberality, and this feeling is much more distinctly to be traced in our poets than our historians. In the lady prioress's tale, there is not one redeeming circumstance for the poor Jews; they are isolated beings, cut off from human society; in the want of all human sympathy, they stand out naked and bare for universal hate and detestation."

44. For a summary of what she calls phenomenological hermeneutics, see Ferster, *Chaucer on Interpretation*, pp. 12–13.

45. Gadamer, "On the Scope and Function of Hermeneutical Reflection," in *Philosophical Hermeneutics*, p. 31.

46. Ibid., p. 32.

47. Ibid., p. 35. Gadamer's emphasis.

7. Chaucerian "Leaving-Taking"

1. Giovanni Boccaccio, *The Decameron*, trans. G. H. McWilliam (New York: Penguin Books, 1972), p. 47.

2. Ibid., p. 830.

3. On the distinction between expressing something ("expression") and finding something expressive, see Alan Tormey, "Art and Expression: A Critique," in *Philosophy Looks at the Arts: Contemporary Readings in Aesthetics*, ed. Joseph Margolis, rev. ed. (Philadelphia: Temple Univ. Press, 1978), pp. 346–61. According to Tormey, for something to be "expressive of" does not require that we assume some intentional state *in* the artist. A reader may find an author instructive without assuming he intends to teach.

4. Boccaccio, *Decameron*, trans. McWilliam, p. 831.

5. Paul B. Armstrong, "The Conflict of Interpretations and the Limits of Pluralism," *PMLA* 98 (1983): 349.

6. See ibid., pp. 346–49, for the argument that literary criticism is an enterprise with "standards and restrictions built into its proceedings, not a field of anarchistic free play where anything goes" (p. 346). Armstrong explains how what he calls the "hermeneutic 'wager'" (p. 349) is negotiated within and between communities of interpretation.

7. Walter Benn Michaels, "The Interpreter's Self: Peirce on the Cartesian 'Subject'," *GaR* 31 (1977): 402.

8. Ibid., p. 401. On subjectivism as a pseudo-problem in interpretation and the idea of the constitution of the self through an interpretive

community, see Stanley Fish, *Is There a Text in This Class?* (Cambridge, Mass.: Harvard Univ. Press, 1980), esp. part 2 ("Interpretive Authority in the Classroom and in Literary Criticism"). See Walter Benn Michaels, "Saving the Text: Reference and Belief," *MLN* 93 (1978): 787, on objectivity: "For the judgment that something is unconvincing, or good or bad, is not an expression of merely personal taste or preference but an invocation of shared values and public beliefs, and the kind of objectivity I thus want to argue for is an objectivity based not on the attempt to match interpretations up to a text that exists independently of them, but based instead on what readers believe."

9. Michaels, "Interpreter's Self," p. 402.

10. Payne, *Key of Remembrance*, p. 89. For Payne's definition of tradition, see p. 46.

11. For Robertsonians, Chaucer's "leave-taking" is read as the key to the moral design of the *Canterbury Tales*. See, for example, Bernard Huppé, *A Reading of the Canterbury Tales* (Albany: State Univ. of New York Press, 1964), p. 9. Huppé's assumptions about allegorical reading and Augustinian stylistics have about them the ring of the scientistic model of interpretation. See also Jordan, *Chaucer and the Shape of Creation*, p. 229. For Jordan, the so-called "retractions" are not only the key to the moral design of the *Canterbury Tales*, but to their architectonic structure as well. Jordan is no less a moralist than a formalist.

12. Michaels, "Interpreter's Self," p. 400.

13. See John W. Clark, "'This Litel Tretys' Again," *ChauR* 6 (1971): 152–56, for the arguments refuting Huppé and Robertson, who, alone among Chaucerians, have maintained that "this litel tretys" does not refer to the Parson's Tale. In reply to Robertson's claim that because the author of the rubrics that precede and follow the "retractions" thinks "this book" and "this litel tretys" refer to one and the same book, namely the *Canterbury Tales*, we ought to assume as much (see Clark, p. 156). See also Howard, *Idea of the Canterbury Tales*, p. 59, who argues that "Chaucer never uses the word 'treatise' to refer to a literary work—a 'book' or song—but always to writings in prose." For Howard's "unawares" theory about the reference to "this litel tretys," see also p. 59: "It looks as though he [Chaucer] began referring to the Parson's Tale but slipped unawares into general reference to the whole of *The Canterbury Tales*. The association is a natural one—talk about the end of a work and your mind goes to the whole of it."

14. Olive Sayce, "Chaucer's 'Retractions': The Conclusion of the *Canterbury Tales* and Its Place in Literary Tradition," *MÆ* 40 (1971): 236.

15. See Howard, *Idea of the Canterbury Tales*, p. 378: "But the tale is not a fable. The Parson himself says so. We do not read it in the same

spirit, for it is not a piece of story-telling that we listen to but a piece of reading matter that we must study and master." For Howard, we have in the Parson's Tale a model by which to judge our responses to the other tales and to our own attitudes and our conduct. As Howard says, "[The Parson's Tale] tells something about the whole book that has gone before, makes us turn from the world of that book and look to ourselves in the world about us" (p. 380).

16. Middleton, "Idea of Public Poetry," p. 110.

17. Jer. 6:16 in Wyclif's translation follows the Latin closely, so that the Parson's gloss is indeed, in its small way, a genuine feature of *his* reading of the text he takes for his treatise: "Stondeth up-on weies, and seeth, and asketh of the olde pathis, what is the goode weie; and goth in it, and yee shul fynde refreshinge to youre soules."

18. Christian K. Zacher, *Curiosity and Pilgrimage: The Literature of Discovery in Fourteenth-Century England* (Baltimore: Johns Hopkins Univ. Press, 1976), p. 123.

19. Although Howard, *Idea of the Canterbury Tales*, argues (p. 74) that after the Parson's Prologue "we are no longer addressed as an audience at a performance"—an argument I, too, would make—he explains (p. 385) that the Parson's Tale "gives a kind of closure" that "is esthetically satisfying only from one viewpoint. It settles everything in the manner of a commentary, by authority, but it throws our attention back to the complex experience on which it comments." In this respect, it, too, is a tale in Howard's broad sense; it is partial and "interior." See pp. 380–87.

20. See Kaske, "Getting around the *Parson's Tale*," in *Chaucer at Albany*, ed. Robbins, pp. 168–9, on Chaucer's and Spenser's pluralism. See also pp. 166–69 for Kaske's discussion of the ways the Parson's Tale "either retained and intensified or replaced by idealistic rigor" the "pessimism about marriage" characteristic of its source (p. 169). See Siegfried Wenzel, "The Source of the 'Remedia' of the *Parson's Tale*," *Traditio* 27 (1971): 433–54.

21. See Melvyn A. Hill, "The Fictions of Mankind and the Stories of Men" in *Hannah Arendt: The Recovery of the Public World*, ed. Melvyn A. Hill (New York: St. Martin's Press, 1979), p. 291: "Storytelling addresses the question of how we understand what has happened from the point of view of the present. The story presents a past experience to us by recalling it to mind, thereby raising it to the level of understanding where we can imagine it for ourselves." See also Hannah Arendt, *The Human Condition* (Garden City, N.Y.: Doubleday, Anchor Books, 1959), esp. pp. 161–67 ("The Web of Relationships and the Enacted Stories").

22. For the distinction between the confessional manual and the sermon in the normal homiletic sense of the word, see H. G. Pfander, "Some

Medieval Manuals of Religious Instruction in England and Observations on Chaucer's *Parson's Tale*," *JEGP* 35 (1936): 243–58. See also Howard, *Idea of the Canterbury Tales*, p. 74. Zacher's argument is that the Parson's "sermon" has a transforming effect on the nature of the pilgrimage to Canterbury that *we* can appreciate and that perhaps, if we imagine the pilgrims finally *in* Canterbury—Chaucer never shows us this—they, too, like real medieval pilgrims, would come to understand. The implication is that the Canterbury pilgrims will in Canterbury shed (try to shed?) their "curious" ways, for which the Parson's Tale is to be heard as a rebuke (and to be imagined as performed).

23. R. W. Southern, "Medieval Humanism," in *Medieval Humanism and Other Studies* (Oxford: Basil Blackwell, 1970), p. 60.

24. See Rodney Delasanta, "Penance and Poetry in the *Canterbury Tales*," *PMLA* 93 (1978): 242, who anticipates me here: "To quicken the pilgrims' conscience into *formal* awareness of their own specific sinfulness, the Parson must first remind them what it is that *materially* constitutes serious sin." See also Russell A. Peck, "Chaucer and the Nominalist Questions," *Speculum* 53 (1978): 759: "Instead of telling a tale, the Parson suggests means of assessing concepts. His sermon is designed to help men to open themselves up, rather than hide behind words. He would use words against words." Donaldson, "Medieval Poetry and Medieval Sin," in *Speaking of Chaucer*, p. 173, has rightly cautioned us not to focus on the Parson's Tale as a "gloss for many of Chaucer's best poetic writings," since we wrongly create stark moral contrasts in a work whose author is anything but a simple moralist. But to heed Donaldson's good sense does not preclude our *using* the Parson's Tale for our own awakening in this world.

25. Howard, *Idea of the Canterbury Tales*, p. 132.

26. Ibid., p. 179. It is important to remember that if we hear Chaucer in the "retractions," as Howard says, "hesitant about the ironic stance," what we are hearing, in Howard's view, is a moment when Chaucer "felt traditional Gower was doing the proper thing and he himself was floundering" (p. 55). We ought not to put the kind of weight on Chaucer's own, perhaps momentary, though serious, "hint of uncertainty and compunction" (p. 55) that would require us to read the entire *Canterbury Tales* in this mood. Indeed, it is only that need to anchor ourselves in moral certitude, our fear of shifting stances—a fear Chaucer has been continuously working against—that compels us to read with the certainty of orthodoxy what we may hear in the "retractions."

27. Howard, *Idea of the Canterbury Tales*, p. 172. See also Lee W. Patterson, "The 'Parson's Tale' and the Quitting of the 'Canterbury Tales'," *Traditio* 34 (1978), on the intellectuality of the Parson's Tale and the effect

on us of "the insistent foregrounding of its metaphysical assumptions" (Patterson's fine phrase): "The practical advice that the *Parson's Tale* offers in its role as a preconfessional meditation is throughout grounded in a careful and consistent theory; we are expected not only to enact but to understand its precepts, indeed to enact because we understand" (pp. 346–47).

28. Douglas Wurtele, "The Penitence of Geoffrey Chaucer," *Viator* 11 (1980): 335–59, hears Chaucer's voice between line 1085 and just past the middle of line 1090—Chaucer's voice disappears after the phrase "to studie to the salvacioun of my soule" (1090). On the scribal rubric separating the Parson's Tale from Chaucer's "leaving-taking," see id., pp. 336–37.

29. See also Sayce, "Chaucer's 'Retractions,'" p. 245.

30. St. Augustine, *On Christian Doctrine* 1.35.39 (trans. Robertson, p. 30).

31. Ibid. 1.37.28 (p. 23): "He lives in justice and sanctity who is an unprejudiced assessor of the intrinsic value of things. He is a man who has an ordinate love: he neither loves what should not be loved nor fails to love what should be loved; he neither loves more what should be loved less, loves equally what should be loved less or more, nor loves less or more what should be loved equally." To be both spiritual and free is never guaranteed by God, but requires an act which is free because it is the spiritual grace of God. St. Augustine's Christianity requires conversion more than once. See also ibid. 1.3.3 (p. 9).

32. See Hannah Arendt, *The Life of the Mind* (New York: Harcourt Brace, 1978) vol. 2, *Willing*, pp. 84–110, on St. Augustine's philosophy of the will.

33. See Sayce, "Chaucer's 'Retractions,'" p. 245.

34. On the etymology of "retraccioun," Chaucer's use of the plural noun ("retracciouns"), and the related verbs (e.g., "revoke"), see ibid., pp. 242–44. Sayce explains that Chaucer has "probably added to a noun derived from French in the sense of 'withdrawal', the meaning of 'revoke' present in the related verbs, and combined this with an allusion to the well-known title of Augustine's work [his *Retractationes*]. The plural form 'retracciouns' and the phrase 'my retracciouns', which is very similar to a title, both point to a deliberate literary allusion" (pp. 243–44).

35. See Howard, *Idea of the Canterbury Tales*, pp. 172–73.

36. On Troilus's location, see John M. Steadman, *Disembodied Laughter: Troilus and the Apotheosis Tradition* (Berkeley and Los Angeles: Univ. of California Press, 1972), chap. 1.

Index

Compositor:	G & S Typesetting
Text:	$11/13$ Caledonia
Display:	Caledonia
Printer:	Braun-Brumfield
Binder:	Braun-Brumfield